MW00668199

Dominican Brothers

Dominican Brothers

Conversi, Lay, and Cooperator Friars

Augustine Thompson, O.P.

NIHIL OBSTAT
R. P. Bryan Kromholz, O.P., S.T.D.
Censor ad Hoc

IMPRIMI POTEST
R. P. Marcus Padrez, O.P., M.A.
Prior Provincialis Provinciae Ss. Nominis Iesu
Die 2 septembris 2017

IMPRIMATUR
+ Michael C. Barber, S.J.
Episcopus Quercopolitanus
Die 19 octobris 2017

The *Nihil Obstat* and *Imprimatur* are an official declaration that a book or pamphlet is free of doctrinal or moral error. No implication is contained therein that those who have granted the *Nihil Obstat* and the *Imprimatur* agree with the content, opinions, or statements expressed.

 Published by New Priory Press,
1910 South Ashland Avenue, Chicago, IL 60608-2903
NewPrioryPress.com

Table of Contents

Foreword

Brother Bruno Cadoré, O.P.
Master of the Order of Preachers

It is with great joy and gratitude that I write this brief foreword for the book that Brother Augustine Thompson has written at the end of his research on the lay brothers (cooperator brothers since the General Chapter of 1958) in the history of the Order of Preachers. I am very grateful to him for agreeing to devote his sabbatical time to this research in response to my request to help the Order situate, in a historical perspective, its reflections on the specific vocation of the cooperator brothers today. But above all, I express my gratitude to him for giving us points of reference in order to learn more about the living out and the diversity of this vocation of brother preachers who, as lay brothers of the Order, cooperate fully in its mission of evangelization for the salvation of souls. With the same deep joy, I now invite readers to share and find evoked throughout these pages, not only the diversity of the "figures" of the brothers encountered, but also how the manner in which they lived out their own vocation has often functioned as an indicator, echoing the efforts of the Order to adjust its mission of preaching to the signs of the times as discerned in the world and the Church. The research of Brother Augustine invites us, in effect, to reread the history of the Order of Preachers through the life and vocation of the cooperator brothers, and from their manner of integration within the body of preachers "totally dedicated to the evangelization of the name of the Lord Jesus Christ."

Each of the recent general chapters of the Order has, in one way or another, addressed the issue of the cooperator brothers' vocation. This has been, often enough, and on the one hand, to regret the decline in the number of candidates for this specific vocation. But it was also, on the other hand, done in order to emphasize the need to think of significant changes in regard to the promotion and discernment of their vocation and formation, and of how to appreciate the brothers' form of commitment in their "consecration to the Word" in the life of the communities. In their evangelical and apostolic testimony, the cooperator brothers make a distinctive contribution to the Order's response to the contemporary challenge of a profound renewal in the Church's mission of evangelization.

Reading the story that Brother Augustine offers us allows us to see more clearly how the diverse ways of being a cooperator brother in the Order illustrate the requirement of a dynamic adjustment of the proclamation of the Gospel—from a personal, but also from a collective, point of view. It seems to me that we can even assume that many of the difficulties they encountered were paradigmatic of challenges that the Order should have engaged—and perhaps must still engage. Under what conditions can large communities be truly evangelical, without reducing some of their members to the status of "servants"? How to integrate artistic creativity within preaching carried out by all? Is it possible to promote an understanding of the faith shared by all in the service of a common proclamation of the coming of the Kingdom, by actually integrating in the same body the diversity of forms of human intelligence, knowledge, and wisdom? How can practical knowledge render more fruitful a more speculative understanding of the world? How can an urban Order really avoid cutting itself off from the rural world? Driven by the desire to follow Christ the preacher, how does the Order give itself the means to be challenged by the poor and the reality of precarious social situations so that its proclamation of the Gospel is prophetic?

It should also be added that, from this reading of the history of the Order from the point of view of the lay brothers, we also come across more "structural" issues: for example, the time required for a "democratic life" that really gives to each the same place and the same voice; or the way the Order's insertion within a culture influences interpersonal and social relations; or, yet again, the hindrance brought by a certain understanding of the clerical status of persons ordained to priestly ministry to the detriment of a more radical understanding of the real link between preaching and ordination, which is to be lived out within a single body, rich in the diversity of its members' vocations.

Sometimes, reflecting on the future of the cooperator brothers, one tries to imagine the Order without them. What would be lost would be a living reminder each day of our call to live as brothers in communion, to be that kind of fraternity which, we like to remind ourselves, was itself called a "holy preaching." The cooperator brothers are not only a reminder that we are "not just priests," but they make this incarnate in our life and work together. They make it true that the Order carries out its apostolic preaching and sacramental ministry precisely as a fraternity, as a religious brotherhood, which seeks to present to the Church and to the world, not just the words of our preaching, but the evidence of our life together, centered on the Word, and living together simply and sincerely in houses of mercy.

Another thing I have noticed is that whenever we reflect on the vocation of the cooperator brother, we inevitably reflect also on the reception and integration into the community of new vocations, both priestly and lay. It is as if the cooperator brothers were not only somehow the guardians of our fraternal life, but are also a point of reference for presenting in its fullness the charism that is the gift God gives the Church through Saint Dominic. How many of our brothers have been attracted to the Order by the simplicity and kindness of cooperator brothers! How often we see that, if we are to speak adequately about the formation of new vocations, we must acknowledge also the vocation of the cooperator brother and his place in the overall mission of the Order.

All these questions have not only marked the history of the Order, but have also been at the heart of the most elaborate reflections within it, during debates and decisions in its general or provincial chapters, in its work of receiving the documents of the Second Vatican Council, and in the development of reflections carried out by several commissions over the last decades. The research presented here gives a precise account of this abundant work, and we can welcome it also as a pressing invitation to extend our reflections beyond the particular theme of the vocation of the cooperator brothers to what is, in reality, a reflection by the Order on its own vocation. To express it in a way that is probably too lapidary, one might say that today it is not a matter of questioning the vocation of the cooperator brothers in order to reverse their declining numbers, but rather to engage in reflection so as not to miss what may be an urgent call to "adjust" the mission of the Order of Preachers even further to the call for renewed evangelization, perhaps even to change the paradigm of that evangelization. Does such a call not ask us to consider in a new way the indispensable lay vocation in evangelization, the building of evangelical communities without making clerical status a central and univocal reference, the strong determination to deploy the "Preaching" in conversation with contemporary cultures where we find intertwined the dynamics of secularization, strong religious traditions, forgotten religious heritages, and new processes for establishing community identity?

Reading Brother Augustine's book leaves me with the conviction that this precise historical research opens the way to a renewal of the vocation of the Order of Preachers today and tomorrow. Done from within the perspective of the vocation of the lay brothers, it should necessarily be guided by the needs of the mission.

Over the course of his study, Brother Augustine allows the reader to meet people, stressing as well and in a very fair manner, that the mission of the Order of Preachers is not a strategic program of action that its members should apply, but one that reveals itself rather through the way people assume in their flesh, their words, and in their acts, and their own share in this service "for the salvation of souls." Behind the many figures mentioned in this book, we can glimpse all the brothers who remained more "anonymous." One of the merits, and not the least, of this book is to awaken in each preacher, as in each reader, the desire to enter into such an adventure where it should be possible to hear the fine murmur of a call to grace.

Preface

Over the past ten years, there has been a growing perception that the role and position of cooperator brothers in the Dominican Order requires not merely theological and canonical reflection, but also a greater understanding of their history. In 2013, cooperator brothers from around the world met for a congress in Lima, Peru. This event culminated a series of regional meetings of brothers around the world. After the congress, the event's conveners drew up a document entitled the *Final Report with Recommendations and Appendices: Presented to the Master of the Order and the General Curia (1 September 2013)*. Among their recommendations is one that reads as follows:

> We recommend that by the Feast of St. Martin de Porres, November 2, 2016, and in tandem with the 800th Anniversary of the Order, a rich history be published on the history, vitality, permanence and presence of cooperator brothers in the life and mission of the Order, including biographies on the Saints, Blesseds, and Martyrs, and personal narratives, since its foundation to the present.

Even before receiving this written report, Master Bruno Cadoré communicated this request to the General Chapter of Trogir in 2013, where I was present. During his visitation of my province in 2015, I agreed to write such a history. Unfortunately, this project was not completed in time for the Feast of Saint Martin de Porres during the eight-hundredth anniversary celebrations, but that makes the project no less important.

In this book, I have tried to observe faithfully the commission just quoted. The goal of describing the "vitality, permanence, and presence" of the brothers has not proved difficult. I have also tried to present the complexity of that story. I made a conscious attempt to include biographies and personal narratives (of more recent friars), and these not only for the saints and blesseds. Those brothers who have been raised to the altar are relatively well known. I have included, as often as possible, something on the other brothers of whom we know more than a name, even if what we know is sometimes meager. Most brothers before the recent past lived a nearly invisible life in the monastery. I have made a special attempt to name and report as much as possible about these hidden friars. When giving personal narratives, I have avoided using in the text the names of living brothers, even of those who gave me "oral history," out of respect for their privacy. I do use the names of living brothers, however, when they were active participants in the historical events I describe.

I need also to explain some of the conventions I have adopted when discussing the brothers. What, if any, special name should be used for the nonordained brothers of the Order is a topic of discussion and debate. I will use the names most commonly applied to the brothers, according to the period I am discussing. From the foundation of the Order until the nineteenth century, the word used was *conversus* (plural, *conversi*), for which there is no good English equivalent. From the beginning, however, the unordained were also called "lay brothers" (*fratres laici*). These are the terms I will use when discussing that period. But the term "lay brother" became more common after the French Revolution and was used, usually in preference to conversus, until the adoption of the form "cooperator brother" in 1958. So, for the modern period, up to 1958, I will use mostly "lay brother" and, after that, exclusively "cooperator brother." This choice has no theoretical or theological loading. It simply reflects common usage.

Next, there is the question of how to render the names of the Dominican friars themselves. I have chosen to use the vernacular name that they would themselves have employed. Thus the earliest brother known by name, is Brother Oderic the Norman, not "Odericus Normannus," as he appears in the Latin sources. I do, however, make an exception for saints, blesseds, and other famous people, like kings and rulers. For these, I generally use the English form. It would be very odd, for example, to use "Domingo" for Our Holy Father or "Simone" for Bl. Simon Ballachi. The one exception is St. Juan Macías, since, even in English, he is usually called Juan, not John.

There are two other terminological decisions that I need to address. Readers will notice that, until the modern period, I regularly refer to Dominican houses as "monasteries." Some might object to this usage on the grounds that "we are not monks." In English common usage, however, a monastery need not be a home for monks—it might be a house of nuns. I could have called these houses "convents" (*conventus*), but in English that means only a house of women. And, indeed, canons regular live in monasteries, and the early friars were not only originally canons; they continued to live like canons until the modern period. Another reason for this choice is to remind readers that, by medieval and early modern standards, modern Dominican priories are, with few exceptions, tiny. In the premodern period, a Dominican house with only fifty members would have been small. The best way to imagine the Dominican house typical of the premodern period is as a monastery, with over one hundred friars, a very large plant (e.g. Santa Maria Novella in Florence), an extensive choral office, and a large indispensable support staff of conversi. That is the image I want the reader to have in mind whenever I use the word "monastery."

In addition, I want to flag my use of the word "American" for the citizens and residents of the United States. I know that there are other "Americans," both north and south of the United States. But the English language has, unlike Italian for example, no specific adjective for citizens of the United States. The constant use of a phrase like "who lived in the United States," would be stylistically ugly and even more distracting than this use of "American." I expect that when this book is translated into other languages, this problem will be remedied when the host language has a suitable adjective. Likewise, I am aware that many modern Dominicans would prefer that we drop the use of the title "father" and refer to all friars as "brother." This preference is reflected in the master's own Foreword. In the historical narrative, however, I have retained the use of "father" because the reader often needs to know which friars were ordained and which were not. This choice implies no position on contemporary usage.

This project was made possible by a year of research leave ("sabbatical") from my responsibilities at the Dominican School of Philosophy and Theology in Berkeley, California. I want to express my deep appreciation to the school and my provincial, Fr. Mark

Padrez, for this permission. There are so many others who have helped me in this project that I cannot name them all, but some deserve special thanks. In particular, I thank Master Bruno Cadoré and the General Curia for the financial support to cover my travel. I also thank them for a warm welcome and assistance at the General Archives of the Order at Santa Sabina. I am also especially grateful to the prior and community of the Dominican House of Studies in Washington D.C., where I spent the first six months of my work. During my "oral history" travels, I enjoyed the hospitality of the brothers of the Polish Province during my time there, as well as that of the provincial and brothers of the Vietnamese Province during my visit there. In both cases, I am especially indebted to those brothers who served as translators. I thank, too, the prior and community of Holy Rosary Priory, here in my own province, for their hospitality and support as I was writing this book. Finally, I thank Brother Ignatius Perkins of St. Joseph Province, without whom I could not have written the part of this book dealing with the period after the Second Vatican Council.

I pray that this book will make the amazing, though often forgotten, Dominican brothers better known to all the friars. This project began as a response to a need; it became a joy and a pleasure.

Augustine Thompson, O.P.
St. Albert the Great Priory, Oakland
Feast of St. Martin de Porres, 2017

Prologue
The First Conversi

The lives of Dominican brothers are often hidden and unnoticed. So it comes as no surprise that their lives, with the occasional exception of the beatified or canonized, have received little or no attention in histories of the Order. But, until the eighteenth century, most clerical brothers (the *fratres communes*) also lived a hidden life in the monastery. Only licensed preachers and masters of theology regularly left the cloister. The "hidden life" of most conversi was, in that sense, not unlike most of their clerical brethren. Nevertheless, even more than the clerical "common friars," the brothers remain unknown. This book is the first systematic attempt to tell their story from the time of Dominic to the present.

Modern Historical Studies

Victor O'Daniel, an American Dominican historian, did produce a slender volume for the use of the lay brothers in 1921, but his historical section is incomplete, consisting of a mere list of names and some brief abstracts of entries found in *Année Dominicaine*, a multivolume biographical encyclopedia compiled at the end of the nineteenth century. There does exist, in English, a short study of the brothers of the thirteenth century, Philip F. Mulhern's *The Early Dominican Laybrother* (1944), which began as the author's doctoral dissertation. Mulhern himself remarked on the lack of any serious study of the brothers, but his own study is now dated and its narrative has conceptual problems.[1] More recent historical work deals with the brothers only in passing, or focuses exclusively on the period of Dominic or the last fifty years.[2]

In addition to the lack of attention the brothers have received, there is also a gap between modern sensibilities and the traditional religious and social culture typical well into the twentieth century. So it is easy to condemn premodern people, including the friars of that time, for not being modern progressives. Those who want to critique contemporary society (and its secularism), are, in contrast, tempted to romanticize and sanitize the medieval and early modern periods. The goal of this study is to understand the brothers' story on its own terms, not to critique our predecessors as unenlightened, or use them as a foil for our own deficiencies. This project requires that we put the early Dominican brothers in the context of their time, if only because "conversi" predate St. Dominic's work of preaching in southern France.

MONASTIC LAY BROTHERS

It is clear historically that the first "lay brothers" appeared in the monastic and canonical orders. [3] Among the Cistercians and Norbertines, the first conversi evolved out of lay domestic servants, who had been granted their own form of vows and habit. Thus, they became members of the community, although living a life of their own, distinct from the choir religious. The admission of simple laymen, who were usually totally illiterate in both Latin and the vernacular, to religious life was a great novelty and an amazing success that addressed a real need. Among the early Cistercians, for example, the number of lay monks surpassed that of the choir monks three or even fourfold.[4] For the first time since antiquity, peasants and uneducated men had a place in religious life. The Benedictines would eventually follow, but the Cistercians, with their need for agricultural labor, led the way. Reformed canons soon also admitted conversi and granted them the "lay habit" and "lay profession."

This lay profession was distinct from the monastic vows of choir monks and canons. When monastic conversi made promises to live the life, they did so on bended knee into the hands of the abbot, a ceremony borrowed from that of knights pledging fealty to their lords. They wore somber dress, usually gray, not the black or white monastic or canonical habit. Outside of Italy, they usually grew beards, unlike the clean-shaven choir monks and canons. Most commonly, these men entered the life as mature adults, often already possessed of a skill or trade. They were totally unlike monastic child oblates, who grew up in the cloister, learned to speak Latin, and became choir monks. These men called themselves "conversi," meaning that they had undergone a "conversion of life" from secular livelihoods to monastic practice.

Although mature and often skilled, these men lacked, as a thirteenth-century canon of Liège noted, the essential skill necessary to be a choir monk: knowledge of Latin. But they were more than mere menial domestics living in the monastery. Among the Cistercians, some managed outlying farms, the granges, and even hired and supervised secular help to run them. By 1200, "conversus" and "brother" (*frater*) had become synonyms among monks and canons.[5]

By 1200, it had become common to distinguish "internal" and "external" conversi. The internal conversi lived in the monastery itself, surrendered all their property to the house, and were bound to celibacy. External conversi lived near the monastery, even on the monastic grounds, but not with the monks. They retained their property, sometimes substantial, and were often married. Some may have practiced chastity, given that they were usually elderly. But this is only clear for those who were widowers or unmarried. If they decided to marry, conversi could leave and do so. The full incorporation of external conversi into the monastic community came only at death, when their property passed to the monastery, and, after burial in the monastic cemetery, they were included in the abbey's suffrages for deceased monks.[6]

BROTHERS OF PENANCE

The number of external conversi steadily declined during the thirteenth century, a development probably related to a new movement, the rise of the "Order of Penance." These brothers and sisters arose as laypeople, usually urban, adopted as a form of piety the practices traditionally laid down for public penitents. These included celibacy, fasting, extended time in prayer, and withdrawal from "worldly" business. The lay penitents usually continued to live at home, or they clubbed together with other penitents. It was not uncommon for such groups of penitents to staff, and even found, hospitals. These men and women usually attached themselves to a church or monastery. They became part of the monastic family (*familiares*). Many lived a life similar to that of the older external conversi. Others remained more independent. The most famous of these "brothers" is St. Francis of Assisi, who was already a "lay penitent" under his bishop before he founded his order.[7] The Church and, in Italy, the cities recognized penitents as "ecclesiastical persons," subject only to the bishop's court and exempt from taxes and military service. With these privileges came greater supervision by ecclesiastical and civil authorities, as well as greater expectations of celibacy. What would later be known as the "third orders" attached to the mendicant friars were being born. The premodern third orders expected celibacy and what came to resemble ordinary "religious" life, albeit more informal and not cloistered. Layfolk who wanted a less demanding form of piety began to join the various confraternities that the mendicants were busily founding.[8]

To understand the first Dominican conversi, we need to keep these earlier developments in mind. When Dominic began his work in southern France, the boundaries between internal and external conversi and lay penitents were still fluid. The language used for these states was itself in flux. As early as 1207, well before the official founding of the Order, St. Dominic was already accepting "brothers" and "sisters" to be associated with the community of his "Holy Preaching" (*Sacra Praedicatio*), which was, at that time, centered on his newly founded monastery of nuns at Prouille, in Languedoc. Dominic was himself the superior of this community, and it included more than the nuns. In that year, we know that he received a Bernard Catolico into the *familia* of Prouille, with the "option of receiving the habit," that is, as a conversus of the nuns' monastery. This resembles the practice of earlier Cistercian nunneries, where men were taken on as external conversi to care for the physical plant.[9]

Prouille's monastic family also included so-called *donati* ("oblates"), who are not to be confused with the later phenomenon of men making third-order promises and living in the community, wearing a kind of religious habit. The monastery cartulary records ten acts of such self-oblation, most before 1224, and all before Humbert's final organization of the monastery. Two were whole families of serfs, including women and children, and two were clerics, probably priests. The rest include both individuals and couples. It is possible that some of these oblates became nuns or friars, but they are simply called "men" (*homines*) and they did not "profess vows." Rather, they "commended themselves" (*se comendare*) to the community.[10]

This self-oblation included a transfer of their property to the nuns, but the donors retained a "life interest," that is, use of the property until death. Adults made life promises of chastity and obedience or loyalty to the superior. They resemble external conversi, but it is best to think of them generically as *familiares*. Such self-oblates have been identified at other (non-Dominican) monasteries.[11] For some there were doubtless financial benefits to the arrangement, and not all seem to have been pristine models of Catholic piety. At least one conversus of Prouille, a certain Pierre-Roger, was reported to have been attending secret Cathar meetings in 1220.[12]

Chapter 1
Early Dominican Brothers, 1216–1300

Before discussing the few early Dominican *conversi* that we know by name, something needs to be said about St. Dominic's "Holy Preaching" itself, as this name has occasioned unfounded speculation about preaching by early Dominican conversi. Similar speculation has arisen from Dominic's desire to call his new movement the "Ordo Praedicantium," which finally became "Ordo Praedicatorum."[1] While it is true the mission of preaching was entrusted to the community and the Order as a whole, no friar received a license to preach by merely joining a Dominican community. The Order as a whole received the license from the pope and gave a limited or extended share in it to individual friars. Eventually, preaching outside the cloister would also need episcopal approval.[2]

Dominican preaching was not "liturgical" in the modern sense of being in the context of the Mass. It was an exercise in itself, whether in the piazza or in the nave of the church. And as a result, its success depended on the drawing power of the preacher. Some friars, indeed most friars, did not have this gift. It is true that until the early 1200s, unordained men were sometimes granted some kind of license to preach reform of life. St. Francis and his first followers were granted such a license by Pope Innocent in 1209. But they were also tonsured, thereby becoming clerics, not laymen.[3]

But by the foundation of the Order in 1216, norms for licensing preachers were changing rapidly. The earliest Dominican legislation did not link public preaching, even in the piazza, with Holy Orders because it was by then taken for granted. Primitive Constitutions 1.24 only envisions nonpriests preaching internally for the community.[4] Even ordained priests could not receive the *officium praedicationis* outside the cloister, that is the license to preach to the people, until they were twenty-five years old.[5] In 1215, the Fourth Lateran Council instructed bishops to associate worthy men (*viri idonei*) with them in the office of preaching. That these men were ordained is clear because they also received faculties to hear confessions.[6] By the 1230s, laymen, even if professed religious, who preached publicly were considered as illicitly "usurping the office of preaching."[7]

This being law and practice in the early 1200s, it is no surprise that we find no hint that the early conversi preached sermons of any kind, inside or outside of the monastery. They did not. While preaching was a community obligation, individual permission to preach publicly was granted by superiors to that small number of priests who had the gift. Those clerics who did not, the common friars (*fratres communes*), stayed home and sang the Office.[8] Occasionally, one of these might be asked to preach internally to the community, which would have been done in Latin. Like these clerics, most conversi in the Middle Ages spent the great majority of their time within the monastery.

Priests with a license to preach were often outside the house for extended periods of time, in fact, so much of the time that service as a preacher was considered incompatible with being a superior. Peter of Rheims was only mildly exaggerating when he wrote that a Dominican preacher "ought never return to his monastery."[9] The lay brothers did not preach externally or internally, as they could not receive the license and they did not speak Latin. The conversi's work was not seen by medievals as "cooperating" in the ministry of preaching. Rather, like the clerical "common friars," conversi were essential to the life of the monastery, which required not just the singing of the Office by clerics, but also a wide spectrum of material needs. These works had clear value in themselves; they did not need to be justified by some vicarious sharing in public preaching.

THE EARLIEST DOMINICAN CONVERSI

When the "Holy Preaching" of Prouille was reformed in 1216 to become the new Order of Preachers, the friars took responsibility for the monastery, its nuns, and its familiars, including the conversi. It is possible that some of the familiars then became nuns, others perhaps the first lay brothers of the Order itself. There were, indeed, four Dominican lay brothers at Prouille in 1225, serving the needs of the nuns, a number that rose to eleven by 1256.[10] Unfortunately, we do not even know the names, backgrounds, or dates of profession of these men. We do know, however, that there were conversi during the very earliest days in Toulouse. For, in 1216, when Dominic and his followers were given the church of Saint-Romain, they also received a cemetery so that they could bury, not only the "canons," as the friars were still called, but also the "professed conversi" of the community.[11]

In 1217, in a famous move, Dominic divided his followers and sent them from Toulouse into the rest of the Catholic world. One group of five left earlier in the year for Paris, the site of the famous university and its center of theological study. Not long after, a second group of seven friars, including Dominic's brother Mannes, followed. They included the first Dominican lay brother whose name we know. Jordan of Saxony gives it and his nationality, writing, "they had with them a Norman conversus, whose name was Oderic." That he was already a conversus in 1217 suggests that he was among the first members of the new Order of Preachers approved in 1216 by Pope Honorius.[12] This is all we really know about Oderic. It has been suggested that he was professed and trained by Dominic himself, that he was the very first Dominican conversus, and that he was part of the original group of Dominicans who voted to adopt the rule of St. Augustine.[13] These suggestions are pure speculation, and the last highly unlikely, as conversi never had a vote with clerics in chapter.

No conversi seem to have been with the four friars sent to Spain in 1217.[14] But the party that went to Spain in 1218 to found houses in Madrid (later given to the nuns) and Segovia, included two unnamed, lay brothers. After initial success finding new recruits, including conversi, this project faltered. None but Brother Adam and the two original conversi stayed with Dominic. We are told that the founder had foreseen these events in a dream, and that, by his prayers, he won back most of the deserters.[15] We also know that the two clerics sent by Dominic to Bologna in 1218 went with an unnamed conversus. The first recruits in Bologna included yet another conversus, also unnamed in the oldest sources.[16] Much later reports name this conversus "Pedro of Spain," and assert that he was present for the miracle of angels appearing with bread for the hungry friars then living at the church of the Mascarella in Bologna. Two other conversi were sent to the first foundation at Milan (1219), and one, we are told, served as Dominic's socius. Except for the last bit of information, which is probably anachronistic, these reports involve speculation, but need not be rejected out of hand.[17]

Soon after, an obituary reports that the conversus Latino of Orvieto, whom Dominic received in Rome, was present for the miracle of the bread at the Mascarella. A provincial chapter later granted him clerical status and sent him to make the Dominican foundation in Todi. After his death, sometime before 1260, the brethren considered him a saint.[18] In his perceived holiness, Latino is like the first conversus in Siena, Brother Landi (†1250), also recruited by St. Dominic. When he was not working, he was praying, and we hear that he died in the odor of sanctity.[19] Better witnessed than these events is St. Dominic's visit, in 1220, to the community of newly arrived Bolognese friars in Florence. There he received another lay brother, Guido the Little, at the hospice of San Pancrazio, where the friars were lodging.[20]

When Dominic later left Paris, in 1219, for Bologna, he had two friars with him, one the conversus Juan of Spain. The *Lives of the Brethren* records an anecdote about this journey.[21] We are told that, while crossing the Alps into Italy, Juan collapsed, crying that he was "dying of hunger." Dominic urged him on, but the brother had no strength. So the founder sent him back to rest on a rock they had passed. There the hungry conversus discovered a marvelous loaf of white bread wrapped in a cloth and ate it. His energy restored, he rejoined the group and asked Dominic where the bread came from. In reply, Dominic asked "Was it enough?" "Yes," said Juan. To which, the founder replied, "Then do not ask where it came from." This same report tells us that Juan himself recounted the story to the brothers in Spain.

As in the case of Oderic, Juan has been subject to much speculation. The *Lives of the Brethren* calls him Dominic's *socius*, which probably means in this case merely "companion." Much later writers identify him as Dominic's *socius* in the technical sense of "official assistant," and even make the unfounded assertion that, in that role, he was the founder's constant companion during his travels establishing new houses.[22] More credible is the report, in the *Lives of the Brethren* itself, that he went with the friars dispatched at the request of Pope Honorius to Morocco, in 1225.[23] Perhaps he died there in 1233.

The most interesting involvement of conversi with Dominic's foundations is that with the house of nuns at San Sisto in Rome during the spring of 1221. This foundation resembled a dual monastery. Along with the house of nuns, there was a community of friars, consisting of Dominic as superior, Brother Eudes as "prior," Brother Roger as "procurator," as well as one other priest and three lay brothers. According to Sister Cecilia, whose memory may have become somewhat confused, when Dominic took over direction of the San Sisto convent, he collected all the nuns' keys. "Then he appointed the lay brothers to guard the convent day and night, to provide food and all necessities for the sisters, and not to permit them to speak with their relatives or other persons, unless others were present."[24]

Before closing this section on conversi and the earliest foundations of the order, we should also mention those conversi who gave their lives in this work. The friar often considered the protomartyr conversus of the Order, Bl. Garcia of Aure, martyred at Avignonet, France, on 29 May 1242, with Bl. William Arnaud and companions was, however, surely a cleric.[25] It is certain, however, that many conversi were among the friars who lost their lives in the Polish, Hungarian, and Eastern European missions during the Mongol invasions of the 1260s. Dominicans have traditionally venerated one group of these men, Bl. Sadoc and Companions, and included among them five conversi, Andrew, Peter, Cyril, Jeremiah, and Thomas, as killed by the "Tartars" at this time. Sadoc's name is unrecorded before 1556 (except as a prior in Croatia during the 1260s), and the names of the conversi only appear in 1606.[26] The immemorial cult of Bl. Sadoc and companions was approved by Pope Pius VII in 1807, and they are celebrated on 2 June. Whatever the facts, Sadoc's conversus companions can stand for the many martyred brothers in Eastern Europe and Muslim lands during the early missions.

So what can we say about Dominican conversi before 1250? First, "conversi" were part of Dominic's community from the very beginnings, even before 1216. Next, after 1216, Dominic recruited conversi as well as clerics. Then, when we have names or numbers for the founding friars of new monasteries, these always include conversi. Conversi also occasionally travelled with St. Dominic on his own travels, at least as members of his entourage. Some conversi were considered to have died in the odor of sanctity, and some gave their lives for the faith. And finally, Dominic seems to have given them a role in providing for the temporal needs and security of the nuns.

Can we detect anything more? Fortunately, we can. We have a report of Dominic's own plans for the conversi, reported by an eyewitness. This witness is Juan of Spain (a cleric, not the conversus), who is also known as Juan of Navarre. In the process of canonization for Dominic, Juan testified about Dominic's proposals during "a chapter." He said:

> In order that the brethren might be more completely intent on study and preaching, Dominic wanted the unlettered lay brothers to be over the learned brethren in the administration and care of temporal affairs. But the clerical brethren did not want the lay brothers over them, lest the same situation result as happened in the order of Grandmont.[27]

This famous passage needs careful parsing to understand its context and meaning. Although this "chapter" is often identified as the General Chapter of 1220 in Bologna, and has been so identified since the days of Galvano Fiamma, this is now known to be impossible. During that chapter, Juan of Spain was in Paris, overseeing a transfer of property to Cistercian nuns. Juan was, however, present with Dominic at a local chapter, in Paris, in 1219.[28] This is the probable venue of the incident, which is related to Dominic's decision to adopt corporate poverty and live on alms, a decision made in Paris at that time. The intention in Juan's testimony is clear: the clerics would dedicate themselves to study and preaching, while the conversi would do the alms begging and supervise expenditures on the temporal needs of the community. So already in 1219, the Paris community had a sufficient number of conversi to take on these roles.

More radically, the brothers would be "in charge" of the funds, that is, a conversus would function as the treasurer of the house, that is, be "over the clerical brethren" in such matters. He would not, however, be the "superior." As treasurer, he would be under the (priest) prior of the community. But he would still be above all the other friars as to temporalities. There is nothing controversial about conversi begging alms and maintaining the physical plant; in fact, they would do this up to the modern age. The last item, being treasurer, was the sticking point.

This corrected dating throws the reference to the Order of Grandmont into clearer relief. In 1219, Pope Honorius III had just finished an intervention into the organization and composition of that order. Grandmont had both conversi and canons, just like the early Dominicans. The conversi were in charge of temporalities, the canons of spiritualities, that is, Mass and Office. The lay brothers far outnumbered the canons, who functioned more like the brothers' chaplains. Honorius tried to limit the number of conversi to no more than two for each canon. He also revised the rule to make the brothers subject to the authority of the canons. This intervention apparently happened after the Grandmont lay brothers murdered a mason that the canons had hired, without the brothers' permission, to build them a new dormitory.[29] The clerical brothers at Paris in 1219 did not want a repeat of that kind of conflict. A similar conflict had already affected the Gilbertines, an English order of canons, nuns, and lay brothers, in the mid-1100s. Like the Grandmont fiasco, the Gilbertine controversy eventually involved the pope and ended with the subordination of the lay brothers to the canons.[30]

During the entire premodern period, the conversi had responsibility for temporalities, just as Dominic wanted. At least in theory, the clerics got what they wanted: the treasurer himself was to be a priest. The surprise is that, in spite of the clerics' objection, conversi were occasionally named treasurers of communities, something contrary to the text of the constitutions. And, when the treasurer is a cleric, he often has a conversus who handles the day-to-day income and disbursements. Some brothers seem even to have kept the books. But at least such brothers answered to the clerical treasurer, or, lacking that, at least to a clerical prior. And the latter is what Dominic seems to have intended.

To complete our overview of the early conversi, can we determine their numbers, or at least their percentage among the friars as a whole? This is difficult, but not totally impossible.[31] It is certain that they were fewer than the lay brothers in thirteenth-century Italian monastic houses, where these numbered about half.[32] An estimate for the percentage of conversi assigned to new houses in southern France in the late 1200s suggests they were between 33% (at Brive) and 18% (Rodez).[33] My calculations, using these south French assignment lists for new houses, suggests about 20% as typical. In the Province of Toulouse, of the 174 friars assigned, 38 (22%) are conversi. In Provence, where numbers are more spotty, 12 of 62 friars assigned (19%) were conversi.[34] Including three lay brothers in the traditional twelve to found a new community seems nearly universal.[35] Necrologies giving obituaries for dead friars confirm this impression.[36] The Necrology of Santa Maria Novella for the period up to 1299 gives obituaries for 172 friars, 39 (23%) of whom were conversi.[37] Other Italian necrologies (Orvieto and Pisa) for before the Black Death show a lower average of about 15%.[38] I think it safe to say that the number of conversi varied from house to house and province to province, but a good estimate is about one-fifth conversi. This percentage seems to remain pretty much constant until the nineteenth century, when modern statistics showing similar numbers become available.

CONVERSI IN THE EARLY CONSTITUTIONS

Along with these narrative sources, our most important witnesses to the life of the early conversi are the versions of the thirteenth-century Dominican constitutions. Extant constitutions of the period come in three major redactions. The "Primitive Constitutions," that is, the earliest form available to us, are conventionally dated to 1228 from manuscript evidence. But the date of the manuscript is not necessarily that of the text presented. And, in one manuscript, there is an interpolation of legislation between 1221 and 1224, which suggests that the text itself is before that date. It seems likely that the Primitive Constitutions represent the practice of 1220, about four years after the founding of the Order.[39] It has been suggested that the legislation on conversi in these constitutions itself dates to 1216, but that is conjecture.[40] The Primitive Constitutions include, at the end, a *Regula Conversorum* that is dedicated exclusively to them. This "rule" will reappear, with minor revisions, in all editions of the constitutions down to the twentieth century. It seems likely that the Regula represents, more or less, what practice was in 1216, but again that is admittedly conjecture.

These constitutions were revised in 1241 under Raymond of Penyafort, the distinguished Dominican canonist. Perhaps the most important single change in this revision is one of language. Raymond changed the term for clerical brothers from "canons" to "clerics."[41] The "Rule of Conversi" of this version parallels that of the Primitive Constitutions, with certain interesting changes. Like the constitutions, extant general and provincial chapter acts for the thirteenth century throw additional light on clerical thinking about the brothers. That this perspective is clerical is important, was well as that it is legislation, not a description of actual practice. It would be very unwise to assume that, just because legislation gives a certain practice or norm, this reflects actual practice. That said, the constitutions and chapter acts do give us a general shape for the life of the early brothers.

It is noteworthy that the treatment of the conversi is called a "rule." The clerical brothers of the Order followed the "Rule of Saint Augustine," which medievals considered a rule for "canons," that is, clerics. This "rule," as such, could not serve as a "rule" for the conversi since they were not clerics, but laymen. Their rule does not, however, spell out every aspect of conversus life. Sometimes, as for example on fasting, the conversus rule simply says that they are bound by the same norms given in the constitutions for clerics, with the proviso that the superior can dispense brothers for the sake of labor.[42] Likewise, when specifying the conversus habit, their rule says that it is the same as that of the clerics, except that the scapular is to be dark and that, in place of the cappa, they are to wear a "broad scapular" of a similar dark material.[43] The one area where their rule is wholly different from the clerical constitutions is their "office," that is the brothers' prayers. Unlike the clerics, who are to sing the Latin choral office, the conversi recite an "office" made up of varying numbers of *Pater Nosters* (Our Fathers). I will deal with this office later.

The referencing of the clerical constitutions suggests thatthe rule was drawn up with those constitutions in mind, rather than simply adopted from some earlier rule for the conversi attached to another order of monks or canons. It has no parallel in the Premonstratensian Constitutions, which were a very important model for the Dominican Constitutions. Sadly, we have very little evidence for legislation on conversi among other canons regular or for possible conversi at Dominic's chapter of cathedral canons at Osma.

One telling norm in the Dominican Rule for Conversi is number 8: "Furthermore, no lay brother shall become a cleric or dare occupy his time with books for the purpose of study."[44] This suggests that Dominican conversi included men who could read, perhaps even read Latin. The early-twelfth-century canon Anselm of Havelberg assumed that all his community's conversi were wholly illiterate.[45] This seems also to be the case for the Cistercians. That some Dominican conversi were Latin literate, or became so, will pose problems about category change that will continue up to the modern period.

With minor stylistic changes, Raymond left the Rule for Conversi basically unchanged in 1241.[46] There are a couple of interesting modifications. Where the Primitive Constitutions had allowed "those conversi who have Psalters to keep them for two years," Raymond dropped this concession, along with the prohibition of changing to clerical status. Raymond seems to have assumed that the conversi now had no Psalters and that it was no longer necessary to worry about them seeking category change. If so, he was mistaken. Just eight years later, a general chapter reinstated the prohibition of Psalters and category change.[47] On a more positive note, Raymond specified that, like clerics, when conversi left the house they were to be accompanied by a socius, who could be a clerical or lay brother.

Other than appearing in assignment lists and the text of the constitutions, conversi are pretty much invisible in early-thirteenth-century chapter acts.[48] Two chapters did regulate conversi carrying money outside the house or having locked money-boxes. The first was prohibited, the second allowed only with permission.[49] We are also reminded that not all conversi followed their rule punctiliously: two general chapters punished grave offenders by demoting them to the lowest place in the conversus "order of religion," that is, their ceremonial ordering according to seniority.[50]

CONVERSI WITHIN THE MONASTERY

Although the few preachers and masters of theology were often away, medieval Dominican houses, with their high numbers of "common friars" and conversi, were large institutions with many to feed and clothe, and extensive buildings to maintain. Without the conversi, this system could not have functioned. They were essential to premodern Dominican life. In contrast to monastic conversi, who often lived outside the monastery doing farm work in far-off granges, the Dominican brothers were part of and lived with the larger community. Humbert of Romans, in a famous sermon, was only slightly exaggerating when he contrasted the status of the Dominican brothers to those of the Cistercians. This passage deserves to be quoted in full:

> Although the Lord has conferred a great grace on those whom he has called to religion, and a yet higher grace to those he has summoned from the lay state, he appears to have granted the highest grace to those whom he has called to the lay brotherhood in the Order of Preachers. In other places lay brothers hear but little spiritual doctrine, and that only rarely; these however hear it continually. Others attend only Mass; these not only hear Mass, but also attend Divine Office, and that every day. Likewise, in other orders, there are distinctions between clerics and lay brothers with regard to food, clothing, medical care, as also with regard to bedding and housing. Others rarely attend chapter or are served by any confessors. Our lay brothers have these habitually just like our clerics.
>
> Likewise, in other places, the lay brothers receive but little consideration; with us they are treated with honor, as appears from the fact they do not go out unaccompanied, nor do they dine apart from the clerics, but are waited on by them, even as they in turn wait on the clerics. Too, other lay brothers have many low tasks assigned to them. In other places, finally, the lay brothers are treated like servants, but ours have the full liberty of sons.[51]

In fact, some Dominican clerics treated conversi as menials and

Servants, and looked down on them. And at least one thirteenth-century provincial chapter had to remind priests to treat the conversi with respect.[52] But Humbert, who always tries to present the conversi in the best possible light, has a point. He explicitly contrasted Cistercian conversi, who were usually unskilled peasants attracted by the status of religious life and "good bread," with the Dominican brothers, who entered at a mature age with useful skills and seem to have generally come from urban backgrounds.[53]

Essential as they are to the functioning of the house, conversi, though distinct from their clerical brothers, were, as Humbert observes, integrated into the community in a way non-Dominican lay brothers were not. Only Franciscan lay brothers enjoyed greater integration. And with time, their position deteriorated. By the later 1200s, the Franciscan cleric Salimbene da Adam would write that Franciscan brothers were superfluous because they could not say Mass, preach, or perform other "useful," i.e., clerical, functions. When medieval Dominicans speak of a conversus as "useless," they mean that he was admitted without a useful skill or could not learn one, not because he was a noncleric.

What was the process by which a conversus was admitted? First, in the Middle Ages, conversi (like clerics) did not simply enter "the Order" or a province, they entered a particular monastery. In theory, they were admitted because they had some ability needed for that house to function. Provincials, therefore, could admit them only for the house where they were to receive the habit.[54] Conversi could, of course, be reassigned to places as needed. There is plenty of evidence for this, but they had to be "useful" to that new community.[55] So, Dominican legislation in the mid-1200s is insistent that conversi are admitted to houses as they are needed, and provincials are to oversee this process. Admission requires permission of both the provincial and the house.[56] It has been suggested that this legislation indicates an oversupply of conversus vocations, but, more likely, it reflects concern over admission of conversi without useful skills.[57]

This is suggested by a growing concern about age of admission. In the 1250s, the general chapter fixed an age limit of eighteen for conversi, and one provincial chapter penalized houses that admitted underage brothers by forbidding them to admit any further conversi for a year.[58] In the premodern period, apprenticeship started very young, and men became independent of their families by their mid-teens. Age requirements essentially prevented the admission of the immature and unskilled. In 1305, the Roman province raised the age to twenty and made this explicit:

> Since conversus brothers who are too young are useless to the order, indeed even destructive and dangerous, we strictly forbid that any conversus be admitted before he has reached twenty years of age.[59]

We should remember that, unlike clerics, whose Latin deficiencies could be made up for during their theological training for Holy Orders, conversi made a one-year novitiate, professed their solemn vows for life, and went to work immediately. Their "formation" (i.e. training in a skill) in this period normally had to happen before admission.

Indeed, there seems to be no question that there were plenty of skilled men interested in admission as conversi. Additional clerics could always be added to the choir (as long as there were the resources to feed and clothe them), but conversi in excess of the temporal needs of the community simply became idle mouths to feed. Friars, both conversi and clerical, needed to be kept busy, lest they waste their time in useless chatter (*confabulationes*).[60] As the century progressed, legislation addressed not only the question of skills but also of numbers. It seems the number of applicants had begun to surpass the need.[61] Humbert of Romans himself warned against admission of conversi beyond those needed for the temporal needs of the community. Only those that can be kept usefully occupied should be admitted.[62] In 1233, the general chapter warned that conversi were to be admitted "moderately"; by 1252, the provincial chapter of Provence urged cutting their numbers.[63]

As Humbert's sermon on Dominican conversi suggests, new conversus vocations were clothed using the same ritual as new clerics. When done in the chapter room (the usual venue), the *Veni Creator*, however, was recited, not sung, and some of the procession was omitted. But these solemnities might still be performed "on account of the excellence of the person" of the new conversus, in which case, the brother could even be clothed in choir.[64] After the papacy required that the Order postpone profession of solemn vows until completion of a year of novitiate, conversi, like clerical novices, spent their novitiate year in the monastery where they were received. The first experiments with provincial novitiates for conversi did not appear until 1326.[65] The brothers' novitiate was separate from that of the clerics, and, like it, was especially directed toward training recruits to live religious life, although, in this case, according to their status as lay brothers. At the end of their novitiate, conversi professed their vows, using exactly the same words as clerics did. Humbert instructed the brothers' master to remind them that their profession was identical to that of clerics and that, as religious, they were "equal to clerics" and subject to exactly the same discipline, unless the Rule for Conversi made an exception.[66]

So far, I, like Humbert, have been emphasizing the "equality in religion" of the conversi. This should be tempered by the recognition that conversi and clerics were very distinct, even different, religious vocations. This difference was reinforced in real and symbolic ways. The most visible of these was a different habit. The conversus habit was "identical to that of the clerics," that is, it includes a long white tunic, a black leather belt, and black shoes. In addition they had two undertunics, like the tunic, of wool, as well as a fur pelisse to wear under the tunic in winter. But, in contrast, brothers wore "a long wide scapular" instead of the clerical cape, the cappa. This "long wide" garment only extended partway down the arm. In fact, it was much like a longer version of the modern capuce, a shoulder cape. Its color was "not to be white like the tunic." They also wore a narrow scapular like that of the clerics, extending just beyond the knees, but gray in color (*grisei coloris*).[67] It seems that beyond this, they also had a "work" scapular to prevent soiling of the habit. [68] Unlike the tonsured clerics, conversi wore only the *rasura*, that is, their hair was trimmed tight, just above the ears, and they were clean shaven. This haircut was renewed every three weeks.[69] Conversi also had "Pater Noster cords," but they did not yet wear these on their belt. And these cords were to be of simple material, not amber.[70]

The habit color specifications proved difficult. Behind these problems is the reality that white sheep produce white wool, but nonwhite sheep produce a variety of colors. This was a problem for the clerics' "black" cappa too. Most likely, the wide scapular would end up being gray, like the narrow scapular. In addition, there was the problem of fading, which made gray ever closer to white. Like clerics, there was also the danger of extravagance and singularity in the habit. By mid-century, the Spanish province was legislating against sartorial extravagance.[71] At about the same time, general chapters begin to deal with conversus habit color and shape. In 1251, the color of the "gray" narrow scapular was defined to be "that of the clerics' cappa," that is, "black." But this brought resistance. The Province of Rome, three years later, required that the black scapulars worn by conversi were to be taken away.[72]

In 1257, a general chapter limited the length of the broad scapular to halfway between the elbow and wrist, and again standardized the color of the clerics' cappa (black). The fathers noted that the brothers' narrow scapular was too often tending to white.[73] In 1282, the chapter at Montpelier chastised conversi of Provence for too white scapulars and ordered priors to remedy this.[74] The chapter of 1289, forbade conversi to wear "broad scapulars" cut like the clerical cappa.[75] Such problems continued throughout the period. In 1294, the general chapter again railed against conversi with scapulars tending to white and forbade those wearing such from serving Mass. It also imposed a penance on the delinquent brothers' priors.[76] And so the problem continued in the early fourteenth century. At Paris, in 1306, the fathers dealt with a controversy in Teutonia and Saxony, where the habits of some conversi were *inordinati*. This was to be remedied before the coming Feast of the Purification.[77] One might wonder if the brothers were being clothed in hand-me-down clerical cappas and scapulars as well as in gray but faded ones. Eventually, the "gray" scapular ended up as "black," principally out of convenience. One simply used the same cloth for the brothers' broad scapular as the clerical cappa.[78]

So much for the legislation. What was the view of conversi about their distinctive garb? Their voices are mostly silent, but we do have the words of the pious brother Juan of Toribio, who died in 1312. The prior of his monastery, Domingo de Rolcedo, who himself died in Juan's arms in 1311, recorded that this brother often said "I could no more take off my habit than relax my self-mortification: that is what the black scapular means to me." Juan always slept in his habit near the statue of Our Lady of Consolation in the conventual church, "so that he could sleep in the arms of Jesus and Mary."[79]

Although, as Humbert tells us, conversi ate with the clerics, they normally had a separate dormitory.[80] This seems already the case in the time of Dominic. We are told that, at Bologna, a conversus was found demon-obsessed at night in the brothers' dormitory. The brothers ran to get their master, who then called on the founder, at that time visiting the house. Dominic ordered the brothers to take the wretch to church, where all the lights suddenly went out. The demon spoke: "I have his power because he drank in town without permission. He drank me with his wine, but I now have to leave because the 'capuciati' [the clerics with their white capuces] are arriving for Matins." They took the brother back to his own dormitory. Found healed the next day, he remembered nothing.[81]

This story also shows that the brothers had their own superior, the master of conversi, who slept with them in their own dormitory, or, in the case of a community with only one dormitory, in their section of it.[82] Sometimes, as at Carcassonne, the conversus dormitory was, like that of the clerical students, in a whole separate wing of the monastery.[83] Along with a different dormitory, the conversi had a different chapter room for their conferences and instruction. The master of conversi had a signal for calling them to their chapter. This was distinct from his signal for calling them, on very rare occasions, to the clerical chapter, which they did not normally attend.[84] Conversus presence at the conventual chapter itself was to happen only because of the utmost necessity and "very rarely."[85] If only because claims have been made otherwise, we should note that conversi had no vote in the conventual chapter, which was composed only of clerics (and not all of them). Humbert is specific that, even in the admission of conversi, clerics alone have a vote.[86]

Within the monastery, the conversi not only formed a separate community with its own chapter and dormitory, they were subject, as already noted, to their own superior, a cleric, the master of conversi. He answered for them to the prior. In his treatise on the life of the monastery, Humbert of Romans discusses this office at length.[87] The master's primary responsibilities were: 1. to serve as the direct superior of conversi, whether professed or novices; 2. to hear or provide for hearing their confessions; 3. to grant them permissions; and 4. to correct their faults. All other clerics, including the prior, only had contact with conversi through the master. Modern authors have noted that this provision served to protect (one would hope) the conversi from clerics who sought to turn them into personal servants.[88]

The master was also responsible for the religious formation of conversi generally and was to explain to them the parts of the rule and constitutions, legislative acts of provincial and conventual chapters, and instructions of provincials, priors, and visitators that pertained to them. Obviously, most conversi could not read these for themselves. During their training, the master was to teach to conversi who did not already know them the Latin prayers they should know by heart: the Pater Noster, the Credo and the Ave Maria. These were the same prayers that Lateran IV expected parish priests to teach (in Latin) and explain to their parishioners. They were the foundation of medieval lay piety.[89] Finally, the master was to make sure that conversi admitted without a skill or trade would be apprenticed to a skilled brother so as to learn one.[90]

As the one responsible for the brothers' discipline, the master was to hold regular chapters of faults, investigating and addressing any accusations against individual conversi, whether by another conversus or a cleric. If a conversus had a complaint about a cleric, the master was to address it in the clerical chapter. And, if necessary, he was to defend in that chapter any conversi accused of misconduct by clerics. In their own chapter, the master was to teach the conversi proper deportment with outsiders, as well as concern and care for the sick. He was especially to reprove and punish them when disobedient, first in private, and then, if necessary, before their chapter. Only if they defy him is he to take the matter to the prior. On a more positive note, Humbert provides that the master give the brothers short but regular conferences on their spiritual and temporal duties. It is unclear whether the master was to hear conversus confessions himself or to delegate faculties (which he had received from the prior) for this to other priests. The latter is most likely, and concern for the brothers' spiritual privacy seems evident. For example, in 1259, some clerics at Pisa had tried to get conversi to give permission to their confessors to reveal the faults confessed. These men, we are told, "were severely punished."[91]

Finally, and very much in the Dominican spirit, the master was empowered to dispense conversi from any obligations of the rule so that they could complete work necessary to the community. If necessary, he would even habitually dispense them from attendance at the community Mass and the Office, with the exception of Compline. They would then say their own office (on that more later) in private. If dispensed from the sung Mass, however, they were to attend a private Mass. It is interesting that the master was to discourage them from attending "too many private Masses," when they have work to do. He could also dispense them from attending Matins, if their workload had prevented them from taking the afternoon siesta.[92]

CONVERSUS SKILLS AND ABILITIES

Before moving on to the life of the brothers themselves, we should examine their status as a separate category within the monastery, not as to their life itself, but as to their abilities. From very early, it is obvious that at least some men with a high degree of culture and Latin literacy chose to become lay brothers, not priests. We know, as already mentioned, that at the time of the Primitive Constitutions, there were conversi who could read and who possessed books. In common parlance, however, "lay," meant "Latin illiterate," as Jordan of Saxony used the word when writing to Diana. He spoke of admitting thirty-three vocations to the order, all of whom were literate, except for two conversi who were "lay."[93] But for friars, "lay brother" did not mean absolutely illiterate, even in the Latin; it simply meant that they were not clerics on the way to ordination.

Occasionally, conversi (or their superiors) wanted to change their category and become clerics. The Primitive Constitutions simply forbade such a category change. This seems linked to their decision to take away the Psalters of Latin-literate conversi.[94] But in his revision of the constitutions, Raymond of Penyafort removed this prohibition and allowed change with permission of the master of the Order. The new cleric's position in the order of religion among clerics was, however, calculated from the date of the change, not his profession as a conversus. Cleric and conversus are two kinds of religious. Some have suggested that Raymond's change reflects a growing number of conversus vocations and a less pressing need to make sure there were sufficient brothers for the temporal needs of the Order.[95] But Raymond's actual motivation is not clear.

The general chapter of 1245 at Cologne changed the discipline once again, requiring not only the master's permission, but also that of a general chapter, to effect a change to the clerical state.[96] And Order legislation shows a continuing concern that conversi not possess books.[97] It seems from the tone of the legislation, however, that the bigger concern is that reading takes time away from work, not that it sows the seeds of category change.

Legislation on category change increases during the latter half of the century. We know from his obituary that Brother Latino of Orvieto was received as a conversus by St. Dominic himself. A provincial chapter later *ordered* his transfer to clerical status and had him ordained.[98] His was among the first of many category changes to come. And there was always a handful of functionally literate conversi. One such was certainly Brother Rainerio of Lucca, also called "of Pavia," because he wrote many books, including the *Liber Papiae*.[99] Admittedly, being a copyist like Rainerio does not imply great literacy. The copying of texts was considered a manual trade and did not necessarily demand a very high level of Latinity.[100] But Rainerio, it seems, had sufficient literacy to read and study on his own.

In the late 1200s, chapters made category change more difficult. In 1282, a general chapter voted to prohibit category change without explicit permission of the master. But the restriction did not get the necessary approbation of three chapters.[101] The same requirement was later enacted again, using even stronger language, but again failed to get the approval of three chapters.[102] Perhaps category change lies behind an enactment of the provincial chapter of Rome at the end of the century that forbade ordinations of candidates who could not read and sing the Latin texts of the liturgy.[103] Or perhaps there were just too many illiterate clerics being presented for orders. The specifics of category change remained ill defined until 1363, when it finally became set law that permission of the master was required.[104]

CONVERSUS SPIRITUAL LIFE

The spiritual core of medieval religious life was the celebration of the Divine Office and Mass, both sung daily in choir by the clerics. This was the primary "work" of the clerical brothers, ordained or not. The primary work of conversi was the temporal upkeep of the house. But, as Humbert emphasized in his sermon about the brothers, they were to share in the prayer life of the community. Humbert exempts some friars from the choir obligation because they have jobs that sometimes require them to be away. Among the jobs normally given to clerics, the sacristan, the treasurer, and the friar responsible for the dormitory must be absent occasionally from choir. His exemption also includes all conversi who have work to complete. In fact, he remarks, it is not an act of piety for a brother to attend a Mass when he has other responsibilities.

Nevertheless, like all friars, the brothers were to hear Mass daily, but they were to hear a private Mass, "without music."[105] And they were normally to attend sung Matins—the medieval night office, which also included Lauds—as well as Prime and Compline. But if they had missed their siesta because of work, they were exempt from Matins. On feast days when they are not working, they, like all other friars, are expected to attend Matins as well as the Conventual Mass, Vespers, and the other minor hours, lest they become idle (*otiosi*).[106]

Until very recently, with the exception of priests, daily reception of Communion was rare. Normally, medieval religious who were not priests received the Eucharist at "General Communions" several times a year. Dominican conversi received Communion with the other friars of the community whenever tonsure and rasura were renewed, that is about fifteen times a year. By medieval standards, this was very frequent. They received exactly as clerics did, at the steps of the altar kneeling, and, like them, before returning to their place, they received a sip of unconsecrated wine from a chalice to purify their mouths.[107] On those days, in some places, it was expected that the master give the conversi a short pious exhortation, a *fervorino*, to prepare them for worthy reception.[108] The conversi, like the clerics, went to Confession much more regularly, sometimes as often as twice a week.[109]

When attending the choral office, conversi had their own "office" to perform. It had a form also found among the pious laity of their age, recitation of sets of Pater Nosters, and the numbers were stipulated in their rule.[110] On entering the church for Matins, Prime, and Compline, they recited quietly, in Latin, as the clerics did, the Pater and Credo. As the choir sang the opening verses of the hour, they were to recite the Latin text themselves quietly. They were to conform their posture to that of the clerics, rising, sitting, and bowing with them.[111] During the singing of ferial Matins, they repeated 28 Paters, and quietly joined the clerics in the recitation of the Kyries before the collect of the hour. On feasts, when Matins was longer, they said 40 Paters. For the other hours, they were to say 7 Paters for each Little Hour and 14 for Vespers. When they did not attend an hour, they said their Paters privately. Contrary to some modern misconceptions, they did not say their Paters together out loud, even when not attending in choir.[112] Finally, "for the blessing at meals, they shall say the Pater Noster and Gloria Patri; after the meal, their thanksgiving shall begin with Pater Noster three times and end with Gloria Patri, or they may say the Psalm *Miserere mei Deus*, if they know it. As they do all this, they shall observe silence in the church and elsewhere."[113]

Certainly, for a great number of the brothers, their participation in the public prayer of the community consisted in their pious attendance and quiet recitation of their prayers in the back of the church, unless they, like the conversi at Milan, had their own stalls in a choir attached to that of the clerics.[114] Certainly, like some laypeople outside the monastery, the involvement of many conversi went deeper. Brother Pierre Bornet (†1292) of the priory at Limoges, France, as Bernard Gui who admired him greatly, tells us, was such a religious. He was obedient and hard working, and, even when dispensed, he never missed Matins. He was scrupulous in his recitation of his Paters and even added Aves on his own. Although he had never studied Latin, he came to understand the readings at Mass and the Office very well. No doubt it helped that French was a Romance language close to Latin. Brother Pierre never broke his monastic fast and never ate meat, even when traveling. He died after more than fifty years of profession.[115] Another conversus of Limoges, Brother Martin Bonel (†1310), inspired similar veneration after his death for his prayer and piety. The friars placed a carved eulogy on his tomb, praising his virtues.[116] Obituaries regularly note the faithful attendance at Matins by respected and holy lay brothers. For example, Brother Taddeo di Giacomo Scalzi, who died in 1256 at Perugia, was remembered for attending Matins every night and staying in church to pray with tears until dawn.[117]

Along with their office, conversi, like their priestly brothers, performed suffrages for deceased friars. The normal thirteenth-century clerical suffrage was one Mass. The constitutions and acts of chapters assigned one hundred Paters as the lay brothers' equivalent. Such a suffrage was not only said for friars, but also for popes or cardinals. By the end of the century, one hundred Aves were often assigned, along with the Paters, but this was not yet universal.[118] One provincial chapter in Dacia even assigned recitation of four Psalters for living friars to both clerics and conversi, suggesting that some were literate, but another chapter there still assigned Paters as the conversus suffrage for the dead.[119] Were the friars as devoted to saying suffrages for deceased conversi as they were for clerics? Perhaps not always. One story in the *Lives of the Brethren* records that the prior of the house in Clermont was reciting his Psalter for the dead in the cloister at night. The (invisible) ghost of a dead lay brother grabbed his arm and complained that the friars were neglecting his suffrages. The prior called the chapter, found this was true, and commanded them all to say the proper prayers for the deceased conversus.[120]

Beyond legislation, we find hints about early conversus piety and prayer. Commonly, these suggest a special devotion to the Blessed Virgin. A least one conversus, Brother Buono of Orvieto (1250–1300), was reported to have received regular visits from the Blessed Virgin, who also revealed "secrets" to him.[121] These secrets were not recorded, if he ever revealed them. In another case, such devotion was rewarded by help in time of temptation. A conversus of Lombardy, whose name may have been Brother Bene, was much tempted to abandon the Order. While praying with tears in the brothers' choir, he is said to have cried out "O Blessed Virgin, you always helped me when I was in the world, have you now abandoned your client?" As he gazed upwards, he saw the Blessed Virgin hovering in the air above him and comforting him. On another occasion, during the Octave of the Assumption, he dreamt he had been kidnapped by two men, and he cried out again: "Lady, help me now, and give me the grace to proclaim your Son's name for my own and others' salvation." At once, the Virgin answered, "Most willingly." A report was sent to the master of the Order in writing, describing both these visions.[122]

Conversus visions of the Virgin could show her protection for the Order as a whole. One Lombard brother, whose name may have been Lantrino, and whom the brethren held in high repute for holiness, lay awake in the infirmary during his last sickness. He reported that the Blessed Virgin appeared to him in company with other holy women. They carried towels and basins for washing. When he asked what this meant, she said that they had come "to cleanse the brethren from the infamy now besmirching them in town." There had been an apostate brother who had passed out some sixty letters slandering the friars, all over town. The sick brother then in his vision saw the holy women cleansing all the brethren. Shortly after, the apostate was thrown into prison and admitted to fabricating the slanders.[123]

Brothers were also rewarded for devotion to Dominican saints. An unnamed conversus of Metz was sick with a swelling of his head. His prior Jacobus visited him on the vigil of the anniversary of the canonization of St. Dominic (3 July), and urged him to trust in the saint. The brother replied, "I firmly believe that, if you command the fever in Dominic's name, it will leave." The prior did so, and the brother immediately recovered.[124] When the friars' church at Arras caught fire, all despaired, but Brother Barthélemy ran and got the relics of St. Peter Martyr. He himself testified that, when he exposed them, the wind suddenly changed and the church was saved.[125] Along with Dominic, conversi are reported to have been especially devoted to St. Catherine of Alexandria, soon to become a special favorite of Dominicans. Brother Matteo of Genoa (†1475), a conversus of Santa Maria di Castello, had asked for the habit when very young. Very observant, his devotion to St. Catherine was well known, and he died on her feast. Brothers put a "B" for "blessed" in the necrology before his name.[126]

Brothers might even be given visions foretelling the deaths of other Dominicans. One conversus—the name given in the manuscript margin is "Juan of Spain"—had a vision of the people of Pavia coming to the Dominican house asking for a friar as their "papa," that is, as their bishop. He told this to the subprior, who passed the message on to the prior, Isnard of Chiampo. Isnard understood the vision: the people really wanted a patron in heaven. So he immediately knelt and confessed his sins. Isnard died a few days later and began working miracles.[127]

So far, these reports involve individual pious conversi, but we also know of a whole group of brothers venerated for their holiness. When stories of the early friars were solicited for the compilation of the *Lives of the Brethren*, the community of Santarem in Portugal sent reports on six brothers, all but one of whom were conversi of the house in the 1250s and 1260s.[128] These brothers confirm the centrality of the saints and the making of a holy death in conversus piety. Brother Martinho, when he lay sick, was placed facing east in anticipation of his death. He predicted that he would not die until a week later. And so it happened. He died on Christmas Eve, as the friars were singing *Christus natus est nobis,* the invitatory of Matins.[129] Brother Gonsales, when very sick, called another brother to hear his deceased mother and sister, whom he heard speaking to him. They promised they would visit him at his death, and warned that he should be prepared for demonic attacks the next day when Jesus would appear to him. Confirmed in his faith, he made a pious death that following day.[130]

The last mentioned of the Santarem conversi is Brother Domingos, who lay ill with dropsy. Twice, a beautiful woman appeared to him and comforted him. He reported this to the infirmarian, who berated him for allowing women into the cloister and began a search for the intruder. Domingo died the next night, the vigil of St. Agnes. He cried out that his hour had come and he then died in peace. The infirmarian then realized that the "intruder" had really been the saint.[131] Deceased conversi could themselves help the sick. At Valenciennes in France, an unnamed brother had a painful malady unresponsive to medicine. So he placed his faith in the recently deceased conversus, Jean of Serlin, and was immediately healed.[132] Unfortunately, we know nothing else about the saintly Jean. Veneration for holy lay brothers even extended outside the monasteries where they lived. Brother Rainaldo, a conversus "of great holiness" with the gift of tears, was beloved by the women of Pisa, who venerated him after his death in the late 1200s.[133] He is not the only brother we will hear of who had a following among townswomen.

CONVERSI AT WORK

Thirteenth-century cultural mores meant that priests, as ministers of the Word and Sacrament, should be exempt from, indeed, should not perform, manual labor. St. Francis expected his followers to support themselves by manual labor, but his original group had few, if any, priests. St. Dominic, after abandoning fixed sources of income, sent his followers begging. Unlike Francis, he never seems to have thought of having them labor for a living. Dominican conversi, however, were laborers by definition. As monasteries could not function without physical labor, conversi were essential to their existence.[134]

The only alternative, given the attitude of the time, was to hire lay servants. But servants seemed not just a violation of poverty, but also a danger to the keeping of cloister. Nevertheless, if lay brothers were not available, paid servants were inevitable. General chapters in 1233 and 1239 forbade them, unsuccessfully, it seems.[135] By mid-century, paid servants seem common, if undesirable. Humbert of Romans takes them for granted, and tells priors to appoint a supervisor to oversee them, correct them, and fire them if they commit "mortal sins."[136] It seems that some clerics were tempted to think of conversi as the same as these paid servants. Thomas of Cantimpré wrote of conversi as "quasi-servants," analogous to the drones among bees.[137]

On the other hand, Humbert of Romans, our major source for the work of conversi, did not think in those terms, and there is no evidence that Dominican conversi, like their Cistercian brethren, had to prove themselves as servants before admission to the novitiate.[138] Humbert, in his *De Vita Regulari*, paints a picture of conversi as true religious, not mere laborers or servants, giving us a paraphrase of his famous sermon quoted earlier.[139] Beyond Humbert, there is evidence that possession of a useful skill made admission of a conversus easier. This was preferable to having conversi who were merely unskilled domestics. This preference was clearly at work in the resistance to the admission of Bl. Christine of Sammeln's brother as a conversus.[140] In any case, it is clear from legislation that conversi were to be kept busy at work to avoid idleness.[141] But Humbert's remarks on "internal gyrovages," that is, friars who wander from parlor to common room, and then to other parts of monastery, bored and aimless, is directed against clerics, not conversi.[142]

Humbert's treatise, although normative more than descriptive, is our best window into the life of early conversi in the monastery. His *Expositio super Constitutiones Fratrum Praedicatorum*, composed between 1263 and his death in 1277, contains extended descriptions of the tasks to which conversi were assigned.[143] Humbert assigns some jobs specifically to conversi: tailor, shoemaker, cook. He lists as normally a conversus the porter and almoner. Finally, conversi can serve as guestmaster and *refectarius* (in charge of food), and are not excluded as infirmarian, *vestiarius* (in charge of clothing), cellarer, and gardener—for each of which the determinate is proper training, not category. If a conversus has no useful skills, then he will have to be assigned as *dormitarius* (the keeper of the dormitory). Finally, he notes that conversi are sometimes assigned to the staff of the master of the Order and of other superiors, roles that risked bordering on being a body-servant.[144] As this chapter is dedicated to the life of conversi within the monastery, their hidden life, I will summarize Humbert's description of their internal work and save the tasks involving contact with outsiders until the next chapter. When possible, I will flesh out Humbert's descriptions with examples from the lives of actual conversi. In short, the duties of conversi in the monastery involved everything having to do with the food, clothing, and shelter of the friars. Without food, clothing, and shelter, friars could not live. No medieval Dominican monastery could exist without its conversi.

The man responsible for overseeing food in the monastery was the refectarius, so called from the refectory, the monastic dining area.[145] At least three other conversi reported to the refectarius: the chief cook, the cellarer, and the gardener. The office of refectarius could be given to any hard-working, responsible conversus or cleric. His responsibilities were supervision of the cooking staff so as to insure proper food preparation, general cleaning, preparation of tables, and timely food delivery to the tables. The servers on rotation would only have to concern themselves with condiments, wine and water containers, bread, fruit, salt, serving spoons, and candles, if necessary. During meals, the refectarius circulated and made sure everyone had what was needed.

In addition, it fell to the refectarius to provide for heating and ventilation of refectory. He controlled late arrivals for meals, and sent food to the sick and to guests. It fell to him to provide for those who needed to eat outside of mealtime. When a meal was finished, he directed the removal of tablecloths and dishes, and he supervised the scullery. He also provided for dispersal of any extra food as alms. This was a large job and so, Humbert tells us, the refectarius had his own office, near the pantry or wine cellar. In many ways, he resembles the manager of a modern large restaurant—Dominican houses with over one hundred friars to feed, twice daily, were not uncommon.

While the refectarius might be a cleric, the cook, who reported to the refectarius, was always a conversus who was, what we would call, a trained chef.[146] When the infirmary was large, there might be a separate infirmary kitchen with its own cook. Given the number of meals provided daily, the cook had a kitchen staff of several other conversi or hired seculars. Although Humbert allowed the hire of a secular as cook, if no conversus were available, later legislation restricted this position to a vowed conversus. But, should they be needed, seculars might be hired to assist him.[147] It was the cook who rang the signal calling the brethren to meals.

Beyond supervision of food preparation, the cook was responsible for training the secular kitchen help, and he corrected their errors. Humbert, however, warned him not to hit or curse them. He supervised the slaughter of animals and saw to the preparation of their feathers and hides for use later. His kitchen might be in a separate building from the monastery itself, and, if so, he was responsible for keeping it clean and secure, closed to outsiders. Beyond cooking itself, he procured all necessary cooking instruments and anything else necessary for food preparation, such as, with the help of the gardener, herbs, vegetables, and so on.

Dominican cooks lived a very hidden life in the 1200s, but we know the name of one of them, Pietro of Assisi, who died in 1279 at Perugia.[148] He was both cook and gardener. Not surprisingly, although Humbert never mentions the task, it fell to Pietro to cultivate the monastery's donors, especially those who supported the kitchen. He said special daily prayers for them, and was "loved by all." We are told that God even revealed to him his time of death so that he could prepare. What procuring food might involve is revealed in a story about a late-medieval Dominican cook, Nikolaas of Holland, who died at Haarlem in 1498.[149] Nikolaas was very exact in obedience; when not serving the brothers, he was in prayer. Once several Dominicans of high rank arrived at his monastery on a winter day in Lent. The prior ordered him to get a fish for them and prepare it. The shops being sold out, he came back empty handed. The prior rebuked him for his "lack of hospitality," and told him to go to the river and catch a fish. Nikolaas stripped off his habit and jumped into the water to try and catch something. Seeing one fish hiding in a hole in the bank, he called out: "The prior has ordered you to come out of hiding and give yourself into my hands!" The beautiful pike came out and offered itself to the brother, who took it home and cooked it up. All, we are told, had a splendid meal. That was a cook who would have made Humbert proud.

Reporting to the cook was the cellar-master, who was to be a friar with a good knowledge of wine.[150] Humbert does not specify that he must be a conversus, although the one cellarer that I have found was. Brother Bernardo, who died in 1382, served the community of Pisa in that capacity.[151] The cellarer oversaw the wine cellar or the beer supply, where wine was not the usual beverage. His cellar was to have an outer office and an inner storage room (where the stocks would be unseen by outsiders). Along with purchase of wine, he cleaned the casks, monitored them for leaks, and refilled them. When supplies were low, he informed his superior, the refectarius, so he could purchase more.

The last of those reporting to the cook was the gardener, who had a highly technical skill because of the variety of plants he had to maintain.[152] Humbert allows a cleric to exercise oversight of the gardens and have a conversus to do the actual physical labor, but it was easier to have a trained conversus in charge. The gardener might have conversi, or lay assistants if necessary. Within the monastery walls, even in cities, it was normal for friars to grow their own vines, fruit trees, and vegetables. Each of these required a different sort of care. The gardener also planted a flower garden for decoration of the altar and for roses to make rose water. He had to have a comprehensive knowledge of both cooking and medicinal herbs. In short, he also functioned as the house apothecary. Whatever he produced in excess, he was to sell. Humbert laconically tells us that the gardener should make sure the garden walls are secure and that there be no way to get over them. This was not an idle instruction. Thieves were always on the prowl. Two Italian conversus gardeners were remembered for their vigilance. Brother Mateolo (†1380) at Siena guarded his plants "like a dog" against entry by thieving youths.[153] While his confrere Colo (†1383), who was "known to all in Pisa as best gardener in town," went after any intruder, shouting at the top of his lungs, and "putting a look of fear on their faces."[154]

A Holy Brother Gardener

Mateolo and Colo sound more fierce than saintly, but their near contemporary, Simon Ballachi, presents us with the model of a holy gardener. Bl. Simon's medieval life is late, dating two centuries after his death.[155] But he was mentioned in the provincial acts of 1307 that reassigned him from the house in Venice to that in Treviso.[156] Born at Archangelo near Rimini, a son of Rodolfo Ballachi, Simon lived a worldly life for twenty-seven years, during which time he served as a soldier. Taking the habit of a conversus to lead a life of penance, he trained as monastery gardener and became an excellent one. When not in the garden, he cleaned house.

Simon's life gives us a window into the penitential life of many conversi, but it tells us nothing about his work as conventual gardener. Simon fasted, not only during Lent and Advent, but also during the popular lay periods of penance called the Lents of the Apostles (June), of the Virgin (August) and of St. Martin (November). Brothers had to rebuke him for fasting so much that he did not get his extra work in the sacristy done. Simon, we are told, tempered his fasts, but because he had been a "sinner in the world," he took the discipline daily and wore a chain discipline. When praying, he did multiple genuflections, a discipline seen in other contemporary Dominican lay blesseds. Brothers criticized his asceticism as excessive, mostly because it weakened him for work.

Like other conversi of the time we have mentioned, Simon was known for his devotion to the saints, especially John the Evangelist, who is said to have appeared to him, along with St. Dominic, St. Peter Martyr, and St. Catherine of Alexandria. This last was his favorite. At the age of fifty-seven, he went blind (supposedly from crying too much during prayer). St. Catherine appeared to him in a vision as he was dying. She asked him to have a monastery built in her honor. His father complied after Simon's death, which suggests that his background was fairly well to do. After his death on 3 November 1319, the crowds were so great that the friars could not bury him until two days later. Bl. Simon's immemorial cult was approved by Pope Pius VII in 1818. Originally celebrated on 3 November, he is now celebrated on the fifth of that month.

Like the refectarius, the vestiarius was a position of great responsibility.[157] He was over the production and distribution of clothing, linens, and shoes of all sorts. He also oversaw parchment production and the making and distribution of bedding. Like the cellarer, he had a two-part office. One part was in the cloister, and one was outside, where he directed any secular employees. The house tailor(s) and shoemaker(s) reported to him. Anything they could not make, he had to procure, either from donors or by purchase. Beyond production, he distributed clothing by season, provided linen for the sick and visitors, and distributed smocks for the kitchen help. He directed the common laundry and the cleaning of shoes. Finally, he was responsible for correcting friars with improper or ill-fitting clothing. The cloth trade was important and lucrative in medieval Europe, and late vocations from it might be men of stature and suitable as vestiarii. Brother Angelo, vestiarius at Orvieto along with another conversus, Brother Pietro, was a wealthy man and brought "many goods" to the monastery as his patrimony.[158] Even more distinguished was Brother Meo, famous in the world as tailor to the wealthy, who entered the Order in old age. He worked as vestiarius for four years at Orvieto before he died in 1329.[159]

Answering to the vestiarius at the production end was the house tailor.[160] Humbert expected that he be trained in his art, have his own workshop, and possess all the tools necessary to his trade. In a large house, he might have conversi or seculars as assistant tailors. Because of his heavy workload in certain seasons, Humbert dispensed him from attendance at all offices except Compline. As the true expert in clothes making, he could even reject as unsuitable cloth provided by the vestiarius. He was that friar's right-hand man, also responsible for reporting his faults to the superiors. Humbert never mentions it, but we know from the obituary of Brother Bondie, the highly skilled (*doctissimus*) tailor at Siena, that some with this office also made vestments for the sacristy.[161] Under the vestiarius was also the shoemaker, a conversus who knew how to cobble.[162] Like the tailor, he had his own workroom or part of a shared one, along with the necessary tools and supplies. It seems that finding conversi skilled in shoemaking was difficult, and Humbert provides for the vestiarius to hire an outsider, if needed.

Humbert also described posts with responsibilities for the physical plant of the monastery, tasks that included care for the different areas' proper functions. The last responsibility assigned specifically to a conversus that Humbert mentions is the dormitarius, who was responsible for the sleeping areas. Before examining the responsibilities of this office, we need to consider other conversi directly involved in plant maintenance whom Humbert, oddly enough, never mentioned. These include those brothers who built or maintained the building itself, carpenters and masons. We know these men principally from their obituaries. They included Brother Benvenuto of the monastery of St. Catherine in Pisa. He was not only remembered as a fine carpenter, but also participated in the construction of the monastery itself.[163] And then there was Brother Giovanni, who served the community at Orvieto, where he built the roof of the church, infirmary, and dormitory. He also undertook major construction at Spoleto, and then at Todi, where he constructed the choir. Giovanni died at Orvieto around 1310.[164] He seems to have been much more than a carpenter; perhaps we would best call him a kind of general contractor. There were certainly other conversi like Benvenuto and Giovanni, and we know of a whole series of masons, even architects, whom I will discuss in the next chapter.

Humbert describes three posts as assigned to clerics, in theory, exclusively. These posts included the sacristan, who not only prepared for liturgical functions, but was also responsible for the physical fabric of the church. Another was the infirmarian, who cared for the sick and maintained the infirmary. These two officials were under the treasurer, who, like them, according to the constitutions and other legislation, was supposed be a cleric.[165] In reality, the rule limiting these tasks to clerics seems often to have been ignored or circumvented. Conversi often assumed them, so I will discuss them here.

Humbert assumes that, because the sick might need anointing or Communion, a priest would normally serve as infirmarian.[166] A couple of general chapters required as much.[167] The infirmarian likewise handled considerable amounts of money, which might be as much as ten percent of the house's income. [168] In addition, the infirmarian, while not necessarily a physician, had to be trained in health care and able to administer, and even determine, what medicines the sick needed. There is nothing specifically clerical about tending the sick and giving medicine. In addition, the infirmarian was to provide for infirmary linen and laundry, hardly a clerical job. He was to have the beds made, the heat regulated, and to have someone read for the sick. He seems to have been on duty at all times, in case of emergencies or administering the Last Rites. There is no reason to assume that most priests had medical skills, and a priest infirmarian would certainly pass off the cleaning and tending to a conversus. Very likely, the "official" priest-infirmarian was simply on call for sacramental needs and for approving expenses.

In fact, many conversus infirmarians appear, with that very title, in our sources. At Santa Maria Novella in Florence, Brother Guido "Galenus" served as infirmarian for several decades in the mid-1200s. His nickname was taken from the famous ancient Greek medical theorist Galen. He may have even been a trained physician before he entered religious life.[169] Andrea of Perugia (†1323), a "late vocation," had been a trained pharmacist in the world. He not only served the Dominican sick, but saw lay patients from the city. When he died, lay people crowded his funeral.[170] Among the holy friars of Santarem whose stories were sent for use in the *Lives of the Brethren*, is Brother Martinho, a physician who was the house infirmarian. We are not told if he was ordained, but he seems to have spent much of his time treating townspeople for free at the door of the infirmary, which suggests he was not. In any case, a conversus, who was working in the infirmary, Brother Pedro, saw Martinho levitate in ecstasy during prayer and heard "secrets," which he was forbidden to reveal. This Pedro himself, we are told, was attacked while in prayer, by the Devil "in the form of a friar." Carried back to the infirmary to be tended by Brother Martinho, he died piously. Those who attended him at his bedside reported that his face glowed with unearthly radiance.[171] In fact, after 1300, we will hear of many other conversus infirmarians.

Like the infirmarian, Humbert assumed that the sacristan would be a priest.[172] Nevertheless, obituaries record conversi with this title. For example, there was Brother Giacomo of Silvalunga, a conversus who was sacristan at Siena in the later 1200s, where he outfitted the entire new sacristy.[173] At least nominally, however, there had to be a priest "sacristan" for certain clerical functions. The sacristan had to know the *Ordinarium* for the Mass and Office to make sure that everything needed was put out for the various feasts. But a literate conversus could do that. A priest, however, had to store and retrieve Communion Hosts, keep the Holy Oils, assist visiting bishops, and take Communion to the sick. As laymen were forbidden to touch sacred vessels and corporals, a priest had to purify and wash them.[174] The sacristan had to be literate enough to receive stipends and offerings, to keep financial records, and to pass on an account of monies to his successor. But, again, a literate conversus could do those things.

Humbert details a long list of duties that the sacristan, in theory a priest, would surely have passed on to a conversus assistant: sweeping and cleaning the church; arranging paraments and decorating for feasts; and maintaining the physical plant of the church, the sacristy itself, and the cemetery. He was also to ring the church bells for offices, fill and light the lamps, and provide candles. He did the lighting, not just for the church, but for the whole house, as he kept the house flint and steel. He kept the church and sacristy clean, and the vessels and reliquaries polished. Finally, before burials, he was to open the grave. It was in fulfilling one such duty that the conversus sacristan at Santa Maria Novella, Brother Bartolomeo, witnessed a purported miracle in the late 1220s. A pious woman wanted to light a lamp at the shrine of Bl. John of Salerno, but told Bartolomeo she had no oil. He told her to go home and check. She did so and found her empty oil stock miraculously full![175]

Humbert tells us that cleaning, airing, and tidying of the sleeping quarters was normally assigned to the table servers of the week. But, if there should be a conversus with so little skill as to be nearly useless (*minus utilis*), he could be assigned as the permanent dormitarius, and we can find traces of such men in chapter acts as well.[176] This office amounts to little more than a domestic drudge, and Humbert seems to envision it as a way to employ a totally unskilled brother. This is, for him, anomalous. To his mind, conversi should be mature men, who bring with them the skills and talents necessary for the functioning of the monastery.

So what would be the responsibility of such a "less useful" brother? He opened and closed the dormitory, and rang the wake-up bell. As dormitarius, he opened and closed the windows according to the weather, being especially attentive to protecting books from water during storms. He made sure the lamps had sufficient oil. It fell to him to provide the books for private recitation of the Divine Office when clerics are unable to attend. He was responsible for the daily sweeping and cleaning of the dormitory and making sure that the beds are made and that the urinal is kept tidy. He did not normally do these tasks himself; rather they fell to each individual friar. When they failed in them, he was to report it, as well as anything "indecent," to the superiors. None of this work seems burdensome or highly time consuming. We may suspect that dormitarii sometimes ended up as general-purpose household help.

CONVERSUS PENITENTS

Penance was central to the medieval understanding of religious life. Men and women entered religion to atone for their sins and to offer their mortifications for sinners, living and dead. Although never mentioned by Humbert, the practice of penance was central to conversus identity. Although the religious life itself was considered in itself penitential, friars, like monks and other religious, added their own personal mortifications. Such practices are especially mentioned in the obituaries of conversi. Brother Bonino of Treviso (†1320), was well known for his piety and austerity.[177] He fasted on bread and water six months of the year, during three of which he ate only barley bread. He went to Confession daily. Brother Andrea Capponi vowed on entering never to eat fresh figs because he liked them so much.[178] He kept his vow until death. Others added corporal penances. Andrea Mancini (†1260), a conversus at Perugia, was mostly remembered for his penances. He fasted daily, wore a hair-shirt (his only warmth in winter), and took the discipline for a quarter of an hour every day.[179] Were our records more complete, we would surely have many other examples.

A good number of men, often late in life, choose to enter as lay brothers specifically to do penance. Older men might also have the ulterior motive of finding a community to nurse them in old age. Chapters warned against such vocations and tried to prevent them. Or, at least, they tried to make sure that older men relinquished control of their property to the house before they were professed.[180] For some, entering came as a natural conclusion to life as a pious layman. Brother Domenico (†1290) had already lived like a religious in the world for decades before entering the house at Perugia. A tailor in the world, he put his skills at the service of friars. But he was always prompt to put down his needle, if a priest needed a server for private Mass. During his thirty-six years as a brother he never missed Matins.[181] Brother Giovanni of Verne (†1330), who likewise never married, had spent his life as a quasi-religious, a servant of the nuns at Perugia. After asking to be admitted as a conversus, he lived out the last eight years of his life as a penitent brother.[182]

Domenico and Giovanni had been celibate in the world, but some penitents became conversi only as widowers. Brother Matteo entered after his wife of twelve years had died. He himself was quite elderly and died while still a novice.[183] In contrast, Biaggio of Perugia (†1267) and his wife mutually agreed to enter religious life, a not unheard-of choice in medieval Italy. She entered the monastery of San Giorgio, while he become a conversus with the Dominicans, where he worked as a gardener. He never ate any fruit while working in the orchard, of such rigor was his practice of "temperance."[184] Not all penitents were townspeople. Brother Niccolò de' Ardinghelli had been a merchant by sea for forty years, before spending the last twenty years of his life as a conversus at Santa Maria Novella, where he died of the plague.[185]

Penitent conversi could be very wealthy men. As such, they may have had guilty consciences from practicing usury. Benintende (†1267), who was extremely rich, entered the house at Perugia as a lay brother, over the "tears and protests" of family and children. He spent the rest of his life piously atoning for his sins.[186] In Germany, Brother Stefan of Metz, who entered in the early 1300s, was not only rich but from a very noble family.[187] Sometimes, a son's vocation inspired a father widower to enter the life. Brother Pierre de Frachet (†1256), father of Gérard de Frachet, the compiler of the *Lives of the Brethren*, became a conversus in 1250. He gave up great worldly wealth to enter the house of Limoges on the feast of the Birth of the Virgin. His son came up from Marseille, where he was prior, for the event. This was also the day of the dedication of the new conventual church, so the new brother Pierre received the personal blessing of Archbishop Philippe Berruyer, who had come to do the ceremony.[188] When a vocation was well connected enough, he might even set the terms of his entry. Feliz Franchiote (†1484) from Galicia in Spain, got the permission of Pope Paul II to unite a church dependent on St. John Lateran to a monastery that he built on his own lands. There he created a new Dominican house where he specially dedicated himself to the service of the sick. This ministry he performed faithfully until his death nine years later.[189]

It was sometimes hard for a rich conversus to cut the link with his money. Peter of Basel (†1420) while in the world had spent two hours each day meditating on the Passion. After his wife died, he entered the Dominican house at Colmar and gave all his money to the monastery. Well, not quite. He held back forty écus (perhaps $5,600 today), which he hid in a sack around his neck. He soon took very sick. In delirium, he had a vision of an ugly woman burning him with a torch. Fortunately, the Blessed Virgin arrived to chase her off. The vicar of the house wanted to see the wound, which proved to be the sack itself. The vicar declared: "This was the demon." Peter surrendered the last of his money and was healed. From then on he lived a perfect religious life as a penitent brother.[190]

Perhaps the most famous penitent conversus of the whole thirteenth century was Carino of Balsamo, best known as the assassin of St. Peter of Verona. He and his popular cult as a blessed have recently been the subject of scholarly study.[191] We know little of the assassin's early life. His baptismal name may have been Caro, and it is unlikely that he himself was ever a Cathar. He was a hired thug, and it was as such that Milanese Cathar sympathizers and opponents of the Church hired him to kill the famous preacher and inquisitor. A Milanese politician, Manfredo, was the architect of the murder, the "principal plotter" of the conspiracy. Carino seems to have been hired because he was a dumb tough, not quite aware of the danger, and greedy enough to risk it. But he was not so dumb as not to demand help. The plotters hired Alberto Porro of Lentate, nicknamed "Il Magnifico," to help him.

Carino discovered that Peter and three companions were going to travel from Milan to Como at Easter (6 April 1252). Refused the use of Manfredo's horse, Carino and Alberto had to run to catch up with Peter, who, suffering from a bad cold, had left two of the other friars behind to eat lunch. Peter and his socius Domenico had gone on ahead. Domenico was not, as is sometimes said, a conversus.[192] Ambush was laid, but Alberto deserted and headed back to Milan. On the way, he met the other two friars and revealed the plot. Carino himself waylaid Peter and Domenico, first murdering the socius with four blows of his axe. Peter prayed, saying, "Into your hands, Lord." Carino attacked him as he began to recite the Creed. Peter was immediately killed by a savage blow to the head. Carino ran off and was intercepted by a farmer who thought he was running for help.

The farmer must have been armed, as he took Carino into custody, and turned him in to the podestà of Milan, Pietro de' Avvocati. The podestà did the initial investigation. Carino ratted out the coconspirators. But, somehow, on the night of 16 April, Carino escaped from the city jail. The assassin seems to have spent several months on the run, until he arrived in Forlì, where he fell deathly sick. He entered the Hospital of San Sebastiano, where the Dominican prior heard his "deathbed" confession. But

Carino recovered quickly and begged to become a penitent in the prior's community. The oblation of the new conversus was approved by the prior and chapter just about the time of Peter Martyr's own canonization, 25 May 1253. In addition, Daniele da Giussano, one of the other conspirators, became a penitent at Sant'Eustorgio, but as a cleric. He was ordained and became an inquisitor. It seems that after his transfer to the Dominican house of Forlì in 1269, Bl. James Salomoni became Carino's spiritual director. There were reports that the assassin experienced ecstacy during contemplation.

Carino died about 1293, after some forty years as a conversus. The exact day is unknown, but the date of his unofficial feast is 22 November. At the request of the people of Forlì, Carino's relics were translated and put in a shrine in the monastery sacristy. They were later joined by those of Bl. James Salomoni and moved to a shrine in the church. The current shrine altar, originally in the Dominican church, was completed in 1658, and has included the relics of Bl. Marcolino of Forlì since 1664. During the unification of Italy, the shrine was moved to the cathedral in 1879. Bl. Carino today enjoys the place of honor in the middle, between the other two holy Dominicans—that is, except for his head. It was given to the parish church of San Martino at Balsamo, his hometown, in the early twentieth century. A petition was made for the recognition of Carino's cult in the nineteenth century, but it has never been approved. Nevertheless, the assassin is probably the most famous conversus of his century, even more so than his fellow penitent, Bl. Simon Ballachi.

Chapter 2
Beyond the Monastery, 1300–1500

In the previous chapter we examined the origins, spiritual life, and the work of *conversi* within the community. Given that the life of conversi was a hidden life, much of it was invisible to those outside the monastery. But, even from the time of St. Dominic, conversi had a visible presence to the world. In the last decades of the thirteenth century, sources for this presence become more numerous. We remember that St. Dominic wanted the friars to live on alms, and that he wanted the conversi to be responsible for temporalities. Although the brothers in 1219 insisted that the treasurer be a cleric, procuring food, supplies, and even monetary alms seems to have fallen principally to the brothers—as Dominic said, priests should be free to pray and study in preparation for preaching. Preachers were, in fact, forbidden to ask alms when preaching or hearing confessions publicly.[1] Dominicans were to be mendicants, but not all friars did much begging.

Brothers as Mendicants

All extant provincial and general chapter legislation, when discussing begging, speak only of conversi. The two lay brothers, when out begging, were always to remain in eye contact with each other, nor were they to allow lay people, especially women, to help them carry what they collected.[2] In one case, a chapter even contrasted fundraising in general (*questua*) from the day-to-day procuring of house necessities, the latter being solely the task of the conversi, while clerics could help in the first.[3]

One famous story about conversus beggars, however, that of Raimundo of Orvieto and Domenico of Viterbo, usually dated to 1221, is not witnessed until much later and so is probably legendary.[4] The brothers supposedly called on the countess of Anguillaria near Rome and received a bushel of meal. Later, the noble lady discovered that her own sack was still full and, thinking that the brothers had refused and returned her gift, she confronted them. But they still had the alms. Her sack had been miraculously refilled. Or so the story goes. We also have a marvel story for another early conversus, Brother Giovanni of Calabria (†1227), who received the habit from Dominic and died at Santa Sabina in Rome. He was in charge of alms collection for all the friars in Rome, a task at which he "joyfully" spent every morning. Legend records that after one less-than-fruitful morning excursion, two angelic figures appeared in the refectory with bread to make up his shortfall. This story, I suspect, may be borrowed from events in Bologna. On the other hand, an early Dominican legend calls Giovanni "blessed," and he was painted with an aureole in a fresco at San Pietro Martire in Naples.[5] In the later 1200s, we hear of another conversus alms-collector, Brother Élie Martel (†1274) of Brives, near Limoges, France. His soft touch, especially in helping the poor, was famous, and he was much beloved by the townspeople.[6]

Conversi not only collected alms; Humbert of Romans assumed that their distribution was a lay-brother responsibility.[7] He wrote that a conversus should be assigned as the monastery "almoner" (*elemonsinarius*), and that the one chosen should be friendly, of good morals, edifying in speech, and prudent. The almoner was, first of all, in charge of almsgathering generally. Although he might beg himself, he was expected to have a team to do this, including other friars as well as lay agents. This alms collection supported the guest house, infirmary, kitchen, and the pay of lay employees (*familiares*). Meat for the infirmary was to be kept clearly separate from other alms.

Sometimes the begging was done by "broadcasting (*clamando*) the needs of the preaching brothers" in the streets and piazzas, but more important was that done by direct solicitation. If the very wealthy or magnates were to be approached, the almoner should consult first with the prior, so as to discern whether he should approach them directly or through one of his agents. Humbert assumes that the house almoner will, with his socius, spend much of his time outside the monastery.

At home, the almoner supervised the distribution of food and other necessities to the poor. Such provisions were to be distributed at set times and on set days. Since food alms were not distributed daily, he was to ensure that leftovers did not spoil, and that they be prepared in such a manner that they could be stored.

The almoner was one of the public faces of the community and so the position was sensitive. He had to be able to discern spiritual needs, not only material ones, and give good words of counsel to those coming to the door.[8] Humbert knew that those asking help could be a tough lot, contentious and rowdy. So the almoner had to be able to deal with this. He was to have the discretion to separate the unworthy from "honorable and shamefaced persons" down on their luck. He was to send away or correct the unworthy, annoying pests, and frauds, in particular vagrants (*trutani*) and rogues (*ribaldi*).

One conversus, Brother Giovanni of Segromigno, well known to the chronicler Tolomeo of Lucca, was sent to the missions in the Holy Land, where he met Teobaldo Visconti, a preacher of the Crusade. Teobaldo took him back to Europe with him. After his election as Gregory X, the new pope made Giovanni elemosinarius of the papal court. He served in the post until he died in 1288.[9]

In the later Middle Ages, reports of highly successful conversus "fundraisers" become common. Two interesting examples appear in the necrology, that is, the collection of friars' obituaries, of Santa Maria Novella in Florence. Brother Giacomo di Andrea Aldobrandini was born in the neighborhood of the monastery and had acquired cooking, and construction skills in stone, wood, and glass while in the world. He suffered from gout and, during attacks, he was known for spending his time in bed reading pious books in the vernacular. But it was in raising money that he really excelled. The fruits of his begging funded major expenditures for decorating the church. These included a beautiful large chalice and a set of silver candlesticks. His work also funded the commission of religious paintings, reliquaries and "many other things" (underlined in the manuscript).

Finally, he undertook the remodeling of the sacristy at the cost of 250 gold florins, the gold content of which would be valued at about $35,000 today, although this probably underestimates the coin's medieval purchasing power. Contrary to legislation requiring that the offices be held by a cleric, Giacomo became treasurer and sacristan of the monastery. He later continued his work in Viterbo and then in Rome, where he died in 1369.[10]

As a fundraiser, Giacomo can be compared to the perhaps

even more successful Brother Niccolò di Michele Bonini of Milan. He was later transferred south to Santa Maria Novella in Florence. There was a reason for this. In the world, he had once been first trumpeter of the city of Florence, which had brought him many noble connections. Assigned to Florence, he became both sacristan for the chapel of San Niccolò, his patron, and chief fundraiser (*questuarius*) of the house. In this latter position, he raised 500 gold florins (about $70,000) to acquire a new altarpiece for the high altar. Unfortunately, this commission has been lost. Giacomo was remembered by a long entry in the monastery necrology when he died in 1467.[11]

Both these almoners raised money for the embellishment of the church, but that kind of fundraising seems a specialty of conversi who served in the sacristy. I have noted that Humbert specified that sacristans be clerics, but they had conversus assistants. Some of these, like Brother Stefano de' Pungilupi of Spina (†1363), simply cleaned (very well we are told) the church and sacristy and took care of the vestments.[12] Or, like Brother Giovanni "Teutonico" (†1488), the assistant to the priest sacristan Father Antonio in Florence, he rang the church bells for Matins and other offices.[13] But others brought a skilled craft to the sacristy. Brother Giacomo di Cristiano, socius of the necrologer of the house in Pisa, not only worked hard in the sacristy, but also crafted fine chalices. He was known to be an expert in dealing with the sometimes demanding women who frequented the priory church.[14] Like Giacomo, his fellow conversus, Pietro was famous for the quality of the vestments he sewed. He, too, acquired a "precious altarpiece" for the high altar.[15]

Pietro's purchase implied that he handled money, and so did other conversus sacristans. Brother Gaddo, of the same house, a "famous conversus," had been a goldsmith before he entered. He seems to have been known for putting the touch on his former clients and other wealthy Pisans. This included acquiring donations of large tracts of land. He died, after thirty years in the Order, in 1322.[16] Conversi could bring in money in other ways. Brother Giovanni di Francesco (†1433) of Siena sat all day in the church of San Domenico there, selling candles.[17] Brother Borghese of Santa Maria Novella (†1419) was famous as a sculptor in wax, embellishing and, we assume, selling Paschal candles.[18] He was for forty years custodian of the sacristy. He was also an expert tailor of vestments, who embroidered them with gold and silken thread so that the ministers "glowed like seraphim." One conversus sacristan, Brother Giacomo de' Bergi, was also house treasurer.[19] He seems to have had financial savvy. He also served as treasurer for the nuns of San Domenico of Cafaggio and for the *Laudesi* Society of Santa Maria Novella. One might call him a professional money manager.

BROTHERS AS THE FACE OF THE COMMUNITY

Even more than the almoner, who was on duty in the alms house only at certain hours, or the sacristan, who worked only in the church, the most public face of the Dominican community was probably the porter, who was on duty all day in the reception area and on call at night. In this role, he was especially responsible for the security of the house and monitoring those entering and leaving the cloister.[20] Humbert of Romans was prejudiced in favor of porters being priests, so that they could immediately serve the spiritual needs of visitors.[21] But practice seems to have been different. Already in the 1240s, general chapters envisioned that porters could be, and perhaps usually were, conversi. This was acceptable, so long as they were mature, discreet, and trustworthy.[22] Humbert himself agreed. Porters should be gracious, without vices, prudent and responsible, pleasant, and not tired out by many questions and delays. The porter must be patient with difficult people and able to avoid scandal.

The porter had his own office next to the main door of the monastery. If a cleric, he might read or write in slack times; if a conversus, he should pray. When answering the door, he should check through its peephole to assure that no troublemakers or women would be admitted inside. There must always be someone on duty at the door. So, if the porter has no assistant, he must sleep in his office, and he may skip Matins. If he did have a socius, the two should exchange turns weekly as to who was on night duty and who went to first table for meals. The porter locked the doors of the monastery at night and unlocked them in the morning.

The most important task of the porter was to serve as receptionist. Humbert explains that he may escort "excellent persons" (bishops, abbots, nobles, benefactors) to the chapter room and there kneel and kiss their hand. Franciscan friars were to be received "with the greatest joy." He was to know all the "friends of the house," that is, benefactors, so that he can treat them properly. Finally, if there were women intrusively frequenting the church or house, he was to send them away with kind (*mollia*) words, or even harsh (*dura*) ones, if necessary. The poor he was to feed at the door "charitably." Finally, Humbert added that he was to attend to all those begging aid, especially poor clerics, and to find housing for pilgrims.

While first reception of clerical or lay guests fell to the porter, their care was really the responsibility of the guestmaster (*receptor hospitium*), a friar expected to have good people skills and to be charitable and hard working.[23] While, in theory, the guestmaster could be a cleric, virtually all his tasks were better discharged by a conversus. When the porter called for him, he was to welcome guests, asking their blessing, if they were priests and he was a lay brother. He was to take care of their books, staffs, and traveling baggage. If the guest should be the master of the Order, he rang the priory bell. For all priests, he was to see that they could celebrate Mass, and he supplied them with office books if they needed them.

After getting guests settled in, the guestmaster was to provide for their meals in the guest rectory. He was to deliver their food from the kitchen and cellar, and make sure they all got their serving of fish or any special foods that the cook had prepared. They were not to be given meat. If possible, the guestmaster should provide that edifying books be read to them while they ate. If they needed clothing, he asked it from the vestiarius. Humbert tells us that the guestmaster, here obviously a conversus, should set up before and clean up after meals, as well as clean the guest bedrooms and lavatory. He also washed the dishes and did guests' laundry, if needed.

In some cases, perhaps most of the time in smaller houses, the duties of almoner and porter logically fell to a single brother, who officially held the two posts. One example of such a porter-almoner, who should be better known, is the saintly Portuguese conversus Pedro of Aveiro (1456–1528).[24] Born in the maritime city of Aveiro of extremely poor parents, Pedro became a sailor. Very pious from his youth, he always confessed before major journeys to priests from the Dominican house of the town. We are told that he avoided "all the sensual sins linked to his profession." Eventually, at the suggestion of his confessor, he asked entry as a conversus.

His asceticism became obvious while still a novice. He drank no wine and ate no meat. Pedro never ceased to think of himself as a "poor sailor," unworthy to wear the habit. Only in his later years in the infirmary did he use a bed. Rather, as his monastery had adopted the early-modern practice of breaking sleep for Matins, he kept vigil nightly in the chapel of the Magdalen until Matins, then returned to the chapel, and slept the rest of the night on the floor. He did what he could to make his food less flavorful and, while working in the laundry, he swapped other conversus habits with his own, if they were in worse condition.

Pedro served his monastery as almoner and porter. In the latter position, he once failed to open the door for the prior because he had been called away by the subprior. The prior severely punished this "failure." Pedro accepted his penance with thanksgiving, but the subprior confronted the superior for his mistake. Pedro, however, insisted on doing his penance in light of his "hidden sins." The townspeople called him "father, defender, and servant of the poor." Pedro went daily, begging food for the poor. He fed them in a kind of soup kitchen attached to the porter's office. After his death a wealthy woman commissioned a fresco of these "banquets" for the church.

After leading this pious, if austere, life for a few years, we understand that Pedro suffered diabolical attacks. The devil once appeared as a pious man, who said that all the brother's penances were worthless as he was damned. Pedro replied: "If I am damned, it is just because of my sins, but God will have mercy on me because of the infinite merits of Jesus Christ his Son." That devil fled. After eight years of interior temptations, the demons attacked him physically at night before Matins, sometimes leaving him bloody. Thinking that relocation might help relieve the attacks, his superiors reassigned him to the house at Evora, where again he was made porter and responsible for the poor.

Unfortunately, this did little to stop the attacks. At Evora, Pedro's reputation for holiness and prophecy began to spread outside the monastery. He was known for the gift of prophecy, mostly concerning the time of people's deaths. He said he would hear a loud knock (in different places for those in different states of life) when someone was about to die. He would then warn them to make their preparations. It was claimed that, in this way, he forewarned the death of seven friars during a plague.

All in Evora wanted his prayers, and the rich and nobles sought him out. Once, the widow of Don Fernando de Castro asked for him and knelt to kiss his scapular. Pedro fell back, crying that he was "just a sinful brother." The priest to whom he was socius, Father Alvarez Mendès, then ordered him to let her kiss it. For him, these visits were like being in prison. King Manuel and Queen Maria of Portugal regularly came to Mass at the house in Evora. The queen always singled out Pedro for conversation and spiritual advice when the community received the royal couple. The royal inspector of monasteries, Father Juan Hurtado, singled out Brother Pedro as the model religious.

At an advanced age, Pedro was found paralyzed in the church one morning and, under obedience, was moved to a bed in the infirmary. He confessed to Father Alfonso Banha and predicted his own death for the next day, Epiphany 1528. The prior was skeptical, but Viaticum was sent for, and the novices were summoned to attend at his bedside. The conversus demanded that they be allowed to take Communion with him. After this, he begged to be taken back to die in the porter's office. After the Epiphany Mass, the celebrant came to visit, and Pedro asked for Extreme Unction. The brother then looked up to heaven and recited the opening of Psalm 56, *Benedictus Deus,* in Latin. He closed his eyes and died. Already in his lifetime, he had been nicknamed "O Santo." In spite of precautions by the prior, word got out of his funeral. Huge crowds attended, invaded the cloister, and refused to leave his tomb. Unable to continue with the community's planned funeral dinner, the prior ordered it be given to the poor. Brother Pedro would have been delighted. His unofficial cult, as Blessed Pedro of Evora, lasted into the modern period.

We have noted a couple of conversi who combined, for example, work in the sacristy or as questuarius with the responsibilities of the house treasurer. This implies, if not true Latin fluency, some ability to do computation and keep simple written (Latin) records. As a lay merchant, Francis of Assisi had this ability. A lack of this kind of basic ability was probably as important as nonclerical status for not appointing conversi as treasurers. But there are hints that some conversi possessed this kind of functional Latin literacy. This seems especially true in the later Middle Ages. Brother Vanno of Verona (†1340), we are told, could not only play the organ and paint very well, he was also skilled in singing Gregorian chant. Brother Giovanni of Bologna (†1494), who died at the house in Faenza, had the community around his deathbed. He joyfully sang the Apostles Creed and other Latin chants as he lay dying.

Did Vanno and Giovanni understand what they were singing? We do not know.[25] We do know, however, that Brother Matteo of the Popolo Santa Maria in Florence, who was vestiarius and tailor of the house in Orvieto, could read and sing the Office, "as well as any clerical brother." He chanted all the offices but Matins with the clerics. But he did attend Matins, and afterwards read the entire Psalter every night before dawn. After the age of fifty, bedridden with gout, he had to be satisfied with simply reciting the Breviary on his own. He died in 1336.[26]

Men like Matteo certainly had the literacy and culture to serve as treasurer, and we know that a number of conversi did, or at least acted as the agent of a clerical treasurer. A document of Santa Maria Novella records a Brother Bruno, conversus, as the house's financial agent as early as 1250.[27] Brother Paolo of Popolo San Gregorio (†1332) was infirmarian for forty years. And he was the legal agent when the *Laudesi* of Santa Maria Novella commissioned a major painting of the Madonna from Duccio in 1285.[28] These men may have been merely agents, but Brother Filippo Manzoli (†1420) was officially treasurer of his monastery and he so appears in documents from 1380 to 1400. He seems to alternate in office with another conversus, Borghese, who died the year before him. Filippo was also infirmarian and sacristan. His obituary says that he was so well educated that he should have been called a "magister," not a "conversus."[29] Again, these men may be exceptional, but the image of medieval conversi as illiterate peasants, found even among some modern historians, needs nuance.

So far, we have focused on conversi who worked inside or mostly inside the community. There were some conversi, who seem, like the preachers, to be almost always away from the monastery. But before we examine them, can we take a guess at how many conversi were assigned, at least in percentages, to various tasks in medieval Dominican houses? The evidence is sketchy, and many obituaries merely mention the conversi's names, not their responsibilities.[30] For three Italian medieval houses, however, jobs are given for a good number of the conversi. For the smaller house at Orvieto, jobs are given for about half the conversi who died before the necrology ceases during the Black Death (1348).[31] Of these eleven friars, the most common position, held by four, was vestiarius. Then there are seven friars, listed as mason, sacristan, bottle-maker, carpenter, copyist, gardener, and barber.

Although the necrology for Santa Catarina in Pisa is too fragmentary to be of use for the period before 1300, it is very complete for the fourteenth century. Jobs are given for 25 out of 27 deceased conversi.[32] The largest group here are the professional beggars (*questuarii*), with six. One suspects that here or elsewhere, many conversi combined this work with some other responsibilities. The next most common are shoemakers (5) and sacristans (4). Then come two vestiarii and two sculptors (more on them later). Then one each for: porter, infirmarian, socius to provincial, tailor, gardener, and cellar-master. Perhaps the biggest surprise, given the needs of Dominican communities, is the absence of cooks and kitchen staff. Perhaps these two houses hired lay workers for that need.

The most extensive necrology available to me in print is that for Santa Maria Novella, and it covers three centuries.[33] The listings for the thirteenth century are too fragmentary to be of use, although a couple of these are "architects," whom I will discuss later. In the fourteenth century, when 36 of the 57 deceased conversi have job descriptions, the largest group by far (10) are involved in the physical plant. These are described as "architects," "masons," or "carpenters." With the exception of the architects, these titles do not seem technical. After these men, the next largest group are the sacristans (6). There are three treasurers, whom I have already mentioned. Then come barbers, shoemakers, and tailors, three of each. With the two vestiarii, clothing seems, after the physical plant, the major conversus responsibility. There are a cook and two gardeners. And a lone "painter." So, during this period, in a large house like Santa Maria Novella, shelter, clothing, and food, in that order, were major responsibilities of conversi. But they were also found in the sacristy. Most of these men probably also did some begging. If I had to guess, I would suspect that this sample is representative of larger houses in this period.

The evidence for the fifteenth century at Santa Maria Novella is somewhat different. We certainly find the kind of jobs we have seen earlier. The percentage of conversi as a whole seems definitely lower than the figures for the two previous centuries, surely a result of the recurrence of the plague. With fewer workers, wages went up and this would have made the brotherhood a less attractive choice for some. At Santa Maria Novella, brothers compose only 18 out of 221 of deceased friars (12%).[34] We know most of their jobs. And I would venture to say that some conversi were "professionalized" in this period. Some brothers hold jobs for very long periods of their lives, and some hold one job exclusively. Three men are not merely identified as beggars, but they are praised for being extraordinary at this work. All conversi probably begged, but these men seem to be committed fundraisers. There were also five infirmarians, each following the other in office. Each seems to have trained his successor. Most interestingly, seven worked as sacristans, and there were three house treasurers. In almost all cases, however, these men often functioned in both positions at the same time. There seems to have been, as with infirmarians, something like a dynasty of sacristan-treasurers, who managed house finances. One of these, Niccolò Bonini, I have already mentioned. There were also two vestiarii, a porter, and a cook.

These necrologies are all Italian, often fragmentary, and probably leave much unsaid. But at least they give examples of conversi at work, often at tasks requiring considerable training and skill, in the monasteries.

CONVERSI OUTSIDE THE MONASTERY

When conversi went about soliciting alms, providing charity in the porter's office, receiving guests, or serving in the sacristy and church, they regularly had contact with outsiders. In all these cases, however, the base of operations for their work remained their monastery. By the end of the thirteenth century, and even earlier, we see brothers with responsibilities outside the house itself. Perhaps the earliest example of this was when brothers were assigned as traveling companions, *socii*, to other friars. There has been some speculation that conversi were assigned to superiors, like the master of the Order, as a matter of policy. Supposedly conversi were the socii of choice for Dominican superiors, bishops, and inquisitors.[35] Actual evidence for this is weak. St. Dominic and Jordan of Saxony had conversi with them when traveling, but there is no evidence of a rule or practice to that effect. Likewise, the suggestion that Dominic had a special preference for conversus companions is unfounded. Probably, most early brothers traveling with Dominican superiors did not have the official status of socius.[36]

This is not to say that conversi did not serve friars out on the road. Jordan had two friar companions with him when he was shipwrecked, a cleric, Gerald and a conversus named Albisius. Both died with him, and their bodies where found on the beach with his.[37] By the 1300s, we find conversi associated with itinerant preachers. Brother Giacomo (†1328), nicknamed "Ave Maria" because of his devotion to the Blessed Virgin, usually held the post of vestiarius. But he was also attached to the famous preacher Remigio dei Gerolami during his provincialate. Giacomo was a man of some learning. He read the canonical hours and those of the Blessed Virgin along with Remigio. He also spent his nights reading the Psalms.[38] Another conversus also served as Remigio's companion. Brother Filippo di fu Dato was first the preacher's lay servant and then admitted to the order as a cook.[39] Records call these men companions (*famuli*), not socii. Another example would be Rainerio, the brother of the preacher, and later bishop, Ambroggio of Rimini, who became a conversus late in life and was Ambroggio's assistant.[40] It is clear, however, that by the 1400s, preachers were regularly being assigned conversi as their socii.[41]

The evidence for bishops receiving conversi as assistants is somewhat better and certainly earlier. After what appears to be initial resistance to loaning out conversi, by the 1240s, we find examples of bishops with Dominican lay brother helpers. These include the bishops Gualtiero of Calabria, Masseo of Chiusi, and Cardinal Latino of Ostia.[42] Brother Giovanni of Fiordimaggio served both Masseo and Latino.[43] Such assignments became common as the fourteenth century progressed. Brother Lorenzo became socius of the Dominican Marco de' Roncioni, who later became bishop of Urbino. He got Giovanni a category change to cleric, which suggests that the brother was a man of some culture. The two died at sea in about 1327.[44]

Brother Giacomo of Ficulle in Umbria (†1330), a bottle maker, became socius to the Dominican cardinal Niccolò of Prato (†1321). He was noted as a questuarius and spent forty years as a brother. Although "illiteratus," he knew how to say the canonical hours and the Little Office of the Blessed Virgin. He was also very diligent in serving Mass.[45] He sounds much like Remigio de' Gerolami's conversus, Giacomo Ave Maria. Pedro of Tarragona (†1330) was socius for the Dominican missionary Bartolomeo of Bologna, the apostle of Armenia. He accompanied the missionary on many journeys and died in Armenia.[46] It seems that some of these conversi actually became house managers for their prelates. The versatile Giovanni di Stefano (†1375), served as sacristan, infirmarian, cook, and cellar-master at Santa Maria Novella. He then became majordomo and stable-master for Cardinal Pietro Corsini, former bishop of Florence. He followed the cardinal to Avignon, and died there, in 1375.[47] Some of these conversi received longer obituaries in the necrologies than those of most friar priests.

These conversus socii sometimes seem little more than servants to clerics of rank. But, beginning in the later 1200s, we discover a new phenomenon in Italy, conversi employed by Church and state as artists and architects. The latter often seem to function more like engineers or general contractors. But this language suggests a modern division of labor in construction that did not exist in this period. Before Fra Angelico, nearly all known Dominican artists and builders were lay brothers.[48] The most notable of these men are the dynasty of architects identified with Santa Maria Novella. These men were responsible for the church and monastery fabric, but much of their work was for outside employers. The first in this series were Brothers Sisto (†1289) and Ristoro (†1283). These men are known from the Santa Maria Novella necrology, where the entries are mostly sixteenth century, but seem trustworthy.[49]

Of the two, we know the least about Brother Sisto. He was born in Florence near Porta San Pancrazio, in the neighborhood of San Sisto, probably in the early 1220s. He died at Rome. Brother Ristoro was born in Campi, between Florence and Prato, perhaps around 1230. It has been suggested that the two men studied under the famous architect Arnolfo di Cambio, or perhaps under Giovanni and Niccolò Pisano, equally famous sculptors, but there is no evidence for this. Both men were certainly trained builders. Most of their work, first in Florence and then in Rome, was done as a team. After Sisto's death, Ristoro returned to Florence. It seems the men entered Santa Maria Novella as conversi in the mid-1250s. If that is correct, it seems that Ristoro had already done work for the commune of Florence, supervising canal construction after the Arno flood of 1252.

After entrance to the order, both men served the city officially as superintendents of buildings. This may have included work on the Palazzo dei Priori, the "city hall" of Florence, where they are credited with construction of the vaulting. Their responsibilities certainly included work on fortifications and bridges, in particular, the Ponte Santa Trinità, after the flood of 1269, and the Ponte alla Carraia, after its destruction by a flood in 1274. In both cases, their work was lost in later floods.

But most of their work was for religious institutions. Ristoro's obituary credits them with the construction of the church of Santa Maria Novella, but this means only the nave, since the chancel was complete in 1246. The nave was begun in 1279. They did not, as is sometimes said, build the monastery itself, as that was the work of two later conversus architects, Giovanni di Campi and Jacopo

Talenti. It is suggested that they had a hand in the church of San Domenico at Prato. Both men served in Rome. The necrology credits them with constructing vaults for the papal palace. The similarity of construction between Santa Maria Novella and the Dominican church in Rome, Santa Maria sopra Minerva, has suggested to some that they supervised that project. Unfortunately, we know only that they did work for the pope and that Sisto died there. What is certain is that the two brothers were famous in their day for their construction work for Church and state, and that they were the principal overseers of the fabric of Santa Maria Novella. They are the first of a line of skilled lay brothers responsible for that monastery.

After Ristoro's death, he was followed in his work at Santa Maria Novella by a group of three even more famous conversus builders. The first was Brother Mazzetto, who is described as a conversus known for his skill in woodworking and architecture. He seems to have entered Santa Maria Novella around 1284 and certainly died there in 1319. It is also suggested that he worked on San Domenico at Prato.[50] Associated with Mazzetto at Santa Maria Novella was Brother Borghese di fu Ugolino (†1313). This Ugolino, Borghese's father, was himself a skilled builder and probably trained his son. Professed sometime around 1272, Borghese was also employed in Rome by Pope Nicholas III (1277-80). His fellow Dominicans knew him as a very pious brother, who "walked in the footsteps of the ancients."[51] The last of this triad was Brother Albertino di Cambio Mazzanti, who died in 1319, after fifty-three years in the Order. Albertino was born at San Michele in Orto and entered the Order in 1266. Again, his exact commissions are not known, and the suggestions that he worked on the hospital of San Casciano and on Santa Maria del Prato are doubtful. But we can trace him in legal documents. He probably came from a comfortable family, as he had to fight his brother Benvenuto for his inheritance—a case that was finally settled by the pope in 1292. He was also agent for the purchase of land for San Casciano, the probable reason for his association with it, and he later witnessed a will and a purchase of linen for Santa Maria Novella.[52]

This trio of Santa Maria Novella architects was followed by Brother Giovanni di fu Bracchetti de' Campi (†1339). It seems, however, that he was not in charge of the fabric of the monastery. He may have had a hand in the construction of the church's campanile, which was completed by Brother Jacopo Talenti. Giovanni was born about 1280 and received the habit in 1317. Most of Giovanni's work was done for the commune of Florence. His most famous work for the city is well documented—his functioning as cappomaestro for the reconstruction of the Ponte alla Carraia, destroyed by yet another flood in 1333.[53] Contrary to some art historians, he did not superintend the Green Cloister, although he is commemorated in a roundel there.[54] We know nearly nothing about Giovanni's successor, Giovannino of Marcoiano del Mugello, who was active in the 1330s and died of the plague in 1348. He had been trained as a painter before he entered the Order. In his work on the fabric, he had an assistant, Brother Matteo Guiducci, who died in 1346.[55]

The last of the great Santa Maria architects is Jacopo Talenti (†1362). Born in Nepozzano, Jacopo, whose brother Francesco was also a noted architect, trained under Giovanni de' Campi as a mason and stone-carver and worked early in his career on the basilica of Orvieto. He is credited in his obituary with construction of the church of Santa Maria Novella.[56] This construction, however, seems to have included only the last two bays before the facade, some of the vaulting, and the bell tower. Perhaps he also worked on various chapels of the building, but there is no direct evidence. Like the other Santa Maria Novella builders, he also worked for the city.

With Talenti, conversus oversight of the Florence monastery seems to end, but we have hints of brothers doing similar work elsewhere. Brother Giovanni the Carpenter (†1310), of the Dominican community in Orvieto, constructed the monastery church roof, the infirmary, and the dormitory. He then moved on to similar work at Spoleto, and at Todi, where he constructed the choir.[57] His younger confrere, Brother Stefano, the "master carpenter," was even better known. After various projects for his Dominican province, he was sent to Rome where he became director (*prefectus*) of the fabric of the Lateran Basilica. After a year in this exhausting post, he died at the Minerva in 1323.[58] Finally, although he is really just a name, we hear of Brother Pedro Gonsales in Portugal, where, with a team of three priest builders, he seems to have constructed bridges.[59]

Looking beyond Santa Maria Novella in Italy, we find evidence of conversus artists already active in the 1200s. The best known of these were both from Pisa and both, like the Florentine conversi, also did work on the fabric of the monastery. The distinguished sculptor Brother Guglielmo Agnelli (c. 1238–1313) entered the Order in 1257.[60] He was responsible for much of the construction of his monastery, Santa Catarina of Pisa. He may have built the bell tower of the Badia of Settimo, where his teacher according to Vasari, Niccolò Pisano, was also active. Niccolò, perhaps the greatest sculptor of his age, took Guglielmo to Bologna in 1266, where they reconstructed the tomb of St. Dominic.

Most visitors do not realize it, but the carving of the miracle of Blessed Reginald's reception of the habit, and the statue of Christ in Majesty on the front of the Arca, are Guglielmo's work. He returned to Pisa in 1267, when he seems to have carved reliefs for the duomo of Orvieto. In 1270, he completed what is his major work of carving, the pulpit at San Giovanni Fuoricivitas in Pistoia. After returning to Pisa, he did work on the facade of the Camaldolese church of San Michele in Borgo.

His Pisan brothers, however, remembered Brother Guglielmo more for an act of pious theft than for all his carving. I will let the entry in the Pisa necrology speak for itself:

> When the most holy body of blessed Dominic was raised into a more noble tomb, which was sculpted by Master Niccolò Pisano, the brother assistant to the said architect, twisted out one of the very holy ribs from the saint's side. This was done forgetting the master's decree of statutory excommunication at the General Chapter of Bologna. He brought the rib to Pisa and reverently hid it in the altar of St. Mary Magdalen.
>
> As he lay dying, he asked forgiveness for this, tearfully revealing his fault. The brothers found the rib where he had predicted and reverently put it in the sacristy. He then died, after fifty-six years in the Order, his life completed, his spirit, without delay, happily passing to the bosom of Abraham.

We note that the brothers did not return the relic to Bologna. Guglielmo was outlived by a conversus artist, who may have been his student, Brother Fazio of Pisa (†1340). Described as a "master sculptor," as well as very devout and discreet, he served dutifully as the monastery porter for many years.[61] This should remind us that even the most famous conversus artists probably discharged domestic duties. This renaissance of Dominican artists seems to have ended about the time of the Black Death. Jacopo Talenti alone lived into the late fourteenth century.

Brother Artists of the Renaissance

By the fifteenth century, however, Dominican conversi again make significant contributions to a number of genera in Renaissance art. None, however, worked in architecture; rather they worked in less monumental arts. One was a conversus contemporary of Fra Angelico, Brother Giovanni of Naples. He was often socius of Antoninus of Florence when the saint was superior of the priory of San Pietro Martire in Naples. Giovanni was remembered as very devoted to the Incarnation and Passion of Our Lord. In his spare time, to avoid idleness, at the encouragement of St. Antoninus, he painted scenes of Christ's life. But he was always faithful to his responsibilities of cleaning the dormitory and toilets. He was also known for his care of the sick. He died in 1450 at the house in Naples. After his death, the Neapolitan friars venerated him as a blessed, and an image of him with rays around his head and the title "beato" was still visible there in the seventeenth century.[62]

At Florence in this period, a number of mostly clerical friars worked as miniaturists in the scriptoria of Santa Maria Novella and Fiesole. But at least one copyist was a conversus. Brother Eustachio, born Tomasso Baldassare, was professed by the famous Dominican preacher Savonarola in 1497. He illustrated two of the great choir books of the house and was well known for his ability to recite long passages from Dante's *Commedia*. It seems that he also executed books for the duomo and for Santa Maria della Quercia at Viterbo. He died in 1555.[63]

More famous than any of these conversus artists was another protege of Savonarola, Fra' Bartolomeo, in the world known as Baccio della Porta (1469–1517).[64] Born in Savignano di Prato,

Tuscany, Baccio received his nickname from the Porta San Pier Gattolini near his home. From about 1483, he apprenticed in the workshop of the renowned painter Cosimo Rosselli. In the late 1490s, Baccio was drawn to the teachings of Girolamo Savonarola, and, under his influence, renounced secular art. While working on a sacred commission, a fresco of the Last Judgement for the Ospedale di Santa Maria Nuova, Baccio decided to become a lay brother and was clothed on 26 July 1500, entering the priory of San Marco.

Fra' Bartolomeo, as he is usually known, renounced painting entirely for several years, but in 1504 his superior appointed him head of the San Marco workshop. He then began to take commissions outside the monastery. The painter Raphael, who was visiting Florence at this time, become close friends with the older Dominican artist. It is the consensus of art historians that Bartolomeo probably had an important influence on the young Raphael's style, and we know that, after the friar's death, he completed two of his paintings.

In 1508 Fra' Bartolomeo moved to Venice to do a painting of God the Father, with St. Mary Magdalene and St. Catherine of Siena, for the Dominicans of San Pietro Martire in Murano. When the friars refused to pay for the work, he sold it to the Dominicans of Lucca, where it can now be seen in the museum. This incident should remind us that conversus artists did not do their work "for love." They did it under obedience, and as a source of income for their communities. At about this time, Bartolomeo also undertook lucrative commissions for the cathedral of Lucca, the Sala del Consiglio of Florence, and the cathedral of Besançon in France.

Finally, in 1513, he moved to Rome, where he undertook commissions for the Vatican. He died at Florence in 1517. As descriptions and images of Fra' Bartolomeo's works are easily accessible in standard histories and encyclopedias of Renaissance art, I will not describe them here. But friars should know that the famous profile portrait of Savonarola, now in the Museo Nazionale di San Marco in Florence, was the work of the young Baccio. He painted it in 1498, the year of the fiery preacher's martyrdom.

At least two later Dominican artists worked in wood. The first of these, Francesco d'Antonio, carved, among other commissions, a large swiveling choir lectern for San Domenico, Siena. It was still in use in the 1600s, although it has since been lost.[65] More famous, however, is the outstanding wood-inlay craftsman, Brother Damiano di Antoniolo de' Zambelli of Bergamo (c. 1490–1549).[66] Born at Zogno near Bergamo into a family of wood-workers, he studied under the inlay craftsman Sebastiano da Rovigo. As was typical of his age, he did not do the designs for his commissions, but just the inlay work itself. His first commission was for *tarsie* (inlay) in the church of Santo Stefano, Bologna. It was paid for by the nephew of the condottiero Bartolomeo Colleoni. This church was destroyed in 1561, but thirty-one of Damiano's panels are preserved in the church of San Bartolomeo, Bologna.

In 1526, he entered the monastery of San Domenico in Bologna as a conversus. His first commission as a brother was the choir of the Dominican church of San Giacomo at Soncino. This work brought him renown throughout northern Italy. His next project was the choir of San Domenico itself, where he was assisted by his brother, Stefano Zambelli. They followed designs by Giacomo Barozzi (called Vignola). The project took from 1541 to 1549. Again using designs of Vignola, and assisted by Francesco Orlandini, Brother Damiano executed wood panels for the chapel of the Château de la Bastie d'Urfé in France. These are now displayed in the Metropolitan Museum of Art in New York. Damiano went on to commissions at San Pietro in Perugia and in the duomo of Genoa.

After his death, he was buried in San Domenico next to his prior, Father Stefano Foscarari, who had for twenty years supported his work. Those who visit the basilica today can see his work there in the retro-choir, to which they were moved after the reforms of the Council of Trent. The original doors of the choir (previously before the high altar) are now those of the sacristy.

Among the fifteenth-century conversus artists, I have saved for last that best known to modern Dominicans, Brother James of Ulm, the only lay brother of the late Middle Ages with an official cult. His life was written by his student, Brother Ambrogino of

Soncino, and has been the foundation of all studies on him until recently.[67] James was born in Ulm, Germany, on 11 November 1407. His father Theodoric had him trained in glass-making, but at about the age of twenty, James asked permission to go on pilgrimage with friends to Rome. They made the journey, visited the pilgrimage sites, and then most returned home. Having no money, James began military service with the army of Alphonsus II of Sicily. After a certain incident, in which soldiers with whom he was stationed broke into a synagogue and took oil from the Torah Ark lamp to cook stolen cabbages, James abandoned the army and made his way to Capua.

There he became the servant of a doctor (or perhaps a lawyer) for about five years. As his father was then aging, he decided to return to Germany, passing through Bologna. There, in the church of San Petronio, he met some soldiers who had been with him on the pilgrimage to Rome. To raise the money for their return north, they enlisted in the communal militia with Captain Tomasso Tartaro of Bologna, head of the city archers.

Unsure how to proceed, James visited the Dominican church of San Domenico and sought advice from the prior. The result of this conference was his decision to enter the Order as a conversus. James was now in his early thirties. His fellow soldiers attended the ceremony to show their support for the decision. His biographer, Brother Ambrogino, says that his informants for this, two elderly lay brothers, Giacomo of Bologna and Giovanni of Parma, were eyewitnesses of these events. After the year of his novitiate, James made solemn profession into the hands of Nicolaus of Catalonia, the prior who had advised him.

As a religious, his biographer ascribes to James the devotional practices we have seen in other devout conversi: he always ate in the refectory, always attended Matins, and was always ready to assist any priest who needed a server for private Mass. He hated idleness and was a hard worker. As to his piety, much of what Ambrogino gives us are somewhat stereotyped examples of the cardinal virtues. But Ambrogino did once ask the pious brother how he prayed. James replied that he simply said the Pater Nosters proper to his station, and that he also prayed daily for the pope and the Order. He did meditate on Christ's Passion, from the

Last Supper to the Resurrection and Ascension, which shows an Easter focus not always common in late-medieval piety. Ambrogino also reports that some friars claimed to have seen James bathed in light during prayer. James kept solemn silence for the twenty-four hours before each reception of Communion.

On one occasion, when Alphonsus of Sicily arrived in the north to participate in a war between Venice and Ferrara, James convinced his former commander to desist and return home. The pious brother was sometimes the butt of jokes. The Dominican bishop Michael of Holland was visiting the friars in Bologna. In jest, he ordered James to take a letter to the master of the Order, at that time in Paris. He expected James to balk. Instead, the brother knelt, asked for the letter and a blessing, and for permission to depart immediately. The bishop ended up the one embarrassed.

What modern friars remember James best for, his glass-making, is only mentioned once in the biography, and this, in the context of a miracle. James had just put a new tray of stained glass into the oven when he was sent an obedience to go out to beg bread for the community meal. This he did, and when he returned, hours later, he found that the glass was not ruined but rather the best he had ever made. The other miracles attributed to James during his life are mostly healings that resulted from his prayers over the sick, in particular for the Genovese friar Girolamo de Aviolo. His prayers cured both Girolamo and his sister, and he once prophesied the success of Girolamo's preaching campaign in Milan. James is also said to have cured a German pilgrim who had been suffering for four months from a headache.

We now know much more about James glass work because of a study done from Bolognese archival and notarial documents in the early 1960s.[68] The author found nothing on James' commissions between 1441 to 1463 and 1476 to 1491, when he was certainly very active, but the evidence for the middle period was rich. These records included those for the windows of the Cappella dei Notai in San Petronio church, his only extant glass. Tradition has it that James also did glass for commissions throughout northern Italy, including the Duomo of Milan, as well as the Palazzo Bentivogli in Bologna, but these commissions are lost.

We know best James' commissions for San Petronio from 1463–64. These not only included the glass for the notaries' chapel, but also windows for the nave. James was hired to create six large round windows (*occhi*), one on each side, for the third, fourth, and fifth bays of the church. In addition, he made the heraldic inserts of the six major windows of those bays. Like the brothers who did inlay, James did not design the windows themselves. The cartoons were by Michele di Matteo. This project brought in £264 bon. (i.e., Bolognese lire) to the Bologna monastery.

This work was followed by that for the notaries in 1464–65. This was an even more elaborate project, and James supervised a team of three Dominican conversi: Matteo di Francia, Giorgio Tedesco, and Ippolito da Cremona. Again, the cartoons were by Michele di Matteo. Ippolito did most of the glass work; Matteo did the leading and metalwork. The program of the window shows: Top Rose: Christ rising from the tomb; the sexafoils flanking the Rose: the Annunciation, with Gabriel on the left and the Virgin on the right. The windows below portray in their upper register: John the Evangelist, Peter, Paul, Luke; in the lower register: Jerome, Gregory the Great, Augustine, Dominic. The total cost of the project was £900 bon. James' community at San Domenico netted £520 9s bon. after expenses. The daily stipend of a master artisan in late fifteenth-century Bologna was 7s, so this represents some 76 days' wages.

It is difficult to translate this into modern purchasing power, but it was enough to cover the entire costs of refurbishing the conventual library, giving it its modern "basilica" form. The work took from 1465–72 and was under the direction of Brother James himself. This shows that he did more than glass. The library was not the brother's first work for the monastery. We know that he had earlier done the rose window of the church (since destroyed). The *Sala Basilicale*, as the library is now called, was modeled on Michelozzo's library at San Marco. James personally did its twenty-one stained glass windows (now lost) and the carved and painted decoration of the columns. From 1474–76, James did work in the church, mostly frescos, but also two round windows.

Tradition says that the blessed was also involved in the renovation of the Chapel of St. Dominic, when the this was done by Niccolò dell'Arca, and that he made windows for church and apse. Sadly, all his windows at San Domenico were removed by the friars in 1730, and replaced with white glass, in accord with the taste of the Enlightenment.

Our last documentary record of Bl. James comes in a decision of the Bologna priory council, dated 1 December 1489. The now "old and decrepit" James was asked to train Brother Francesco of Soncino, conversus, in the making of stained glass "lest the skill be lost to the monastery." The result of this motion is unknown. But James had trained his biographer, Brother Ambrogino Tormoli of Soncino (1437–1517), as a glazier.[69] He was active all over northern Italy. His work is preserved at San Giacomo of Soncino (the Annunciation window), Santa Maria delle Grazie, Milan (priory windows), and San Giovanni et Paolo, Venice (frescoes).

James of Ulm died on 12 October 1491. As he lay dying, his prayers healed friar Dionisio of Belluno, whose constant diarrhea had kept him from celebrating Mass and Office. Dionisio held James in his arms as he died; the conversus sang the *O Spem Miram*! The Bologna prior determined that James be buried anonymously in the cemetery cloister. But, after exposing his body to crowds of lay people, James was entombed aboveground in the chapel of the chapter room. One week after his death, with permission of the bishop of Bologna, the friars relocated the relics to the chapel of St. Thomas Aquinas in the church. During this translation, his body was found to be incorrupt. Today, it remains so, and it is displayed under his altar in the north transept of San Domenico.

The process to raise James to the altar as a saint began almost immediately, with the recording of miracles. Out of the twelve recorded by Ambrogino in his biography, eleven were healings (one of a man named Giovanni afflicted for four years with the "French Pox"). The last healing was done for James' fellow conversus of Bologna, Brother Stefano. That brother had been charged with caring for a mule that was to carry a certain preacher general on a campaign to Piacenza. The night before departure, the mule collapsed, and the veterinarian declared it dead. Stefano spent the night praying at James' tomb. He dozed on the floor. Then, at midnight, a familiar voice woke him, ordering him: "Feed the mule!" Stefano went and found the mule alive and well. The next morning, Brother Stefano led the preacher on his mule to Piacenza, "rejoicing the entire way." In the end, Bl. James enjoyed only a popular, that is, unofficial, cult. But, when it was officially approved by Pope Leo XII in 1826, it spread to the whole Order. He is celebrated on 11 October.

BROTHERS IN THE MISSIONS

From the earliest days of the Order, conversi had responsibilities outside of the monastery in the missions. Dominican missionaries traveled to areas where there were no monasteries: they had to establish them. This meant that friars, clerical or lay, had to adapt to unusual and changing circumstances. Sometimes, the "mission" was in Christian areas. Jordan describes how the first friars were sent to England in 1221.[70] This expedition probably included conversi, although they are not mentioned. Brother Juan of Spain, who, we remember, almost died of hunger when crossing the Alps with St. Dominic, went with the missionaries to Morocco and was martyred there, probably in 1233.[71] Although not raised to the altar, he is probably the lay brother protomartyr. And we know of two conversi from Santa Maria Novella who went to the missions in the Holy Land. One, Luppo of Cascia, died at Acre in 1291.[72] Brother Matteo of Popolo San Lorenzo, who went to the Holy Land with Bishop Aldebrandino Cavalcanti of Urbino, escaped the fall of Acre and the dangers of sea travel, only to die on arrival home in 1292.[73] And there were, of course, the many friars, including conversi, who participated in the missions in eastern Europe. These included those lay brothers martyred by the Mongols, whom we remember under the title of Blessed Sadoc and Companions.[74]

Already in 1221, the chapter at Bologna had sent a friar Solomon to Scandinavia, along with a lay brother as his socius. After many adventures, traveling north by way of Cologne and suffering a shipwreck in Norway, the two finally reached Copenhagen. There, the archbishop of Lund gave them land for a monastery.[75] Perhaps the best known conversus of these northern missions was Brother Gerhardt of Stommeln, in the world known as Sigwin, who died around 1310. He was the brother of Bl. Christina of Stommeln, who mentions him in her letters to Peter of Dacia. Seemingly very simple and of sweet disposition, Christina was able to convince the friars to admit him as a conversus in spite of hesitations about his lack of skills. Berthold, the prior of Eckholm, gave Sigwin the habit on 20 August 1282, changing his name to Gerhardt, because "Sigwin" seemed too strange to the Italian missionaries. When Peter of Dacia became prior of Wisby, he took Brother Gerhardt with him. As often in the missions, necessity overruled strict law: Gerhardt had unrecognized management abilities, and so he became, in practice, the community treasurer. Peter wrote of Gerhardt that "he has care of the temporalities of the house and all its expenses pass through his hands." He noted that Brother Gerhardt raised all the money needed to feed and clothe the community.[76]

Among the best known of the early Dominican missionary efforts was the province of the "Pilgrim Friars," the evangelists sent to central Asia. The Pilgrim Friars were recruited from all over Europe, but above all from Italy. In the east they recruited not only local Latins, but also Greeks and Armenians. The first mention of this group is in the acts of the General Chapter of Toulouse in 1304, at which point they were already a kind of congregation. By 1312, they had a vicar general, Franco of Perugia. First in Constantinople and then in Trebizond, by 1330, they had missions in Greece, Turkey, Georgia, Persia, India, and Armenia. All but the Greek and Armenian missions were destroyed by the plague. The Pilgrim Friars lived on, however, as the Congregation of the Orient until 1857, when it was disbanded. These friars pioneered linguistic studies and attracted native vocations. John of Qrna, an Armenian monk, translated Latin liturgical books and the constitutions into his native language. Brother John made profession as a Dominican in 1344. After his death, Giovanni of Florence, bishop of Tiflis, in Georgia, took over the project.

This Giovanni of Florence illustrates the unusual situations in the missions.[77] Giovanni had entered Santa Maria Novella as a conversus and served the community as shoemaker. An exemplary religious, he was tapped for the mission to Armenia, probably about 1310. Along the way, during the journey through Greece and Asia Minor, this lay brother discovered his gift for languages. He became fluent in Greek and Arabic. On reaching Armenia, he added its language. Brother Giovanni first translated the sermons of his clerical brothers, but eventually took up preaching and catechizing himself. His admirers observed that he spoke, "not with grammar," but with "the wisdom of the holy doctors." His tongue-tied brother priests soon allowed Giovanni a category change to clerical status. He seems to have been ordained a priest in the East, where he helped organize the "Friar Unifiers," the province of converted Armenians dedicated to reunion of the Eastern and Western Churches. Summoned home in 1318, he was consecrated a bishop, probably at Avignon, in 1318, along with a group of other missionary bishops. His first mission east after consecration was to take the pallium to Bishop Franco of Perugia, who had been sent as the first archbishop of Sulthanyeh in Persia. Pope John XXII then named Giovanni archbishop of Tiflis in Georgia, under the *in partibus* title of Smyrna, on 19 October 1329.[78]

On the death of the vicar Bartolomeo di Poggia, bishop of Marahah, Bishop Giovanni became the head of the entire Armenian mission. It was under his guidance that John of Qrna converted to Catholicism and undertook his translation of the Missal. Giovanni then appointed him superior of a community of Armenian monks who had joined the Catholic Church, the future "Friar Unifiers." Giovanni himself seems to have translated a theological work by his predecessor Bartolomeo into Armenian. It is possible that Giovanni of Florence also became responsible for the see of Nakhitchenvan in Armenia, otherwise vacant after his death until appointment of Thomas of Djahouk, a Friar Unifier.

From 1343 to 1345, Archbishop Giovanni was back in Europe, organizing a new mission to Persia. In the latter year, he requested permission of the pope to make a pilgrimage to the Holy Land as he returned home. The pope gave him permission to do so, along with thirty other friars, granting them a plenary indulgence as well. It seems that Giovanni never reached Palestine. He died in 1347 at the Dominican house in Pera, across the Golden Horn from Constantinople, and was buried there. His tombstone, which reads simply "Johannes de Florentia," is now in the Franco-Byzantine collection of the Archeological Museum in Istanbul, Turkey.

THE CRISES OF THE LATER MIDDLE AGES

I mentioned that the number of known conversus artists drops to none after the mid-1300s and remains that way for over fifty years, until the comeback in the early 1400s. I suspect that one of the reasons for this was the effect of the plague, which arrived in Europe in 1348 and reoccurred regularly into the early modern period. Notoriously, this demographic disaster produced a religious crisis. Doubts would grow about God's providence, and about the wisdom of a Church that could not explain its seeming absence. On the eve of the plague, concerned capitulars, that is, members of the chapter, were already urging preachers to refute the apocalyptic message of Fra Dolcino and his followers.[79] Decline in fervor and observance was older than that. While perhaps overly romanticized, the first generation of Dominican friars, the age of Dominic and Jordan, was marked by excitement and enthusiasm. After Jordan, things changed. The life of large communities, which were already the norm during Dominic's life, easily led to institutionalization and functionalism. There were just too many things that had to get done to keep the community running. And providing for those material needs fell mostly on the conversi.

The second generation, that of Raymond of Penyafort and Humbert of Romans, has been characterized as the age of strict (as opposed to enthusiastic) observance.[80] For the first time, we see legislative concerns about poverty and obedience. This was, however, a golden age, if not for piety and holiness, for respect and influence. Both of these pleasant realities could encourage complacency and self-satisfaction—in short, pride. Here are hints of laxity, even in small matters. After Humbert, chapters and masters of the Order begin to worry about "abuses," and to take measures against them. The 1279 General Chapter complained that it was senseless to legislate, if friars did not obey. Provincials were ordered to police delinquents.

The general chapter of 1309 was reduced to disciplining priests, deacons, and subdeacons, who refused to wear albs when celebrating private Mass and even left them off at solemn Mass.[81] It seems they just took off their scapulars and made do with their white tunics under the vestments.[82] The result was growing authoritarianism. Sometimes, it seems, by the early 1300s, the major concern is avoiding public scandal.

Lay brothers could be as delinquent as clerics. In 1301, Brother Rainerio of Arezzo, conversus, was put in chains by order of the provincial chapter at Todi. We do not know what enormities he had committed with the four clerics who were punished with him. The chapter fathers seem to have considered the priests as more at fault. They were expelled from the Order entirely as "incorrigibles."[83] The next year, the conversus "R. Costa" was exiled from his own house in Lérida, Spain, to that of Catania in Sicily, for the "grave damage" he had done his community.[84] It seemed the best way to deal with the brother was to get him far out of town.

By the middle of the fourteenth century, long-bothersome problems had become acute. The General Chapter of 1354 codified these issues in a long comprehensive "reform statute," that was renewed in 1355 and then dropped in 1356. Capitulars then replaced it by an even longer piece of legislation in 1359.[85] "Studies are defunct in many provinces"; Friday abstinence needs to be enforced; there are houses without lectors; dispensation is overused; friars have bedrooms outside the cloister. There are *vagi*, friars absent from the monastery without leave, everywhere. Friars who commit secular capital crimes are to be jailed for life. This chapter called on provincials to establish up to six "reformed" houses of strict observance in each province. Conversi are not mentioned in this legislation, but they too were affected by it. Eventually, it became obvious that reformed houses needed to have a measure of institutional independence. In 1390, the master Raymond of Capua formed the reformed Italian houses into an independent reform congregation.[86]

Behind the seeming turn for the worse in mid-century is, in part, the effect of the plague. The Plague Year, 1348, stands out in Italian necrologies. At Pisa, 31 members of the community died; at Santa Maria Novella, 81.[87] Observance ceased, as friars feared contact with the infected. At Pisa, only one friar, the cleric Fazio

Gualandi, continued to eat in the refectory, and then he, too, died.[88] At Siena, 49 friars, 7 of them conversi, died.[89] Loss of clerics created problems, but in the typical huge monastery, the loss of conversi meant that the mechanisms for providing food, clothing, and shelter broke down.

In the later 1300s, these issues became harder to deal with as the plague returned again and again. Especially bad was 1363, when 33 friars died at Santa Maria Novella.[90] The dying abated in the 1400s, but did not go away. In 1479, a conversus, Brother Andrea, himself died while nursing plague victims in the Santa Maria Novella infirmary.[91] The result of religious turmoil and death was a major vocation crisis and lack of manpower. By the early 1400s, capitular legislation would have to address problems with celebration of the sung choral office in houses with under ten friars.[92]

Chapters were constantly urging friars to promote vocations. Given the urgency, great vocation promoters received high praise in their obituaries. And these promoters are virtually all conversi, not clerics. At Santa Maria Novella, the highest accolades were bestowed on Brother Filippo, "who called many young men to the Order," before he himself died during the plague of 1363.[93] Brother Giacomo di Bernardo, the monastery shoemaker, who also labored in the sacristy, was singled out at his death in 1387 for his promotion of vocations.[94] Examples could be multiplied. Perhaps this should come as no surprise: the mortality, as I have noted, probably had a greater effect on the daily life of conversi than that of clerics. Likewise, in their work as porters and door-to-door beggars, conversi had more direct contact with young men than many clerics.

Provinces began to put pressure on local superiors to admit more men. The Province of Aragon in 1378 ordered every prior to admit at least six novices, four clerics and two conversi, in the next year. General chapters issued the same kind of instructions.[95] This meant admission of younger and less qualified novices. Provincial chapters in Aragon and Lombardy openly admitted that the plague reduced vocations, and that the manpower shortage resulted in admission of immature men as lay brothers. The age limit of eighteen was to be strictly observed.[96] The fruits of laxity in admissions can be seen in the general chapter of 1417. It stripped priests who did not know how to say Mass (*missam legere nescientes*) of their voting rights; and those priests who did not know enough theology to hear confessions were deprived of faculties.[97] Such problems were probably even greater for conversus admissions: taken too young meant "unskilled," and unskilled meant "useless."

Breakdown of discipline and drop in vocations intensified after the outbreak of the Western Schism in 1378. Like the Church, the Order was divided, as competing masters were elected in the two obediences—one obeying the Roman, and the other the Avignonese, pope—and excommunications were issued against the friars of the rival obedience. The general chapter of the Avignon obedience, meeting at Avignon itself, was the first to censure the other, branding Raymond of Capua an "anti-master" and excommunicating all superiors subject to him.[98] Competing obediences meant that disobedient or unhappy friars could simply decamp and join the other obedience. Or, they could become *vagi*, wandering about until they found a community with observance, or the lack thereof, to fit their taste. Within a year, the Avignon obedience was condemning to ecclesiastical prison friars who attempted to defect.[99] Such defectors included conversi. Brother Filip de Garcia was among a group of fugitives who decamped and left their Avignon-obedience province for greener pastures elsewhere.[100]

It comes as no surprise that evidence for serious reform is pretty much lacking in general chapter legislation of either obedience until the schism was coming to a close. I only find one example, an attempt by the Avignon obedience to forbid friars from having personal paid servants.[101] Only in 1405 and 1406 do the two obediences issue comprehensive reform statutes. The infractions listed seem grave in both cases, beyond anything we have seen earlier: simony, unchastity with women, unlocked dormitories, chronic absence from office and refectory, engaging in trade and commerce, extravagant retinues traveling about on horseback.[102] The schism in the Order finally ended in 1418, with the election of a single master, Leonardo Dati of Florence, which was announced by a joyful encyclical letter.[103]

We can best trace the breakdown of discipline among lay brothers in the provincial chapter acts of Aragon for the 1300s, which have been edited and are very complete. The editor traces the rise in gross numbers of penances from the low point in 1314 to the high point in 1357.[104] In that latter year, 20 friars were penanced, of whom four (20%) were conversi. One of the most telling examples of lay brother delinquency happened in 1353. The issue was meat eating. One conversus, Joan Estella, who had been regularly eating meat outside the house, was deprived of all meat (normally allowed when friars were bled, which was then a monthly practice) for six years. If he, or others, did not mend their ways, they might even be jailed in the ecclesiastical prison.[105]

Random meat eating might seem trivial, but, in 1353, six friars from the monastery of Cervera raised their dietary infractions to the level of public scandal.[106] Although he seems to have been egged on by five clerics, the conversus Bernat de Pinyana was at the center of what the chapter acts call a "conspiracy." Four friars, including Bernat, had gone about stealing chickens and hens. It seems it was the conversus who actually did the deed. They then roasted and ate the fowl publicly. These thefts and picnics were public knowledge and caused a major scandal. Not only did Bernat provide hens for other clerics inside the monastery, they even ate them during the penitential seasons of Advent and Lent. And they took oaths to keep the business secret from superiors.

The five clerics were assigned to other monasteries, made to fast on bread and water four times a week, and forbidden any meat for five years. Three lost voting rights for five years, two for two years. Although at the center of the affair, Bernat was merely required to fast on bread and water for twenty days, a penance he was to complete within four months. At other times, delinquent conversi seem to get harsher punishments than clerics, so we might wonder if poor Bernat was viewed as simply a tool of his priestly betters.[107] The prior of Cervera was charged to keep an eye peeled for similar conspiracies. More seriously, in 1344, at the Dominican house of Orange in southern France, the conversus brothers Rostagno Ernaldi and Giordano Dregoli were involved in the mishandling of the prior's property, causing "great damage to the brothers" and "grave scandal among seculars." The exact damage done is unclear, but it seems that it was financial, as well as to the community's reputation. The general chapter at Le Puy imposed on them the penalty of a grave fault.[108]

Conversi could also turn violent. In the house at Catania, Sicily, Brothers Francesç Peyoni and Bartomeu Capit got into a fistfight in the cloister; over what, it is not recorded. Bartomeu knocked Francesç down and began to kick him and beat him. Francesç grabbed a rock and used it to brain his fellow conversus, stunning him and causing him to lose his ability to speak. Finally, other friars arrived and broke up the melee. The chapter left it to the prior to determine the severity of the brothers' penances.[109]

Such conversus altercations could become potentially deadly, since all friars carried their table knifes on their belts. At the same house in Catania, two conversi, Gundisalvo Pulcromonte and Garcias de Biossa, got into a knife fight in the public square of town in front of a crowd of lay people. They wounded each other severely and ended up in the public jail. The prior got them out and investigated. It seems that Gundisalvo was the instigator, as he was the only one penanced. I should note, however, that conversi were not the only ones involved in such fights. The same chapter also penanced two clerics for a knife fight in the refectory.[110]

RESPONSES TO THE LATE MEDIEVAL CRISES

The Order did attempt to address the problems of conversus recruitment and discipline just outlined. Our knowledge of the response is made more difficult because most provincial acts, at least those that have been edited, such as those of the German provinces, never mention the brothers, not even in legislation on suffrages. In Italy, we can trace changes of assignment for brothers, but that tells us very little.[111] Many of these sources are fragmentary; there may have been legislation that has been lost. Extant acts, however, do allow us to trace Dominican attempts to address issues affecting conversi, at least in general terms.

Even before the Black Death, the admission of ill-prepared men as conversi was widespread enough to need addressing. Already in the 1280s, general chapters sought to restrict recruitment by requiring provincial permission for each admission. In contrast, some provinces passed legislation against admissions by the provincial without the approval of the local community.[112] Restrictions were also imposed on category changes.[113] The Roman province in 1305 raised the age requirement for conversus novices to twenty, because "young conversi are useless to the Order." They also forbade ordinations of men under twenty-five.[114] The problem of immaturity was not unique to the brothers.

Alternatively, houses might have provided "vocational training" for young novices so as to render them "useful." What to modern people would seem a logical course of action, however, was late in coming. The earliest example of legislation proposing such training dates to 1372, well after the vocation crisis of the plague.[115] At the General Chapter of Toulouse in that year, the friars finally seem to have recognized that admitting ever younger men to supply for the temporal maintenance of the house meant that they had to be trained. Yet the next time I have found an example of concern for the formation of conversi comes only a hundred years later. The 1497 chapter of the Province of Holland, noting that in several houses the conversi seemed to be ill-formed, mandated the appointment of a master for the younger men. He was to take charge of their formation and hear their confessions once a week.

In Italy, too, weekly Confession for conversi was also on provincial agendas.[116] The master was to hold weekly chapters to instruct them and correct their faults. They were to learn to serve private Masses. On the other hand, he was also to prevent their access to books and teach them to reverence priests. The issue of boundaries comes to the fore. The master is to make sure the brothers' hair is cut and does not resemble a tonsure. They are not to act like clerics, sitting and reading books in church, lest people think they are priests.[117]

I have already discussed in Chapter 1 the ongoing debates over allowing conversi to change category and become clerics. By the late Middle Ages, probably with considerable misgiving, as this was a class-ordered society, such changes were permitted. I suspect it was a result of the priest shortage produced by the plagues. But unclear boundaries for medieval people were not just problematic; they were dangerous. Order, in a disordered time, meant keeping people in their place. If a conversus became a cleric, the friar had to be enculturated in the new category before being given voice in the chapter. Typical of late-medieval restrictions of this sort was to grant voice only five years after the change, and then only after ordination.[118] And, keeping order of religion tidy, former conversi only had seniority as clerics from the time of the change, not their lay profession.[119]

This legislation conceals somewhat the real danger: conversi who took it upon themselves to change category. The concern about conversi "passing" did not go away. In 1510, the master of the Order, Tomasso di Vio, better known as Cajetan, intervened in the Province of Holland, where contrary to their superior's will, several conversi had presented themselves as having his permission to change categories. He cassated, that is made void, the resulting category changes and announced that he would no longer grant any such permissions. He also revoked the permission he had given to the Province of France to allow such changes on their own initiative.[120]

The same concern about boundary clarification manifested itself in reinforcement of the differences between the clericaland lay state. Functions proper to clerics were not to be usurped by conversi. Late-fifteenth-century provincial chapters made this clear. "Honorable" offices, that in the past had occasionally been entrusted to conversi, were now to be given exclusively to clerics. One visitator in the Province of Holland summed up the problem in his 1489 report. The honorable offices, like treasurer, vestiarius, and infirmarian might have to be occasionally given to conversi, but only as a very last resort. And the conversi serving were not dispensed from Matins and the Great Silence after Compline.[121] Within the clerical state, the boundary of ordination was also reinforced. An Italian provincial chapter forbade the practice of allowing unordained clerics to give sermons to seculars.[122]

If conversi had to be given honorable jobs, at least theycould be kept distinct from clerics in appearance. The post-plague period saw a new wave of legislation on the brothers' habit. It seems that conversi were regularly wearing the white scapular. In

1323, the capitulars of the general chapter complained that the brothers' narrow scapulars were sometimes so light as to be mistaken for those of clerics. In addition, the brothers seem to have abandoned or modified their broad scapulars without permission. Priors were to police this abuse.[123] The general chapter at Narbonne in 1354 thundered: "Conversi are not to dare wear the clerics' habit."[124] If they do wear them, the 1366 general chapter declared, they *ipso facto* incur an excommunication whose removal was reserved to the master of the Order or his vicar.[125] This problem may, in part, have been the result of superiors giving lay brothers clerical hand-me-downs, but it also reflects the apparent practice of allowing the white scapular to conversi as a reward for excellence in their work. This honor was only to be allowed with explicit license of the provincial, so decreed the chapter of 1370.[126]

At least one province, Holland, addressed the issue of hair-styles. It seems that here some conversi were being given permission to wear the clerical tonsure. In 1468 and 1470, this was absolutely forbidden, along with the possession of Latin books. The conversi were simply to get their hair cut (short) four times a year, without any *corona*.[127] But, in fact, the community, by a two-thirds voice, and with the consent of the provincial vicar, could grant license for both use of Latin books and tonsure to individual conversi.[128] It was hard to enforce strictly even symbolic categories. The fathers of the Avignon obedience, meeting at Rouen in 1388, admitted that the practice of granting white scapulars to certain conversi was perhaps impossible to eradicate. But, they declared, this honor did not mean they could be promoted to orders, and such brothers were under no circumstance allowed to vote in elections!

In short, it did not involve category change or the blurring of that boundary. This required a whole separate legal procedure.[129] Four years later, the fathers of the Avignon obedience reminded the brethren that the proper color of conversus scapulars was to match the clerical cappa, or at least be "gray."[130] Two years later, for the first time, at least in the Avignon obedience, it seems that the habit of the conversi was defined as consisting of the white tunic, the dark scapular, and (like the clerics) the black cappa.[131]

This signals the beginning of the disappearance of the "broad scapular" in the late Middle Ages and the first appearance of something like the "modern" brothers' habit.

Perhaps surprisingly, late-medieval chapters issued few directives on conversi in strictly disciplinary matters. The one exception, which coincides with the schism, is the punishment of vagi, friars who wander about or abandon communal life. Aragon repeated the requirement that any leaving the monastery be accompanied by a socius.[132] In Lombardy, unsuitable novices, expelled from one house, were never to be received into the novitiate of another.[133] And, as this period ends, the Lombards also attempted to regulate the contact between conversi and the "youths" hired to work in the kitchen, tailor shop, and other places in the monastery open to outsiders.[134] And any friar, conversus or cleric, who threatened another brother, even of the Third Order, with violence, was to be gravely punished.[135]

We lack full texts of provincial chapter acta for the fifteenth century like those for the fourteenth century in Aragon, so it is hard to find concrete examples of actual delinquency and its punishment. And general chapters now do not normally deal with individual malefactors. The one example I have found is in the Rome-obedience general chapter of 1405. The fathers declare that a conversus, Brother Lawrence, "committed horrible enormities," and that they expel and cast him out of our Order as an abominable member.[136] Perhaps what he did was better left unsaid.

After the close of the schism, the most common, indeed virtually the only, legislation concerning conversus concerns suffrages. By the 1300s, the conversus suffrage for the dead of one hundred Pater Nosters had become normative and was usually supplemented with a hundred Aves. There had been intermittent attempts to add the "Angelic Salutation," the Hail Mary, to the suffrages, starting in 1266.[137] But it only became universal by 1304, after which, this combination was repeated by virtually every chapter.[138] The only oddity is that this conversus suffrage requirement disappeared in the 1360s, only to return in the 1370s. If the provincial acta of Aragon reflect typical practice, the same discipline was imposed at the local level.[139] The major change in the early 1400s was that conversi not only say their own suffrages, but also supplement the suffrage Masses of priests by saying a number of Paters and Aves, usually forty.[140] By the late 1400s, the recitation of the hundred Paters and Aves by conversi was being stipulated not only for the dead, but for other purposes. For example, it was stipulated as part of the terms for receiving indulgences granted to the Order.[141] Or as a thanksgiving suffrage for living popes.[142]

To modern readers, this combination of Paters and Aves in conversus prayers immediately brings to mind the modern Rosary. That prayer, in its modern form of three sets of five Paters, each followed by ten Aves, with each "decade" connected with meditation on a mystery from the lives of Christ or the Virgin, first appeared in the late 1400s. Its first appearance in Dominican legislation seems to be in 1498. On that date, a general chapter imposed it as a penance on an unlicensed preacher guilty of peculation, Henricus Dremet of the Province of Saxony.[143]

But it was the conversi who seem to have immediately taken up the prayer. Brother Angelo of Naples, who died in 1500 at the monastery of San Pietro Martire, was a precocious practitioner. He was fervent and joyful, even after an accident that caused third-degree burns to his face and blinded him. He accepted this disfigurement with fortitude and, until his death, spent every day from dawn to dusk in church, constantly praying the Rosary. Both friars and laity, we are told, were edified greatly.[144]

Chapter 3
Reformers, Missions, and Martyrs, 1500–1650

Events in the early sixteenth century would bring changes to the life of the *conversi* and the Order as a whole. At the center of this development was the Catholic (previously called "Counter") Reformation, and the rise of Protestantism. The year this book was written, 2017, was the five-hundredth anniversary of Martin Luther's protest against the abuse of indulgences in Germany, which triggered what we know as the Protestant Reformation.

This is not the place to treat these events in detail. Fortunately, among the books appearing this year in English, there is an excellent one, *Reformations* by Carlos Eire of Yale University, which readers may consult for more information on the background of the history of the Order in the 1500s. It not only represents recent scholarship, but gives adequate coverage of the Reformation in the Catholic Church that was well under way fifty years before Luther. We are still waiting for studies, like that of Eamon Duffy for England, to give us a better idea of what lived Catholicism was like in all its regional diversities before 1500, but such background is not essential to the story of late-medieval and early-modern conversi.

I ended the last chapter with the Order's attempts to address the vocations drop and discipline crisis that affected the friars in the late fourteenth and early fifteenth centuries. The vocation crisis and decline in numbers that affected the Dominican Order seem to have eased in the 1500s. Where we can find statistics, the impression is that numbers have stabilized or increased. We know that in the 1500s the Lombard province counted about 2000 friars in some 63 houses, meaning that the average was about 30 friars per house. Aragon, with about 1100 friars in 53 houses, numbered about 20 per community.[1] Although the numbers for before the Black Death were certainly higher, these averages suggest that most houses were substantial and some very large. The number of friars seems to have increased further in the 1600s.

Chapter acts no longer legislate honors for friars attracting vocations, and the concern over very young recruits fades away. The percentage of conversi per house seems to have remained constant or even increased. The one case where I can make a tally, the published necrology of the Roman Province for the late 1600s, lists 430 priests, 68 novices, and 186 conversi, with a total of684 friars. This would put the percentage of lay brothers at 27 percent, up considerably from the average of about 20 percent before the plague.[2]

The religious change and turmoil of the early-modern period in Europe eventually resulted in the suppression of Catholicism and the practical disappearance of the Order in much of the German-speaking lands, Scandinavia, and Great Britain. It also resulted in confessional fragmentation and conflict in Ireland, France, and much of Eastern Europe. There the Order continued, but under conflicted conditions. Only in Italy, Iberia, and the Spanish Dominions did religious life continue without great upheaval. The rapidity of this change can be seen in the acts of the General Chapter of Valladolid in 1523, just six years after Luther's theses against indulgences. This is also the first chapter to mention the reformer, calling on friars to write and preach against his errors. The only provinces represented at the chapter were those of Italy and Iberia. Attendance from the others was rendered impossible "through war and plague."[3]

The institutional response to these events only becomes visible in Dominican legislation with the general chapter of 1564, when the reforms mandated by the Council of Trent (1545–63), start to appear.[4] The most comprehensive and balanced history of this council, for readers who want to pursue it, is still probably that of Hubert Jedin, published from 1951 to 1976, and available in an English abridged edition as *A History of the Council of Trent*. Before 1564 and on to the end of the century, conversi appear rarely in acts of general chapters, nearly always as subjects of assignments.[5] The tantalizing penances of delinquent conversi that mark fifteenth-century general chapters are completely absent.

REFORM LEGISLATION ON CONVERSI AFTER TRENT

The Bologna chapter of 1564 stipulated that no friar was to receive the habit before the age of fourteen and that none was to be professed (solemnly, we remember) until the age of seventeen. This actually relaxed the higher age requirements of the late Middle Ages, and probably reflects the pressure of the ongoing late-medieval vocation crisis. Local provinces with more rigid requirements for conversi probably kept them, given the problem of internal training in skilled crafts. When, after 1600, Tridentine reforms began to affect the brothers' life directly, conversus novices, by papal decree, had to be twenty years old and already proficient in Christian doctrine. A quarter-century later, the Order itself forbade the clothing of conversus novices who did not already possess training in some skill (*arte*).[6]

Council fathers of the same period also addressed haphazard novitiate training. Although conversi continued to be accepted for individual houses, not for provinces or for the order as a whole, they were all to make novitiates in large formed communities, even if they were later to return to the smaller houses they had been accepted for. The smaller houses themselves were to supply their novices with clothing, and the newly professed were to be assigned to the house they were received for, and not reassigned elsewhere "unless scandal required it."[7]

The growing centralization of the Order in the 1600s meant that general chapters also confirmed provincial legislation. So we know of similar local legislation in the Province of Aragon.[8] In 1629, the Province of the Kingdom (i.e. of the Two Sicilies in southern Italy) requested approval of their decision to set up what amounted to a provincial novitiate for the brother candidates admitted "privately" by smaller houses at one of their larger houses in Naples. The general chapter approved it.[9] For the first time, the Order sought to regularize conversus admissions and their novitiate training, as had long been the case for clerics. But laxity in admissions continued in many places, and attempts at more stringent procedures, such as approval of admissions by higher superiors, especially for converts, continued into the 1700s.[10]

A revolution was soon to occur in conversus formation. Already in the 1500s, experimentation had begun on probationary periods before admission of men to the brothers' novitiate. We know that already by 1530 members of the Third Order, wearing the habit of that order, were living in various Dominican monasteries, doing manual labor like most conversi.[11] In 1592, the general chapter ordered provincials to oversee the bestowing of the habit on both conversi and such members of the Third Order, and to make sure that they had received religious formation necessary "so that they might serve their houses in manual work," before they were clothed with the habits.[12]

As these members of the Third Order will play a role in the history of the conversi from this point on, we need to know something about them, their rule, and their form of life. Since the early 1400s, Dominican lay penitents had followed a rule ascribed to the late-thirteenth-century master of the Order Munio of Zamora. We now know that this rule was actually composed about 1405, almost certainly by the biographer of Catherine of Siena, the Dominican priest Tomasso Caffarini. He then got it approved as the penitents' rule in 1415. This is the point at which the lay penitent movement most influenced by Dominican piety, the "Black Penitents" or *Mantellate* (called after their black mantle), were for the first time officially aggregated to the Order. This was also the first time such penitents were officially called the Dominican "Third Order."[13]

Medieval lay penitents were celibate (often widowers or widows), lived an austere life of prayer, wore a kind of habit, and had status as ecclesiastical persons. Such penitents predate the mendicant orders.[14] Their habit, which much predates the Third Order Rule of 1415, was a white tunic, black leather belt, and a black cape, the "mantle." Women wore a white veil.[15] The modern phenomenon of "Third Order Regular" sisters wearing a white scapular is extremely rare before the nineteenth century. I only know of one grant of the scapular before 1660, that to a group of tertiary women holding a common purse in Venice during the early 1600s,[16] and then, in 1667, Pope Clement IX allowed it to women penitents living in community. But male tertiaries did not wear it, even when living as donati in the monastery.

Although celibate—the married needed their spouse's consent[17]—tertiaries did not make public religious vows; rather, they used a formula saying that they "expressed their will to observe the rule."[18] Although this included the promise of celibacy, the act did not invalidate an attempt at marriage, should a member abandon the penitent life. Nor was their obedience absolute like canonical religious. It was personal to their confessor, who might happen also to be the superior of the house of a religious order. Finally, although they lived simply, tertiaries could own personal property. Tertiaries often worked to support themselves, and this commonly involved service in hospitals or other charitable work. A good number practiced considerable ascetical discipline and spent much time in prayer.

Canon law did not impose severe penalties on penitents if they abandoned their way of life. The only juridical punishment for those abandoning the life was loss of their status as ecclesiastical persons subject only to church courts. They also lost the secular privileges (exemption from taxes and military service) that most cities, at least in Italy, usually granted them.

Tertiaries had their own office, much like that of the conversi, consisting of set numbers of Pater Nosters and Ave Marias. Their rule stipulated 28 Paters/Aves for Matins, 14 for Vespers, and 7 for the other hours—unless the penitent was a cleric. Clerical tertiaries simply said the Divine Office. For the dead, the suffrage was 50 Paters.[19] Unlike conversi, they were not bound to attend any part of the liturgical office sung in a church or monastery—although many did. We already hear, in the fourteenth century, of penitents performing services and perhaps even living in Dominican houses. These men were bound only to quarterly Confession and Communion.[20] And, again, unlike the vegetarian conversi, they could eat meat every Sunday, Tuesday, and Thursday outside of penitential seasons.[21]

The presence of Third Order brothers as a category in the community provided a way to regularize the "probationary period." In one of the most important reforms of this period, the Valencia General Chapter of 1596 mandated that no conversus was to receive the lay-brother habit immediately. Rather, he was first to be given the habit of the Third Order and to make promises as a tertiary. These men are to wear that habit for three years before a decision was made as to granting of the conversus habit and admission to the novitiate. These brothers, like the others of the Third Order living in the community with no intention of entering the novitiate, are here called, for the first time in Dominican legislation, *donati* ("oblates"). Both groups would be known by this name into the modern period. In 1656, it was determined that all donati, as well as all conversi, were to be examined, not only before vows or promises, but every year on their morals, doctrine, and religious spirit. If deficient, they were to be corrected; if rebellious, punished. And, if necessary, they could even be expelled and returned to "the world."[22]

This temporary tertianship was to be a period of testing, formation, and discernment of character and ability. Superiors who did not impose and enforce this new discipline were punished. Those conversi clothed with the brothers' habit in circumvention of it were to be stripped of the habit and expelled from the Order.[23] There would now be two kinds of "lay brothers," living in community, the tertiaries and the conversi, each with a different habit and different rule. Some tertiaries were "permanent," others "transitional," hoping to enter the novitiate and become conversi. This system would be confirmed by general chapters and masters of the Order on various occasions, and it remained in force into the twentieth century, albeit with minor changes. For example, in 1784, the master of the Order Baltasar Quiñones extended this probationary period to four years.[24] Later, in 1862, Pius IX required three years of "simple" or "temporary" profession before perpetual solemn vows, but this new probationary period did not eliminate the preliminary period that a conversus spent as a donatus. For the first time, conversi now had a "formation" period, albeit before their novitiate and solemn profession, analogous to that of the clerics between their own profession and ordination.

REFORMS IN CONVERSUS FORMATION

The post-Tridentine period saw increased concern about conversus formation itself. Since the earliest days of the Order, conversi were subject to their own superior, the master of conversi. Even the prior was supposed to deal with them through this official. Post-Tridentine legislation strongly emphasized this friar's role as the spiritual and disciplinary formator of the conversi. It seems that there had been some negligence in appointing to this office, as the Chapter of Valladolid in 1605 reminded priors of the obligation to appoint them.[25] The chapter of 1644 codified medieval legislation on the master in what seems to be the most extended description of his responsibilities.[26]

That chapter, above all, emphasized his responsibility to train the conversi, not only in the external ceremonies of the Order and their work, but also to form their internal piety and to instruct them in mental prayer (*oratio mentalis*). Provincial visitators and priors were to make sure this was done. The master was to hear the brothers' confessions, lead them in spiritual exercises, and insure their fruitful reception of sacraments. At least once a month, he was to hold a chapter of faults. When voting on them for admission to vows, the "vocals," that is, the friars with voting rights, were to use the same secret voting method, black and white beans, that was used for clerics.

The chapter was also concerned about clerical abuse of the brothers. They wrote:

> We admonish and most severely forbid clerical brothers and other priests to molest the conversus brothers. They are not to hold them in contempt, lack good will towards them, or molest them. Rather they are to accept them charitably as sons and brothers. And they should strive to edify them by their example of kindness, without censures, rather than bully them.

Furthermore, the master was to examine them on their knowledge of Christian Doctrine and, by the 1700s, give them weekly spiritual conferences. Later chapters repeated this legislation in whole or in part.[27] It is telling that the occasion of this strongly worded legislation was the same chapter that announced the death of Brother Martin de Porres. One senses that there is a connection between its celebration of that holy brother and the new concern for the well-being of lay brothers generally.

Perhaps the most surprising event of the mid-seventeenth century was another obituary, this one published with the acts of the Rome 1650 Chapter. It records the death of Brother Giacomo of the Roman Province.[28] The friars noted his simplicity and his zeal in religious observance. These qualities had led the province to give him responsibility for the nurture and instruction of the conversus novices in order to "train them in religious perfection." As a brother, he could not be the master of conversi, but, even without the title, Giacomo is the first lay brother known to have served, in practice, as an assistant novice master.

The seventeenth-century chapters also addressed the nature of the offices, sometimes explicitly clerical, traditionally held by conversi. The chapter at Valladolid in 1605 summarized the responsibilities of the porter, an office open to both clerics and conversi. These were the same as those listed by Humbert, but to them were added the porter's obligation to have a board with the names of all the friars of the house, and to mark which are out and which have returned home. The fathers add that the porter is to edify all comers by spiritual conversation.[29] That conversus porters were expected to do this suggests that the renewal of their training had given at least some of them the basic religious culture to engage in helpful spiritual conversation.

The same chapter renewed the traditional legislation on the office of treasurer, emphasizing the requirement of keeping written records of income and expenses. This accounting literacy does not seem to have prevented the continued appointment of conversi as treasurers, a practice only strictly forbidden in 1777. But even then they could still serve as assistant treasurer and even draw up the annual financial report.[30] One new conversus job first appears at the Rome 1670 chapter. The fathers decided that every master of sacred theology, and all former provincials, were to be assigned a conversus as his servant (*pro eorum servitiis*). Later, because this use of lay brothers as servants had led to "abuses, especially in Italy," the practice was discontinued at the Rome 1694 Chapter.[31]

In earlier chapters, we have seen conversi serving unofficially as infirmarians and, sometimes it seems, officially as well. Similar examples multiply in the early-modern period. Such men might be highly skilled. For example, Brother Sebastião de Goes (†1597) of the community in Bemfica, Portugal, was trained in the world as a surgeon. He became wealthy and respected through his practice of that profession. Then, at the height of his career, he became a conversus. He was inspired to do so by the friars, including conversi, who were tending plague victims during the horrible outbreak at Lisbon in 1569. His decision shocked his fellow doctors, who urged him not to give up his great wealth, and to continue practicing in the world. His entrance amazed the entire city. Sebastião spent the last nineteen years of his life serving as house infirmarian and providing seculars with free medical care.[32] One wonders how his fellow doctors reacted to that.

In the next generation, we hear of Brother Jean Gervais, professed of the priory of Avignon, who served in the infirmary, perhaps as assistant infirmarian. In response to the city's request to the prior, Father Jean Carquetto, for nurses to work in the hospital during the plague of 1629, every conversus in the house volunteered, including Jean. As this was more men than needed, Jean alone was sent as socius to Father Pierre de la Bastide, perhaps the official infirmarian. Delighted that he had been given such an honor, Jean made a General Confession in preparation for his possibly lethal ministry. The two friars served throughout the plague, but Jean did not survive. A crazed plague patient had fled the hospital and was drowning in a ditch. Jean dove in and saved him. Perhaps from a contagion in the water, the courageous brother died the next day, 27 October 1629, at Hôpital de Champ-Fleuri, near Avignon, France.[33] Still, even after such sacrifices, the Chapter of Valencia in 1647, when treating the responsibilities of the infirmarian, continued to insist that this office be held only by a cleric.[34]

Nevertheless, even after that chapter, conversi, even if not officially infirmarians, dedicated their lives to the sick. And more brothers sacrificed themselves during later outbreaks of plague. Many of these men are little more than names to us. The general-chapter obituaries of 1650 give us some background on two such brothers.[35] The conversus Domènec Geros of the Aragon Province was observant, humble, and rigorous about poverty. He was especially remembered for his devotion to the Holy Rosary and to the poor. He expended himself in their service, tending poor plague victims and orphans. Juan de Aguirre of Santo Domingo in

Betica, similarly died serving plague victims. The "whole city" attended his funeral. We also know of self-sacrificing conversus nurses in the missions on Crete. Four conversi of the Venetian missionary province of Greece served at Candie. There, brothers Niccolò, Giovanni, Felice, and Giovanni-Baptista all died after contracting plague while nursing its victims in 1649. A tertiary donatus, Francesco, also died with them.[36]

In the end, one suspects that most conversi continued to do much the same kind of work they had done since the thirteenth century, perhaps adding on the earlier-mentioned role of assigned servant. Brother Gaudioso of Cava, who died in 1639 at Naples, had been assigned to the new Dominican rector of the seminary at Naples through the request of Cardinal Alfonso Gesualdi. But his brothers remembered him for centuries as the model lay brother. He lived up to his name, which means "joyful." He had served diligently as refectarius for many years, was always hard working and pious, and never missed Matins, for which he rang the bell. When the cardinal died, Brother Gaudioso simply returned from the seminary and resumed those duties.[37]

Like the reforms of the immediate pre-Reformation period, those of the seventeenth century show what to moderns seems an obsession with category violations and a mania for reinforcing the boundary between clerical and lay brothers. The general chapters of 1596 and 1608 strictly forbade anyone from calling or allowing conversi to be called "father" like a priest. The 1589 chapter forbade provincials from permitting conversi to wear the clerical white scapular. They also forbade prioresses to grant the white choir-nuns' scapular to lay sisters. Such grants produced confusion and many "inconveniences."[38] Backtracking, however, the 1611 chapter reminded the brethren that, if a conversus were given a clerical scapular, he was still to do manual labor. Nor could he be considered for ordination without the permission of the master.[39]

It seems that the white scapular was often given to brothers as an honor, or as a step toward clerical status and ordination. Or, perhaps, treasurers were just being cheap and decided that conversi had to make do with what was on hand. An early-seventeenth-century chapter reminded the provinces that it fell to them, not the transfiliated brother, to provide a habit that matched those of the native members of the province.[40] Eventually, in 1694, a general chapter even ordered vestiarii to pay for conversus habits.[41] Clearly, some had left the lay brothers to their own devices as to clothing. As with habits, so with hairstyle. One late-sixteenth-century chapter legislated at length on conversus hairstyle, their rasura: to be over the ears and coming down exactly one inch lower in the back.[42]

On the other hand, in one aspect, the conversus and clerical habits converge during this period. We have already noted that around 1400 the Avignon Obedience replaced the conversus broad scapular with the black clerical cappa. It has been suggested that this change became universal under the master general Antonio de Monroy of Mexico (1677–86). [43] But the change clearly happened earlier. In art, the "modern" habit already appears in the "Dominican Blesseds Altarpiece" (1424) by Fra Angelico, now in the National Gallery, London. By 1551, a general chapter required all conversi to wear their cappas when receiving Communion and when serving private Masses.[44] In any case, the fathers found the idea of conversi wearing clerical habits, especially at their own choice, highly offensive. Such a delinquent was not only punished by deprivation of his own black scapular for six months, he was incarcerated in the ecclesiastical prison for a year.[45]

An example of what the fathers were worried about had happened in the 1510s. The conversus Andrea of Ragusa had adopted the clerical habit, abandoned his monastery, and managed to get himself ordained. When this was discovered, he—now a priest—was suspended *a divinis* and jailed in an ecclesiastical prison by order of the master of the Order and the cardinal of San Sisto. Somehow, he managed to escape and, for all the council fathers knew, was out plying the trade of a priest somewhere. They ordered his recapture and incarceration until a decision on him could be made by the cardinal protector as to his fate.[46] One scholar has observed this kind of boundary policing is especially marked in the new edition of the constitutions promulgated by the master Antonin Cloche in 1690.[47] These repeated the legislation of Pope Clement VIII requiring a second, clerical, novitiate before category change. But it also allowed unordained clerics to be busted down to conversus—without a new novitiate—as a punishment for very grave faults.

Category change to cleric remained possible under very restricted circumstances. The reform chapter of Bologna in 1564 laid down the rule for the early-modern period. Conversi might become clerics and even ordained, but only when there was serious necessity, and only with explicit permission of the master.[48] Any category change without permission of the master was void.[49] Prohibitions of change in category reached their high-water mark in the late 1600s, when two popes forbade them absolutely.[50] But it still happened. Given this reality, the reception of full clerical rights had to be regularized. Since the early fourteenth century, former conversi had taken the order of religion from the date of their clerical profession, not that as a conversus. And at the chapter of 1605, a full twelve years in the clerical state was required before the former conversus received voting rights, a requirement renewed in 1629.[51]

THE RENEWAL OF PIETY

In this period, conversus suffrages, correlated with priests' Masses, continue to be composed of some number of paired Paters and Aves. Most commonly, there were to be thirty for the living and a hundred for the dead, although sometimes both suffrages are just thirty, sometimes both a hundred.[52] Another change during the mid-1550s in the brothers' office, done explicitly to free up conversi for manual labor, probably also freed up time for conversi to adopt new forms of piety. The General Chapter at Salamanca in 1551 reduced the burden of the conversus office of Pater Nosters.[53] At Matins, the 40 Paters on feasts was reduced to 28, as on other days. Those of Vespers were reduced to 12, but the other hours remained at seven. The conversi substitute for the Penitential Psalms was reduced from 100 Paters to 25. Suffrages were also reduced. In the second half of the century, the same Paters and Aves continue as the usual form of conversus suffrages, but the numbers are reduced to, most commonly, ten for the living and thirty for the dead.[54]

Perhaps the most important development in Dominican piety of the early modern period was the rise of devotion to the Rosary.

At the end of the last chapter, I mentioned the first conversus known for his devotion to the Rosary, Brother Angelo of Naples (†1500). For the first half of the sixteenth century, the Rosary remained a private devotion, unremarked in chapter legislation. Starting in 1571, general chapters began to urge or require friars to preach about and promote the Rosary.[55] Three years later came the first legislation promoting the Rosary Confraternity, as well as the institution of the Feast of the Holy Rosary by Pope Gregory XIII. Previously, this had been in May and only observed in the Province of Aragon.[56] The 1580 chapter hailed the papal institution of the feast on the first Sunday of October and commanded its observance by the whole Order. In the wake of these developments, in 1583, the General Chapter of Rome first introduced the Rosary for conversus suffrages. The standard brothers' suffrage for the dead became one third, that is, five mysteries of the Rosary. But prayers for the living remained ten pairs of Paters and Aves.[57] This will be the form of the conversus suffrages into the next century. After 1605, the Rosary suffrage is under formal precept for the brothers of any house in which a friar has died.[58]

The Rosary became a distinctive aspect of conversus piety about this time, in contrast to the clerics, whose daily Marian devotion was still the Little Office of the Blessed Virgin. An example of this can be seen in the life of Brother Jacques Grou (†1647), who was born in Lagny-en-Brie, France, and became a soldier. A late vocation, he entered Annunciation in Paris as a conversus. He recruited many men to the order and served the poor and sick. His Marian devotion was pronounced; to his office of Paters and Aves he added a daily Rosary and the Little Office. His Eucharistic devotion was also noticed by the brothers. On days he was to take Communion, he attended three Masses, the first two as spiritual preparation for reception of the host at the third. In his obituary, the brothers recorded his well-known saying: "Our virtues are linked to our actions, our actions to each hour, each hour to each day, each day to each week, each week to each month, each month to each year; each day is the image of our life, and the best way to perfect it is to attend to our daily activities." Assigned as socius to Father Étienne le Brun, the almoner of the count of Ronorantin, he departed for the Middle East, but on arriving in Malta, he fell sick and died. After death he appeared to his nephew, "looking like an angel."[59]

The Rosary is even more pronounced in the piety of another holy French conversus, Brother Pierre des Forges, who died in 1679 at the monastery of Saint-Jacques. "Guileless, pure, and poor," he even attended to the needs of the paid secular servants of the community. At the age of seventy, he asked permission to go on pilgrimage to all the major saints' shrines in France. About three or four years before his death, he went blind, but remained tranquil, never sad, and ever prayerful. He was always at Matins. But it was his devotion to the Rosary that most impressed the brothers. He was never seen without it in his hand, and never ceased reciting it, except to sleep. As he lay dying, Pierre sang the *Veni Creator Spiritus* in a loud voice.[60]

The new Rosary Confraternity not only promoted the devotion among the laity, it became a source of lay brother vocations. The most memorable example of this would be Brother Jean Charrancin of the Dominican house in Lyons, France. Born at Longessaigne and baptized at the parish church, his family was respectable but of modest means. From his earliest youth, Jean was active in the Confraternity of the Rosary, which had been established in his parish when he was three years old.[61] The archivist of the house at Lyons, André Ramette, recorded the holy brother's life and his devotion to the Rosary.[62]

As an adult, Jean supplied butter and eggs to the house. Edified by the life of the friars, he petitioned to become a conversus in about 1648, at the age of 43. When he had finished his years of probation as a donatus, the consensus of the chapter was that he should be rejected for the novitiate because he had no useful skill. But when it came to the actual vote, all voted yes. Jean ascribed this "miracle" to the Blessed Virgin, whose Rosary he had prayed constantly as the chapter debated his admission. He took the religious name "Jean du Saint-Rosaire," and made solemn vows on 13 January 1688. Jean was regular in attending Matins, "took the discipline" by scourging himself for two hours daily, and then attended with devotion the earliest low Mass of the day. He served as porter, always reading devotional books and praying the Rosary when not busy.

As socius to priest-confessors, he spent much of his day visiting and helping the sick poor. Jean begged money for them, buying bread and distributing it daily to beggars. This work became well known during the horrible grain shortage of 1694, when it seemed he could multiply bread. "If I can eat dry bread," he said, "the poor deserve no less." After an attack of chest pains, Jean died on 28 July 1702. A huge crowd of poor arrived, not asking for alms, but simply to honor their benefactor. His body seemed incorrupt, and his crowd of admirers ripped up his habit for relics. The friars had to find a second one for his burial. In hope of his canonization, Father Dominique Duchesne (prior, 1698–1701) sent a report on his life to Rome in which he described his feeding of four to five hundred poor a day during the famine as a miracle. The Revolution seems to have put an end to the canonization process.

The sixteenth century witnessed a strong turn in piety toward interiority, a revolution that gave the Church mystics, such as the Dominican spiritual writer Luis of Granada (1505–1588) and the Carmelite mystic John of the Cross (1542–1591). Prayer was taking on its modern character as a mental activity, rather than the medieval verbal forms typified by the brothers' recitation of Paters and Aves. Even before legislation was passed encouraging the daily practice of mental prayer, we find conversi practicing it. For example, the humble lay brother Gonsales do Santa Maria of the community in Guimaraens, Portugal, was remembered by his community for his long periods of prayer, during which he struggled with diabolical attacks and received divine consolations. He died, in 1522, in the odor of sanctity.[63]

In the spirit of the times, the general chapter of 1571, for the first time, ordered all friars to practice mental prayer (*oratio privata*) for fifteen minutes minimum, after Matins, Nones, and Compline. Priors were not "to dispense this easily."[64] This legislation certainly delighted another Portuguese brother, Brother Reinaldo do Santa Maria of Amada, who died in 1574, three years after its promulgation. Reinaldo was a contemplative who loved solitude and never left the house except under obedience for business of the community. Although very busy, not only as cook, but also as porter, refectarius, infirmarian, and chief alms-collector, Reinaldo was always up to serve the first private Mass of the day. He then did an hour of meditation in the tribune that faced the Holy Name Altar. When not praying, we are told, he was serving the community.[65]

Reforms and strict observance movements in the seventeenth century institutionalized these practices. The Rome Chapter of 1650 expanded the mental prayer requirement to a full hour of "pious meditation" between Matins and the first Mass of the day. It also approved the practice of breaking sleep to celebrate Matins in the middle of the night, something first instituted by the chapter at Valencia in 1647. The result was the creation of a long quiet period between Matins and Prime, which could be used by non-sleep-deprived brothers for meditation and mental prayer.[66] Although these rules seem to have applied only to clerics, conversi could take advantage of them, if they had no work to do, something always true for the time after midnight Matins.

Brother Bernardin Heraud of the community in Béziers, France, had already impressed the brothers during his donatus postulancy and novitiate. Serving as cook, he always stayed after Office for the periods of prayer. On Christmas of 1652, he spent the entire night in mental prayer and received "great spiritual consolations." He died six days later.[67] His older confrère, Brother Jean Chapon (†1640), the carpenter of Annunciation in Paris, was remembered as simple, prayerful, hardworking, and obedient even as a child. During the time available to him as a brother, he added various prayers and devotions to those required by the rule. Given his duties as carpenter, it comes as no surprise that these devotions often centered on St. Joseph, a newly popular saint in that period.[68]

A final example of the growing importance of spirituality and piety in early-modern conversus life can be seen in the biography of Brother Raymond Texier (1602–1689) of the Dominican house in Béziers, France. Born in the village of Nisas, his pious family educated him at home and he became known locally for his works of piety. At the age of thirty, he asked admission to the community. Raymond was assigned to the kitchen, where he served for fifty years as cook. When friars did not eat all their allowance, even out of abstinence, he accused himself of badly preparing the meal. He was especially devoted to the priests and other guests passing through the house. He was known for tranquility of soul, even when dealing with the larger-than-average number of difficult brothers in the community.

He was constant in attending prayers and became known for his frequent ejaculation: "Gloire à Dieu!" The phrase became his nickname. Even when rushed, he always had meals ready, which he ascribed, not to himself, but to God's help. The friars remembered him for his special graces in prayer, his gift of tears, his great reverence for Eucharist, his fervent preparation for Communion, and his devotion to the Virgin Mary in the Rosary. A contemplative domestic, in his fifty-eight years as a religious, he never left the house. Raymond died reciting the Rosary at the age of eighty-eight, on 21 October 1689. At least one member of his family claimed a miraculous cure through his intercession.[69]

The lay brothers' new life of private prayer and Marian piety is summed up in the obituary of Brother Louis Croisson of Albi. The brothers remembered his fervor for regular observance and his refusal to eat meat, even when old and sick. Above all, they admired how, when free, and later when too old to work, he spent all his time praying in the church. He was always up earlier than the other friars, so that he could do an hour of mental prayer before Matins. And he was always the first to arrive for the community's common meditation period at 4:00 in the morning. His great delight, along with meditation, was praying the Rosary, which he always carried with him. He treated his body harshly and wore the worst habit available. When he died in 1685, at about the age of 80, he rose from bed to receive Viaticum on his knees. The "whole town" showed up for his funeral, all wanting to touch their own Rosaries to his body.[70] Within twenty years of the deaths of these pious brothers, the need of spiritual nurturing for the conversi as well as clerics was recognized by the provision that lay brothers, too, make spiritual retreats before their vestition and before profession.[71]

Beyond the new focus on meditation and mental prayer by seventeenth-century conversi in provincial obituaries and order legislation, we have a new source of information for the brothers themselves. Beginning with the General Chapter of 1608, the published chapter acts include notices about certain "brothers or sisters because these enjoyed a reputation for holiness."[72] Thus we can identify more conversi than previously, who were respected and admired by their communities, even if their lives were relatively hidden. Most of the conversi commemorated do not receive elaborate biographies. The focus is generally on their asceticism, humility, and obedience. For example, Brother Giacinto of Amalfi had no cell and slept on the floor.[73] Brother Francesco di Sant'Agostino was a "mirror of observance." The laity mobbed both their funerals.[74] The French provinces also compiled obituaries, mostly unpublished but summarized for us in the nineteenth-century biographical encyclopedia *Année dominicaine*. There we hear of Brother Durand Aragon (†1537) of Couvant Saint-Jacques, whose piety so impressed the friars that they erected a plaque to his memory in the choir.[75] Other provinces kept short obituaries, too. For example, the Province of Portugal remembered Brother Pedro do Santo Domingo (†1548), who was a servant of the brothers and a "slave of Jesus Christ."[76]

BROTHERS AS "ZEALOTS OF PIETY"

The sixteenth and seventeenth centuries saw Catholic reforming movements within the orders as well as renewed Catholic political action, participants in which have received the name "zealots of piety," or just "zealots." The French brother Gervais Thonat (†1632) for example, was dissatisfied by the observance of his community and directly approached the master of the Order Niccolò Ridolfi. He begged to be reassigned to Avignon, because there they observed the constitutions to the letter. That community remembered him as a model religious, especially for his service to the sick during plagues.[77]

But perhaps the most famous, even notorious, zealot conversus of the period has to be Brother Jacques Clément (1567–1589), the conspirator and assassin of King Henry III of France.[78] Jacques was born at Sorbonne, in today's Yonne department, in Burgundy. He became a Dominican lay brother during the French Wars of Religion. Fanatically pious and an ardent partisan of the Catholic League, which opposed both Protestantism and moderate "political" Catholicism, he constantly spoke about the evils of heresy and the need to exterminate the Huguenots. He and other League-connected laymen formed a plan to kill the king, who was a "politique" Catholic and a tolerant absolutist. This project received the support of the League, in particular, of Catherine de Guise, the duchess of Montpensier. They promised Jacques worldly rewards if he succeeded, and eternal bliss if he failed in the attempt.

He obtained forged letters addressed to the king on 31 July 1589 and set out. He reached Saint-Cloud, the headquarters of Henry, who was besieging Paris, on 1 August 1589. He approached the king disguised as a priest and asked for a private conference to deliver the letters. The attendants withdrew, and Brother Jacques stabbed Henry with a dagger, as he was whispering in his ear. The king shouted in pain, and attendants ran in and killed Jacques. Henry died the next day. The conversus' body was quartered and burned. Some partisans of the League viewed him as a martyr. Paradoxically, the assassination brought to the throne the Protestant "politique," King Henry of Navarre.

As in the past, early-modern lay brothers sometimes came from backgrounds other than the peasantry or poorer skilled labor. Their obituaries give evidence of this. Brother Claude Paradis (†1644) of Lyon, France, was the son of the wealthy and powerful Louis Paradis, squire, councilor, notary, and secretary of the king at Lyons. Claude had lived and traveled in Germany and Italy. For two years, the young aristocrat petitioned to be admitted to the Order as a conversus. Finally, the community relented and accepted him in March 1636. Professed, he served the community until his death.[79] Even more interesting is the background of Jean de Lapa of Saint-Maximin, France. He was born in Scotland in 1580 and raised a strict Calvinist. While in France as a young man, he abjured heresy and, after much study and practice of the faith, asked for the conversus habit at the age of forty. This former Presbyterian so impressed the community that they professed him after just a year of novitiate, skipping the probationary donatus period. He served the house as sacristan and then as vestiarius. He always took the worst habits, and once had to be commanded to put on a better black scapular and capuce. Like other contemplative brothers of this period, he prayed and meditated for extended periods at night before Matins. Jean lived to be 83, when, after some 43 years in the monastery, he died in 1663.[80]

We can also detect early-modern conversus involvement in activities outside the monastery, some in tasks already seen and some in new ones or on a greater scale. Although not as impressive as the accomplishments of the fifteenth-century artist brothers, these conversi made notable contributions in the arts. An example is Brother Charles Rasteau of Annunciation, in Paris, who, although of an illustrious family, entered the monastery as a tailor. His piety was conventional for the age: he was noted for his gift of tears and fidelity to attendance at Matins. They called him a "zealot of observance." But he was chiefly remembered as a calligrapher. He copied and decorated all of the house's large choir books in a beautiful hand. Like other pious brothers, he was remembered also for his love of serving Mass. Accepting his final illness as a penance, he died in 1655.[81]

At Saint-Maximin further south, Brother Vincent Funel, a young vocation, proved to be an excellent sculptor and woodworker in the tradition of Brother Damiano of Bergamo. His embellishments and decorations of the community choir stalls still exist today. He died in 1694, at the age of forty-seven.[82] Perhaps the most significant among these seventeenth-century French conversus artists were Claude Borrey and Jean Raymond, active in mid-century at Toulouse. Both were also known for their piety. Most important among their commissions was the new shrine for the relics of St. Thomas Aquinas. Regrettably, this monument of late-Baroque stone carving was completely destroyed during the French Revolution.[83]

BROTHERS IN NEW FORMS OF SERVICE

Perhaps the most remarkable example of the brothers' creativity of this period was the rise of a dynasty of conversus herbal pharmacists or, in Italian, *speziali*. The necrology of the Roman Province records the new importance of this skill. Among the 36 brothers for whom skills are given, the largest group, nine brothers, are listed as speziali. The only trades close in numbers were sacristans and farmworkers, each of which counted five conversi.

The first, and most famous, of these men was Brother Angiolo Marchissi of Santa Maria Novella. In 1612, he founded what is today known as the Officino Profumo Farmaceutica di Santa Maria Novella, the "Pharmacy of Santa Maria Novella." We should remember that "pharmacies" in seventeenth-century Italy not only compounded drugs and herbal remedies, they also made prepared spices and perfumes. This shop, long secularized, continues to operate at Santa Maria Novella and is a magnet for tourists. Brother Angiolo superintended the construction of the pharmacy itself, crafted silver vessels and storage containers, and planted the spice garden. The income from this project was enormous and, in great part, supplied for the needs of the monastery. Within his lifetime, Brother Angiolo's work was famous throughout Europe, and it eventually came under the protection and patronage of the grand duke of Tuscany, Ferdinando II de' Medici. In reversal of the usual spice trade of that age, the Pharmacy exported products to India and China.[84]

Brother Angiolo was followed in this work by Brother Giovanni Cavalieri, speziale at Santa Maria Novella until his death in 1694. Patronized by bishops and cardinals, he also brought in great revenue for the house. Some of these funds were used to refloor the business and purchase more silverware.[85] The success of the pharmacy in Florence inspired conversi to undertake such work elsewhere. Across town, Brother Giovanni Vicenzo of Foiano (†1660) managed the rival pharmacy of San Marco.[86] Outside of Florence, Brother Ambroggio founded a pharmacy in Pistoia, and died, much respected for his skill, in 1679.[87]

We also know of at least one seventeenth-century conversus outside of Tuscany who served his community as a pharmacist. This was Brother Cosimo de la Tour of Spatola, the pharmacist of the community in Soriano near Naples, Italy. He was one of the two conversi who, along with their prior, survived the horrible Calabria earthquake of 1659 that killed eighty of the friars. Soriano was an observant house, to which many friars transferred seeking greater religious discipline. Brother Cosimo was originally simply a donatus of the house. His industry and piety convinced the community to profess him as a lay brother and give him charge of the pharmacy. He also served in the infirmary, dispensing the drugs he himself compounded. The other conversus who survived the quake, Brother Gregorio of Gemilliano, became house sacristan and was known for his service of the poor. Quiet and prayerful, he bore with patience a paralysis of the tongue that left him mute in his later years.[88]

In the early modern period, one service we have seen undertaken in the medieval period by conversi seems to have become their exclusive responsibility: begging. This task often became something more, and resembled modern fundraising. When we hear of priest brothers begging in this period, it seems more an act of devotion or a ritual humiliation. Legislation on *questua* in the Province of the Kingdom in southern Italy seems typical. There beggars went out in pairs, not larger groups, and were to be exemplary religious. They were to be "conversi or tertiaries," not clerics. Doing this work was considered an honor, perhaps because of the constant contact with outsiders, sometimes very wealthy. A beggar guilty of a grave fault might be stripped of his "office" as a punishment.[89]

We know the names of a couple of these star beggars. Brother Giuliano of Burgo San Sepulcro, conversus of San Marco in Florence, was originally a rich noble. He astounded his family and friends when he gave it all up to enter the monastery. He spent the rest of his life begging, door to door, to supply bread for the house.[90] Of more humble background was Brother Filippo of Viterbo (†1575), of San Pietro Martire in Naples. He entered young and was so effective in his daily begging that he was put in charge of the porter's office. There he impressed friars and lay people by his tender love of the poor, who came to beg bread from him.[91] In that service, he resembles another porter brother of the next century, Brother Manueto Vitry of the Roman province. Manueto also served the poor as porter and was a great alms collector. But what caused the province to send his obituary to the general chapter was probably his patience in illness and his ascetic mortification. He was known for flagellating himself around the cloister every night.[92]

The great exemplar of such work is the "blessed" conversus

Giovanni of Amalfi, Italy.[93] After what seems to have been a worldly youth, Giovanni asked admission to San Domenico in Naples as a lay brother, claiming that he did not have sufficient education to be a cleric. Friars already recognized him as a model religious during his postulancy and novitiate. He usually spent long periods in prayer each day and, if too busy, did his meditations and prayers at night. Known for his austerity, he ate only once a day, except Sundays. He had no cell but the church, where he slept on the altar steps after taking the discipline. But it was in raising funds that he excelled. He was known throughout Naples for his effectiveness in bringing in donations, not only food, but large amounts of cash. When the prior rewarded his work by allowing him to dispense the alms himself, the first thing he did was to spend them on the redecoration of the chapels of the Blessed Sacrament and of Saint Dominic, to both of which he was very devoted. After being made sacristan, his fundraising continued. His fame reached the point that people he had never met brought or sent him money and goods.

This celebrity status seems to have bothered his humility. He hated honors. The count of Lémos, viceroy of Naples, and his wife both considered Giovanni a saint and, much to his discomfort, regularly came to him for spiritual advice. Stories of miracles circulated. Once, when filling cruets for Mass, he was summoned by the prior. Putting down the wine bottle in haste, it tipped over. Rather than take the time to right it, he went off for his new obedience. Later, when it was righted, the friars found that not a drop had spilled out! The notary of the monastery, Father Amadeo Graziano, once claimed to have seen him levitating in choir. After his death in 1633, public demand required a solemn public funeral. The crowds who attended reported intercessions and miracles and considered him a saint. "Beato Giovanni Buono," they called him, "Blessed John the Good."

As we have seen, it was not uncommon for these fundraising conversi to do what could be called poor relief and social service. We know of other early-modern brothers who did this without being known as great beggars. The friars remembered such conversi in their obituaries as "Fathers of the Poor." We know of two such men in Italy. Brother Gregorio de' Santi, a friar in Sicily, was known as a saint and slept on the floor of the conventual church.[94] His contemporary, Brother Raimondo (†1668) of Naples, came from a distinguished family and was well educated. An ascetic typical of the spirituality of the age, he wore a hair shirt and took the discipline daily. The house almoner, he earned the title of Father of the Poor through his work in the refectory. He carefully gathered up leftovers and served them to those who came begging at the door. When there were few remains, he simply gave the poor his own serving. He himself would be satisfied, he said, with merely "a bowl of potage."[95]

Brother Raimondo does not seem to have put his education to use as part of his service, but at least one other French conversus of the time did. Balthasar Carayol was born in Le Quercy of a pious but not wealthy family. They did have sufficient funds to send him to school, where he studied humanities and philosophy. At the age of twenty, he dropped out and joined the army, a choice we have noted in so many other conversi. He grew to hate the service. When on maneuvers near Gap, he became ill, and was finally released. The experience renewed his piety and he began to frequent the Dominican church at Gap, where he became a domestic servant. While fulfilling those obligations, he asked to be admitted to the Order. He did so with permission of the provincial and professed as a conversus. The friars remembered him as obedient, careful in his observance of the constitutions, and charitable. He helped with the rebuilding of the monastery after it had been destroyed by Protestants during the religious wars. Like the other conversi we have been considering, he did begging, solicited money, and so helped support the house.

So far, he sounds rather conventional. But while working in the porter's office, on his own initiative, he opened a school where he taught reading and writing to poor children. This school did more than teach trades or elementary reading and writing. Taking advantage of his own higher education, he also taught Latin. One day, the prior came upon him correcting a student's Latin composition exercise. Shocked, the superior asked Balthasar how he was able to teach such an elegant Latin style. The shamefaced conversus admitted that he had completed advanced studies in Latin literature and in philosophy. The prior wanted him to petition for a category change, become a cleric, and be ordained. Balthasar refused, "out of humility." He wanted to be nothing more than a servant of all.

Something more seems to have been going on here. The brother asked that he be able to expand his school and teach more advanced subjects, like philosophy. The prior consented, and this "junior college" became Balthasar's primary work. He was soon famous throughout the city as an educator. The wealthy came asking that their sons be able to study (alongside the poor) in the friar's classroom. His excellence in teaching came to the attention of the bishop of Gap, and then to the master of the Order. The master sought to take him to Rome, but the bishop intervened and insisted he remain in Gap, as he was irreplaceable as an educator. In addition to teaching, Balthasar served as sacristan, treasurer, gardener, and baker for the community. He was assiduous in prayer, which included chanting the choral office along with the clerics and passing long nights in meditation before the altar. We have come across many intelligent and educated conversi, but Balthasar seems unique for his intellectual apostolate and public stature as an educator. In October of 1664, suffering from what seems to have been a cancer on his arm, the learned brother asked for Viaticum and Extreme Unction. On the eighteenth of the month he died in the odor of holiness. His funeral was mobbed. In the crowd were the canons of the cathedral chapter of Gap and, as his obituary proudly noted, all the local Franciscans.[96]

BROTHERS GIVING WITNESS AS MARTYRS

Initially, the life of conversi in the early modern period was relatively unchanged from the late Middle Ages, except for their formation and some new forms of service. The post-Reformation period also brought two earth-shaking developments that changed the life of conversi in radical ways. First, the Wars of Religion and the persecution of the Church in non-Catholic lands, especially in the seventeenth century, meant that conversi, along with all the other friars, experienced martyrdom on a scale unheard of since antiquity. These martyrs, especially in Ireland and Eastern Europe, are often forgotten. They should not be.

After the discovery of the New World in 1492, conversi participated in missionary work on a scale unheard of at any time in the history of Christianity. This had already begun in the sixteenth century. Here, too, there were to be countless martyrs, including some conversi who have been beatified and canonized. As the Asian missions are, in a way, a prelude to the great missions of the Spanish Dominicans in America, we will examine the Asian missions here. The next chapter will be devoted to those in the New World and the Philippines.

The first known conversi martyred by Protestants in Europe were in the Low Countries during the 1500s. A violent Reformation began there in 1566, when Protestant mobs sacked churches and burned images. Persecution of Catholics began in earnest soon after William the Silent adopted the Reformed faith and began the "Eighty Years War" against the Spanish and their Dutch and Walloon Catholic allies. The conversi who died during this period might be considered the forgotten companions of St. John of Cologne (†1572). The general chapters of 1569 and 1571 were the first to mention the Dominicans killed by the Dutch Calvinists. These friars were Walloons, from the area now in Belgium. The master of the Order, Vincenzo Giustiniani, included a personal letter with the 1569 acts. He asked the provinces to train novices and send them to areas, like the Low Countries, devastated by Protestants. The chapter of 1582, which published the obituary of St. Louis Bertrand, stopped listing individual names of martyrs—they were too many—and simply reported that *plures* had been killed in the Netherlands.[97] Happily, we know the name of one conversus who suffered with these martyrs, Brother Jan Vercruyssen, killed at Ghent in 1581.[98] Sadly, all the acts give is his name.

The next century saw the two most violent persecutions of Catholics of the early modern period, both in the 1640s. One wave of persecution occurred in Ireland. It happened after the English Civil War, when Oliver Cromwell attempted to eradicate Catholicism and replace the Irish Catholics with Scottish Protestant settlers.[99] Systematic persecution began in 1646, at which time the Irish Province counted about sixty friars. When the persecution ended, there remained only about fifteen. The general chapter of 1656 included a martyrology of these friars.[100] For us, again, some brother martyrs are only names. For example,

Brother Cormac Egan (or MacEgan)[101] and Brother Raymond Keoghe,[102] both killed by the Protestants in 1642. Later we hear of Brothers James Moran, Richard Overton, and Dominic Black (perhaps a donatus), all martyred about 1650.[103]

The worst year of persecutions was 1648, and we know a few more details of the conversus martyrs from two Dominican houses. Sometime during the military conflicts of 1648, soldiers of Murrough O'Brien, later named First Earl of Inchiquin, occupied the priory of Kilmallock at night. Most of the friars had fled, but two refused to flee. Soldiers found conversus David Fox and a clerical student kneeling before the altar, reciting the Rosaries they wore around their necks. Enraged by this act of Catholic piety, the soldiers cut the brothers down with the sword and left their mutilated bodies in the church.[104] Paradoxically, Earl Inchiquin would convert to Catholicism in 1656.

We also know something of a Kilmallock brother who escaped this massacre. Brother William Gormain had professed as a conversus of the monastery in the early 1600s. During the attack, he retreated to the bell tower and vigorously defended himself until Catholic troops drove off the attackers. Afterwards, William fled to Spain and entered the house at Valladolid, where he was remembered as an excellent tailor. The friars there believed him to have "healing hands," and he imposed them on many people sick with scrofula. Later sacristan of the church of Nuestra Señora de Atocha, he was eventually named procurator general (legal representative) of the Province of Ireland at the Spanish court. A surprising appointment for a tailor, which suggests he was an educated man. He died in 1665, at Madrid.[105]

Another slaughter occurred at the Dominican house in Roscommon, far in the west. There two conversi confessed their faith, although at different times. In 1648, the area was occupied by Protestant troops. Brother Donald O'Naughton refused to stop wearing his habit, and hide. He went around in public, always carrying his Rosary in hand. The occupiers seized him, beat him, shot him with arrows, and finally decapitated him.[106] Taken at about the same time, Brother Bernard O'Kelly was arrested and imprisoned. In prison, he was restrained in such a way that he had to undress himself to reach the bits of bread put out for him. Thus humiliated, we understand that he died of neglect and starvation in prison, although other reports say he was later condemned to death and hanged in Galway. Whichever the case, he died in 1653.[107]

To close this summary of the Irish conversi during the turbulent seventeenth century, we should mention one who was not a martyr. Edmond Bourke came from a well-to-do family. After a wayward youth, he underwent conversion and entered the Dominican house at Burishool in County Mayo as a lay brother. He had, he confessed, wasted his time in "hunting, games, and loose conversations." Brother Edmond was remembered as a *Speculum Perfectionis*. He wore chain disciplines, used a rock as his pillow, and slept little. He always rose for Matins, after which he flagellated himself. He perpetually fasted on bread and water. Above all, he was devoted to the Blessed Virgin and the Rosary. It is reported that, when the Protestants suppressed his house, they let him go out of respect for his piety and humility. He continued to practice religious life in private and died in 1653 at "great old age."[108]

More numerous, but far less well known to modern Dominicans, are the seventeenth-century martyrs of Eastern Europe, who were mostly of Polish background.[109] They were active in the huge region of the Polish-Lithuanian Commonwealth, which included modern Poland, Lithuania, and much of Ukraine. In 1615, the general chapter divided this enormous province between the Poles and the "Ruthenians" because of ethnic tensions. The new "Russian" Province received five houses. By 1648, the region had three provinces, Poland, Guardian Angels (Lithuania), and St. Hyacinth (Ukrainian and Russian speakers).[110] In the disasters that were to come, Dominican presence in the eastern part of this region would nearly cease to exist.

Conflict had not always been inevitable between the Dominicans and the Russian Orthodox and Muslims of this region. For example, in the early 1600s, Father Tymotka Maholinski of the Province of Poland and his lay brother socius Aleksy, a tailor, travelled to the Crimea on the Black Sea. He planned to undertake a mission to the Jews of the region and so had learned Hebrew. On entering the Muslim parts of what is now southern Ukraine, they encountered large numbers of captive Christians, to whom they ministered. Father Tymotka died serving Christian plague victims. After his death, he was found to be wearing a chain discipline. Brother Aleksy continued the work among the sick, whether Christian or Muslim, until he too died of the plague. The Muslim "Tartars," to whom Tymotka and Aleksy ministered, attended the funerals of both these "martyrs of charity" in great numbers. This contemporary usage, "Tartar," meant the Turkish-speaking peoples of the Kahnate of the Crimea, then a vassal state of the Ottomans. The two friars died about 1620.[111]

Conditions changed in the 1640s. Political instability in the region precipitated a chaotic period of wars between the Commonwealth, the Russian Empire, the Ottomans, and the Crimean Tartars. Many Dominican houses were in towns with historically large Jewish populations, and these bore the brunt of the violence along with the Polish friars. The most horrible atrocities of these wars, against Catholic clergy and Jews, were committed by the Orthodox Cossacks, who had revolted with the intention of separating the Ukraine from the Commonwealth. The conflict is commonly known as the Cossack-Polish War, or the Khmelnytsky Insurrection. It continued until 1657, but the worst period was 1648 to 1649.[112]

The general chapter of 1650 listed 66 friars martyred by the Orthodox during the revolt, of whom 16 were identified as conversi. This puts the number of conversi at one out of four friars, even though there are probably some conversus martyrs who did not make it into the report.[113] As communities seem to have fled before the attacks, this may indicate the lay brothers were more likely than clerics to stay behind and guard the buildings. We know little about these brothers, except, occasionally, how they died. The locations of the destroyed priories are now mostly in Ukraine, so I identify the towns under their modern names.

The brothers' names should also be remembered. In some houses, only a conversus was martyred. At Busko, the elderly Brother Maciej was killed by ax blows; at Pidkamin, Brother Marian was tortured to death; at Letychiv, Brother Maciej was pierced by a lance. In other places, the brothers died along with one or two priests or clerical brothers: at Lviv (then Lemberg), the conversi Piotr and Placyd were hacked to death;[114] at Mostyska, Brother Jakub was killed at the door of the church; at Bar, Brother Inocenty was captured, beaten, and burned, while his companion, Brother Feliks, was decapitated; at Kiev, Brother Inocenty died along with a lay brother novice. In other places, four or five clerics stayed to die with the brothers: at Yezupil, the Cossacks killed Brothers Marcel and Jan; at Czernihów, Brother Jan; and at Chernobyl, Brother Stefan was tortured in prison and drowned in the Prypetz river.

The greatest atrocities occurred at Novgorod-Siverskyi, where eight friars were killed along with Brother Jakub. And at Tulchyn (then Nestervar), where nine clerics died with Brothers Filip of Lagow and Placyd of Szensko. And at the house of studies in Starokostiantyniv (then Constantynów), two priests and four students died with the conversi Brothers Paweł and Fortunat, who were martyred in the church. At other houses, between one and three priests died.[115] There were also many martyred nuns.

The killing stopped after the treaty between King John Casimir and the rebels, but revolts returned under King John Sobiescki in 1672. Between 1648 and 1672, some thirty priories were burned. The last conversus martyr known by name was a causality of Muslim, not Orthodox, hostility, during the revolt in 1672. Brother Symplicjan died along with four other friars of the Province of Poland. Their bodies were found near Lviv (Lemberg), the clerics in the forest, by a canon of Rescow named Massabski. Brother Symplicjan's body had been riddled with arrows and was found in a field. Other members of this community were taken prisoner by the Tartars and enslaved.[116]

BROTHERS IN THE ASIAN MISSIONS

Outside of Europe, brothers journeyed long distances to risk their lives in the Asian missions. These include seven who would be raised to the altar. In 1571, the acts of the General Chapter of Rome included, for the first time, an extended report on missionary activity in Asia. Father Fernando do Sancta Maria sent it from Goa, in India, on 26 December 1569.[117] It says nothing about his lay brother companions. Nine years later, in 1580, the chapter passed, for the first time, extensive legislation on the

Asian missions. These regulations were issued *motu proprio* by the master of the Order, Paolo Constabile of Ferrara.[118] Again, the acts said nothing about conversi, but the motu proprio is a sign of the growing independent power of the master during this period. From this time on, independent initiatives of the master take on much greater importance than in the past.

That year, we hear of the death of the earliest conversus missionary in Asia for whom we have a record. And his story is colorful, to say the least. Pedro de la Magdalena was born in Lisbon and took the habit at the Dominican house in Lisbon. In 1548, he joined the expedition of Father Diego Belmudez to found the Congregation of the East Indies. That expedition arrived in India at "Morumbin," now Mumbai. There, he was a member of the founding community of the monastery of Santa Bárbara. From there, he was transferred north to the mission in Daman, a region today in Gugjarat state. The Portuguese had occupied the area in 1531. When Brother Pedro arrived, the Order had already established a community there dedicated to the Indians and the "blacks" or "Moors," as the Portuguese called the Muslim Indians. These were subject to the Grand Mughal, whose realm covered most of central and northern India.

The town and its Portuguese garrison was weakly supplied and suffered almost daily attacks by the "Moors." The Mughal Empire had as king the powerful Akbar, its greatest ruler. At home in Portugal, young King Sebastian died in battle in 1578, and the country was convulsed by a succession crisis which ended with the Spanish monarch, Philip II, taking the throne in 1581. The Portuguese governor during this period, Luís de Ataíde, did his best to organize troops to defend the town. The men made a sortie against the "Moors," but were quickly demoralized and retreated toward the city. Brother Pedro went out to meet them, carrying a cross on his lance, and he proceeded to rally the troops. They turned and gave battle, dispersing or killing all the attackers. Brother Pedro did notsurvive to enjoy the victory. He died, on 15 February 1580, of the many arrows he received while serving as the Christian standard bearer.[119]

Somewhat later, further east, in what is today Myanmar, we hear of two other Portuguese conversus missionaries who gave their lives for the faith. The vicar general of the Congregation of the East Indies sent Brother Pedro de los Santos to accompany priest missionaries into what was then called Syriam in Burma (now Thanlyin, Myanmar). Most of the missionaries, when they found that country at war, decided to return to Málaga. Others, including Brother Pedro, decided to land and attempt a mission. Many died of plague. Brother Pedro and his companions were captured by Muslims and stripped of their habits. Then, on 30 April 1600, they were whipped to death.[120]

A decade later, the famous Portuguese captain Felipe de Brito managed to build a fortress on the coast near the city of Bago, then called Pagou, in what is now Myanmar. This captain asked for missionaries to found a house and evangelize the region. The conversus brother Gonçalo was among the friars who responded. But the king of "Ava" (now a region of coastal Myanmar) attacked and conquered the mission. He enslaved or killed nearly all the friars. The priest Emmanuel and Brother Gonçalo alone remained. They defied King Min Khamaung, a Buddhist this time, who ordered them killed by lance thrusts. Brother Gonçalo died for the faith on 2 April 1613.[121]

The lives of these Portuguese missionary-martyrs seem remarkable, something from a romantic adventure. But even more amazing were events taking place at the same time in Japan. There, the initial missionaries had been Portuguese Jesuits; the Spanish friars arrived later. The number of martyrs in Japan is extraordinary, and includes two conversi who are the first non-European friars known to have suffered martyrdom for the Faith. In fact, all the conversus martyrs of the Great Japanese Persecution were native Japanese, and they seem to have been professed in prison while awaiting their deaths.[122]

The background of these events was the establishment of what has become known as the Tokugawa Shogunate, the military regime that ruled Japan until the nineteenth century. The first shogun, Tokugawa Ieyasu (ruled 1603–1605) and his successor Tokugawa Hidetada (1605–1623), had an ambiguous religious policy, sometimes accepting Christian missions, sometimes expelling or repressing them. But during this period the Catholic missions thrived, reaching their greatest success. Later, in the last years of Hidetada's reign, repression, expulsion, and persecution began with the mass execution of missionaries and Japanese Christians at Nagasaki in 1622. This persecution continued under his successor, Tokugawa Iemitsu (1623–1651).

The first group of conversus martyrs died during this persecution between 1622 and 1628, either at Nagasaki or Omura. Five conversus martyrs of this persecution were beatified with Alphonsus Navarrete. They were Dominic of the Rosary Magoshichi (†10 September 1622), Peter of St. Mary (†29 July 1627); Mancio of the Cross (†29 July 1627), Thomas of St. Hyacinth (†8 September 1628), and Anthony of St. Dominic (†8 September 1628).[123] The second group, that during the persecution of 1633, included two conversi, both of whom died at Nagasaki. They were canonized along with St. Dominic Ibáñez de Erquicia. These were St. Francis Shoyemon (†14 August 1633) and St. Matthew of the Rosary Kifioye (†15 August 1633).[124] Two of these martyrs, Mancio and Peter, are commemorated in the martyrology issued by the general chapter of 1644, along with, among others, Bl. Alphonsus Navarrete and St. Dominic Ibáñez de Erquicia.[125]

The story of Christianity in Japan is remarkable, spiritually extraordinary, and has been told many times.[126] The first missionary to Japan, St. Francis Xavier, arrived in 1549 with two Jesuit companions and a lay Japanese. For the next forty-nine years the Jesuits were the only missionaries there. The Franciscans arrived in 1598. Already by the 1580s, there were an estimated 130,000 native converts. However, the positive conditions that Christians had earlier enjoyed, finding tolerance, if not support, from local lords (*daimyo*) under the ruler Toyotomi Hideyoshi (1537–1598) were coming to an end. Suspicions of foreigners and Christians began late in his reign, and the first persecutions began. These reached their peak after 1603. Between 1607 and 1612, the first Dominican priests, including Bl. Alphonsus Navarrete, arrived in Japan. Dominican missions were centered in Nagasaki, and the Dominican martyrs recognized as saints and blesseds are all from that region.

The first conversus martyr died during the purge of Christians at Omura, a castle town near Nagasaki. Brother Dominic of the Rosary, born John Magoshichi, was arrested with two priests and a cleric and imprisoned. He was a native Japanese, born about 1601, and raised Catholic. So, at the time of arrest he was about 21 years of age. As these friars went to prison they sang Psalm 116 *Laudate Dominum Omnes Gentes*. The prisoners were eventually joined by many other Christians. These included other Dominican friars, among them Alfonso de Mena, the vicar provincial, and his eventual successor as vicar, José de San Jacinto. They established a community in the jail and were even able to sing the Office daily, including Matins.

On 10 September 1622, their execution was announced, and the prisoners were brought to Nagasaki. They were held outside the city with a great number of other Christians, including Dominican secular tertiaries and members of the Rosary Confraternity. Brother Dominic of the Rosary and the other native Japanese were condemned to be burnt alive. But fires had been prepared to burn only the twenty-five Europeans, so the Japanese were beheaded. It is reported that as the executions began, the martyrs began to sing the *Te Deum*. In all, ten friars died, including four who had been clothed with the habit just before the execution.[127]

The next group of conversus martyrs gave their lives in 1627–28. Brother Peter of Saint Mary and Brother Mancio of the Cross died together on 29 July 1627, as companions of Bl. Louis Bertrán y Exarch.[128] Louis Bertrán was the nephew of the saint of the same name. He had arrived at Nagasaki in 1623 with other missionaries and quickly became fluent in Japanese. He was captured on 26 July 1626. In his letter from prison to Father Antonio del Rosario, administrator of the diocese of Macao, he wrote that, during the year and a day he had spent in prison, he was always able to celebrate daily Mass. Brother Peter and Brother Mancio may have converted in prison; we do not know. But we do know that they were clothed with the habit, did their novitiate, and made profession there under the direction of Fr. Louis Bertrán. These three friars, along with other Christians, were taken to a hill called "Socabata," where Christians were normally executed, and killed there on 29 July 1627.

The last two conversus martyrs of this persecution died a little over a year later. They were Brothers Thomas of St. Hyacinth and Anthony of St. Dominic. They were martyred with the priest Dominic Castellet Vinale. He was captured and taken to Nagasaki, where he was imprisoned along with Brothers Thomas and Anthony, who were native Japanese conversus novices, and twenty-three secular tertiaries. Thomas, at the time, was about thirty years of age, Anthony about twenty. In prison, the group was able to live something of a regular life, and Father Dominic was even able to say Mass for them. They recited Matins in the dark.

After three months in prison, twelve of the prisoners, including Father Dominic, the two conversi, and four children, were chosen to be burned alive. Another ten were to be decapitated. The sentences were carried out on a hill outside the city of Nagasaki on 8 September 1628.[129] The blesseds Dominic of the Rosary Magoshichi, Peter of St. Mary, Mancio of the Cross, Thomas of St. Hyacinth, and Anthony of St. Dominic were beatified among the companions of Bl. Alphonsus Navarrete-Benito by Pope Pius IX in 1867. Originally celebrated on 1 June, their current feast day is 6 November.

The persecutions then relaxed somewhat. But in 1632, the shogun Iemitsu began an even more ruthless persecution, determined to exterminate all the native Christians and kill or expel all the European missionaries from Japan. The only choice for a Japanese was apostasy or death, usually after atrocious torture. The last two Dominican conversus martyrs died a little over a year later at the peak of this holocaust. The first, Brother Francis Shoyemon, is associated with St. Dominic Ibáñez. Dominic Ibáñez had come to Japan from the Philippines in 1623, during the Great Persecution, and had worked underground for ten years. He was much helped by two Japanese Dominican priests, James of St. Mary Kyuchei Gorobioye Tomonaga and Thomas of St. Hyacinth Hioji Rokuzayemon Nishi, who would also be martyred. His translator was the Japanese Christian Francis Shoyemon, who also served as a lay catechist.

The group, traveling in disguise on a Chinese junk, arrived at the port of Nagasaki and disembarked at night. James of St. Mary knew the area, but Dominic and his companions did not. They found the local community with difficulty. A controversy broke out among the Chinese sailors and some of them betrayed the captain (who would be baptized in prison) and missionaries to the authorities. The court ordered a search for those at large. After some of the Christians and those who had been hiding them were arrested and tortured, Dominic and Francis were discovered and arrested in July of 1633. They were imprisoned at Nagoya. They were then sent to Nagasaki. While in prison, Dominic professed Francis as a lay brother. The friars were tortured "in the pit" for some thirty hours. After this, having refused a bribe to apostatize, they were martyred together on 14 August 1633.[130]

The second conversus martyr of 1633 is associated with the Dominican missionary Luke Alonso of the Holy Spirit. Fr. Luke Alonso had arrived at Nagasaki along with Dominic Ibáñez and, like him, worked underground for ten years. During the last year of his work, he was much assisted by his young Japanese catechist, Matthew Kohioye. He received the Japanese as conversus at the age of 18, giving him the name of Brother Matthew of the Rosary. On 2 October 1633, Rosary Sunday of that year, Father Luke was arrested, along with nine other Dominicans, and sent in chains to the governor of Nagasaki. Jailed under horrible conditions, they were offered freedom if they apostatized. All in the prison refused.

The authorities, having decided that the Dominicans were the ringleaders of the resistance, ordered Father Luke, Brother Matthew, and a secular tertiary named Dominic tied to stakes upside down in a pit up to their waist. They were then pressed with boards piled with stones. In spite of the torture, they spent the day praying and praising God. Extracted and returned to prison, they were again offered release for apostasy, and again refused. Finally, on 19 October, the three were again tortured. Dominic died immediately under the torture. But Father Luke and Brother Matthew had to be tortured twice more before they expired, faithful to the end.[131] Francis Shoyemon and Matthew Kohioye were beatified, as companions of St. Dominic Ibáñez de Erquicia, on 18 February 1981. They were then canonized with him on 18 October 1987 by Pope John Paul II. Their feast is celebrated on 28 September.

Chapter 4
Iberia and New Worlds, 1550–1700

I have deliberately omitted from the last chapter the early-modern Spanish provinces and their worldwide missions. To have included them would have overburdened that chapter and overwhelmed the story of the brothers in the rest of Europe. In this chapter, we will first examine the life of the brothers in Spain itself and then trace their role in the Spanish colonies. The extra-ordinary expansion of Spain in this period parallels the extra-ordinary vitality in the Spanish part of the Order. The worldwide growth of the Order in the Spanish dominions required not just colonial expansion but also a revitalization of the Order. This revival of the Iberian Dominicans began before Columbus, and the Dominican world missions grew out of it.

The vitality of the Spanish friars began with a major reformation of the Order in Castile during the twenty-year reign of King Henry IV (1455–1474). The driving force behind this reform was the Dominican cardinal, Juan de Torquemada (1388–1468). The principles of the reform were strict observance of the constitutions within the monastery and the revitalized monastery itself as a center for evangelization and preaching.[1] In short, the post-Reformation revival of the Order in the rest of Europe had, like the Catholic Reformation itself, already begun in Spain a generation before Luther.

The Model Spanish Brother

For the sixteenth and seventeenth centuries, the sources for Spanish *conversi* surpass those for the other European Provinces, even those of Italy. These reports give us, if not a picture of the actual life of the Spanish brothers, a sense of the model of piety they were expected to emulate. In great part, these reports are probably more indicative of what clerics expected and admired in their lay brothers, but they are still useful, because they show us the model presented for imitation to conversi themselves.

The obituaries appended to general chapter acts sometimes

give us only a name, as, for example, in the case of Brother Lorenzo de Santo Tomás, who died in Segovia.[2] Often the compilers seem satisfied with a list of generic virtues. Francisco de San Miguel (†1643) of Penna-di-Francia, we are told, was "patient, humble, and obedient."[3] Brother Juan Guerrero of the community in Ibraléon during the 1640s was "hardworking, obedient, and joyful."[4] Sometimes, we simply hear that the brother was "holy," something validated by reports of miracles at his tomb, as, for example, in the case of Brother Pedro de la Cruz, of Valladolid, who lived in the later 1500s.[5] Or, again, Brother Tomás Pirolle (†1574), originally from Sicily, of the monastery of Valencia, who predicted the date of his own death.[6] Sometimes we are simply told that a reputation for holiness led to lay people demanding relics or even stripping the holy friar's corpse to get them, as they did to Brother Diego de Jesus, who died at San Pedro Martír in Ronda during the 1600s.[7]

Occasionally, the brother's portrait is more specific and describes the brother's work in the community. For example, Brother Cristóbal de Pesquera of San Pablo in Valladolid was a model of "prayer, penance, and labor, much devoted to silence and humility." These virtues were especially admirable in one who was the community cook.[8] This kind of eulogy is so common that we can be sure that conversus holiness during the Spanish reform was very much linked to their faithful execution of their assigned work and responsibilities within the monastery. We are told that Brother Cristóbal de Todos los Santos (†1648), of Málaga, was modest, pious, and always slept on the floor. But more importantly, although charged with the whole temporal administration of the monastery, he still did the usual manual labor and "never had an argument with any outsider." He was a model both within and outside the community.[9] One brother was remembered as so dedicated to his work, that of gardener, that he merited a hagiographic *vita* after he died and he even enjoyed a local cult. The Catalan brother, Juan de Dios, who died in 1556 at Llutxent near Valencia in the Province of Aragon, managed the garden and grounds of the house dependency at Barranco. He worked day and night, carrying all the water needed for the plants and living more or less as a hermit on the property. His was a life without idleness, wholly taken up by prayer and discharge of his duties.[10]

After faithful discharge of his duties, the most remarked-on quality of a brother was asceticism, perhaps not a surprise given the emphasis on personal mortification among the reformed Spanish friars. Mostly this expressed itself in fasting. Brother Jaime Bon (†1648) of San Pablo, Seville, fasted every Friday on bread and water. He was "poor, obedient, very observant of constitutions on silence." His mortified body remained flexible even after his death, as the crowds at his funeral noticed when they touched and moved it.[11] We hear of many brothers, like Cristóbal de Todos Santos of Santo Domingo Malacitano in Betica, who fasted every day and never slept in a bed. In spite of that, he worked hard "and avoided all disputes."[12]

Severe penances seem especially emphasized in the large number of conversus obituaries from the seventeenth century that were recorded at the General Chapter of Valencia in 1647. Even in his final illness, Brother Cristóbal de Troyes (†1600) of Santa Catalina Martír, Jaén, never moderated his penances. He spent his nights in prayer, took the discipline, wore chains, and fasted.[13] Brother Ildefonso de la Cruz (†1646) of San Luca of Barrameda was "virtuous, chaste, silent, and exact about the rule." To mortify the body he made a cross studded with nails and wore it under his tunic, with the points embedded in his flesh.[14] The conversus Domingo González of Toledo was praised for his harsh penances. Along with a nailed cross like that of Brother Ildefonso, he also wore a hair shirt. We are told that his "spiritual wisdom" so inspired the laity that they flocked to his funeral to kiss his feet.[15]

Considered as a whole, the aspect of model conversi that received, if not most common mention, the most extended attention in their obituaries, was prayer and experiences in prayer. This reflects the new interiority that marked early-modern Catholic piety in Iberia generally. Often, it is indicated only by the record that the brother was never missing from Matins, in spite of his heavy work internally and externally. For example, Brother Gabriel de Palacios (†1600) of San Pablo, Seville, we are told, never missed the night office, even though he spent long hours making or repairing clothes for the poor.[16]

More often noted and praised was the practice of long periods in mental prayer, something that we have noticed already in obituaries of lay brothers from the 1500s.

But interiority and practice of prayer could not replace simple hard work in the model conversus. Brother Servacio de Santo Tomás, a sixteenth-century brother of San Pablo, Valladolid, was the cook of his monastery for thirty-six years. On top of directing the kitchen and cooking, he did an hour of mental prayer every morning and evening. If his workload meant that he had to postpone his holy hours, he stayed up for two hours after Compline to complete his spiritual exercises before falling asleep. In addition, he spent time every day in spiritual reading. We are told that this pious discipline allowed him, even in the midst of overwork, to maintain his inner tranquility. Even when aged and infirm, he begged his superiors, who wanted him to retire from service as cook, to allow him to continue on in the kitchen, at least as an assistant, so that he could exercise charity to the community.[17]

Another cook of the same period, this time from the community at Salamanca, Brother Matías de la Paz (†1535), may not have spent as much time in mental prayer, but he was scrupulous about attending the choral office. He was totally illiterate, but he did not satisfy himself with simply reciting his Pater Nosters. To the amazement of the friars, by carefully listening to the chanting, he memorized the words of all the major hours of the entire week in Latin and was able to chant along with the clerics. He also memorized, by rote, the entire Little Office of the Blessed Virgin and the Office of the Dead, both recited in choir by clerics during this period. Brother Matías faithfully served as cook at Salamanca for thirty years. When he died, the friars buried him in the section of the cemetery reserved to masters of sacred theology. It was common in those days to reuse graves after a certain period of time, but no one dared disturb his resting place for decades after his death. When it was finally decided that his tomb should be reused, an earthquake shook the monastery just as the first blow of the hammer struck the chisel to open the slab. That put a stop to that![18]

Perhaps the most extraordinary example of the new emphasis on prayer and spirituality in the life of the reformed Spanish brothers is found in the life of Brother Domingo González of San Pedro Martír at Toledo.[19] I think it fair to call Brother Domingo a lay brother parallel to Bl. Henry Suso. Domingo entered the order at the age of thirty. His life was marked by extraordinary penances. He seems never to have held any responsibility in the community other than as a domestic, with occasional periods spent serving the beggars and poor who arrived daily at the porter's office. He was noted for his tender conscience and his strong devotion to St. Dominic, Mary Magdalene, Bernard of Clairvaux, Francis of Assisi, Catherine of Siena, and, above all, to Joseph and Mary.

His biographers pass over these exemplary qualities and focus almost entirely on his visions and locutions. As these, like Brother Domingo himself, are not well known today, I will describe some of them. Once, when on duty serving the poor, Domingo was assigned a lazy brother to help him, but ended up having to do all the work by himself. Begging help in prayer, he had a vision of a big commercial city with two ships on a voyage of trade. One ship arrived at the city with songs and joy, the other, to the horror of its crew, sank into the abyss of the sea. The holy brother then understood that the city was the world; the first ship, the soul of the pious and provident; the second was that of the impious and slothful. Although the vision lasted six hours, Brother Domingo finished all his duties on time.

He also had visions of the saints to whom he was devoted. On one occasion, during Matins, as the choir was singing the words *Te ergo quaesumus* of the *Te Deum*, St. Francis of Assisi appeared to Domingo as he prayed before the saint's altar. The brother fell down in tears and kissed the saint's feet. St. Francis then told him that his humility was pleasing to God, and that he should persevere in the form of life he was leading.

The largest number of Brother Domingo's recorded visions concerned his favorite devotion, the Holy Rosary. During one of these visions, Jesus Christ appeared to him and revealed what the "Secret of the Rosary" was. This was the model of Christ as "the Way, the Truth, and the Life." The fifteen Mysteries of the Rosary symbolize the steps of the spiritual life by which the Christian is conformed to Christ. The Joyful Mysteries symbolize the action of divine grace in the soul. The Sorrowful mysteries symbolize the difficulties and trials of the spiritual life. Brother Domingo never recorded the "secret" of the Glorious Mysteries, perhaps because they concern the final union of the soul with God, something that is beyond words.

On another occasion, while reciting the Rosary, at night, in the church, Domingo cried out to Our Lady: "Holy Virgin, if you are my mother, help me quickly!" Although he had meant the prayer to be a pious invocation, Domingo became convinced that his prayer was presumptuous. He prostrated before the tabernacle and begged forgiveness. Suddenly, an angel appeared and rebuked him. In penance, he took the discipline until blood was running down his back. Suddenly the Blessed Virgin and a group of saints appeared to him around the tabernacle. Each saint was holding an instrument of the Passion. The Lord Jesus Christ stood in their midst as judge of souls. One angel standing before Christ began to recite Domingo's sins in a loud voice and challenged the brother to acknowledge them and any other sins he had committed. The brother then heard the terrifying words: "Every tree that does not bear fruit shall be cut down and burned."

The saints then offered to Christ the Judge the instruments they were holding and, with the Blessed Virgin, began to beg Christ for mercy. In response, the Lord declared that he had granted Domingo pardon "because of the merits of the Passion." Profoundly consoled, Domingo realized that he could always receive mercy, if he practiced penance and asked for it. This vision began a period of his life when the brother undertook ever more severe physical penances. These included wearing a cross with nails, carving the name of Jesus and Mary into the flesh of his chest, sleeping on the stone floor, and very severe fasting and abstinence.

In another vision, a woman and child appeared to him and gestured for him to follow. They crossed a wide river. Domingo sought to follow, trying to use the trunk of a huge tree as a raft, but he could not lift it. Suddenly he found himself on the other bank, along with the woman and her child. They led him up a mountain to a beautiful garden and then disappeared. Brother Domingo realized then that the woman was the Virgin Mary and that the child was Jesus. The only thing necessary to follow them was to abandon his own will, which had been symbolized by the tree trunk. If he did that, they would take him to heaven without danger. So he moderated his penances. This river appears again in another of the brother's visions. In it, he saw himself beside a wide river, on which there was a white cloud. As he contemplated it, he realized that the cloud was the soul of Jesus, hiding within the depth of his love, which was always ready to help souls cross the river.

One last vision of Domingo's reminds us of a similar passage in Dante at the beginning of the Comedy, but now applied to the spiritual life. In it, Domingo found himself on a long journey during which he encountered three animals: a wolf, a bear, and a lion. God revealed the meaning of these frightening animals. The wolf symbolized the difficulties experienced by beginners in the spiritual life. These difficulties create unnecessary anxiety, like that of the Holy Women who, coming to anoint Jesus's body, worried about who could remove the stone. The bear was the human repugnance for doing penance, something found even in the spiritually more mature. Finally, the lion was the desire for human respect and honor, a flaw that remains even among those most spiritually proficient. It is the greatest spiritual danger.

Finally, having escaped the beasts, Domingo arrived at a tent decorated with rich draperies. At its door, a venerable woman was holding a mirror. She invited him to enter and rest. Entering, he saw a poor child, whose glance cut him to the heart. Whereupon, an angel in human form appeared, followed by a seraph looking upon the face of God. The Lord revealed to Domingo the vision's meaning. The woman with the mirror was the soul searching for rest and meditating on the life of Christ. The rich tent and its draperies were the soul's merits that would compose its heavenly crown. The poor child was evangelical poverty, the angel stood for meditation on the divine law, and the seraph symbolized the soul beholding the mysteries hidden in God that are revealed through meditation.

Two weeks before the feast of St. Dominic, Brother Domingo had a premonition of his own death. He redoubled his penances and, taking a violent fever, he died on 7 August 1629. Huge crowds, we are told, mobbed his funeral, after which he was buried in the church of San Pedro Martír, Toledo. For long afterwards, Domingo enjoyed a popular cult as a saint among the people and friars.

CONTEMPLATION IN ACTION

The theme of prayer and contemplation is marked in the obituaries of early-modern Spanish lay brothers, but it needed to be completed by bearing fruit in action. One might say that the ideal conversus of this age had to fulfill the motto of the Order: to give to others the fruits of contemplation. In contrast to contemporary conversi in the rest of Europe, who performed many kinds of service, the Spanish brothers seem to be remembered, almost exclusively, for their work in the porter's office. Such service moved the friars of the Province of Aragon to send obituaries of holy conversi for inclusion in the acts of the general chapters of the 1640s. Brother Rodrigo de Santa Maria of Burgos was remembered in 1644 as very devoted to Our Lady and for his care for the poor while serving as porter.[20] In the acts of the chapter of 1647, we hear of Pablo de Santa Maria of Santo Domingo, Murcia, whose charity and poor relief brought crowds to his funeral who acclaimed him as a saint.[21] Similar accolades marked the obituaries of Brother Juan Robledo of San Isidoro, Cartagena, and Brother Dalmacio Ciurana of Girone, Catalonia.[22] Finally, the chapter acts commemorate Brother Pedro de Quiroga (†1649) of San Pedro Martír, Lucente, Andalusia, who was venerated for his service to the poor while serving as sacristan. He died reciting the Ave Maria.[23]

This combination of prayer and service is best exemplified in the life of the "blessed" Pedro d'Ochoa of Santa Catalina, Jaén. He was born about 1561 in Biscaye.[24] Pedro's father was a wealthy gentleman, Juan Diaz, his mother, a woman of great piety, Maria Ortiz de Zarete. He was their oldest child. The future conversus was conventionally pious. He was very scrupulous about guarding his chastity, and, from his youth, avoided women, even his brother's wife. While young, he already fasted every Friday on bread and water and slept on the bare ground or a board. Although he avoided women, Pedro carried on an extensive spiritual correspondence with a female cousin who was a nun. These letters still existed in the nineteenth century; they discussed the Holy Rosary and Dominican life.

At the age of twenty-two, although of aristocratic background and sufficiently learned to be a cleric, Pedro chose to enter the order as a conversus. At first assigned as assistant sacristan, he discharged the office to great praise. He learned to anticipate the sacristan's needs before being asked. When not working, he spent his time in prayer in the chapel of the Rosary. He took the discipline nightly and would have preferred to live as a hermit. Being sent into town was for him a great penance. While in early middle age, Pedro was struck with some form of paralysis, perhaps a stroke. He moved with great difficulty and had to use a cane. Pedro tried to continue in his sacristy work, but constantly fell down, suffering bruises and other wounds. When he could no longer move about at all, he told the friars: "Fathers, for the love of God, in acknowledgement of your charity, I will pray the Rosary to the Blessed Virgin for you." The superiors decided that, in light of his immobility, he should serve as porter so that he could remain seated most of the time. This proved an excellent decision. He not only served the poor and beggars, but gathered children in his office and taught them catechism, "a child among children."

His paralysis seemed to let up a bit, but then came a turn for the worse. Pedro remained bedridden for the last eleven years before his death, viewing this as a gift of God. Perhaps he was then, finally, able to live the contemplative life he had always been drawn to. On 3 January 1616, he felt sudden weakness and knew he was dying. He asked for Viaticum and Extreme Unction. Sensing he would die the next day, he spent his last hours in prayer and spiritual conversation. He died the following day, at age of fifty-five, in the odor of sanctity. The "entire city" attended the humble catechist's funeral and took bits of his habit for relics. Reports of miracles followed his death, and he enjoyed a traditional cult into the modern period.

Other Spanish friars of the same period not only did poor relief, but were known as *questuarii*, which, as we have seen, might be translated as "beggars," but probably better as "fundraisers." Three very successful "beggars" of the Province of Betica all died in 1648. Brother Gregorio de Santa Maria, of San Lucar, Barrameda, was especially known for his love of the Virgin Mary. He spent all twenty-six years of his life as a conversus in the streets and houses of the town, procuring for the needs of his community.[25] In his efficiency, however, Gregorio's confrere Brother Ildefonso Marin, of San Pablo y Domingo, Ecija, completely overshadowed him. Ildefonso raised, we are told, over 10,000 ducats (perhaps about $1,680,000 today), more than enough to refurbish every altar in the conventual church. He "hardly kept an obol for his own use."[26]

The spiritual dimension of work with the poor is especially emphasized in many memorials of early-modern Spanish conversi. That of Brother Vicente de Santo Domingo (†1548) of San Pablo, Cordoba, tells us that the brother devoted himself wholly to prayer and to work as community porter. So much given to prayer was this humble brother that, when dealing with outsiders, whether in need of material or spiritual help, he never said an unnecessary word. So much was he devoted to silence that he preferred to use gestures or speak in a very low voice. This quiet, but very public, brother died in the odor of sanctity, beloved by the townspeople.[27] Vicente's near contemporary at Santa Catalina, Jaén, Brother Gregorio de Arazza (†1556), born at Archiona, was at first viewed by his clerical brothers as ignorant and unspiritual. But his "ignorance" proved to be filled with Holy Wisdom. He manifested such perfect obedience to the rule, and to even the most minor requests of superiors, that he finally earned universal respect. In the porter's office, where he seems principally to have served, he was beloved by both priests and laity. Gregorio never left the monastery, but townspeople came daily, asking to consult with him. He did give spiritual advice, but only after receiving a particular obedience to do so, even when the inquirers were members of his own family. Like Brother Vicente, he died in the odor of sanctity, especially venerated by those whom he had counseled.[28]

This theme of spiritual counseling, something not usually associated with conversi in the Middle Ages, is explicit in the lives of two later holy porters. Brother Juan Gorjón (†1640) of San Pablo, Seville, was remembered as obedient, respectful ofpriests, candid, and simple. As porter, however, he came to be best known for his deep knowledge of the mysteries of the faith. We are told he was much admired by learned theologians, who came to him for advice. When he died, the huge crowd at his funeral stole his habit and tore it to bits for relics.[29] This kind of consulting could even develop into something like spiritual direction and exhortation. Juan's confrere, Brother Jacinto Miranda (†1646), also of San Pablo, Seville, was equally remembered as a humble porter who loved the poor and miserable, caring for their corporal needs. He rose every night at 3:00 a.m. for Matins, and made frequent Communions. But he was also known for his impromptu *fervorini*, little spiritual conferences, to the poor, urging them to bear their trials with faith and patience.[30]

For most holy and beloved conversus servants of the poor, we have little more than names, dates, and houses of assignment. But for one remarkable early seventeenth-century Spanish conversus, we have enough information to reconstructan outline of his life and ministry. I will close this section on the forms of holiness of early-modern Spanish brothers with the most celebrated of them all, a man sadly forgotten by nearly all modern Dominicans, Brother Pablo de Santa Maria of San Pablo, Seville.[31] Pablo was born in Ecija, near Seville, and baptized by the parish priest, Juan Ramirez, on 15 September 1583 at the church of Santiago el Mayor. His parents were Pedro Martín Rabadán and Isabella González. His family seem to have been farmers. From the time of his youth he wanted to be a religious, but he was judged to have neither the intelligence nor the physical stamina for the vocation. Finally, mostly because of his piety, he was at last admitted to the postulancy. During his novitiate, his novice master detected no skills or ability, compounding the problem of his seeming bad health. The chapter agreed and decided that Pedro was to be sent back to the world to "prove himself."

The biography, prepared for his canonization process, tells us that Pablo spent the night before the friars were to vote on his admission to vows in prayer, begging God that he somehow might be admitted. In the middle of the night, the community porter heard a loud knock at the priory door, but found no one there. Rather he heard a loud voice saying: "The father prior forbids taking the habit away from Brother Pablo!" The next day, when the novice master was informed of this, he revested Pablo with his habit. Later, the prior seeing the brother back in his habit, asked the master why Pablo had not been told to leave the monastery. The novice master replied: "Because you forbade his dismissal." He then told him the story of the voice in the night. The prior, taken aback, took it as a sign from God and said: "Well, then leave that good religious alone. If he cannot do anything to serve the community, he can at least pray for us to God." The chapter then reversed its vote and approved Brother Pablo for his vows. He made profession in 1565.

The newly professed brother proved himself to be no more adept than he had been as a novice. Finally, not knowing what to do with him, his superiors sent Pablo to tend the sick in the infirmary. Feeling that he was doing very little as a nurse, he redoubled his prayers, spending the time from Compline to Matins in the church praying every night. He only went to bed when the choir began Matins. His intercessions remained hidden from the community until one day a large crowd dragged a possessed man into the church for an exorcism. When Pablo arrived with the rest of the community, the demoniac cried out: "Oh, I know you! You are the one who was piously praying last night in the church of San Pablo. I tried to distract you by sounding a great bell, but you acted as if you heard nothing. Cruel, cruel enemy!" Pablo ran off humiliated, but the friars recognized the confirmation of the prior's unwitting prophecy at the time of his profession.

If not highly skilled, the young conversus could always be counted on to share what he had with the friars. He always took the worst habit and patched it with black or white thread indiscriminately. During cold weather, when he was ordered to get a cloak from the vestry to wear over his habit, he did so, but then gave it to any friar who seemed to be colder than he.

After five years in the infirmary, Brother Pablo was reassigned as porter, a post he held until his death twenty-seven years later. It was in this work that the "useless" brother became famous. He convinced the brothers to give ever greater quantities of food, not just the leftovers, for him to distribute to the poor. Stories began to circulate throughout Seville about the multiplication of bread and wine as he distributed them. On one occasion, the quarter of a fish he had given off his plate to a poor man became four by the time he got home to his family. Once, just before Vespers, a friar entered the porter's office to check on the food for the next day's distribution. He found there a large hamper of fine white bread. Asked about where he got it, Pedro equivocated until forced to admit that he had found it in the trash, after praying to God for something to distribute the next day. As porter, Brother Pablo always called the poor he served "the children of God," and he treated them as his masters, even when they were rude and demanding.

The sick and the poor reported healings after eating their portions. A woman with dropsy, having heard these reports, came hobbling all the way from her rural village to ask Brother Pablo for bread. She was cured, we are told, after eating it. So many were the demands by the sick and beggars for food from Pablo that he was eventually made almoner. As such, he earned the title "Father of the Poor." Other stories of healing followed. A woman, Agnés de Rosalés, came to the porter's office with a horrible cancer on her face. Her family wanted Brother Pedro to touch it and pray. He refused to do so, until ordered by the prior. The cancer disappeared without a trace. Constanza, the sister of Jerónimo Guillé, one of the friars of the community, was also healed of cancer, again after the prior's vicar ordered Pedro to pray over her.

Brother Pedro had a gift for spiritual healing as well. He predicted the deaths of those who needed to repent so that they could confess in time. On one occasion, he predicted to two unfaithful novices that they would leave. In contrast, to one friar, who was convinced he was damned, he promised that God would give him the gift of perseverance. This ended his despair. By the end of his life, it was commonly reported that the sick could be healed by merely kissing his hand. We can just imagine how the conversus reacted to such approaches.

Brother Pablo felt a special calling to pray for and help travelers and pilgrims. This calling was the occasion of his most celebrated miracle. A Sicilian pilgrim had been robbed and was being beaten to death by the robbers. As the man prayed for help, a Dominican lay brother appeared out of nowhere. The friar covered the man with his scapular and commanded the robbers to leave. They did. The brother then accompanied the man to a fork in the road. Asked who he was, the apparition said to the man, "I am Brother Pablo of the house of Seville," and he disappeared. When the man reached the monastery to thank his liberator, he immediately recognized him in a group of friars. But Pablo insisted that he had nothing to do with the delivery. It must have been an angel, he said. Those present immediately knew that the angel had been sent in answer to Pablo's constant prayers for travelers.

In 1597, a horrible plague attacked Seville. While serving the dead and dying, Brother Pablo contracted it. He knew by inspiration that he was dying. He received the last sacraments and asked forgiveness of all his brothers. As the community recited the prayers for the dying around his bed, he held a candle and made the responses with them. On 20 December 1597 he died at the age of sixty-three. The people of the city, including noblemen and women, attended the funeral, all hoping to kiss, if not the saintly brother's hands, at least his feet. The burial itself was delayed because of the press of those wanting to touch his body.

It was reported that he appeared after his death to several of the faithful, and prodigies, both spiritual and physical, were ascribed to him. The holy porter's tomb became a place of pilgrimage, and a process for his canonization was soon opened.[32] Images of him were painted for churches, including one above his tomb in the house chapter room. For reasons, it seems, of expense, his process stalled in the 1680s and, although open today, it has not been pursued.

It is interesting that the traits we have identified as those of the ideal early-modern Spanish conversus—industry, deep and even mystical prayer, poor relief, and fundraising—are exactly those of the most famous brother of the century, St. Martin de Porres of Lima. This should not surprise us as he belonged to the same, albeit colonial, religious culture. But before we consider him, we need to follow the friars, clerical and lay, to the New

World.

BROTHERS IN THE NEW WORLD

The story of the Spanish arrival in and conquest of what is today Latin America has been told many times, and this is not the place to do so again. Fortunately, readers who lack a background in these events now have an eminently readable narrative that takes advantage of modern scholarship. I strongly recommend, among his other books on the topic, Hugh Thomas's *The Conquest of Mexico*. For those who want a short summary of the missions themselves, I would suggest Stafford Poole's contribution in *Christianity Comes to the Americas*. The Dominican missionaries to the Caribbean and what is today Central America and Mexico came mostly from San Esteban in Salamanca. Christopher Columbus had himself stayed with that community between 1486 and 1487, during which time he gained the support of the Dominican Diego de Deza, who would become bishop of Palencia and then archbishop of Seville.

The first Dominicans intended as missionaries to America, fifteen in all, were dispatched by Cardinal Cajetan in 1507, but only four of them actually reached the New World, in 1509. In 1512, some forty more arrived with Father Pedro de Cordoba and founded the first house on the island of Santo Domingo, in what is now the Dominican Republic. Pedro de Cordoba was a noted reformer and would later play a major role in defending the rights of the indigenous peoples.[33] Among these first friars to America, we know the name of one conversus, Brother Juan García, who died with another (unnamed) conversus at Cumaná in modern Venezuela about 1515.[34] By 1530, there was a sufficient number of friars in the Caribbean to establish the first province in the New World, that of the Holy Cross of the Antilles.

We know of a second conversus who died in the "West Indies," which probably means the province of the Holy Cross. Brother Alberto Garnica, like many of the early missionary friars, lived much of his life in Spain. By training a master accountant, he received scholastic training from his brother, who wanted him to take orders. Instead, he entered the house at Valladolid as a conversus. Recognizing his talents, his superiors made him not only treasurer of the community, but the procurator (legal representative) of the province at the Royal Chancery in Valladolid. He was the first brother to serve in that capacity. Although he lived in humility—remembered especially for his "vile" habit—he went on to serve as procurator at the Spanish court itself. His administrative talents were probably the reason for his assignation to the West Indies. He died there in 1580.[35]

The Province of St. James in Mexico followed that of the Holy Cross two years later, in 1532. These early settlements were torn by a debate over whether the friars should imitate the form of life back in Spain, with houses of at least thirty friars and formal religious observance, or establish smaller settlements in the countryside dedicated principally to pastoral work. For the most part, the latter would be the rule in the missions. In 1539, the Province of John the Baptist in Peru was founded. Dominican missions were initially most numerous in what is today southern Mexico and Central America. In 1551, the Province of St. Vincent of Chiapas was established by the general chapter that year in Salamanca. It also reorganized the missions in what is today Venezuela, which eventually became the Province of St. Antoninus.[36]

These provinces were very large. For example, that of Chiapas included four dioceses covering all of modern Chiapas, Guatemala, Nicaragua, and Honduras. That of St. James extended from Oaxaca in the south all the way to what is today the states of Florida and Texas. The chapter of 1551 gave this province responsibility for the missions to Asia. Dominican expansion was southward from the Province of St. James in central Mexico. Eventually, the friars were the most numerous missionaries in what is now southern Mexico and Central America. Divisions came later in the century. In the 1580s, the Provinces of St. Catherine the Martyr in Ecuador and of St. Lawrence in Chile were hived off from the Province of Peru, while in the north, St. Hippolytus in Oaxaca was separated from Mexico in 1592.

Thus, by 1600, there were seven Dominican provinces in the New World, as well as the missionary Province of Our Lady ofthe Holy Rosary, centered in the Philippines. In 1656, the Province of the Angels in Puebla would also be separated from Mexico. In the latter part of the century, Philip II demanded that friars accept the administration of more small mission stations in remote Indian villages. The Mexican Provincial Chapter of Zacapulas had already in 1587 rejected this demand for additional administrative and pastoral responsibilities on the grounds that the Dominican Constitutions forbade such commitments because they limited itinerant preaching and regular observance. In the end, throughout Latin American, the compromise would be large houses in the cities and small mission stations in the countryside.

By 1550, in Mexico, there were large houses in Mexico City, Oaxaca, Puebla, Veracruz, and San Juan de Ulloa, and some twenty-two smaller filial houses.[37] This is significant for our study because virtually all the conversi found in contemporary records lived in the large urban houses or were with traveling missionaries. There were certainly conversi in the small churches of the countryside, but they are mostly invisible to us. There may be a reason for this. It seems, from the diary of friar Tomás de la Torre, that during the early days in Mexico, conversi were indeed sent to rural mission houses and given complete control of the temporalities, so that the priests could travel about to various mission stations. Father Tomás reported that many of these brothers simply disappeared and went native, in contrast to those in the cities, who lived in the large houses and remained stable.[38]

The piety of the missionary friars was imported from Spain and always carried a peninsular Spanish flavor, even after large numbers of indigenous people were converted. Dominican and Franciscan missionaries did learn the native languages and studied their culture, but the goal was to facilitate conversions, not preserve those cultures. In 1650, for example, the general chapter regularized this practice by appointing preachers general fluent in the native languages for the Province of St. James: four for the Nahuatl speakers, four for the major dialect of Zapotec, three for the northern dialect, and one preacher each for the Chontal, Chinantec, Gavia, and Mixtec populations.[39]

In fact, this "indigenization" did preserve many aspects of the Indian culture, even in religion, but that was not the intention of the friars. The goal was assimilation and integration into Spanish Catholic society. This manifested itself in the piety that the friars promoted. From the very beginning, they preached the Rosary—

an important part of conversus spirituality—as a way of evangelizing. The first provincial of St. James in Mexico, Father Betanzos, ordered all friars to wear the Rosary around their necks. This practice would spread to the whole of the Spanish Dominions. The friars established confraternities of the Holy Rosary and of the Holy Name of Jesus in the New World as early as 1548. The 1573 provincial chapter in Mexico mandated the establishment of Rosary Confraternities in all Dominican churches.[40] And a century later, in the Province of Ecuador, for the first time, it seems, choral recitation of the Rosary was instituted on a daily basis for all the friars.[41]

EARLY BROTHERS IN MEXICO

The first conversus of Mexico whom we know by name was Brother Gregorio Castaño of Chiapas, who was remembered as devout, humble, and a lover of the poor. He died on 5 August 1564.[42] We can assume that he, like the friars' piety, was transplanted from Spain. That was certainly the case for the other sixteenth-century conversi of New Spain that we know. These men were mature vocations, often penitents, who entered after many adventures. One of the earliest was not a Spaniard at all. Brother Gonçalo of Andrade, a Portuguese of aristocratic background, had come to Mexico as a merchant and became very wealthy. Near the end of his life, perhaps suffering from a heavy conscience about his financial dealings, he spent the last six years of his life as a conversus in the principal house of Mexico City. His life was marked by poverty, obedience, and charity, as well as great devotion to St. Catherine of Siena, whom he constantly invoked during his last illness. The chronicler of the Province of St. James, Agustín Dávila Padilla, was present at his deathbed on 20 October 1584.[43]

We know something of the lives of two other adventure-seekers who became conversi in the Province of Saint James at about the same time as Gonçalo. Their lives are very suggestive for the kind of men attracted to the lay brotherhood in Mexico during the Golden Century.

Brother Miguel of Zamora, so called from his birthplace in Spain, came to Mexico with the early *encomenderos* in search of wealth and fame. Disgusted by what he saw, he underwent a dramatic conversion. He gave away all his money, dressed in penitential rags, and returned home to Spain. It was the opposite of the Parable of the Prodigal Son. His father threw a fiesta to celebrate his son's return, but, on seeing Miguel, he immediately began to berate him for his vile appearance. The young man realized, we are told, that this proved that his family valued his wealth more than his person. So he put on rich garments and returned to the party to universal applause. Taking the floor, we are told, he announced: "Since you value me only for my wealth, you will get none of it; it will be shared with the poor." Miguel does not seem to have given his possessions away immediately. Rather he married and took his wife back to Mexico. There he did well, but lived a reserved and austere life.

When his wife died, he placed his son, Alfonso, with friends and became a hermit penitent. He spent five years with an unnamed companion, living in the cold mountains of Tlaxcala. Realizing that they could not live this life into their old age, the two men made their way to Mexico City, looking for observant religious communities to enter. His friend entered the Franciscans, but Miguel chose otherwise. Taking the twelve-year-old Alfonso with him, he asked admission to the Dominicans as a conversus, and the status of clerical aspirant for his son. Friars remembered Miguel as a hard-working brother who practiced the presence of God. An able architect, he was involved in the construction of several new foundations. Always considering himself a penitent, he refused to wear a new habit.

Reassigned to Oaxaca, then still part of the Province of St. James, he engineered irrigation works for the city and the monastery, for which he earned great praise and admiration. Miguel's later years were marked by two painful illnesses, but he did not relax his fasts or vigils until a very advanced age. He died at Oaxaca in the later 1500s. His son proved adept in several native languages and served the friars as interpreter for sermons and catechism, although it seems he never made profession in the Order. Alfonso was alive when Agustín Dávila Padilla added his father's biography to his history of the Order in Mexico.[44]

The same conflicted relationship with worldly success and wealth marked the life of the other early Mexican conversus whose life has come down to us. Francisco García was originally from Galicia in Spain. As a young man, he went to America to seek his fortune. He made it in silver mining, but, like Miguel, he became alienated from the colonial culture. Perhaps he was disgusted by the treatment of the natives in the mines. He repented and sought entrance as a donatus postulant at the house in Puebla. He remained, however, hesitant as to whether this was the right decision. He placed at interest much of his silver fortune as a fallback, should he not persevere. In the monastery at Puebla, he became the chief cook and had supervision of the garden. But the memory of his worldly life of ease and honor was a constant temptation. At last, he gave it up, discarded his habit, and returned to the world and his money.

As a postulant donatus, this was technically not a violation of any vows—Francisco was not yet even a conversus novice. But this backsliding did not last long. He took his fortune, returned to the monastery, and gave all the silver as Mass stipends for the souls in Purgatory. He made a General Confession of his transgressions to the prior, who then sang a Requiem Mass for Francisco's intentions. He was clothed in the conversus habit and made a fervent novitiate. Brother Francisco professed his vows on 10 February 1559. He became a model of poverty, obedience, and prayer. His principal duty, until his death, was begging, most likely at the doors of his former rich friends. Indeed, he was remembered for the large sums he brought home as alms.

In 1586, Brother Francisco was sent to serve the missionaries active at the mines near Taxco. Running out of food, he stopped at the house of a wealthy woman, who took the poor brother in. Almost immediately, his health declined and he asked for a priest to give him the last sacraments. It was Holy Week, and, on the evening of Holy Thursday, the woman went to visit Francisco on his sickbed and see if he needed anything. We are told that she found the room bathed in light, this visible through the cracks around the door.

Assuming that he was reading, and not wanting to distract the sick man, she did not enter. Asking around, she discovered that no one in the house had given the sick brother a lamp. A maid sent to check also saw the light but was afraid to open the door.

Eventually, this light disappeared and the woman entered his room. Asked how he was, Francisco said that while meditating on the Passion of Christ he had learned that he would die on Easter Sunday. And so it happened. Brother Francisco died on 6 April 1586. Fifteen priests, we are told, arrived for his funeral, none aware of any of the others, and none by invitation. Those present took this as a sign of the brother's holiness.[45]

MISSIONARY BROTHERS IN FLORIDA

At the same time as these penitent brothers were experiencing conversion and seeking religious life, other conversi were leaving the monastery and embarking on far-flung missionary travels. This is best documented for those who went to the Florida missions. This region was at the time among the most active missionary areas of the Mexican Province. The first explorers arrived in Florida under Ponce de León in 1513, but found the indigenous people hostile. They returned to Puerto Rico.[46] In 1523, another expedition under Pánfilo de Marváez arrived with the Franciscan bishop-elect of Florida. The ships separated in a storm, and this group found itself abandoned. Their trek back to Mexico was one of harrowing adventures. In 1539, a large expedition with some six hundred settlers, including twelve priests, arrived under Hernando de Soto near modern Tampa. Finding no gold, they went overland to Mexico, discovering the Mississippi River along the way. Finally, in 1549, the first Dominican mission, that under Luis Cáncer de Barbastro, arrived. Influenced by Bartolomé de las Casas, they intended a peaceful settlement without a military presence. It was short lived. Father Luis was almost immediately killed by Calusa Indians and the mission abandoned.

The largest of these missionary expeditions departed Mexico in 1559 under Tristan de Luna. It included thirteen ships, five hundred soldiers, a thousand colonists, five Dominican priests, and one conversus. That brother may be the most colorful of the whole sixteenth century. Bartolomé Matéos came from Spain as a conquistador and attached himself to the party led by Francisco Pizarro to Peru in 1532. There were some Dominicans in Pizarro's party, and it is perhaps at this time that Bartolomé first met the Order. In Peru, he was involved in the conquest, the consequent brigandage, and the resulting conflicts and violence, which included the killing of Pizarro himself. The power struggle between the conquistadors and the viceroy became an open civil war. The conquistadors, led by Pizarro's brother Gonzalo, rebelled against the New Laws, which had granted relief to the Indians. They defeated and executed the viceroy Blasco Núñez Vela in 1546.

Conditions in Peru had reached such a point that, the following year, Emperor Charles V dispatched an expedition under a soldier priest, Pedro de la Gasca. This put down the attempt by Gonzalo to set himself up as king of Peru. Bartolomé was imprisoned in chains with the rest of the rebels. While awaiting his execution, the wily soldier of fortune managed to escape his prison. He made his way by boat up the coast to Panama. He then went overland to Mexico City. On arrival, he immediately presented himself at the door of the Dominican monastery, asking to be received as a penitent conversus. Hewas granted the habit and put under the direction of Father Cristóbal de la Cruz, a highly respected religious, who was also the director of a good number of the conversi whose names have come down to us.

Under that spiritual guide, Bartolomé did penance night and day. He gave himself up to prayer, and proved himself well disciplined and observant of the rule. He impressed the entire community by his harsh penances: use of cord and chain disciplines, sleeping on a board, and fasting. Most noted was his humble deference to all the friars, including other conversi. When the provincial was selecting the friars to join the 1559 expedition to Florida, he asked the priests which conversus he should assign. Unanimously, they chose Brother Bartolomé. After receiving instruction from his spiritual director to prepare himself for this new mission, Bartolomé set sail with the convoy for Florida.

The expedition first tried to establish a mission near what is now Pensacola, but the settlement was destroyed by a hurricane. The next attempt, in what is today Georgia, met the same fate. Throughout these trials, everyone was impressed by Bartolomé's prudence, discipline, and prayerfulness. We are told that native converts considered him a holy man. It was decided to send some of the expedition by ship to Spain to recruit more settlers for the struggling colony. Brother Bartolomé went with them. This vessel was lost with all hands in yet another horrible storm in late 1559. His director, Father Cristóbal, always considered him a saint.[47] Two Dominican priests from this Florida mission would eventually become bishops, Pedro de Feria in Chiapas, and Domingo de Salazar in Manila.

The conversus eventually sent to replace Brother Bartolomé in the Florida mission was, like him, born in Spain and originally a soldier of fortune in the New World. Again, like Bartolomé, he underwent a conversion, although perhaps not so dramatic. Brother Matéos de la Madre de Dios originally entered the Mexico City community about 1554 as a cleric, so he was a man of some education. There, he was directed by the same Father Cristóbal de la Cruz who had so influenced Brother Bartolomé. He also became friends with another older brother, Juan de Sena, who had been, in 1538, among the first professed conversi of the community. We do not know if he was close to Brother Bartolomé, but their similar background and the overlap of their time in the monastery suggests this is possible. In any case, we understand that soon after admission, Matéos changed categories and became a lay brother "out of humility." Brother Matéos de la Madre de Dios was remembered as a "model religious," principally employed in the infirmary.

Luis de Velasco, viceroy of New Spain, planned a new expedition to Florida to reinforce the earlier one of 1559. It was intended to become a permanent base in North America. Matéos landed with this expedition, which was led by Domingo de Salazar, already mentioned, at Gulf Station in April of 1561, only to receive word that the project was cancelled. They returned to Mexico City late in the year. There, Brother Matéos served the community for forty years, principally as infirmarian. Brother Juan de Sena, who was much older, died on 10 July 1602, Brother Matéos having nursed him in his last illness. The younger conversus died just a month later and was buried with Brother Juan. Both were venerated as saints by the people of Mexico City.[48]

The most hair-raising adventures of any of these explorer conversi happened, not on an expedition to unsettled areas, but during an attempt to sail to Spain. We know by name two of the lay brothers involved, Marcos de Mena and Juan de Mena, who may have been blood brothers—the evidence is unclear. Marcos, we know, was born in Villar del Pedro near Talavera, Spain. We also know his parents, Pedro Diaz and Maria de Mena. The family was well off, and Marcos was sent to the University ofSalamanca. In spite of his education, he chose to enter San Esteban as a conversus. He received the habit in 1544 and was professed a year later on 29 April 1545. Almost immediately, he was sent to the Mexican mission, where he apparently worked in various houses of the province and in outlying stations among the Indians.[49] During that time, Juan de Mena, whose origins are not reported, entered the same community, also as a conversus. He served there as infirmarian.[50]

In 1553, the two conversi sailed from Veracruz for Spain with several other friars and a number of lay people. The reason is not clear. Perhaps they were giving up the mission, or perhaps the friars were returning on province business. In any case, they only got as far as modern Louisiana, where, after a storm, they were shipwrecked off the "River of Palms," now known as the Mississippi. This was in what was then called West Florida. Almost immediately, the stranded party was attacked by Indians. Brother Marcos and two sailors managed to make an escape. When they returned to the site of the ambush the next day, they found all the Spaniards there dead or dying. So the three took off after some other survivors, who had fled westward. The three caught up with them the following day. The party then traveled southwest, hoping to find their way back to Mexico. After twenty exhausting days on foot, they reached a river, probably the Trinity River in what is today eastern Texas. During this journey they had seen no one, whether indigenous or Spanish.

While camped on the banks of this river, they were again attacked by Indians. The leaders of the expedition and Brother Juan de Mena were killed by arrows. Marcos and some of the group managed to hide in some undergrowth, but he was attacked by huge ants. He bolted from the bush and managed again to escape the natives. Returning the next day, the survivors found the bodies of their comrades but were too exhausted to bury them. Instead, they continued southwest. While they traveled, the Indians continued to harass them. Brother Marcos took seven arrows, one in the face, and fell to the ground. The Indians disappeared. The grief-stricken party buried the inert conversus in the sandy riverbank.

The next morning Brother Marcos woke up, buried alive. Fortunately, the sand was soft and the grave not very deep. Marcos dug himself out. He found himself bloody, naked, and riddled with arrows. Ahead, he heard what seemed like sounds of rejoicing. He crawled through the underbrush, hoping to find his companions. Instead, he found only their corpses—and the Indians celebrating their victory. He was now alone. In an unbelievable trek, not even considering his physical condition, Brother Marcos made his way overland, some seven hundred miles, to the Pánuco River in central Mexico. There he collapsed in a bloody heap on the bank. What seemed to be two Indians arrived in a canoe. They wrapped Marcos in a white sheet and took him twenty miles downstream to the settlement at Tampico near the coast. There the Indians disappeared, after gesturing that he should go into the nearby town. On returning to Mexico City, Marcos underwent painful surgery to remove the arrows. The whole adventure had taken between twelve and eighteen months.

Brother Marcos always kept the white cloth as a relic ofwhat he considered a miraculous rescue. The next twenty-one years Marcos spent in the Mexico City monastery, much admired for his courage and his humble service of the friars. One day in the 1570s, a Dominican professor from Spain, Bartolomé de Ledesma, arrived to teach at the university in Mexico City. About five years later, he was transferred to teach at the University of San Marcos in Lima, Peru. He chose as his socius Brother Marcos de Mena. In 1581, de Ledesma was appointed bishop of Oaxaca, but, because of age and infirmity, Marcos stayed on in Peru. The chronicler Dávila Padilla met the aged brother at his community in Lima. He noticed a votive painting hanging in the brother's cell. It showed someone being rescued by two angels in a canoe. Dávila asked who the man was, and the venerable conversus told him that it was himself. Brother Marcos de Mena died at Lima in 1584. It was men like these brothers that the provincial of Mexico had in mind when he wrote to Master Vincenzo Giustiniani (1558–1570) about the excellent quality of the conversi of his province.[51]

Historians usually speak of the Mexican province of the next century as having undergone a decline in fervor and discipline.[52] Perhaps it was true. Certainly, we no longer hear of heroic lay brothers like those of the 1500s. In fact, the only Mexican conversus of the 1600s for whom I have found records is Brother Francisco Montes of Mexico City. We are told he was humble, hard working, practiced physical penances, and never ate meat. He was also a spiritual man, known for constantly reading the works of Luis of Granada. He was admirable, perhaps, but much more conventional than his predecessors. He died in 1661.[53] In contrast, the seventeenth century will be the great century for the lay brothers elsewhere in the Spanish Dominions. This will be the heroic age of the Province of Our Lady of the Holy Rosary in the Philippines and of St. John the Baptist in Peru.

BROTHERS IN THE FAR EAST

The previous chapter dealt in part with the earliest friars in Asia, at first mostly Portuguese, but later, in Japan, mostly Spanish. These Spanish friars came mostly through the Philippine Islands, which were formally under the Province of Mexico until the creation of the Province of Our Lady of the Holy Rosary in 1596.[54] These Spanish missionary brothers normally came along with groups of missionary priests. An early example would be Brother Pedro Martínez, who was born in Segovia to a comfortable farming family and received a good Christian upbringing. A devout and docile child, he frequented the sacraments and had great devotion to the Blessed Virgin. He sounds like a typical pious Spaniard of his time. While still young, he became convinced that the Virgin Mary wanted him to seek the habit as a conversus at San Pablo in Cordoba. There, the great missionary priest, Juan Cobo, developed a great admiration for the young Pedro because of his prayerfulness. When Cobo left for the Philippines in 1588, he took the young conversus with him.

On arrival in Manila, Brother Pedro was made porter of the newly founded community. The friars nicknamed him "Rezador," "The Man of Prayer," and "The Holy Brother." He was, as typical of conversi of the age, especially devoted to the Rosary, which he recited along with his office of Pater Nosters. But, we are told, he sometimes took as long as an hour to recite each decade of the Rosary, which was perhaps an exaggeration, as five hours of prayer a day would have taken him away from his manual labor.

Brother Pedro seemed to have had a special, infused knowledge of the faith that surprised even learned theologians. The pious brother was able to discern spirits. On one occasion, the governor of the Philippines heard the brother explaining the mysteries of the Rosary and declared it the best presentation he had ever heard. Along with his busy work as porter, he was eventually made sacristan. Assigned to Pangasinan Province on Luzon, he contracted a bad fever on arrival and died on 9 December 1591, while holding his Rosary and reciting the Hail Mary.[55] He seems very much a transplanted Spanish brother of the Reform.

Within five years, there would be sufficient friars in the East to establish a province. In 1611, the general chapter at Paris dedicated much time and effort to organizing the Dominican presence in the Philippines and Macao.[56] But the takeoff was slow. Still, in 1615, the capitular fathers at Bologna were warning other provinces against taking in and assigning missionary friars on the way to the East Indies. They were only to do so if the friar in question were sick, or they had received special permission from the vicar for the Spanish Dominions. Many of the priests in the Philippines were on loan from other provinces. This chapter ordered that they were not to be recalled until they had done at least ten years of service in the mission.[57] Within a decade or so, things had become established enough so that the Philippines could send missionaries to Japan. This was right in the midst of the Great Persecution, which was described in the last chapter.[58]

The Philippines, like the Spanish Dominions in the New World, posed great linguistic challenges for preaching and teaching. The clerics may have known Latin, but this was of little value for anything other than administering the sacraments or singing the Office. Sometimes, it was the brothers, with their closer contact to the people, who ended up as translators. The conversus Domingo de San Blas, professed at San Pablo of Seville, asked to go and serve the brothers in the missions.[59] He was named the companion of Father Ambrosio de la Madre de Dios and sent to New Segovia (i.e. the Philippines). There he learned several indigenous languages and served not only as translator but also as a catechist. Father Ambrosio recognized in him the usual lay brother virtues of humility and recollection, but also acknowledged his indispensability in preaching and teaching.

As a brother who spoke their languages, Domingo seems to have established close friendships with natives. Some of these encounters were later recounted as marvels, if not miracles. One year, on the feast of St. Dominic, when the only food available for the banquet was boiled vegetables, Brother Domingo prayed and—out of nowhere—a native arrived with a beautiful fish of a species "unknown in those parts." Domingo prepared it for dinner. "The whole community praised God for the regal repast."

A second marvel happened that very day. A native convert had asked Father Ambrosio for permission to mourn a pagan native who had died suddenly in the fields. Ambrosio went to check that the native was truly dead. Domingo, who was with him, was shocked to see that this was the very native who had brought him the marvelous fish. In sorrow, the brother knelt and prayed over the body. The dead man promptly resurrected and asked to be baptized. The natives knew that the miracle was due to the brother's intercession "because of his love for the natives." Brother Domingo's work with the indigenous peoples continued for many years, until one day he collapsed, it seems of sunstroke. The beloved brother was taken to Manila for treatment, but, after receiving the Last Rites, he died on 20 June 1600.

Unfortunately, and perhaps more typically, contact with the indigenous peoples sometimes resulted in violence when the native way of life was disrupted. Conversi could end up in the cross-fire. Brother Onofre Palao of Manila was assigned as socius to the missionary priest Ildefonso García in 1622 and sent to New Segovia. The place of evangelization assigned them was considered among the most dangerous in the Philippines. The two friars tried to move the Mandagos natives out of their traditional mountain areas and make them live in houses within the mission compound. The Indians resisted and could not be made to live in the mission station without coercion. Some bolted and returned to the mountains.

Others resisted their friar tormenters. On Trinity Sunday, 1625, they attacked the mission itself. One native killed Brother Onofre by a knife blow to the head; others badly wounded Father Ildefonso. His servants carried the priest back to the residence, intending to take him on to civilization by boat. He actually recovered enough to say two of the Trinity Sunday Masses at the mission. But the natives returned en masse later in the day and killed him, "leaving his body to be eaten by wild animals." It was reported that he died with such piety that, even though he had lost his translator and was not fluent in the native language, he was able make his forgiveness evident enough to his killers that they were moved. By the following year, these natives had converted and built a chapel in his and Brother Onofre's honor.[60] It seems that eleven other Dominican priests died in this uprising.

Often, it seems, the work of the conversi with the natives went unnoticed by their priestly collaborators. When Brother Francisco de San Agustín died on 12 September 1650, in the province of Cagayon of the Philippines, large numbers of natives crowded his funeral. They venerated his body, kissed his feet, and prostrated before his bier. The fathers had considered him a pious brother, but never paid much attention to his work with the poor natives. While admitting the brother's piety, purity, and simplicity, they simply could not understand the natives' devotion. In their ignorance, they could only ascribe it to some kind of divine inspiration![61]

The kind of service rendered to other races by the conversi in their ministry to the poor and sick comes across clearly in the life of Brother Juan de San Dionisio.[62] Born Juan Héredia in the village of Aguilar, Spain, he entered the Córdoba monastery of Scala Caeli as a conversus and pursued a life of "humility, charity, and manual labor." His principal duty was begging for the needs of the community. His demeanor and holiness made him much loved, and he brought in many alms. "A zeal for souls" eventually caused him to volunteer for the Philippine missions. But the revenues he generated for his house and the charities of the city caused his prior and the bishop, Pablo de Laguna, to object. This was overcome by the Dominican archbishop of Manila, the famous sinologist, Miguel de Benevides, who asked for him as his socius.

On arrival in Manila, Brother Juan received his attribute "de San Dionisio" because it was not the practice there for religious to use surnames. Appointed porter, Brother Juan became known as a "father of the poor" for his charity and alms. When feeding the poor, many of whom were natives, with the leftovers from refectory, he would read chapters of Luis of Granada to them as they ate. Juan also served in the hospital of San Gabriel, which had been founded by the Dominicans to serve both Spanish and Chinese. Although he never learned Chinese, Brother Juan's love and care for them caused many Chinese to ask for baptism. We know this from the report of Father Francisco de San José, the Dominican rector of the hospital.

Age and physical decline caused Brother Juan to be recalled to the monastery to serve in the lighter responsibility of porter. Nevertheless, after full days in the porter's office, he still got up for Matins. Eventually dispensed from the Office because of age, he instead took up rising two hours before dawn so that he could visit the altars of the conventual church, especially that of the Holy Rosary, where he would pray until Prime. He then attended several low Masses. Brother Juan kept up this regime until he was ninety years old. After his death on 5 September 1638, the only possessions found in his cell were a blanket and a rough tunic.

Although the early conversi of the Philippines, in contrast to the former conquistadors of Mexico, seem to have been pious men recruited back in Spain and dispatched there, there is one conversus whose adventures recall those of some of the early penitent brothers in Mexico. He was probably not unique. Juan Estrada, born about 1596, had arrived in the East as a young man and become a rich merchant in Manila.[63] Recognizing his intelligence, many Spanish and Chinese entrusted their commercial dealings to him. Although very conscientious, jealous detractors raised questions about his integrity. He was arrested and thrown in jail. He endured this loss of liberty, which destroyed his reputation, for three years. Eventually he was vindicated and released from jail, but the experience had led him to question the whole pursuit of wealth. Instead of reopening his business, he went to knock at the door of the Dominican house in Manila and asked to be admitted as a conversus. Accepted and professed, he proved an exemplary religious. He was prayerful, humble, self mortifying, and edifying to the community. Brother Juan died in the house at Manila in 1662.

The 1600s seem the golden age of the Holy Rosary Province, not only at home, but also in the Asian missions. Although he was not a friar, I need, before moving back to Latin America, to mention the Rosary Confraternity member, St. Lorenzo Ruiz (1600–1637), the Protomartyr of the Philippines. Of mixed Filipino-Chinese ancestry, he came from the kind of background served by the conversi just described. In the following century, we hear little of conversi in the Philippines. The one whose obituary made it into general chapter acts of that century was Brother Juan Peresio, of Santo Domingo in Manila. We are told he loved the rule and had a very good reputation.[64] There were doubtless others like him, but they have been forgotten.

THE DOMINICANS IN PERU

As I have already mentioned, Dominicans arrived in Peru with Pizarro himself. The history of the Church, the missions,and the Order in this region has received less attention from historians than events in Mexico.[65] Peru, indeed, starting in the late 1500s, saw a veritable renaissance of conversi. Overshadowing them all is St. Martin de Porres and, to a lesser extent, St. Juan Macías, but they are only part of this story. In this study, while certainly not ignoring these two men, I want also to focus attention on the other lay brothers who lived with them in the houses of Lima, El Rosario and La Magdalena. We can trace in those communities three generations of remarkable conversi. They begin with Brother Marcos de Mena, whom we have already met, who arrived about 1580, and extend to Brother Simón García, who died in 1652.

This seventy-year period is the brothers' golden age in the history of the Order. I call this group the "Lima Circle," a phrase I borrow from the recently published, and first truly scholarly, life of St. Martin, Celia Cussen's *Black Saint of the Americas*. The centrality of the Order in the evangelization of Peru is symbolized by the Dominican Jerónimo de Loayza y González (1498–1575), originally bishop of Cartagena, and, from 1541, the first bishop, and then archbishop, of Lima. He founded in Lima both the

University of San Marcos and the first hospital in Peru. He wrote instructions on the ordering of the *doctrinas*, the mission stations among the indigenous peoples. His two provincial councils (1551–52 and 1567) not only organized the work of the archdiocese, but produced the first pastoral document with a normative character on the Christianizing of the native peoples. Although he sought to defend the native peoples from the encomenderos, he determined that they be taught prayers and doctrine in Spanish, not their own native languages.[66]

The Province of St. John the Baptist in Peru predates the great bishop's arrival, as it was established in 1539. It seems to have been slow to develop, and, in 1571, the general chapter was still allowing Peru to recruit friars from other provinces, although limiting the number to ten from any individual province.[67] But within ten years, the major houses in Lima were very large, both in physical size and numbers of friars. El Rosario, for example, was home to over three hundred.[68] Given the percentages typical in this period, we can assume about sixty of these friars were lay brothers, to whom we may add at least ten or more donati.

Such establishments required a large labor force to maintain the fabric and provide for the needs of the residents. All the offices described in Humbert of Romans's ordering of the monastery, which I outlined in chapters 1 and 2, were necessary for these communities to function. El Rosario had three separate religious communities, that of the clerics, that of the conversi, and that of the donati. The clerics and conversi each had their own cloister garden, but the donati did not. Each had its own separate dormitory, chapter room, and chapel. Each group wore a distinct habit. Resident lay servants and employees (*familiares*) lived in the donati section of the house. All three groups shared the monastery church and the refectory.

Some donati were transitional, undergoing the three-year postulancy before entering the conversus novitiate, while others were permanent and remained tertiaries for their entire life. The conversi and donati were, in great part, the public face of the monastery. They did the begging for daily needs, and they served the temporal (and sometimes spiritual) needs of the poor and broken who frequented the church and arrived daily at the porter's office. These brothers preached by their actions, not usually their words, but their activities made them well known throughout the city.[69]

The first generation of remarkable Lima conversi can be considered to begin with Brother Marcos de Mena, who arrived in Lima in 1580 and died there four years later. I have already discussed his adventures at length. Living at El Rosario in this period was another brother, Jacome de Acuña. He was a poor Spaniard, but skilled in administration. He was the community's jack of all trades. He served as porter, commissary, and head nurse of the infirmary. In addition, he was administrator of the *haciendas* attached to the monastery at Limatambo and Palpa. His purchases, including slaves, for those properties can be found in El Rosario's records.[70]

The most noted conversus of this first generation, Brother Miguel de Santo Domingo, was, like St. Martin a mulatto, born in Cusco out of wedlock to a black mother and a Spanish father.[71] Like his mother, he was born a slave. He did, however, receive a good education. He came to the attention of the viceroy, Don Francisco Alvarez de Toledo, because of his ability to read and calculate. The viceroy made Miguel his personal secretary. Miguel had, by this time, become functionally free, since his master had returned to Spain and abandoned him to his own devices. When Don Francisco left office in 1581, he offered Miguel preferment, either in Spain or the Indies. The gifted mulatto, however, entered El Rosario, first as a donatus postulant and then as a professed conversus. His profession had already taken place when Martin de Porres arrived at El Rosario in 1594. We can only guess at the future saint's experience of this remarkable brother, and about Miguel's influence on Martin.

Given his skills, Brother Miguel was made treasurer of El Rosario, and so served for fifteen years. He was remembered as always at Matins. Then he went to sacristy to set up for the private Masses, because he also worked as sacristan. Miguel had excellent calligraphic skills and transcribed the great choral books of the monastery. We understand this was his favorite task, as it allowed him to pray and meditate while he worked. His careful observance of the rule and his prudence led to him being named the depositary responsible for the goods of all the friars of the community. After Matins and preparing for the private Masses, Miguel kept vigil before the Blessed Sacrament, being satisfied with just two hours of sleep a night. He died, at the age of eighty-seven, on 7 September 1642. We should remember that there were some sixty other conversi in the community with Brother Miguel. For lack of records, however, we know nearly nothing about them.

The oldest member of the second generation of remarkable brothers in Lima is also its most famous, St. Martin de Porres. The sources for Martin's life have mostly been published, and he has been the subject of many books and studies.[72] This older work has been mostly rendered obsolete by Celia L. Cussen's *Black Saint of the Americas* (2014), the first attempt to reconstruct the "Martin of History."[73] While methodologically sound, Cussen's decision to relegate all reports of miraculous phenomena to the section on the saint's canonization and cult renders the biographical section of the work very incomplete. Martin's reputation for the miraculous had already arisen in his lifetime and has to be treated, albeit critically, when reconstructing his own life. For this reason, this book needs to be read along with the older classic biography by Giuliana Cavallini (1961), written for Martin's canonization process. My treatment of the saint is much indebted to both of these works, and readers desiring more on Martin should consult them directly. I have made no attempt to reproduce all the information in them.

Before discussing Martin himself, we need to consider two issues—often tied together—that have played a large role in discussions of the saint. These are Martin's race and his "humility." Both were important themes from the beginning. When Bernardo de Medina wrote the first biography of Martin in 1673, nearly thirty-five years after his death, he placed special emphasis on both themes. They fit together. Martin's mixed-race status was for Medina a positive. For Creoles like Medina, Martin was a "model of humility and reliability."[74] These traits allowed Bernardo to present his hero as a model of holiness for blacks, natives, and mixed-race Peruvian Catholics. The brother's humility was not only a spiritual virtue, it inculcated in his nonwhite devotees the docility and meekness that the ruling elite of Spaniards considered proper to them in a very class-conscious and hierarchical society.

Martin was, no doubt, "humble," but he was also able to use his mixed status to his own benefit and that of his work—it allowed him to cross social boundaries. Also, we should be on guard when we read that Martin entered El Rosario as a donatus and chose to remain one simply because he was "humble." Perhaps humility played a role, but, as we will see, Martin's donatus status also gave him greater autonomy than he would have had as a conversus. We need to remember that "humility" is not only a virtue, it is also a hagiographic stereotype: all saints are supposed to possess it. I think Martin did, but what that meant is complex.

The vicious racism of late sixteenth-century Peru is also invoked to explain choices in Martin's life. Consider, for example, his status as a donatus. We should be on our guard here again. When Martin entered El Rosario, there was at least one professed conversus who was a mulatto ex-slave: Brother Miguel de Santo Domingo. There was, as yet, no "color line" that imposed the "inferior" status of donatus on Martin. Miguel came from an even lower class than Martin, who was never a slave, and he was a fully professed brother. When Martin entered El Rosario in 1594, as when he professed religious vows in 1603, the Order as a whole, and the Peruvian Province in particular, did not yet have any legal racial restrictions on admissions. This is not to say that the society—and the friars—were not racist. They mostly were, and racial and class distinctions obsessed them. Already in 1605 a general chapter had to arbitrate between "Peninsulars," those born back in Spain, and "Creoles," those born in Mexico, regarding who could serve as provincial in Mexico: it stipulated that the office was to alternate between the two groups.[75]

The first Order legislation forbidding *mestizo* (mixed-race) admissions would not happen until two years after Martin's profession, and it applied only to the province of the Holy Rosary in Asia.[76] Two years later, similar legislation was approved again, but this time only for the Provinces of Portugal and Betica. This forbade admission to the Order of former Muslims, Jews, heretics, and those who had been placed under penance by the

Inquisition.[77] Nothing was said about blacks or mulattoes. That would wait until 1618, when such a bar was approved by the general chapter for the Province of Peru itself.[78] This same bar was approved for Mexico in 1622, and for Ecuador in 1628.[79] Perhaps these new restrictions lie behind the apparent shortage (*penuriam*) of conversi in Peru, where, in 1629, the province decided to profess new lay brothers after a single year of novitiate, without the three-year period of donatus probation.[80] I have taken the trouble to review this, not just because Martin faced racial prejudice, but because such color bars are sometimes evidenced as determining factors in his vocational choice to become a donatus.

SAINT MARTIN DE PORRES

Martin de Porres was born in late 1579 in Lima. His mother's name was Ana Velázquez, as we know from the entry of his baptism in the register of San Sebastián Church, on 9 December 1579. Ana was a manumitted slave from Panama, who probably came to Lima in the household of a wealthy Spaniard as a domestic servant. No father is listed in the register, but we do know his name. He was a well-to-do Spaniard, Juan de Porras (note the spelling), who had at least one other child with Ana. Her name was Juana. Martin's "social zone" was "ambiguous." His father was well to do, but there is no evidence that he was noble, a governor, or a member of the Knights of Alcántara.[81] These assertions arise very late, and they reflect the old hagiographic stereotype that holy men must also have noble blood.

Juan de Porras took special interest in his natural son and got him apprenticed as a barber surgeon. This was a not uncommon way for Afro-Peruvians to advance socially. Pedro de Utrilla, another mulatto barber surgeon, would testify for Martin's canonization process. Like his mixed race, his education put him beyond neat category boundaries. His social status has rightly been called as much one of "ambiguity" as of "discrimination." Martin later seems to have taken advantage of the limited ability to "pass" given him by his family background and education.[82] Beyond this we know little about the saint's youth.

In 1594, when he was about fifteen years of age, Martin asked to be admitted to the El Rosario monastery as a donatus, a *donado* in Spanish. This meant he was officially a member of the Dominican Third Order and, as such, wore its habit: a white tunic, black leather belt and shoes, and a black mantle. He also, like other Dominicans in the Spanish Dominions, wore a Rosary around his neck. At some point, he also took to wearing a black wooden cross on a cord, as can be seen in his oldest portrait. It shows him as quite elderly, and he has lost all his teeth. This is how the saint was always attired.

Martin and the other donati did not, as I said, have a cloister of their own, but lived in the area of the monastery where food was prepared and laundry done. They lived with the familiars, both free servants and slaves. This section of El Rosario was on the north side of the monastery, facing the river. The wing also housed the carpentry shop, stables, chicken coops, livestock corral, and foundry. The wing had its own entrance, the *porta falsa*, at which Martin nursed or helped those in need. They could be introduced into the building there without violating the formal cloister of the clerics and conversi.[83]

Whatever speculations have been made about Martin's decision to become a donatus, Martin never explained his decision himself, or, if he did, the information has been lost. He certainly knew of Brother Miguel, who came from an even lower class, who had entered as a conversus (after his transitional period as a donatus). Juan Meléndez, in his hagiographical biography of Martin, relates a story about a sudden appearance of his father at El Rosario. Supposedly, two years after Martin's entrance, Juan arrived and protested his son's second-class citizenship as a donatus. He demanded that Martin be allowed to make profession as a lay brother. Giuliana Cavallini's opinion was that "Martin firmly refused" to acquiesce to his father's protests since they "were inspired only by wounded pride and vainglory."[84] Perhaps this is true, but again we have no contemporary witness to Martin's motivations. Whatever was the case, Juan's supposed protest was of no avail: Martin was not given vows or made a conversus on this occasion.

Whatever the case, we learn that some nine years after his admission as a donatus, Martin was permitted, on 2 June 1603, to make solemn profession of religious vows, "something very rarely permitted to donati at that time," to quote the canonization documents drawn up after his death.[85] The Book of Professions of El Rosario simply states that Martin "hizo donación de sí." He signed the book as "Ermano Martín de Porras." Nothing is said about a change to the category of conversus, and the title "brother" was used by donati as well as conversi. All the evidence, in particular the portrait of Martin in old age, indicates that he remained a donatus, albeit one who had made profession of religious vows. His status was unusual, but not unheard of.

Modern scholarly literature remains confused on this.[86] The problem is, in part, the result of an anachronistic projection of the modern canon law of profession back into the 1600s. At that time, there were no "temporary vows." There were only two kinds of vows: promises made privately—like those of the tertiaries—and those made solemnly and publicly before the Church—like those made by monks and friars. That one made a public vow did not automatically turn a tertiary into a conversus. It simply made a private promise into a public and binding vow, and thus made it an impediment to marriage. The promises of tertiaries did not impede vows of marriage. In any case, the exception made for Martin was extraordinary and shows that, after less than a decade in the monastery, he had won the esteem of the whole community.

What Martin did was to make a solemn, that is, public, "vow of religion." This is very significant because it meant that Martin, as a donatus, retained the ability to handle money, as was implicit in the rule of the Dominican tertiaries. He was also, unlike conversi, not bound to attend the choral office. He did, however, have to recite his Paters as a tertiary, just as the conversi did as vowed brothers. Martin would take advantage of his special, more autonomous, status. Whether he actually refused conversus status because of "humility" is unremarked in contemporary records. In any case, the seventeenth-century process for Martin's canonization, and the nineteenth-century bull approving his beatification, both call him a "professed religious tertiary," not a "conversus" or a "lay brother."

The choice had advantages. Within the monastery, his first biographer tells us, Martin, "wearing the donado habit from his priory, exercised the duties of infirmarian, barber and surgeon."

This description fits the way Martin was viewed by the friars and people of Lima. His major form of service to others was medical. He combined both Spanish barber-surgeon training and the herbalism and natural medicine practiced by Afro-Peruvians. The marvel stories reported of Martin show that he was not only a skilled practitioner, but one who addressed the spiritual needs of his patients. Martin was in high demand among the Lima elite as a "healer," a *sanador*. This role was Martin's "public face" outside the monastery during his life.[87]

In addition, Martin was a social healer. His mixed-race status allowed him to serve not only the Spanish aristocracy, but also the enslaved African population. We know that he was especially devoted to, and loved by, the slaves of El Rosario's Limatambo hacienda. Famously, his compassion and care extended even to animals, and many of the stories circulating about him, even before his death, recount his ability to communicate with and heal domestic and wild beasts. In fact, in the testimonies of witnesses for Martin's first canonization process, it is the animal miracles that take pride of place. Later, in the 1679–85 Roman canonization process, the saint's healing miracles are front and center.[88]

Martin's work was not a merely personal ministry; he used his considerable network of wealthy admirers and patrons to raise the funds necessary to build and endow the first foundling hospital and the first orphanage in the city of Lima. Always tactful, he funnelled donations from rich admirers to poor priests under the cover of Mass stipends, so that they could receive the charity without being shamed by it. Although he never seems to have officially held the office, Brother Martin functioned as the almoner of El Rosario. Martin never turned his back on his own family. He used his connections with the well to do to arrange a fine marriage for his niece, Catalina de Porras. She married a wealthy Spaniard, entered the upper class, and signed her documents as "doña." Martin took good care of his family.[89]

Martin was also a force for decency and charity within his spiritual family. Father Cipriano de Medina, who gave a long testimony for the seventeenth-century canonization process, recalled how Brother Martin skillfully reprimanded other friars who mocked Cipriano for his short stature and unattractive face.

Cipriano also witnessed several of Martin's miracles while the saint was still alive, including his ability to pass through locked doors. He is the origin of the story of Martin's bilocation to Asia and the stories of the humble donatus's savage penances. He recounted these for the inquest of 1660, which also contains the oldest reports of Martin's ability to communicate with animals.

When Martin died on 3 November 1639, his funeral was a great civic event. The visiting archbishop of Mexico City and the viceroy of Peru were among those who carried his coffin. Others were chosen from the canons of the cathedral and the council of the city. The popular cult began immediately after his death.[90] His fame was not limited to Peru. Martin has the privilege of not one, but two, obituaries in the acts of general chapters, those of 1642 and 1656—and they are longer than any priest commemorated.[91] The second of these gives his name as "Frater Martinus de Porras, donatus," using the spelling he himself used during his lifetime. Both emphasize, along with his piety and penances, his healing and care for the sick poor. Martin's canonization process was initiated in 1660, and the last depositions were taken in 1683. But nothing came of this inquest, and the Order was still urging his canonization in 1777.[92] The holy brother was not beatified until 1837, when he was declared blessed by Pope Gregory XVI. Pope John XXIII would canonize him on 6 May 1962.[93] Previously celebrated on 5 November, his feast day now matches that of his death, 3 November.

The best testimony to Martin's stature and holiness is contained in the legislation of the general chapter of 1642, which published his first obituary. That chapter declared "the many very severe ordinations forbidding admission to mestizos, Indians, and Africans, through one parent or both, are everywhere abrogated, wherever they exist."[94] And in 1670, legislation for Mexico was approved that declared that nationality or indigenous status was to play absolutely no role in the ranking of the friars.[95] It is hard to believe that Martin de Porres was not on the minds of the fathers who passed these strongly worded condemnations of their own previous racist enactments.

One last issue remains before we move on to the other conversi that shared St. Martin's life at El Rosario. That is the origin of the mistaken idea, found also in art, that Martin was a conversus, not a donatus. Cussen, in her biography, reproduces a selection of images of Martin produced in the 1600s and 1700s.[96] All of these show him in the tertiary habit. One even shows other friars, in clerical and conversus habits, watching the pious donatus levitate. Only one image, dated to the late 1700s, shows him in a lay brother habit, and it may be misdated and actually later. Only in the 1800s, after his beatification, do we find Martin dressed in the wrong habit and being called a "lay brother." How this error came to pass would make an interesting study, but is beyond the scope of this work.

THE BROTHERS OF EL ROSARIO

Three conversi made profession in Lima within a year or two of St. Martin's profession of vows. As a group they give us a good idea of what kind of men were part of the Lima Circle. Of one of these brothers we know relatively little. Brother José de Rueda was born about 1595 and received the habit at El Rosario on 24 February 1608. He then did his novitiate at La Magdalena, but he was assigned to El Rosario. There he was principally known as a contemplative. He prayed at night in the chapel and then visited all the altars in the cloister. When he became old and infirm, he made himself a little collapsible wooden bench, which he took with him to sit on as he made his rounds. Before returning to his cell to sleep, it was his habit to take holy water and sprinkle all the other cells, the cloister, the chapter room, and the cemetery. Every night at 8:00 p.m. he rang the monastery bell to remind people to pray for the dead. He died on 4 April 1658, after fifty years of profession.[97]

Of Brother Martín de Barragán, to whom Martin de Porres reportedly appeared in a vision, we know much more.[98] His adventures remind us of the early conversi of the Province of Mexico. Born to poor parents in Spain, Martín went to seek his fortune in the Indies. He first passed through Mexico, which he found "too easy and delicate." He felt drawn to wilder climes. He went on foot to Acapulco, eating only wild game along the way. He was armed with a battered arquebus. At the port, he found no ship, so he continued on foot to the Réalejo, where he found a ship bound for Peru.

The ship beached on a desert island during a storm. He and the six surviving members of the crew asked the natives for permission to get water and collect wild fruit. But when they returned, they found that strong winds had pushed their boat back to sea. They were marooned. They built a hut, set up a cross, and killed some sea lions for their pelts. Desperate, Martín turned to prayer. But, instead of consolations, he heard voices chanting "You are going to die here." And: "You will never escape from here." Convinced these were demonic, he ignored them. The small band were reduced to eating sea lions.

Martín convinced his companions to make a vow to Our Lady of the Rosary that they would go, barefooted and in sackcloth, on pilgrimage to a church consecrated to her, if they escaped. Two years later, she finally heard their plea. The viceroy of Peru had sent out a ship to find them. It arrived on the first Sunday of October, the feast of Our Lady of the Rosary. Taking their cross with them, they set sail for Callao, the port of Lima. Offered hospitality by the viceroy, they asked first to fulfill their vow. Having no sackcloth, they wore sea lion skins. But they did walk barefoot. Their destination was El Rosario, where they were received well by the friars and allowed to make their thanksgiving at the altar of the Holy Rosary.

Their vow fulfilled, Martín asked to be accepted as a conversus. As a novice he proved obedient, austere, prayerful, and modest. He made profession about 1607, at the age of fifty-three. After a period of service at La Magdalena, he returned to Rosario, where he was made porter. Initially, he found the going and coming of people a distraction, but eventually he dedicated himself to helping the poor and became skilled at identifying fakers. Like St. Martin, perhaps imitating him, he became known for serving the poor and sick. On one occasion, a black woman with a rotting ulcer arrived at the door. Surgeons had declared her incurable. Even the beggars avoided the stink. Brother Martín received her with charity, cared for her, and in a couple of days she was healed. He seemed a model porter. Nevertheless, one night the blessed Martin de Porres appeared to him in a dream and rebuked him for passing off his service of the poor to other brothers. He accepted the rebuke and henceforth always strove to see God in those he helped.

Martín spent twenty years at the house in Lima. He rose before midnight to pray in the chapel of the Rosary until Mass at 5 a.m. He was occasionally seen in rapture before images of Christ and the Virgin. Like Martin de Porres, he undertook severe penances. He wore a hairshirt of steel wool, a chain with nails twisted into it, and took the discipline nightly to blood. His principal devotion was the Rosary, and he made them for the poor.

In the estimation of the friars, he had the spirit of prophecy. On one occasion, Lucia and Clara de la Daga, foundresses of the convent of St. Catherine of Siena, arrived very discouraged. He urged them to "collect the flowers" of their tribulations because their project would succeed. On another occasion, he was praying in the chapel of the Rosary with friar Blas Martinez. Martín there told Blas that he would not leave the chapel till he died. After spending the night in prayer there, Martín heard Mass, knelt to adore the Blessed Sacrament, and had a stroke. He died in the sacristy, after receiving Viaticum and Extreme Unction. It was the vigil of St. Dominic, 3 August 1627. His corpse was reported to be incorrupt and supple. During the funeral, his habit had to be replaced twice because of people cutting off pieces for relics.

The last of this El Rosario group is Brother Bartolomé de los Santos, another great wanderer and imitator of St. Martin de Porres.[99] He was born in Palencia, Spain, but when young he came to Peru, perhaps with his father, to seek his fortune. Bartolomé entered El Rosario as a conversus on 17 October 1609. His time in the Order was short as he died 6 on February 1616, but he made a powerful impression on his confreres. Even before his admission he was known for his asceticism. He fasted daily on bread and water, sometimes going for days without water, even in the Peruvian heat. Often assigned duties outside the monastery, he still kept a strict silence. He had no cell, so he spent the night in church praying for sinners.

After only a few years, he felt inspired by God to transfer to the Province of Mexico. Perhaps with Brother Martín already busy at work at El Rosario, he thought that one Martin de Porres imitator was enough. He embarked with just his habit. On arrival in Mexico City, his piety and austerity were immediately recognized: he wore a cross with nails under his tunic. But he was mostly remembered for his skill at collecting alms. These he passed on to the sick, the poor, and beggars. Like Martin de Porres, he became famous among the rich and poor of the city. His prior asked him, under obedience, where he got all the money for his charity. He ascribed his success to his habit of always praying before the image of the Blessed Virgin in the choir. She had promised to help him get whatever was needed. He was placed in charge of procuring food for the rectory. He rose early, swept the monastery, and went off to get supplies. By midmorning his two large begging bags were always full.

Just before his death, he asked to be relieved of his work in the porter's office and sent to the infirmary. There he correctly predicted the date of his own death and that of another sick friar. He died on 6 February 1616. As in the case of Brother Martín, Bartolomé's funeral was mobbed, and people tore his habit to bits. One devotee even stole one of his fingers. His body was reported incorrupt. Father Antonio González, procurator of the Province of Peru, opened his case in Rome, the third of that province in the century, this along with Martin de Porres and Juan Macías. But, unlike the holy mulatto, Brother Bartolomé has never been beatified.

THE BROTHERS OF LA MAGDALENA

Although the lives of nearly all the Lima conversi overlapped, I have divided them by generations so that we can get some sense of how the backgrounds and life of the brothers changed over the nearly seventy-five years of the Peruvian renaissance. The first brother of the "third generation" is chronologically part of the second generation—he died in 1619, but his house of affiliation, La Magdalena, is shared with all the later brothers. The most interesting development of this later period is that the notable conversi all come from La Magdalena, the monastery of St. Juan Macías, not El Rosario, the monastery of St. Martin de Porres.

La Magdalena, a daughter house of El Rosario, was founded in 1606 as a house of strict observance. It originally had only four priests and three conversi, but grew to twelve friars within a year. It later became quite large, but in this period it was more a "house of recollection" than a large complex like Rosario. As a house of discipline and prayer, it attracted penitents. For example, the conversus Brother Pablo de la Caridad was a noble born in Spain and well educated. Seeking his fortune, he came to Lima and lived a dissolute life for some twenty years. Having repented, he entered La Magdalena on 7 December 1611, five years after the foundation.[100]

Four years later, another penitent conversus entered La Magdalena, Brother Antonio Rodriguez. He died at El Rosario, however, and he so is a bridge between the houses.[101] He was, by origin, a Portuguese shepherd born in the mid- to late sixteenth century. He reported that, while tending his sheep, the Blessed Virgin appeared to him in a vision. She told him that he would one day become a religious, but that he would first have many adventures. Like so many early New World conversi, he joined the army and departed for Mexico. The troops he was with spent most of their time fighting and subjugating the natives. One day his detachment conquered a village and set fire to a large house. In the conflagration some three hundred Indians, including women and children, perished. In horror, Antonio tried to enter the house to save at least some of the children. He only saved a couple. Then, what he saw happen to the other soldiers was, in its way, equally disturbing. The natives killed some with poisoned arrows, others drowned in rivers, and still others fell to their deaths off rocky cliffs.

At the urging of his conscience, the young Portuguese abandoned the army and made his way to Peru. In Lima, he heard about the highly observant Dominican community at La Magdalena. He asked to be admitted there as a conversus, even though he was now quite elderly. The prior, Father Bartolomé Martinez, saw before him just another elderly, weather-beaten soldier looking for a place to retire. Antonio turned to God in prayer and asked that his white hair be restored to its original color. When he awoke the next day, it was its original dark brown. The younger-looking Antonio was then admitted to La Magdalena, and so the Blessed Virgin's prophecy was fulfilled. Antonio received the habit from that same prior on 29 September 1615. The penitent conversus dedicated himself mostly to prayer (but was always ready to leave off, if ordered to do something), ate only a small piece of bread a day, and practiced many other penances.

After just four years in the monastery, Brother Antonio fell sick and, not wanting to be a bother, asked the prior's permission to die. Given permission, he retired to the infirmary at El Rosario, made a general confession, received the Last Rites, and died, gazing on an image of the Infant Jesus. As he died on 2 March 1619, it is possible that his caregivers included St. Martin de Porres.

These were not the only impressive lay brothers in early-seventeenth-century La Magdalena. They were soon joined by Brother Simón García (†1652), about whom we would love to know more.[102] The brothers remembered him as devoted to the poor and a lover of poverty, who never asked for a new habit. Like the other conversi of La Magdalena with a reputation for holiness, he served as porter. He became a martyr of charity while nursing a sick mulatto woman. From this ward, he contracted what modern historians think was Erysipelas, a horrible bacterial infection of the skin also known as "St. Anthony's Fire." This infection spread to the rest of his body. He endured his sufferings with great patience. At his death, the provincial chapter of Peru considered initiating a cause for canonization.

SAINT JUAN MACÍAS

The most celebrated of the La Magdalena porters, however, is St. Juan Macías. This saint has received far less scholarly attention than Martin de Porres.[103] Like Martin, however, the major sources for his life have been edited and published.[104] Among the modern biographies, the closest to a scholarly study, that of Salvador Velasco (1975), adds little to the *vita* prepared for his canonization by the modern postulator of his cause, Tarsicio Piccari (1975), who drew heavily on the early-modern chronicler of the Peruvian Province, Juan Meléndez. My summary of the saint's life draws on these two authors.

About Juan's youth in Spain we know relatively little. He was born on 2 March 1585 at Ribera del Fresno in Extremadura, the home of so many conquistadors. He was baptized at the parish church. His family came from the poor peasantry who had been "ennobled" during the Reconquest, but this brought them little benefit other than some tax breaks. His father was a familiar of the Holy Office, so we can assume the family was pious. But their influence on Juan was minor, because both of his parents died when he was four years old. He was adopted by a maternal uncle, whose surname, Macías, Juan adopted.

While tending that uncle's sheep herd, he spent much of his time praying the Rosary. We are told that while in the fields, the pious young man had a vision of St. John the Evangelist, who told him to go to Jerez de la Frontera. There he seems to have lived by begging and day labor, a pious vagabond. It was there he first met the Dominicans. Juan then went on to Seville, and then by ship to Cartagena in modern Colombia. Little is known of his stay there. He soon moved on to Bogotá, then to Quito, and finally to Lima. Juan himself would later report that the whole trip took four and a half months. In Lima, Juan first worked for a merchant, who fired him because he was "illiterate." By his own admission, he remained unlettered, but he could, in fact, write short notes in Spanish. Juan then found work with a rich ranch owner, Pedro Jiménez Mancho, in the barrio of San Lázaro. The young former shepherd had enough ability to become the rancher's "mayordomo," that is, his chief shepherd. Mostly, however, Juan worked in the Lima slaughterhouse.

At this time, Juan underwent a conversion and decided to enter La Magdalena as a conversus. We know little about this decision, but it is clear that it was in part the result of his growing friendship with that house's "first porter," Brother Pablo de la Caridad, the repentant Spanish nobleman whom we have already met. Juan received the habit from the prior, Salvador Ramirez, on 22 January 1622, at the age of thirty-seven. He never made a donatus postulancy, but he was professed after the one-year novitiate. Juan's novitiate was spent as assistant to Brother Pablo de la Caridad in the porter's office. Juan became Pablo's protégé. The future saint was quoted as saying:

> I spent my first year of probation as second porter in the excellent company of Fray Pablo de la Caridad. O great and merciful God! So good and so penitential was my companion, and so charitable towards the poor, that I find no words to express it! With his holy example, I, a sinner, began to pray six or seven hours daily, and truly, the time seemed like fifteen minutes.

Brother Pablo was eventually transferred to El Rosario, and Juan became first porter of La Magdalena. This become his major responsibility, although he seems also to have worked in the kitchen.

Under Brother Juan, the porter's office at La Magdalena became well known in Lima as the place to go for help, no matter what the seeker's race or condition. Juan became famous for passing out little *cartas* of encouragement and advice to those he cared for. His work was both spiritual and material. If the inquirer was not in need, these cartas often contained a request for alms. Like so many other premodern conversus porters, Juan became famous as an almsraiser. Sometimes his advice was very practical. To a down-and-out inquirer, Alonso Martín, Juan recommended that he start a bakery. It turned out to be a great commercial success, and Alonso became a major benefactor of the monastery.

Hagiographers remark on his gift of counsel and prophecy, and they give some examples. On one occasion, asked for alms by an inquirer at the porter's office, he read the man's heart and recognized him as a runaway priest. Early reports also list his miracles: mostly visions of the saints and of souls he had prayed out of purgatory. It was reported that he had the gift of invisibility. But he was mostly remembered for his healing, charity, and, above all, his wise spiritual, vocational, and business advice. These activities are a window into the often down-to-earth practical services provided by conversus porters.

Like Martin de Porres, we also hear stories about Juan's familiarity with animals. For example, he is said to have trained a donkey to make the daily alms circuit on its own—something that sounds a bit more practical than similar stories about Martin de Porres. Famously, Juan is also remembered as a friend of St. Martin. It does seem that the two pious brothers made "days of recollection" together in the country at the haciendas belonging to El Rosario, but that is really all we know about their relationship.

About Juan's own piety we are much better informed, although these reports resemble the kind of piety that seems stereotypical for holy Spanish conversi. Juan was obedient, vigilant about his chastity, humble, and devoted to the Eucharist.

More specifically, he meditated on Christ Crucified and had devotions to the Blessed Virgin and his patron St. John the Evangelist. We are told that his penitential practice of flagellating himself was once so severe that he needed an operation to repair the damage. He confessed this incident on his deathbed as one of his faults. As a conversus, he did not normally attend the sung community Mass, but he did attend as many as twenty Low Masses each morning, perhaps several at once, as conversi often served more than one Mass at a time.

As he was dying, Brother Juan Macías made a public general confession of his life and experiences. This recounting lasted several days. It is the source of most of the visions and miracle stories told of him. He died on 16 September 1646. Like Martin de Porres, he was, by the time of his death, a famous personality of the city of Lima. The archbishop, Pedro de Villagomez, and the viceroy, Don Pedro de Toledo y Leyba, both helped carry his coffin. His first recorded miracle occurred during the funeral, when a deaf priest, Antonio de Alarcon, had his hearing restored after he used the holy porter's hand to bless his ear. Juan's cell became a shrine.

Like St. Martin, Juan's road to the altar was long. His name, but not Martin's, was included in the solemn petition of the master of the Order in 1656 to move forward the processes of Louis Bertrand, Ambrose Sansedoni, James of Mevania, Catherine de' Ricci, and Rose of Lima (who, it seems, contrary to legend, was not an acquaintance of the holy brothers).[105] The Order repeated the call for his and Martin's canonizations in 1777.[106] But Juan Macías was only beatified by Pope Gregory XVI in 1837. Pope Paul VI canonized him on 28 September 1975, and his feast is celebrated on 18 September.

Like the Philippines, the Province of Peru and much of the Order entered a period of decline in the 1700s, something we will discuss in the next chapter. But we should not end the story of the famous conversi of Latin America without a word about two holy brothers of the Province of Quito. Brothers Domingo de San Miguel and Domingo Frayre were commemorated at the Genoa general chapter of 1642.[107] Both were remembered as men of great penance, simplicity, and chastity. Friars revered them as saints, even before their deaths. They were mentioned again in the acts of the general chapter of 1644.[108] Their lives, in contrast to those of the Lima Circle, were mostly hidden in the monastery. In this, they are like the greater number of conversi of the Spanish Missions, and so they fittingly remind us of those many other forgotten, uncanonized, brother saints.

Chapter 5
Revolution and Restoration, 1700–1960

The Catholic Church of the eighteenth century, the age of the Enlightenment and the French Revolution, has recently been the topic of several good historical surveys in English.[1] For the purposes of this study, the most important developments in this period were the Church's increasing subjugation to the Catholic absolutist states in Europe and the suppression or decline in fervor of the missions in the Spanish Dominions. The perfect symbol of these events is the suppression of the Jesuits. First, the Catholic powers, who viewed them as supranational and a block to enlightened absolutist policy, expelled them, seized their assets, closed their schools, and destroyed their missions, most famously in Paraguay. Those in authority—the monarchs, the aristocracy, and the colonists—shared in this plunder. The indigenous peoples entered a new period of exploitation and enslavement.

The Dominicans, like the other mendicant orders, experienced these tragedies to a lesser degree, but, after the amazing renaissance described in the last chapter, this period seems an age of growing formalism, declining fervor, and retrenchment. The conversi we know from this period fell, in most cases, short of the remarkable and holy men of the sixteenth and seventeenth centuries. Indeed, none of the eighteenth-century conversi who merited commemoration by the brothers served in the missions. All served in Europe.

Lay Brothers of the Enlightenment

The general chapters of the 1700s, fewer than in previous centuries because of the increased power of the master, a pale reflection of the absolutist monarchs, have nearly nothing to say about the lay brothers. When the brothers appear, it is almost always in the context of legislation on suffrages. This basically repeats older legislation, stipulating the requirement that the brothers' suffrage for dead friars consist of five decades of the Rosary.[2] The chapter at Rome in 1756 did, however, pay some attention to conversus formation, repeating older provisions that masters of conversi give the brothers spiritual conferences on major feasts, instruct them in piety, devotion in the workshop, and, above all, to make sure that they show respect for priests and avoid idleness.[3]

The brothers we can identify in this period were nearly all remembered as pious contemplatives hidden within the monastery. One, at least, Brother Pierre d'Orange, from Toulouse, was praised as a model for brother sacristans. He had taken the donatus habit at Valence in Dauphiné in 1659, and professed as a conversus four years later. Assigned nearly his entire life to the house in Toulouse, he was sacristan for twenty-five years. We hear nothing about his interactions with the laity. Rather, he was remembered as pious, humble, prayerful, devoted to the Blessed Virgin, and very respectful of priests. It seems his master of conversi did a good job forming him according to the Order's directives.[4]

Four other known conversi also fit the model of contemplative laborers inside the monastery. Brother Félix Brun de Saint-Antoine (1648–1721), of Le Thor in Vaucluse, southern France, had been a shepherd for seven years after elementary school.[5] He developed a love of solitude, a fear of mortal sin, and a devotion to St. Peter. At the age of twenty-three he became a conversus. He was so retiring a personality that his superiors did not even send him out to beg. He worked as cook and general domestic for the community, practiced traditional forms of penance—fasting, sleeping on the floor, and spending much of the night reciting the Rosary before the tabernacle. He died at the age of seventy. In Italy, Brother Domenico Delfini of the Congregation of Santa Sabina in Lombardy was especially remembered for his hard work and avoidance of idleness.[6] He never left the monastery, preferring to spend long hours on his knees before the crucifix. He was remembered for his great fervor when receiving Communion. He died on 17 March 1751. It would be hard to distinguish these men from Benedictine lay monks.

The two Spanish brothers who merited a mention in the general chapter acts, both of those in 1756, were late-vocation penitents, again known for piety, not activity. Brother Juan de

Todos Santos was born at Villanueva near Plasencia.[7] He served in the army, but "kept his chastity." He thought of becoming a Franciscan, but the Virgin appeared three times in dreams and instructed him to become a Dominican. He did so at Santo Domingo in Plasencia. He had no equal in piety: he wore a chain discipline, fasted, and spent vigils in prayer. We are told that demons tried to break his recollection, but that, when he rebuked them, they fled. He often said that he would happily be crucified, if it would save the souls of the brothers. He died in the odor of sanctity in 1744.

Brother Cristóbal Quevedo, born at Cártama in Betica of pious parents, worked on their holdings and married. At the age of forty, he received his wife's permission to enter religious life. He found his vocation serving the community as a farm laborer and by constant prayer. He was totally obedient to his superiors and rumored to be able to read hearts. Unlike the previous conversi, however, he was well known enough outside the monastery for his funeral in 1748 to be crowded with townspeople.[8]

One of Brother Domenico's confreres in the Congregation of Santa Sabina breaks this mold of the hidden contemplative lay brother. Giacinto Giacchetti was remembered like the previous brothers for his piety, which included mystical experiences, the gift of tears, and a love of the Blessed Sacrament.[9] But he was famous for his "unlearned" spiritual erudition. Even the most learned theologians were amazed by his insights and doctrine, and considered his understanding a supernatural gift. Among his admirers was Cardinal Niccolò Caraccioli, who spent long periods in conversation with him and sent him letters asking spiritual guidance. The cardinal preserved the brother's replies and often quoted the brother's opening salutation, "Amiamo Gesù!" Brother Giacinto also became a spiritual adviser to the Dominican cardinal Pietro Francesco Orsini. The two continued to exchange letters, even after the cardinal's election as Pope Benedict XIII. The pope wanted to move Giacinto to Rome, but the local bishop objected. The holy brother was allowed to live out his vocation in the south. He died in 1734. If his letters still exist in the Vatican Archives, they would certainly reward study.

The most celebrated eighteenth-century conversus was, however, Brother François Romain, who is better known among historians of engineering than among his modern Dominican brothers.[10] François was born at Ghent on 22 March 1647. When he died in 1735, his obituary appeared in the *Mercure de France*. François had received training in what we would call civil engineering before entering the Order. As a conversus, his first major commission outside the order was by the Estates of Holland in 1685. He was chosen to supervise the construction at Maastricht of the Pont Saint-Servais over the Liége channel. When completed, it was a structure in nine arches. The bridge tookfour years to finish. The Dominicans of Arras then employed him to design and construct their new monastery and church—the old one had been razed during the expansion of the city wall. He completed this project in 1687. His church was notable for the large windows, and the monastery he designed was noted for his vaulting of the refectory. Brother François also supervised the construction of the church of Saint-Didier at Asfeld.

His fame as an architect and engineer grew, and because of difficulties encountered in construction of the Pont Royal in Paris, King Louis XIV summoned him to Paris to superintend that work. To complete it, he invented a new form of dredging to set the piles of the bridge, the caisson system, which is often mistakenly ascribed to much later engineers. He finished that project, which still stands today, in 1689. In that year, Brother François's friend, Count Louis Phélypeaux de Pontchartrain, became comptroller general of finances for the kingdom of France, and he put the brother to work on royal projects, in particular bridges and highways. Brother François also worked on the count's chateau and the fortifications in his fiefdom. The general comptroller considered him absolutely trustworthy financially—unlike most lay contractors.

Brother François's work so pleased the Sun King himselfthat he appointed him royal inspector of the bridges and public buildings for the Paris region. François's Dominican communities greatly benefited from the pensions assigned to him by the Crown. The industrious brother also worked for the Church, superintending the reconstruction of the Abbey of Jouy in 1691.

According to the obituary written by his provincial, he was responsible for a total of 110 projects, including 41 bridges and many roadways and palaces. His last project, in 1728, was the reconstruction of the facade of the Dominican monastery in Ghent. Brother François was also remembered as a good religious, humble and unaffected by his public honors and fame.

In 1723, because of age and infirmity, Brother François gave up most of his responsibilities, retaining only responsibility for the areas of Dreux and Montfort and the chateau of Pontchartrain, where he lived. Three years later, worsening health dictated that he move to the Dominican house in Paris. He had lived much of his life outside of community, and it was not until 1732 that he finally relinquished all his public functions as inspector of bridges and highways for the Crown. Brother François Romain died at the age of eighty-nine on 7 January 1735 of diarrhea, piously invoking, we are told, the Blessed Virgin Mary. He died at the Dominican General Novitiate in Faubourg Saint-Germain, Paris, where a Latin epitaph on his tomb commemorated his works and piety. It is suggestive of the age that Brother François, the last notable conversus before the French Revolution, was best known for his service to the state, not the Church.

The last general chapter of the eighteenth century was held in Rome in 1777. Its only mention of conversi was that they were not to be admitted without a vote of the house chapter, just as clerics were.[11] Unlike the previous two general chapters, this one included no obituaries, but it did include a long note on the missions and martyrs in China, including martyrdom of the companions of Bl. Peter Sanz.[12] None of these seems to have been a lay brother. Perhaps the most important notice in these acts was that Charles III of Spain would provide financial support to the Province of St. James in Mexico to staff the fourteen remaining Jesuit missions in Baja California. These missions had been founded by the Jesuits, whom King Charles expelled from his Dominions in 1767. The Franciscans took over the missions in 1769. The first Dominicans had arrived in 1773 to relieve the Franciscans so that they could go north to Alta California.

The chapter fathers determined that the king's funding would be sufficient for twenty-three priests and two conversi, which seems to be just about the number of Dominican missionaries still in Baja California at the time. It is interesting that the percentage of conversi funded was about half that typical in earlier Dominican houses. The friars were also to build two new missions in the northern part of Baja for instruction of the natives.[13] There was no direct mention of conversi in that last chapter before the French Revolution. The next general chapter would not meet until 1832.

REVOLUTION AND REFOUNDATION

The Revolution began at Paris in 1789 and resulted in the overthrow of the monarchy and the suppression of the Catholic Church in France. It also began a series of wars and other revolutions that would convulse nearly all of Europe until 1815. The result was the near destruction of the Order. Under the revolutionary regimes or under French domination, Church property, including that of the Order, was seized, religious life forbidden, and clergy killed or exiled. The destruction was nearly complete, except in the Iberian Peninsula and in southern Italy. The Order did continue to function in the Spanish Domains, but there too, during the wars for independence in the early to mid-nineteenth century, secularizing liberal regimes in Spain and the newly independent colonies seized Dominican houses and abolished religious orders. Even after the restoration in France, the religious orders would be suppressed and Church property seized by the state at least twice, the last time in 1905.

This is a story that does not have to be retold here. The magnitude of the destruction can be seen in the first general chapters held after the Revolution and the wars. The chapter of 1832 in Zaragoza, Spain, under the Spanish vicar Francisco Usagre, was attended only by friars from the provinces of Spain, Aragon, Betica, the Canaries, and the far-off provinces of the Philippines and Oaxaca. The next chapter, at Rome in 1838, was better attended and even included a diffinitor from the Province of St. Joseph in the United States. In Spain, however, the old absolutist settlement remained: when the master of the Order was not Spanish, the Spanish provinces were to be under a Spanish vicar, who answered to the Crown. The 1832 chapter had nothing to say about lay brothers (as they are now generally called), and that of 1838 only mentioned them when dealing with suffrages for the dead.[14] The chapters of the 1840s continued this lack of interest in the brothers. Again, they are only mentioned in decisions on suffrages and, once, in the assignments for southern Italy.[15]

We do know something about two lay brothers who lived through this period, and their lives are instructive. Brother Guillaume Verdoy, born in 1760, entered the Province of France at Saint-Omer on the eve of the Revolution. When the Republic established the "Constitutional Church," with its bishops and priests vowing obedience to the state instead of the pope, he refused to swear obedience to the "constitutional" bishop. He was not executed, but he managed to flee to Italy, where he joined the community at Iesi. His life there reminds us of the "contemplative" brothers of the old regime. He hardly ever slept and seemed to spend all his time in the church praying. He attended all the morning low Masses and recited five Rosaries a day. He is probably typical of the many refugee religious who fled the terrors of the Revolution.[16]

Another French lay brother shows us the alternative to flight. Pierre Bussat was born 25 February 1736 at Petit-Bornand in Savoy, then part of the Kingdom of Sardinia.[17] In 1761, he entered religious life in the house at Chambéry, where he did internal domestic work until the Revolution suppressed the community, and seized its property, in 1793. Brother Pierre chose not to flee to Italy or Spain, but lived out his vows privately. He became a teacher in the Chambéry parish school. This parish had a vital religious life, even during the Revolution, thanks to the legacy of St. Francis de Sales (1567–1622). The holy bishop had reevangelized the area and founded the parish Confraternity of the Holy Rosary, of which Pierre became an active member.

Pierre was especially remembered for saving his community's relic of St. Vincent Ferrer from destruction by the revolutionaries. He took it with him to Chambéry, which was very fitting, as St. Vincent had once preached in the parish church. Thanks to the former brother, the parish developed a fervent devotion to the great preacher. Pierre Bussat died on 9 January

1804 at the age of 68, while Savoy was still under the revolutionary regime. We know about him thanks to the memoir of the pastor of Chambéry who, in 1875, noted that there were still elderly members of the parish who remembered the saintly brother who had taught them their catechism lessons.

In the midst of these dislocations and disasters, the lay brothers did have something to rejoice about. In 1807, the beleaguered Pope Pius VII approved the Mass and Office of the martyrs of Sandomierz commemorated under the name of Bl. Sadoc and Companions. The traditional list of these martyrs included five conversi. Pope Pius, in 1818, approved the Mass and Office for Bl. Simon Ballachi, the pious gardener and earliest conversus remembered at Mass by name. The recognition of the cult of James of Ulm followed in 1825 by decree of Pope Leo XII. Then came the long-awaited beatifications of Martin de Porres and Juan Macías by Pope Gregory XVI in 1837. These two were the first brothers to be officially beatified. The last of these new lay brother blesseds came in 1867, when Pope Pius IX beatified the five conversus companions of Alphonsus Navarrete, martyred in seventeenth-century Japan. It must have been satisfying that, after so many centuries of service to the Order, holy lay brothers were finally to be officially recognized and celebrated at the altar.

The confusion of the times and the unsettled vocation of the lay brothers is beautifully symbolized by the life of the one nineteenth-century brother for whom a formal process of canonization was opened, Bartolomeo Concordia. He hardly functioned as a lay brother at all.[18] Born on 21 February 1835 at Nepi, near Viterbo, in what was then the Papal States, Bartolomeo's parents were peasants. One of his two siblings who survived infancy, his sister, became a nun. The miraculous marked his life from the beginning. He seemed stillborn, but he was revived through the imposition of a relic of St. Francis Xavier, whose name he received at baptism. As an infant, he was fascinated by the images of saints and, at four, he asked his mother to teach him the Rosary. At his parents' request, he became a choirboy at the cathedral, where he was educated for six years. Even as a youth, he often gave away his food to the poor. During the insurrections of 1849, when he was thirteen, he went to Rome to retrieve his sister following the suppression of her convent.

The following year he was apprenticed to a cooper, who worked him very hard. Finally, in his late teens, he became a lay brother of the Vigna Pia, a school for poor children founded by Pius IX outside of Rome. In 1853, after taking a cold during a procession of Our Lady of the Rosary, his health declined so much that he was dismissed from the congregation. He recovered and began the search for a new vocation. He entered the Jesuit novitiate, but was again dismissed for bad health. Back home, during an attack of fever, he saw the Blessed Virgin and two other saints. Mary promised him good health, if he entered "her order." So, on 10 October 1857, he received the habit at Santa Sabina from the prior, Sebastiano Gramondo, a collaborator of the master Alexandre Vincent Jandel. Having completed a two-year novitiate (he seems never to have been a donatus), he professed solemn vows in October 1859. He lived just over three months as a professed lay brother, dying on 15 January 1860 at Santa Sabina in Rome.

His actual life at Santa Sabina is completely hidden and unknown. His fellow friars remembered him as extremely prayerful and dedicated to the Rosary. After his death, his body remained flexible, seemingly incorrupt. In 1869, the holy brother's relics were translated to a tomb in the old Rosary Chapel of Santa Sabina. Pius IX declared him venerable on 9 March 1869. The ensuing verbal process for his canonization consists almost entirely of testimonies of healing though his intercession. It seems that this pious brother was, like St. Dominic, more useful to the brothers after his death than when alive. I understand that the current postulator general is not pursuing the cause.

REESTABLISHING THE ORDER

After the chaos of the late eighteenth and early nineteenth centuries, the real reestablishment of the Order would come only after 1850, under the leadership of two French friars, Alexandre Vincent Jandel (1818–1872), appointed vicar in 1850, and then master general in 1855, by Pope Pius IX, and Jean-Baptiste Henri Lacordaire (1802–1861), the famous French preacher. As we have seen, in the premodern period, Dominican life was characterized by large monastic communities, with many friars who never left the cloister, other than the extremely busy itinerant preachers. During the refoundation, Jandel focused on the reestablishment of the regular life, while Lacordaire focused on preaching and pastoral activity. What had been a "both/and" understanding of the Order in the medieval period tended to become an "either/or" dynamic in the modern age.

One province established during the refoundation of the Order in France was explicitly intended to revive the medieval monastic ideal according to the spirit of Alexandre Jandel, the Province of Lyon. It was initially called Occitania after one of the provinces destroyed in the Revolution, and its friars tried to recapture that lost world. The first house of this province, at Lyon, was detached from the Province of France in 1858. It became the nucleus for reestablishing a monastic life of strict observance. Provincial status arrived in 1862. By 1870, the province had forty priests, twenty-four lay brothers, and thirty-six clerical students. Even counting the students, the percentage of brothers was over 30%, high even by prerevolutionary standards. This reflected the material needs of the larger monastic communities.

The way of life of its lay brothers, and how it changed by the early 1900s, has been traced in a document preserved in the archives of the Province of France.[19] The author of this text describes the life of the brothers in the refounded province as quiet, hidden, and totally dedicated to internal domestic work. The obituaries of brothers printed in the acts of the Lyon provincial chapters are stereotyped descriptions of their regularity and piety. The brothers passed their entire lives in one house and never seem to have left the monastery. In fact, these obituaries are often repeated verbatim, only changing the brother's name and date of death. The brothers of the pre-World War I period generally entered in their 30s and died in their 50s. Only three in this period were under 30 when they entered. Only one lay brother had any notice outside the monastery. Brother Giles Brossette (†1892) was a distinguished organist and a noted worker in stained glass, as was also Brother Arbogaste Heinie (†1918), who, exiled after the 1909 suppressions, long served as porter at Rijckholt.

The crisis of the Paris Commune in 1871 and the suppression of religious orders that followed produced great disruptions though confiscations and exile. Many friars, including Jacques Falquet, one of the province's first lay brothers, left for the provincial mission in Trinidad. Others went to foundations in Jerusalem and to the exiled house of studies at Rijckholt in Holland. Still others moved to houses in Fribourg, Switzerland, and in Cuba. When reestablishment came after World War I, the province was vastly different. Houses were smaller and very much pastoral in focus. Lay brother vocations were nearly all very young, some men not even in their 20s. They also lived longer, mostly into their 70s. But most important, there were seldom more than one or two in a community. In addition, they moved from house to house, and were even more dedicated to domestic work, serving priests who focused on pastoral ministry.

Ultimately, it was Lacordaire's activism that came to dominate. Outside of the houses of study, the typical modern Dominican house was much smaller than those before the Revolution. That this was already becoming the norm in the mid-nineteenth century, as can be seen in the so-called Jandel Constitutions of 1867. New or refounded houses required a mere nine friars; priory status required twelve, of which ten were to be clerics. When this was actually the case, the numbers preserved the earlier proportion of about twenty percent lay brothers. While traditional in the sense that a new community with twelve friars, of which two or three were lay brothers, was typical of the thirteenth century, modern priories were seldom much larger than that unless they were "major priories." These were to have thirty friars.[20]

This would have a great effect on the life of the lay brothers. Where previously, conversi formed a true community of their own in the large monasteries, modern lay brothers, as often as not, lived alone or in twos, with a group of priests. Other changes in the wake of the commercial and industrial revolutions made full-time gardeners, tailors, and shoemakers unnecessary. The availability of paid workers would make lay-brother cooks, masons, and carpenters ever more superfluous. That paid *familiares* were becoming common is seen in the Jandel Constitutions

(1867).[21] These required that familiars not live in the community, unless they are "necessary," in which case they must be at least twenty years of age. If so, they should make temporary vows—which makes them sound like donati. These rules seem to have been observed mostly in the breach.

On the other hand, the Jandel Constitutions simply reproduced, virtually unchanged, the *Regula Conversorum* of Raymond of Penyafort's constitutions.[22] The three changes made, however, are very significant. Pope Pius IX had, in 1862, introduced temporary "simple" vows as mandatory for the three years before a religious made perpetual solemn profession.[23] This regime was grafted into the constitutions. Conversi were now to spend three years as a transitional donatus, then one year as a lay brother novice, followed by three years of temporary profession. Finally, they could make, if approved, solemn perpetual vows.

Lay brother formation, in effect, would last seven years. No donatus was to be admitted unless he was at least twenty years old. So lay brothers could not make solemn profession until they were twenty-seven years of age.[24] Although the constitutions do not say so, at least one Dominican canonist of the period commented on the requirements for potential lay brothers: they were already to know the principal teachings of "the Catechism," and, "if possible," to have training in some skill, before receiving the tertiary habit.[25]

The constitutions also addressed this new longer "formation" period. Lay brothers were now to do their novitiate (and implicitly their three years as a donatus) in "a house of stricter observance where the clerical novitiate is located." Admission of transitional donati to the brothers' novitiate required the approval of the prior of the house, the provincial, and two-thirds of the vocals.[26] At the beginning of the novitiate, the new lay brother would put off the tertiary habit and receive the lay brother habit.

The Jandel Constitutions repeated the medieval regulations on the conversus habit with its two gray scapulars, but a footnote confirms this is no longer the practice: the lay brother habit is now identical (as it had been for a couple hundred years) with the clerical habit, except for the black scapular and capuce. This meant, given the nature of the donatus habit, that vestition as a lay brother meant "receiving the scapular" over the white tertiary tunic and belt.[27]

The actual "formation" was not specified, but the same canonist's commentary prescribed "instruction in Christian doctrine" once a week and allowed the brothers, as the constitutions provided, permission to have a few "inexpensive" pious books.[28] The implication, of course, is that the typical lay brother is now literate, at least in the vernacular. The institution of this new regime reflects the modern reality of small houses. It was simply impossible for each small modern priory to admit, form, and profess its own clerics and lay brothers. Formation was now a provincial responsibility, conducted in a "major priory," the modern provincial "house of studies." This made professed lay brothers (like priests) a provincial resource, to be assigned and detailed according to the decisions of the provincial. It is hard to imagine any other system, given the realities of the postrevolutionary Dominican Order.

Unlike the clerics, lay brothers did not have to stay in the house of studies or the priory of the novitiate after simple profession. They could be immediately assigned out, although this was to be to a priory whose chapter could vote on their solemn profession. The form of this profession, was, as it always had been, identical to that made by clerics. And illiterate conversi could still sign the profession book with a simple cross, something that, given the rise of mass elementary education in the nineteenth century, was becoming unheard of.[29]

The constitutions also addressed the situation of individual brothers in small communities of priests. No lay brother was to be assigned to serve a single priest. They were to be under the direction of the master of lay brothers (*conversorum*), who was to see to their ongoing formation. He was, in theory, to give them a spiritual conference a couple times a month and to make sure that on feria, when they did not rise for Matins, they do an hour of meditation before serving the private Masses. This spiritual formation could be incorporated into their weekly spiritual conference and their chapter of faults.[30]

In practice, after novitiate, the brothers learned their house functions simply by doing them. As there was no provision for teaching them a trade or skill, this meant most brothers did simple domestic work, unless they came in with some kind of technical training. One indication of the expectation that lay brothers would be doing unskilled domestic labor is a remarkable change in the rules on the brothers' office of Pater Nosters. While repeating the early-modern reduction as to the number of Paters said for Matins and the major hours, and adding an Ave to every Pater, the Jandel Constitutions provide that, if a lay brother is solemnly professed and supported by the community, he is completely dispensed from the brothers' office because the "sweat of his brow" suffices for the obligation.[31] The contrast with the sometimes highly skilled prerevolutionary conversi, their elaborate regular life, their attendance at the clerics' chanted Divine Office, and their periods of formal mental prayer is dramatic, to say the least.

But what about the religious ethos and spirituality of the lay brothers in the restored Order of the later nineteenth century? The constitutions themselves tell us very little. They emphasize the old virtue of humility and remind the conversi that they are not to be called "father." They are to show reverence for priests, devoutly serving their Masses and going to confession weekly. They are to stay in their place: should they wear the clerical habit, or, God forbid, fraudulently receive ordination, the punishments are severe.[32] In contrast, a delinquent cleric can be punished by being "broken down" to the status of lay brother. The premodern hierarchical structures seem, if anything, even more rigid. But perhaps this is partly because the social and educational gap between the typical lay and clerical brother has narrowed. As a gap narrows, the tendency is to make distinctions stricter, lest the gap be blurred.

The Brotherhood in the United States

The lay brothers to whom the constitutions were applied lived under vastly different circumstances than those for whom Raymond of Penyafort wrote them. The single greatest change, even more perhaps than the Industrial Revolution, was the size of nineteenth-century houses and the number of lay brothers living in these communities. We have decent statistics for the United

States, where the foundations were admittedly "missionary."[33] But throughout most of Europe, because of the suppressions during the revolutionary and liberal regimes, the reestablished provinces were, in a sense, "missionary" too.

For the Province of St. Joseph in the United States, from its founding in 1805, 49 lay brothers had entered and died by 1920. Until the 1870s, there were only two prioral houses, St. Rose (Kentucky) and St. Joseph (Somerset, Ohio). About 25 brothers lived in those two communities. This might seem like a large number, but their entries are spread over a sixty-year period. It was rare that either of these larger communities ever had more than five brothers living together at one time. Nearly all the brothers were employed in farm work. In the late 1800s and early 1900s, the remaining 20 or so brothers were spread over nine communities. With the exception of the house of studies in Washington, it was rare for there to be even two brothers living in a community at a time. In short, only in Washington was there anything like a large "monastic" community. In California, there were only two communities with brothers commonly assigned, San Francisco and the house of studies in Benicia. Neither house ever had more than two or three brothers.

The men who entered in Kentucky and Ohio were nearly all from rural agricultural backgrounds in the United States or Ireland.[34] Two came with skilled trades: one was a mason, another a shoemaker. Four had some education, one even classical studies, another a schoolteacher. One, Brother Simon Brady, a late vocation from a well-to-do family, actually brought with him a "dowry" large enough to build the priory in Somerset. As the province established houses in the eastern cities, the background of the brother changed. Some, like Brother Joseph Huggins, had already learned a skilled trade. He was a mason, and he superintended the building of St. Dominic Church in Washington. All the brothers were literate. One, Brother Charles Sandin, a convert from Lutheranism, had sufficient education to be ordained but was not, because he was deaf. None of these later vocations came from a farming background. In short, once the province was established, brother vocations were not "peasants," but urban and possessed of at least an elementary education. But, with a few exceptions, they did not enter with training in a skilled trade.

The most striking evidence for these developments comes in the form of the first book I have found that was written specifically for lay brothers. The author assumed that the brothers receiving the book were all literate, at least in the vernacular, and able to read his treatise for themselves. This book, *Religious Institutions of the Lay Brothers of the Order of Preachers* (1879) was composed by Father Francis Sadoc Vilarrasa, a son of the Province of Aragon and first provincial (1850) of the Province of the Holy Name in California.

Vilarrasa was a man in the tradition of Jandel, in contrast to the cofounder of his province, the Dominican archbishop of San Francisco, Joseph Sadoc Alemany (1814–1888), who was an activist in the spirit of Lacordaire. This made for occasional tensions. I mention this because of the monastic model that lies behind Vilarrasa's little book. The author explained that his reason for writing was to meet the needs of the lay brothers, who cannot read the Latin Constitutions of the Order for themselves.[35] In great part, the work is a paraphrase of those constitutions, with a running commentary. Most of it deals with matters that affect clerics as much as lay brothers, and one might wonder if it was also intended as an aid for clerics with mediocre Latin skills.

The book also reflects accommodation to modern conditions. Given the nature of what Vilarrasa called "present circumstances," superiors can allow friars to ride stagecoaches and trains and to "easily" carry necessary money with them.[36] Likewise, although he does not like it, he recognizes that there are two kinds of Dominican houses, those "of the common life," where all goods and money are managed corporately, and those "of the private life" where friars control their own income, finances, and expenditures without any need for permissions.[37]

Vilarrasa's image of the brothers is traditional, but it also reflects the nineteenth-century reality of the brothers, not as essential to running a large monastery, but as servants who free clerics for pastoral work and—as the author is a Jandelian—for their choir obligations. He wrote:

> The object of receiving Lay Brothers in our Order is that they may perform the manual and corporal labor necessary and useful to

> the community, in order that the Choir-Religious may devote themselves to the duties proper to them. They are committed to labor by their profession and should, other than recreations and other duties, fill their time with it.[38]

His spiritual elaboration on this is interesting. He introduces an idea that, common as it became afterwards, does not appear explicitly in any earlier legislation or writings on conversi. He wrote:

> It will be a great help to the Lay Brothers in their discharging faithfully and cheerfully their duties to reflect that by their corporal labors they are working for . . . the good of souls and are partakers of the merit annexed to it.[39]

And again:

> The object of the Order is to procure the salvation of souls. Every member of the order, the Lay Brothers included, labors for that great object. . . . Hence, a Lay Brother, by discharging faithfully the employments imposed on him, labors for the salvation of souls no less than the priests.

Although the language will not appear until the next century, Vilarrasa is clearly suggesting that lay brothers are to find their spiritual meaning by "cooperating" through their manual workin the pastoral ministry of priests. It is certainly an elevated vision of the brother's role, but the result is to subordinate the vocation of the brothers to the ministerial activity of the ordained in a way that would have been very strange to friars of the previous centuries. The brothers have, in a way, lost their independent identity and function within the Order.

On the other hand, Vilarrasa is a good Thomist, not a functionalist. He writes that the brother's vow of poverty is not an end itself; rather it should lead to the virtue of religious poverty, which is something much greater. Rules exist to foster right attitudes and virtues.[40] This is a noble vision. One might wonder how well his readers appreciated it.

The first sixteen chapters of *Religious Institutions of the Lay Brothers* deal with the constitutions and capitular legislation then in force on a great number of disciplinary and spiritual topics. Only in the last two chapters does the author deal with the brothers directly. Chapters 17 and 18 on the brothers' work and training summarize, as I have done, those topics in the Jandel Constitutions. In the final chapter, Vilarrasa treats the community life and prayer life of the brothers, the contemplative and monastic part of their vocation. This is his principal contribution to the life of the brothers. And, as a faithful disciple of Jandel, it is his longest section.

Vilarrasa knows only the Brothers' office of Paters, which are traditionally paired with Aves, and he allows no dispensation from this office for work.[41] The recitation of the office is central to the brothers' piety. He is emphatic about the lay brothers' mandatory attendance at the clerical choir office. They go daily to Compline, make the evening meditation, and attend the procession for the dead that followed the weekly Requiem Mass. It is a general custom (i.e. has force of law), that they attend the Major Hours and the Sung Mass on Sundays and Holy Days. They, like clerics, make weekly confession, and they receive the Sacrament, with the clerics, at the General Communions on Sundays and the dozen or so major feasts of the year. Brothers must make a ten-day spiritual retreat every year (no exceptions!) and do mental prayer for thirty minutes (of which fifteen may be the Rosary) each morning and each evening.[42] In spite of the changes brought by modernity, Vilarrasa's brothers are above all religious in the older sense. They may "cooperate" in the priests' apostolate, but personal sanctification by prayer is the essence of their life.

When Francis Sadoc Vilarrasa wrote his little manual for lay brothers, there were only about twenty-five lay brothers living in the United States, five in his own general vicariate of the Holy Name, and another twenty or so in the Province of St. Joseph. One of these brothers, who may well have read Vilarrasa's book, deserves to be remembered because he broke out of the assumed brotherly duty of domestic service.[43] Thomas Anthony Hickey was born in Ireland about 1844. As a young man he came as an immigrant to the United States. The country was in the midst of the Civil War, and Thomas volunteered with an Ohio regiment in 1862. As a foot soldier, he participated in General William Tecumseh Sherman's devastating "March to the Sea" from Atlanta to Savanna, Georgia. He was with the army up the coast and inland to Columbia, South Carolina, the birthplace of secession.

The blood, death, and destruction of the war seem to have affected him deeply. Settling in St. Rose, Kentucky, the oldest foundation of St. Joseph Province, he made a considerable amount of money as a grocer. A pious man, he loved reading, especially about Catholic doctrine and theology. Finally, in 1869, he presented himself to the fathers at the Priory of St. Rose as a lay brother postulant. As he was literate, had some Latin, and was proficient in basic theology, the fathers pushed him to enter as a cleric. He refused "out of humility." We might wonder whether the blood of the war, some perhaps shed by him, did not play a role, along with humility, in his decision. Thomas went to workalmost immediately, running the priory grist mill. This brought in agood income from grinding neighbors' grain. He took a course in agronomy and reorganized the priory farm. He also offered training in modern methods to local farmers.

But what made the former Union soldier famous was his charitable work for former slaves. He took advantage of his own education to open the first school in St. Rose for teaching the newly freed blacks to read and do figures. Even more surprising, in a state that had been evenly divided between Unionists and Confederates, he worked tirelessly to reconcile the local ex-soldiers of the two armies. The hardworking lay brother was probably the most famous, and revered, Dominican in the town of St. Rose, perhaps in all of Kentucky. He died on Christmas Eve 1914. Nearly the entire population, Protestant as well as Catholic, black and white, attended his funeral. Most had to stand outside the crowded little church. A new province of the restored Dominican Order had produced a modern lay brother who deserves to be remembered with the famous names of the past.

THE BROTHERS IN CANADA

But elsewhere, domestic service, often in parishes, was becoming the norm for brothers. An example can be seen in the first lay brother of the Province of St. Dominic in French Canada.[44] The first friars arrived in Quebec in 1873, and official status as a province came in 1911. The brothers of the Canadian Province deserve special attention. The Canadian province would, by the

1950s, have the highest number of lay brothers in the entire Order. It still has the highest percentage of brothers today (20%), although most are now very elderly.

Brother Hyacinthe was born Alfred Rousseau on 17 December 1857, at Sainte-Claire, Quebec. His family was poor. His mother died when he was in his early teens. He then left home "looking for adventures." This quest lasted only two years. When he returned home, the local pastor took him in as a domestic servant, to relieve his poor family of the burden of supporting him. In 1878, while driving the buggy for the parish priest to visit the sick, Alfred suddenly fell sick. The priest ran to get the oils and a doctor. Returning, he gave Alfred Viaticum. Suddenly, while changing his stole to do the anointing, the priest himself died of a heart attack.

These traumatic events seem to have triggered Alfred's investigation of religious life. He went to work for a Dominican parish priest and then asked admission to the Order as a lay brother in 1879. Now Brother Hyacinthe, he lived first at the church of Notre Dame, where there were only a couple of priests, no lay brothers, and some lay employees. The young postulant replaced the lay parish cook, who had gone blind. In 1880, a lay brother, Jean-Marie Closse, arrived from France with a new pastor for Notre Dame. So Brother Hyacinthe began his six years of "formation," after receiving the donatus habit on 15 August 1880. Before the year was out, Brother Jean-Marie was moved to Lewiston, Maine. Brother Hyacinthe was left to supervise several other untested new brother postulants. He was himself moved in 1884, and then, on 2 June 1886, having finally completed a canonical novitiate, he was professed. The author of his obituary, Father Thomas Gonthier, commented on the "irregularity" of his formation, but this kind of makeshift training as a lay brother seems to have been rather common, if not the rule.

In his thirty years as a lay brother, Hyacinthe was assigned variously to Lewiston, to Ottawa, and then to Fall River. In those parishes he served as porter, sacristan, cook, gardener, driver, and laundryman. The parish priests remembered him as quiet, obedient, and retiring. In old age, during a final hospitalization, he told a visiting priest: "You don't realize how sick I am." As it was obvious that he was dying, Brother Hyacinthe was returned home, where he received the Last Rites. He died 24 June 1916 at Lewiston, Maine. The quiet brother's example was credited with many priestly vocations.

Brother Hyacinthe resembles, in his responsibilities, another Canadian brother of the same period, who also served in many houses, doing internal domestic work, Ange Lemay.[45] Father Lacroix, his biographer, wrote of him: "Il fut le frère convers idéal." He defined that "ideal brother" as "without profane education, but intelligent, spiritual, a friend of order and regularity, solitary in work and prayer." Ange was born in 1879 to a large, pious family. After parochial school, he entered the minor seminary, but he did not stay. Instead he chose, in 1901, to enter the Dominican Order as a lay brother. His entire life was dedicated to manual labor and prayer. He served first as gardener for the vast grounds of the monastery of Saint-Hyacinthe. The rest of his life was spent as sacristan, gardener, and cook at Fall River, at Montreal, and at Lewiston. When not busy, he made Rosaries. Known for enthusiasm and humor, his only recreation was fishing, by which he supplied Friday dinner for the community. He did have an independent streak. Once, when the prior said that the cost of a fishing license was just "money thrown in the water," he proved that he made back the cost of the license, many times over, by his catches of fish. The prior relented and gave him the money for the license. When he died, after a short illness on New Year's Day in 1949, his cell was found barren, his bed the worst in the house.

A good example of a later parochial brother in this tradition would be Venant Valcourt.[46] He was born in Fall River, Massachusetts, in 1893, and died there in 1957. A product of parish and public schools, he first worked in local piano and cloth factories. At the age of twenty-one, he was received at Saint-Hyacinthe. Immediately after his first profession, he was assigned out, eventually living in Ottawa, Fall River, and Lewiston. He functioned as gardener, sacristan, cook, and housekeeper. His favorite work was in the larger Ottawa community as the porter. When called away from that work and made refectarius against his own preferences, he did not complain.

The makeshift formation, the shuffle of assignments among small parish ministries, and the jack-of-all-trades domestic work that marked the lives of Brother Hyacinthe, Brother Ange, and Brother Venant were typical of many lay brothers in the twentieth century. On the other side of the Atlantic, the same sort of random assignments and responsibilities mark the lives of the fourteen lay brothers of Lyon serving in the 1920s for whom we have death notices. With the exception of just one, Brother Emmanuel Armand (†1925), a missionary in Trinidad, all did internal domestic work. Even Brother François Monechon (†1932), whose health problems kept him as a tertiary donatus for fifteen years, served tables and washed dishes. The friars were amazed when, on his deathbed, the dying brother could recite long sections of the Psalms from memory.[47]

Not all of these "traditional" brothers were uneducated men. In the Province of Lyon, Brother Amand Pittie (†1951) was, in fact, very intelligent and well educated. The procurator general of the order called him to Rome in 1908 to serve as his assistant. He handled most of the Order's banking and postal affairs. But, his biographer emphasized, he remained a "good Occitan" in clothing, speech, and habits, even after many years in Rome.[48]

A good number of the Lyon brothers found the shift from the older monastic model to the newer pastoral focus difficult. Father V. Paragot, the chronicler of the Lyon brothers, observed that when the friars returned from dispersal abroad and in the missions during the 1920s, they returned to houses that had been, in their youth, very monastic.[49] These houses were now busy parishes and often ran elementary schools. Some conversi, like the elderly Brother Bertrand Besson (†1938), lamented: "These parish priests are never at Office. They have to go play with the children instead of hearing confessions."[50] Brother Bertrand, known as the "Provincial of the Conversi," mostly served, both in exile and at home, as assistant to a provincial who served four consecutive terms. In later years, he divided his time between receiving inquirers in the porter's office and saying his Rosary in chapel.

Father Paragot called Brother Bertrand an "old-school

Occitanian conversus," and compared him to another long-suffering older brother, Giles Giband (†1941). This ascetic practiced strict poverty and ate only other friars' leftovers at meals. Brother Giles left the monastery only twice in his life, both times on the orders of the superior. Paragot thought that many of these older brothers lived the old life as best they could, and that they never really adjusted to new demands. They did, however, get a French translation of the constitutions in 1931, some sixty years after the work of Vilarrasa in the United States.

The one task where the old monastic model did not differ much from the newer one of small, active houses was that of porter. One of the most celebrated of these men in the Canadian province was Brother Marie-Alphonse Brousseau.[51] Born in 1883, he only went to elementary school. He then helped his father on the farm. The parish priest noted his piety and suggested he consider the Dominicans. Alphonse entered in 1902, at the age of nineteen. He received the tertiary habit and entered the brothers' novitiate three years later. He made final profession in 1909. Originally the gardener at Saint-Hyacinthe, he went to Ottawa as porter, where he served in that post for forty-two years. He also helped out as sacristan, refectarius, and gardener.

Brother Marie-Alphonse may not have been well educated, but he was very intelligent. He was perfectly fluent in both English and French. He was remembered for his maturity and his respectful and affable personality (a "true gentleman"). He never cursed or used hard words with difficult people, and he remained patient and helpful to the poor, even during the Depression. After Ottawa, he counseled alcoholics at Fall River. He was justly proud of the men he brought back to sobriety. He preferred the personal touch to simply giving out money, taking beggars to refectory rather than giving them the handout of "a dime for coffee."

Practical and pious, his biography leaves little doubt that his diligence at the door saved the priests much aggravation and trouble. When his health began to fail in 1948, he still served the community by washing dishes. He died in 1960, after a long illness. He was the kind of man who inspired the Canadian brothers' vocation boom of the mid-twentieth century. By the 1960s, the Canadian brothers numbered over one hundred, the most of any province in the Order.

RETHINKING THE BROTHER'S VOCATION

Father Paragot linked a drop in Lyon brothers' numbers in the 1930s to the growing emphasis on pastoral work and smaller houses after World War I. Perhaps he is right, but we need to examine the extant statistics. This is especially so because the drop he saw in the province of Lyon would, at about the same time, affect the whole Order. Starting in 1876, the Order has published, at varying intervals, directories listing all the friars of the Order, organized by provinces. These allow us, for the first time, to get good figures for the numbers of lay brothers in the Order and in each province or entity, as well as their percentage of the total friars.[52] The last such directory was published in 1992, but I also received statistics for 2015 from Santa Sabina.

I have tabulated statistics from these publications in Appendix A (p. 288). In 1876, out of a total of 3289 friars, 567 were lay brothers, that is, 18%. The percentage fluctuates between 18% and 20% until 1931. Although the number of lay brothers continues to increase to a high of 1219 in 1967, from 1931 to that date the percentage drops from 20% to 15%. This is because of the larger recruitment of clerics in that period. After 1967, both the total number of brothers and their percentage drops. The most recent figure (2015) is 310 brothers, 5% of all friars.

If we look at the period before 1930, we have a period during which, in percentage terms, the number of brothers is stable and comparable to that of the premodern period, which I have already estimated as about 20% or slightly more. The modern brothers were not evenly distributed though the provinces. In 1930, some provinces had well over 20% lay brothers: Ecuador (44%), Bohemia (41%), Spain (32%), Naples (38%), Austria-Hungary (36%), and Teutonia (33%). Other entities have very low percentages: St. Joseph USA (8%), Sicily (10%), France (10%), Holy Rosary (11%).

The statistics for Naples and Sicily are strange. Sicily had a high number of brothers, only to have it drop. In the case of Naples, it was exactly the reverse. This may reflect movement of brothers from the poorer to the (somewhat) more prosperous province. If the numbers are combined, the result is high. Holy Rosary may be low because, as a mobile missionary province, priests were more needed than brothers, and because native vocations were not accepted until 1929.[53]

In any case, the higher percentages seem to concentrate where the economy is more agricultural. Among such provinces, the highest levels are also in Spain and southern Italy, where the effect of the Revolution and Liberalism was not so drastic. The liberal regimes of Latin America clearly had a huge impact on the Order in those regions: the numbers are all low, and the Province of Mexico simply ceased to exist during the Mexican Revolution (1910–1920). The lowest numbers are in the most modernized (urbanized, mass-educated) areas: the United States, France, and England. These are also areas where, as we have seen, the move to small houses also brought greater involvement in parish work.

The counter example is the growing number of lay brothers in Canada, which had heavy commitments to parishes, but also some large traditional monasteries. Canada would, during the twentieth century, recruit large numbers of brothers. This recruitment was so effective that, even after the effects of aging and deaths, the brothers' percentage is twenty percent today, the highest in the Order. Even after recognizing the diversity of numbers, the trend in the twentieth century has been down, first, since 1930, in percentage, and then, after 1967, in gross numbers. This development deserves careful study.

The early 1900s also saw a reworking of the Dominican Constitutions that had an effect on the life of the brothers. The central event of the period was the promulgation of the 1917 Code of Canon Law and the eventual promulgation of the 1924 Constitutions, which had been revised in light of the Code. Within the Order, late-nineteenth-century chapters said nothing significant on the brothers.[54] But, in 1910, the fathers were concerned that, between first and final profession, brothers be assigned to a fully functioning priory.[55] Succeeding chapters paid considerable attention to brothers' formation. Perhaps there had been too many vocations whose training was like that of Brother Hyacinthe Rousseau.

In 1913, the old system of a three-year period as a donatus, then the novitiate, followed by simple vows for three years, and then solemn profession was modernized. There was to be a prenovitiate of two years, a novitiate of one year, six years of simple profession, and then solemn vows. Brother aspirants were to be twenty-one years of age or older.[56] This reproduced the directives of the decree *Sacrosancta Dei Ecclesia*" (1 January 1911), which would eventually enter the new Code. It seems that some provinces kept some aspects of the old donatus pre-novitiate. At least in the two American provinces, the men in the pre-novitiate wore a version of the old tertiary habit even into the 1950s. That used in St. Joseph Province was identical to the traditional habit; in Holy Name Province, the aspirants also wore a black capuce. Oddly, the St. Joseph aspirants wore the habit only while working; for church services, they changed in and out of a black suit.[57]

The 1913 chapter also tried to regularize the formation program. New brothers were to receive regular instruction from their postulant and novice masters. The masters were to discuss both spiritual matters and constitutions: in particular, deportment, prayer, the forms of manual labor, and obedience. The last item received the longest treatment in the legislation. The capitulars also reminded priests that they were to treat the brothers with respect.[58] Although the period as a transitional donatus before the novitiate was now gone, the chapter still assumed that there would be permanent donati. These donati were to be formed, along with the lay brother postulants, in priories with good regular observance. This would make it easy for them to learn "humility, piety, work, obedience, and fraternal charity."[59]

Incidentally, the abolition of the transitional donatus period for lay brothers in 1913 makes it possible to estimate the numbers of permanent donati in the modern period. The Order directories produced from before this change show that the percentage of transitional and permanent donati before the abolition was about 2 or 3 percent, rising from 95 in 1876 to a high of 155 in 1910. These directories do not distinguish between the two types of donati. Nevertheless, a safe guess is that during this period, transitional donati outnumbered permanent ones by ten to one. This is evident from later directories. Beginning in 1931, when we can be certain that all listed donati are "permanent," their percentage averages only about 0.3 to 0.4 percent, the total number rising from 15 in 1931 to 37 in 1967. Donati are no longer listed in the 1992 directory, but their numbers were clearly dropping precipitously. This is mostly due to the reconfiguration of the Third Order as the Dominican Laity, which made the idea of a "donatus" problematic. I know of only one donatus alive today.[60]

When the constitutions of 1924 were published, they contained these substantial changes. These constitutions also integrated the treatment of the brothers into the body of the text instead of in a separate *Regula Conversorum*.[61] The implication was that lay brothers and, at least implicitly, all friars were to be understood as religious in the same way. Indeed, the new constitutions said as much at the beginning of the treatment of the brothers: "Conversus brothers, like the other clerical brothers, are true religious."[62] That this should not be the case would probably have never occurred to a medieval Dominican. Now, with the growing subordination of the brothers to priestly ministry as a kind of support group, it needed to be stated explicitly.

As the 1938 chapter in Rome emphasized, the lay brothers were still understood to be very different from clerics. They were a separate "category," and they should have their own chapel and recreation room. They did have to admit that contact with clerics, given modern apostolic houses, was impossible to avoid due to the brothers' work.[63] This characterization of clerical and lay brothers as "the same but different" created a tension in the lay brothers' status that is still with us today.

The 1924 Constitutions implicitly recognized the growing understanding of lay brothers as primarily domestic servants, and this is reflected in the treatment of lay employees. When there are "insufficient" brothers to do essential domestic work—maintenance, cooking, laundry—then the house can hire lay workers to do it. Superiors are to see to the employees' spiritual welfare and make sure that they frequent the sacraments. These same responsibilities fell to their master in the case of lay brothers.[64]

That those performing domestic functions need not be highly skilled is reflected in changes in the 1913 formation program. The two-year postulancy (a relic of the old donatus years) is now gone.

There is still to be a postulancy, but it can be of any length. And the age of admission is lowered to 17 from 20. After the one-year novitiate, brothers were to make temporary vows twice, each time for three years. Then they were to be solemnly professed. The formation period was thus reduced from nine years to as little as six; the age of solemn profession was lowered from 29 to 23.[65] The old medieval fear of admitting "untrained youths" was gone entirely.

The final significant change instituted in 1924 concerned the lay brothers' life of prayer. Gone is the requirement that they be present for Matins and the Major Hours, if only on Sundays and feasts. They are now required only to attend Compline, the Salve Procession, and the weekly Procession for the Dead. In recognition of the now near-universal literacy of the brothers, they may replace the traditional Office of Latin Paters and Aves with recitation (in the vernacular) of the Little Office of the Blessed Virgin. The recitation of Paters and Aves remained for suffrages; likewise, the traditional Rosary for the dead.[66]

Chapters during the period between the World Wars added little on the brothers, sometimes not mentioning them at all.[67] In most specifics and general structure, the Book of Constitutions as reedited in 1932 would remain in force until after the Second Vatican Council.[68] Several significant decisions were made in 1938, however. Novice brothers were to have their own master, and not be under the clerical novice master. Their time in simple vows was to be in a priory, not an unformed house. Finally, Blessed Martin de Porres was declared the patron saint of the brothers.[69]

The 1920s saw the publication of new books for lay brothers about their life and vocation. These are the first I have found since Father Vilarrasa's work in 1879. Two of these were published just before the actual promulgation of the new constitutions. Victor F. O'Daniel of St. Joseph Province in the United States published *The Dominican Lay Brother* (1921) and Henri-Dominique Noble of Le Saulchoir published *Le Frére-Convers dominicain* (1920), which was translated for use in England in 1931. Noble's booklet seems, in part, intended as vocation literature for brother vocations at Le Saulchoir. Although published a year earlier, Noble's vision is more expansive. Perhaps that is the reason that it was later published in English.

O'Daniel's work was meant for the brothers themselves, much like Vilarrasa's. But the change between Vilarrasa and O'Daniel is stark. Vilarrasa's brothers are essential to the functioning of the monastery, and their life as contemplative religious is central to his presentation. O'Daniel's brothers do their reception at the door, sacristy work, general cleaning, and cooking so that priests can be freed from domestic drudgery to focus on the preaching and the apostolate. St. Dominic, O'Daniel tells us, instituted the brothers to "give their clerical brethren greater freedom for a more vigorous prosecution of their vocation."[70] In return, the Order provides the brothers with a religious life, so they can be holy and go to heaven. But prayer is quite secondary. O'Daniel is blunt. The lay brothers are to do their required devotions and then give themselves to labor and "think little more of prayer," because a brother doing that is "better in the sight of God than one who slights his work to pray more."[71]

Father Noble, in comparison, anticipates the new constitutions in his insistence that lay brothers are "real religious" and "real Dominicans." They make the same vows as clerics and, like them, live a real Dominican life.[72] Both brothers and priests labor for the salvation of souls in their own diverse way.[73] Although he does not use this language, O'Daniel thought that the major difference between clerics and lay brothers is their differing "education and employment." This distinction as to education is explicit in Noble's booklet: "For admission into the Order of St. Dominic as a Lay Brother you need not have done your studies, but you must be in fairly good health, without infirmity that would unfit you for material work."[74] Although not explicit, lack of academic preparation, or inability to do it, has become the marker of a lay brother vocation.

In one important sense, both authors are still working out of the monastic vision of Dominican life that characterized Vilarrasa. When describing the daily round of a brother, O'Daniel gives that of the fifteen lay brothers in the house of studies of his province. They rise early, attend a private Mass, and receive Communion.

They join the clerics for meditation in choir until breakfast at 7 a.m. They then work till 11 a.m., when they get an hour off, followed by lunch and recreation. Then they go back to work until 5 p.m., when they join the clerics for Vespers (unless they are busy), which is followed by supper and the house common Rosary. Then they may have another recreation, do spiritual reading, or hear a conference from the master of brothers.[75] Strangely, O'Daniel never mentions Compline!

Noble also characterizes "real Dominican life" as focused principally on monastic observances, prayers, and penance. "The Lay Brothers in a Dominican Priory share to the full in all prayers and monastic observances. Only a few accidental modifications separate them from their priest brethren." That is to say: "They substitute manual work in place of study."[76] The brothers do, like cloistered nuns, pray for the priests engaged in active pastoral ministry and preaching.[77]

O'Daniel's vision of the work done by lay brothers reflects the internal domestic focus increasingly typical since 1900. In fact, he remarks that lay brothers in the past did catechesis and were "veritable apostles among children, the poor, and the ignorant." They were especially useful for this "in foreign missions where there were few priests." The implication is that such "apostolic" work by brothers is a thing of the past, unneeded in the modern age.[78] Similarly, Noble's primary vision of brothers is as serving to support a large community. He wrote: "A house as huge as a monastery calls for a large number of services." Priests cannot do these because of time or "ineptness." So the lay brother is "indispensable to the [priests'] apostolate."[79]

Like O'Daniel, Noble presents as typical the work of brothers in his own academic community, Le Saulchoir. They serve that large community by serving as porter (receptionist), as sacristan (setting up and serving the many private masses), cleaning the building, and working in the kitchen and refectory.[80] In both cases, the work of brothers is basically unskilled. It is telling that Noble's short life of Martin de Porres makes him illiterate and unskilled. Martin's work for the poor consists of distributing food and alms. It is hard to recognize the skilled healer, fundraiser, and organizer of hospitals and orphanages.[81]

The vicar provincial of the Province of Canada, Father Mannès-Emmanuel Marchand, in the obituary of one of the brothers of this period, wrote that the means of sanctification for the brothers was "to work much, to work always; with renunciation, silence, and forgetfulness of self; for the common good, that is to say for the house." He was eulogizing a conversus who personified that kind of self-abandonment, Brother Marie-Gabriel Vaillancourt.[82] Born in 1889, at Sainte-Anne-des-Montes, he was one of thirteen children in a pious family. At twenty-four, after a parish mission, he asked the Dominican preacher to admit him as a brother. His parents were opposed, but he promised the priest that he would resist them.

Assigned first to Quebec and then to Notre-Dame-de-Grâce, his principal work was manual labor and plant upkeep. Brother Marie-Gabriel would stay up all night planing boards or fixing machinery. He was porter, refectarius, plumber, laundryman, gardener, steam-fitter, blacksmith, cabinet maker, "and even architect, contractor, and bookkeeper." The brothers best remembered him for making beautiful furniture. When asked to do work in individual cells, he always obeyed but was known to say "Very well! I will do what you wish; but I am going to have to undo it when another father replaces you in this room." He died at Notre-Dame-de-Grâce, Montreal, in 1946, at the age of fifty-seven.

Brothers assigned to plant maintenance in this period often had very little time to pursue their own talents, but some did. In Canada, Brother Jean-de-la-Croix Boucher (1908–1946), served as porter and refectarius at Ottawa, Quebec, Ottawa again, Montreal, Quebec again, Ottawa again, Montreal again, Quebec again, and finally at Saint-Hyacinthe. But the skill at which he excelled was bookbinding. He even wrote and bound a booklet modeled on the *Imitation of Christ* for his own devotion.[83] And in Lyon, there was Brother Symphorien Chastel (†1945), who was an excellent photographer.[84] In both cases, these talents enriched the brothers' communities.

THE BROTHERHOOD AMIDST WAR AND CONFLICT

We must look a bit far afield for a brother whose talents, beyond those domestic and merely manual, were put to work under obedience of his province. Brother Manes Wichrowicz, the uncle of a now elderly priest of the Polish Province,[85] was working as a sacristan in the 1930s. Brother Manes used to lead the other brothers in recitation of the Little Office of the Blessed Virgin. The provincial, sensing hidden abilities, reassigned him to Lwów (now Lviv in Ukraine), where the province published its journal, *Szkoła Chrystusowa* ("The School of Christ"). The brother was there trained as a master printer, and other lay brothers were assigned as his assistants so that he could teach them the craft and run the provincial press. Running the printing presses, which did much more than print the journal, remained a major responsibility of the Polish lay brothers until after World War II, when the Communists vetoed such religious publications.

The more typical domestic service, irreplaceable (without some expense), marks the last of Brother Marie-Gabriel's contemporaries at Ottawa.[86] He may fittingly stand for the many other brothers we have no space to consider. Brother Raymond-Marie LaRose (1916–1944) came of a devout family (his aunt was a missionary in Japan), and after completing his novitiate in 1939, he was assigned to Ottawa where he lived until his death. He tended the furnaces, kept the parish shop, and worked as carpenter and domestic housekeeper. Like many brothers, he kept his piety as hidden as his life. It was only on his death that copies of his prayers and meditations were found among his effects. Among them was an oblation prayer modeled on that of St. Thérèse of Lisieux. The brother therein offered an oblation of himself to the Virgin, asking her help and that of St. Dominic. In it, he pledged himself a slave of Mary. This card he carried over his heart on the day of his profession, 2 July 1940, and for the following four years until his death in 1944.

Some readers might find the lives of these mostly domestic friars somewhat tedious, but one more needs to be considered before looking outside the monastery for brothers who broke this mold, if only because his canonization is under consideration. This man entered the Province of Our Lady of the Rosary in the Philippines very soon after the Dominicans there began taking native vocations in 1929. Brother Gregorio Hontomin was born in 1909, one of six children of devout parents. As a young man, he worked as an orderly in a Manila hospital.

Gregorio entered the Order in 1936 and took final profession in 1944. Until it closed in 1959, he did plant maintenance at Rosaryhill and cooked. From there he was sent to the University of Santo Tomás, where he became head of plant maintenance for the university hospital. On 6 July 1982, he collapsed at his workbench while doing watch repair. He died that evening. Nevertheless, his holiness is so respected in the Philippines that the 2002 Cooperator Renewal Meeting there urged his canonization.[87] His model inspired seven native lay brother vocations at Rosaryhill before it closed, although in the turmoil of the 1960s only two finally professed.

As these brothers were quietly serving their communities and provinces into the late 1930s, storm clouds were appearing on the horizon that would prove to be the lead-up to World War II. Central among these was the Spanish Civil War (1936–1939). This war between the Nationalists of Francisco Franco's Falange, supported by Germany and Italy, and the Republicans, supported by the Soviet Union, was exceptionally bloody and involved countless atrocities and civilian deaths. At least 4,000 of those martyred by the Republicans were priests, along with similar numbers of religious brothers, sisters, and nuns.[88] Some 107 Dominicans, including the former master general Bonaventure García y Paredes, were among those killed.[89] The Spanish friars killed in this conflict represent the largest group of Dominican martyrs in the history of the Order, far surpassing those killed in Ireland, or even in the Ukraine, during the persecutions of the seventeenth century.

Of these friar martyrs, many were lay brothers, of whom 24 have now been beatified. The first group of six were beatified on 11 March 2001 by Pope John Paul II and are celebrated on 22 September as the companions of Bl. Hyacinth Serrano López. The second group of 18, beatified on 28 October 2007 by Pope Benedict XVI, are celebrated on 6 November as companions of Bl. Bonaventure García y Paredes. I provide a complete list of the beatified lay brothers in Appendix B (p. *290*). Their biographies and pictures, along with those of martyred clerics, can be seen on the Spanish Province website.[90] There were other cooperator brothers martyred as well, who have not yet been beatified, in particular those who died in Barcelona and Catalonia.[91]

Although many brothers were captured and shot by Republicans individually, most died in three large massacres. The mass killings of brothers began in Madrid during July 1936 and continued into the fall. Nine of the beatified brothers were members of the communities at the houses of El Rosario and Santo Domingo El Real. One brother, not included among those yet beatified, Manuel Rodriguez, was pressed into service as an orderly at the Republican military hospital, and later he was taken out and shot when he was no longer needed.

A second large group died at Almagro Theological College in August 1936.[92] Most of these brothers died, along with a great number of priests and seminarians, on the Vigil of the Assumption. Two were in formation, one was a novice; the rest were domestics at the college. Of the two cooks who were shot, Brother Arsenio de la Viuda Solla (born 1903) died shouting "Viva Christo Rey!" A last large group were martyred at Santander later in December 1936.[93] They included two sacristans, the porter, and the cook-infirmarian. The five brothers killed were all very young, the oldest being twenty-six, the youngest only eighteen.

Less well known than the Spanish Civil War martyrs are the eight Polish martyrs of Lwów (now Lviv, Ukraine), who were massacred by the Soviet NKVD Police in 1941, after the German invasion of the Soviet Union. As the entire community of Czortov, near Tarnopol, was killed, these martyrs would have included the lay brothers. The beatification process for them was commenced on 19 November 2006.[94] During the chaos of the War and the long period of Communist repression that followed, these were, certainly, not the only lay brothers who bore witness to the faith, even at the cost of their lives.

THE BROTHERS IN THE POSTWAR PERIOD

Concern over the relative drop in vocations, the increasingly advanced intellectual culture of the brothers, and their integration into the apostolic life of the Order, all clearly evident in the legislation and writing on brothers between the World Wars, greatly intensified after World War II. In part, especially in the United States, lay brother vocations were often veterans, mature men with good educations and military technical training. In addition, the priests of the "vocations boom" of the 1950s were seldom men who had received the rigorous classical education typical of earlier clerics. In a major break with past centuries, clerical brothers could rarely speak Latin well, if at all, and some found the recitation of the Breviary with understanding difficult.

The great wall of Latin literacy that previously separated the lay and clerical brothers was crumbling. To some extent certainly, the relative decline in lay brother vocations was the result of these changes. During the vocations boom, the spread of mass education, as well as lesser standards for clerical Latinity, meant that the percentage who sought a priestly vocation could and did go up. And this meant the percentage of brother vocations went down. Intoxicated by the large numbers of postwar vocations, Dominican formators and superiors often seem to have failed to recognize these realities.

The general chapter of 1946 reminded the friars of the then-current legislation on lay-brother formation, in particular, the importance of their theological training in a priory.[95] But the first full-scale institutional attempt to address the life of the brothers occurred at the Washington General Chapter of 1949. The chapter fathers expressed strong concern over the decline in brother vocations, and over the perceived lack of respect for the brothers by many clerics.[96] The genesis of this legislation is clear in the work of the chapter commissions and the verbal process of the chapter itself.

It is interesting that nearly all commission discussion of the lay brothers occurred in the commission on vocations. The context of the discussion was clearly the relative decline in vocations and concern about its causes. This was set out in the initial discussions of the commission.[97] Commission members were concerned that the acts emphasize that lay brothers were an "essential" part of the order, and that priests come to understand this. The commission identified an overemphasis on manual labor, to the exclusion of spiritual aspects of the brothers' vocation, as being at the root of the problem. This discussion occurred in St. Joseph Province, and one wonders if the vocals had in mind Father Victor O'Daniel's little book. This problem, they thought, could be addressed by better spiritual formation and improved prayer life, in particular, the promotion of the Little Office over the recitation of Paters and Aves.

The final report of the Vocations Commission included the proposals of its Third Session (13 September 1949), that on the brothers.[98] The fathers drew up a list of the "special difficulties faced by conversi." These fall into two groups. First, they detect insufficient respect for the excellence of the brothers' vocation. To remedy this, the brothers' master should give them better spiritual and intellectual instruction during the novitiate. Then, they are to be assigned, after first vows, to a full-fledged priory, where community religious life is truly lived. They are not, it is understood, to be assigned to a small house just because it needed an additional domestic worker. The second issue identified is more dire. It is the "insufficient adaption of their way of life to aspirations fitting the modern mentality."[99] They list various social, economic, and human developments to which the brothers' vocation had not been adapted. The brothers needed a greater role in their communities through better specialized training and a formation that imparts better knowledge of Christian doctrine. The fathers hope that this will eventually facilitate their participation in the choral office. Or, if that is not possible, at least in their own common recitation of the Little Office of the Virgin. However, they admit that not all are ready for this; if necessary, some may continue saying Paters and Aves.

This report was discussed in Session Nine of the chapter.[100] The discussion opened with the brothers' vocation crisis. The fathers discussed and voted on, as a block, the proposals that would go into the acts. They accepted the proposals on training and spiritual formation, and the brothers' progressive inclusion in the choral office—or, at least, their use of the Little Office. For the future, the most important change was the adoption of proposed language about their vocation. This summary of the brothers' vocation passed into the acts of the chapter. It reads: "Since conversi are true religious, undertaking manual labor, they cooperate in the ministry of priests and the salvation of souls." For that reason, their vocation should be promoted.[101] The fathers went so far as to recommend that every province have a promoter of lay brother vocations.

What can we know about the brothers and their formation in the early 1950s? Careful readers have probably noticed that I have said virtually nothing about what the conversi, the lay brothers, thought about themselves and their work. The fact is that nearly everything we know about the brothers comes from priests writing about them and legislating for them. In the period after World War II, this suddenly changes. It is still possible to talk to brothers who lived through the 1950s, that is, to do their oral history. And, by the 1960s, the brothers began to leave their own written, sometimes published, record. Oral history gives an opportunity to see some of the realities behind the legislation of chapters and the writings of clerical theologians, spiritual writers, and canonists. The living voice of brothers themselves throws light on their motivations for choosing the brotherhood, the kind of formation they received, and the work they were involved in during the decade before the Second Vatican Council. A full list of those brothers interviewed for this book may be found in Appendix D (p. 293).

I focus on brothers from the United States because the Washington Chapter was held there, and it was there that the tensions I have been describing became the most pronounced, although similar tensions also appeared in Canada and much of Western Europe. When young men thought about a brother vocation in the 1950s, they could be very young. Since 1924, a recruit need only have been seventeen years of age. And men entered that young, as seen among the brother martyrs in Spain. Their postulancy might be quite short. One brother, who entered in 1953, had already tried the Brothers of Mercy, a nursing order, before he applied to the Province of St. Joseph. He did not even have a high school diploma, as none was required. There was no formal admissions process, just "rolling admissions."

Another wrote asking to enter, arrived at the house of studies, and became a postulant, wearing the old donatus habit. There was no formal screening. Postulants worked along with the lay brother novices doing long hours of plant maintenance. Prayer was the Little Office in common in the brothers' chapter room. The brothers attended the morning office and went right to work.

The hours were long, but this brother did enjoy working in the laundry.

A last example of the admissions process at the time: One brother was directed to the Dominican house in New York City by his secular parish priest, because the boy seemed to have a religious vocation. The young man rang the bell and was met, unplanned, by the prior provincial. The provincial simply told him to write a letter and apply. He did, but he got no answer. He wrote to the (clerical) vocations director. Nothing happened. Finally, he called the provincial, who said he would check. Two days later the young man received an acceptance letter.[102]

During the postulancy, one St. Joseph Province brother remembers, there was a Sunday afternoon class each week on the *Baltimore Catechism*. Since all the brothers had already studied it in parochial school, he thought this was "pretty silly." "But that was just the way things were."[103] Another brother of the same province, who entered soon after, also applied before high school graduation. The only screening was a medical and dental exam, followed by reception of an acceptance letter. He went to the province six-month postulancy program. Brother postulants wore the old donatus habit and had catechism once a week. He gave an example: "The father would ask, 'Brother, what are the seven virtues?' A silly program since we already knew the answers from Catholic school."[104] The tension between low intellectual expectations and actual preparation was marked, even after decades of concerns about improved formation for new brothers.

Another brother who entered at Washington in 1952 commented that the goal of the postulancy program seemed to be to supply extra workers to care for the physical plant, to do domestic work, or to type. He remembers doing fourteen hours a day in the laundry. Most of his fellow postulants had no high school diploma. He got together with them, and they asked the postulant master if they could earn high school diplomas at night. He refused, so nine of the thirteen postulants left.[105]

Another brother, of the Holy Name Province, who entered in 1953, did have a high school diploma. In fact, he had already gone through the prenovitiate juniorate with the Christian Brothers before graduating from high school. He had left the Brothers because he felt no call to teaching and had always had mediocre grades. He applied as a Dominican brother immediately after high school graduation and spent a year as a postulant in the old donatus habit. The postulants went to prayers and did manual labor around the provincial house of studies. There were no classes or conferences. On entering the novitiate, the brothers' novice master gave the classes in constitutions, spirituality, and dogma specified in the constitutions.[106] It seems then that, after 1949, formation and assignments were still haphazard; not much had changed since fifty years before the World War II.

The revision of the constitutions in 1954 did begin to reflect the work of the Washington Chapter.[107] These track the earlier constitutions, but shorten them and incorporate the growing desire to integrate the brothers more fully into the life of the community. They also assume that the modern brother will be literate in the vernacular and have at least an elementary education. Given the growing emphasis on the brothers' equality in religion, these constitutions introduce some language that reaffirms their identity distinct from clerics. The brothers "constitute a special group (*specialem coetum*), apart from priests, students and novices."[108] Indeed, the brothers' dedication to manual labor means that they are to be "compelled (*cogantur*) to learn a trade (*artem*) useful to the monastery."[109]

That the brothers' state is subordinate, even inferior, is preserved in the legislation by which a cleric may be punished by reducing him to a lay brother, not merely because of inability for studies, but even as a punishment for misbehavior.[110] Otherwise, the constitutions do reflect the concerns for better formation, a more developed spiritual life, and greater presence, if not participation, in the liturgical life of the community. The chapter of 1955 did little to develop the new ideas about the brotherhood. Rather, it was concerned about too much integration: brothers are not to be present in the house chapter, except perhaps in special sessions on lay brothers' acceptance into the novitiate or admission to vows.[111] The extent to which this rethinking of the brothers' life in the order was reflected on the local level remains less clear.

Turning again to the Canadian Province, which was undergoing the height of its lay brother vocation boom in the 1950s, we have a remarkable book, Father Benoît Lacroix's *Compagnon de Dieu* (1961), which beautifully summarizes the changing theological and spiritual reflections on the brothers from the 1920s to the 1950s. This book is long—280 pages without the obituaries—and intended for the use of the brothers themselves. It is a theological and spiritual treatise on the brotherhood. That something this long and sophisticated would be published for the use of the brothers themselves shows how their culture had changed since the writings of O'Daniel and Noble. Lacroix assumes a literate and theologically sophisticated reader.

The book has three parts. The first is a reflection on the brothers' vocation as one of service to God and the salvation of souls. The second elaborates on how brothers authentically live the religious life and pursue their work for the good of souls and the glory of God. Finally, Lacroix presents Jesus, the Virgin Mary, and St. Dominic as models for brothers. These three holy models make up, with the brothers themselves, the Body of Christ, active in the world. The book is devotional but also theological. The author draws on Scriptural examples, and gives concrete examples from the life of the Holy Family and that of the Church. The result is a series of spiritual conferences, meant not only for reflection and meditation, but also to be put into practice.

Lacroix's major thesis is that the brothers are "coopérateurs" and "auxiliaires" of priests. Brothers and priests are both "Servants of the Word." By the will of St. Dominic, lay brothers are just as much religious as priests and clerics.[112] Lacroix develops this "equality in religion," which we have noted since its first appearance in the 1920s. To show that the salvation of souls is the work of all members of the Order, Lacroix places texts of the constitutions in flanking columns. The result shows that the treatment of brothers and priests is parallel. All that is said about the priest's work of study and preaching finds a parallel in the brother's work of prayer and manual labor.[113] Both categories "cooperate" in the salvation of souls by doing different works for the same common good.

As in work, so in prayer. Lacroix tells the brothers to follow the Mass and to "listen to the readings." He may not be assuming that they can understand the Latin, but he certainly assumes they can read and follow a bilingual hand missal. "The Mass is an affair of the whole Mystical Body."[114]

The treatise is quite conservative in its preservation of the older model of the brother.[115] Lay brothers do manual labor. Each category has a distinct duty and these complement each other. Brothers need the sacraments; priests need the time to administer them. Work is not inferior, says Lacroix. Jesus the carpenter did manual labor, so did his father Joseph, and so did Our Holy Father Saint Francis. He quotes Francis himself from his Testament: "I worked with my hands, and I want the brothers to work."[116] Lacroix's book is marked by a tension he probably never really noticed; a friar who could read this long, sophisticated treatise might not find a life of manual labor and plant maintenance very satisfying, even if it did bring about the salvation of souls.

ON THE EVE OF THE VATICAN COUNCIL

Conversation with brothers who entered in the later 1950s shows that Lacroix's higher expectations as to education and theological preparation were accurate, at least for North America. By that time, admission without secondary education was rare. Take an example from the early 1950s. One candidate of Holy Name Province, who actually always thought he wanted to be a priest, did have a high school diploma, but he was never very good in school. The brotherhood was attractive because it lacked the stress of college and theological studies. He wrote an application immediately after high school and got an acceptance telephone call as soon as the application was received. He did not even have an interview.[117] Contrast that with a later example in St. Joseph Province. This brother entered, aged 22, at the very end of the decade. He not only had a high school diploma, but two years of business school. There has been a remarkable change in educational background.[118]

Early in the decade, the postnovitiate formation program could be minimal, thus the concern about assignment to a prioral house that we have noticed in legislation. In St. Joseph Province, simply professed novices were normally sent to the farm in

Somerset, Ohio, or to the clerical novitiate. Both were large enough communities to fulfil the constitutions. Somerset meant farm work, mostly milking cows. "Farm work for a Bronx Boy!" one brother remarked on his experience.[119] He was happy to be sent back to the laundry in Washington.

Another brother, who entered in 1953, was considered too frail for farm work. He was left to himself and spent much of his time reading theology in the house library. This brother had always thought of being a missionary, but his province had left their China mission after the Communist takeover. The province was then collaborating with the Italian Dominicans on a mission in Pakistan, but the brother had not finished three years in a "formed house," that is, a functioning priory. A priest told him: "Oh, just write to the provincial." Within a week—mail was faster in those days—he received a letter from the provincial assigning him to Pakistan. So much for formation.

Another St. Joseph Province brother remembers being assigned as the sacristan for the huge community of priests teaching at the province's liberal arts college in Rhode Island. He had received no formation or training for that. The brother served that community as sacristan for twenty years. This meant setting up and, even serving, some ninety private Masses a day. This was before concelebration was permitted. Even after that permission, he remarked with a smile, he was still very busy. "Concelebration still meant much setup work; less work for concelebrants, but not much less for the sacristan."[120]

One Holy Name Province brother remembers his assignment after vows. It was a priory, but he was the only brother. He did domestic work and was chauffeur for the fathers. Strict categories meant that he recreated by himself and could not talk to clerical novices or priests, except under unusual conditions. When told that he was going to be trained to service the boiler, he had a year of crisis. This ended when he was sent to learn typesetting and help a brother who did printing at the house of studies.[121] We will return to that printer brother in the next chapter.

All these examples are from the United States, but the testimony of a Vietnamese brother, who entered the French vicariate in the north run by the Province of Lyon in the early

1950s, sounds very similar.[122] Born into a very pious Catholic farming family, his parish priest, sensing a vocation, introduced him to a Dominican. The Dominican introduced him to the vocation director. After a chat, the director accepted him as a lay brother. His postulancy and novitiate were well in advance of the programs in the United States. His novice master gave him and the two other novices not sent back to France classes on canon law, Scripture, spirituality, and religious life.

After profession, in 1954, the friars fled to the south because of the Communist takeover. There this brother was assigned to the Priory of the Holy Rosary in what was then Saigon, his only assignment. He made profession, and worked as assistant treasurer, and then as treasurer himself. This unusual assignment resulted because the French priests of the house did not have enough Vietnamese to do the shopping. When Vietnamese priests began to be ordained and the province was founded, he became driver for the provincial. Then he was, once again, in charge of the physical plant at Holy Rosary as assistant to the treasurer. Eventually, he served as porter and handled charity needs of many kinds. More recently, before retirement, he became sacristan. This was the work he has liked the best because of its closeness to God and the chance to help people who met him in church. But this takes us much ahead of ourselves.

It is fitting to end our discussion of the brothers in the period from World War II to 1960 with the General Chapter of Caleruega in 1958, the last chapter of the 1950s. In a sense it summed up the changes and tensions we have seen and pointed the way to the age of the Second Vatican Council. This chapter was the first in history to have a commission dedicated exclusively to the lay brothers. It also had a full session dedicated to them.[123] One petition at the chapter reminds us of the shrinking gap between the culture of lay brothers and that of clerics. At one of the opening sessions, a diffinitor asked that capitulars be able to speak in their own languages instead of Latin, because "professors speak Latin, others do not." There was discussion, but a decision was deferred.[124]

The thrust of the commission on the brothers and the session on them was, above all, to integrate the brothers into the prayer and apostolic life of the Order. In response to discussions in which vocals urged that the brothers be brought directly into pastoral work in parishes, at least in the catechesis of youth, the chapter passed legislation to that effect.[125] This was the first time that this work, in which brothers had, as we know, been active for centuries, was authorized officially. The decision was not even controversial. There were also to be symbolic moves toward equality. Lay brother professions were to be done with the same solemnity as those of clerics. Brothers, like clerics, were to have annual spiritual exercises.[126]

The gap between clerics and lay brothers within the community was debated, and here the divisions became more evident. There was sympathy for greater "fraternal religious activity (*conversatio*)," but a motion to admit brothers to the house chapter with active voice failed, as only eight vocals supported it. The capitulars did allow that the brothers "could be heard in the chapter on matters pertaining to them." This was a long and tense discussion. The original version, which proposed that the brothers "should be heard," failed.[127] In the same session, the vocals approved a provision that brothers, with permission, could fulfill their office obligation by reciting the Divine Office itself, as opposed to the Little Office or their traditional Paters and Aves. This matter was referred to the Liturgical Commission, which was to prepare a version of the Office suitable for brothers "within a year." The fathers also congratulated the Provinces of Lombardy and Aragon for their new programs at Bolzano and Pomplona, dedicated specifically to formation of lay brothers.

A symbolic but important matter that ended up deferred was a reform of the habit. While the chapter did end the distinction between lay sisters and choir nuns, and so abolished the black scapular of the lay sisters, the fathers did not consider it opportune to change the brothers' scapular.[128] That was left to a future chapter. This seems a relatively small result for so much discussion, but the chapter also produced something very important for future reflection, although not included in the acts themselves. This was a list of questions on the brothers to be dealt with at the next chapter.[129] There were twenty-one of these, and, while none was really new, the whole amounted to a program for greater integration and better formation of the brothers.

Of the greatest lasting significance was the chapter's decision to abolish the terms "lay brother" and "conversus." Henceforth those called by those names were to be called "cooperator brothers."[130] This change came at the petition of the diffinitor of Poland, who remarked that "many find the word 'conversus' offensive." This change in language actually happened slowly in some provinces. One St. Joseph Province brother remarked: "In my province, they kept calling us lay brothers until 1968 or even after in some cases." Categories remained very strict, too, he said, even after their abolition in 1968.[131] So, the long reflection on the brothers' "cooperation" in the work of the Order and in the apostolate of priests would now be signaled by their name. I will use this new form exclusively from now on.

Chapter 6
The Brotherhood in the Age of Vatican II

While many changes had occurred in the life of the brothers from the refoundation of the Order in the nineteenth century until the 1950s, the most significant religious event of the twentieth century, the Second Vatican Council, would make these developments seem insignificant. Much has been written on the Council, but less on its aftermath and Dominican responses to it. And there is virtually nothing on the Dominican Order's history during the following half-century.[1] This makes writing a history of the brothers after 1960 difficult, and anything I write here will be very provisional.

An entire book, or several, could be written on the brothers of each province over this period. An oral history, with contributions of all the living brothers, would be a massive undertaking. What is most needed are histories, and oral testimonies from the brothers, for each province and entity. This is something best done by the friars of each province themselves. I apologize for the incompleteness of this chapter and its many lacunae. Let it stand as a challenge to further research. When such books have been written, this chapter will have to be revised. Or, perhaps, a whole book should then be written on the modern period.

That said, the 1960s began with great enthusiasm and excitement. The conclusion of the last chapter shows that, even before the Council, theological and spiritual developments were already far advanced, most of the canonical and constitutional changes of the post-Conciliar period were being discussed, and the cooperator brothers had begun to minister in new ways and outside the confines of the local house or priory. Perhaps the single most exciting event of the early 1960s was the canonization of St. Martin de Porres, the patron of cooperator brothers, by Pope John XXIII on 6 May 1962. After centuries, the brothers could finally count among themselves a canonized saint. He would not be the last.

LEADING UP TO THE COUNCIL

The decade of the sixties began with the back-to-back general chapters in 1961 and 1962. These came soon after John XXIII's announcement of the Council in 1959, and that coming event colored the capitulars' concerns. The chapter at Bologna in 1961 passed virtually no legislation on the cooperator brothers. And the chapter had no commission on the brothers as such. They did, however, require that the constitutions and other documents of the Order be revised to use exclusively the new name "cooperator brother."[2] That change would become final with the third reading of the legislation in 1962. The chapter also determined that the cooperator novice master be equal to the clerical one, not subject to him, and an ex-officio member of the house council.[3] The master of the brothers at this time, however, still had to be a priest. The final decision was, perhaps, a step backwards. The annual retreat for cooperator brothers was only required in houses with three or more brothers.[4] This does not mean that the council paid no attention to the brothers. Much to the contrary, they were a lively topic of interest, as we can see from the petitions to the council and the verbal process of the discussions.[5] The most important development of the 1961 chapter was the establishment of a commission to draw up proposals for an *aggiornamento* of the brothers in anticipation of the chapter to be held in 1965.

In the petitions and discussions about the brothers, the friars of Spain, Lyon, and the Holy Land were the most engaged and active. Some petitions simply reiterated previous legislation or clarified it. For example, one petition requested that the brothers' novitiate be separate and parallel to that of the clerics, and that their period of simple profession be reduced to five years. Some petitions completed changes already begun. For example, the brothers could already say the Little Office in the vernacular, so now those not saying it should be able to say their Paters and Aves, as well as their suffrages, in the vernacular, as well.

Two issues, however, were more contentious. One was the petition from the (clerical) friars in Dalmatia, Lombardy, Brazil, Spain, and the Holy Land to abolish the cooperator habit and give brothers the white scapular. The friars from Dalmatia called the black scapular a "humiliation" that hurt vocations. A number of friars from various provinces pointed out that it was "not the habit given to Bl. Reginald," and so, in their opinion, not really a Dominican habit. Friars of the Holy Land noted that many cooperators were equal in education to the clerics—so why a distinction in garb? Institutionally, even more significant was the proposal that the brothers be given active voice in house chapters for matters that concerned them (Belgium-south, Saulchoir, Spain, Holy Land, Lyon), or even for all matters discussed (Teutonia).[6]

The issues raised in these petitions were of major symbolic and canonical importance. They remain with us today. The verbal process of the chapter, which does not include summaries of the debates, shows that in both areas, the friars of the chapter were hesitant to move quickly. The motion to grant active voice to the brothers in chapter failed 12 to 44. And "no agreement was reached" on changing the habit.[7] The Belgian provincial, in response to these two nondecisions, declared: "In our regions, the case of the cooperators is lost."[8]

Categories were still strong. The Holy Land motion to allow the brothers to come to clerical recreations occasionally did not make it to a vote. On the other hand, the less concrete motion of the Holy Land, to promote the dignity and explain the excellence of the cooperator vocation, and to make it clear to clerics so that they could encourage and appreciate work of the brothers, passed. As the Bologna chapter had set up a commission on the brothers for 1965, the next chapter, at Rome, in 1962, restricted itself legislatively to giving third approvals to earlier legislation. Brothers did not have a commission, and do not seem to have been a topic of discussion in 1962.[9]

As the chapter fathers temporized, change had long been coming quickly on the ground in the provinces and in the missions. The St. Joseph Province brother who was assigned in 1956, shortly after his simple profession, to the mission in Pakistan, found there a very different world from that in his home province.[10] He would stay in Pakistan for thirty-three years, only returning to the United States in 1989. The priests in the mission were all young, and he was immediately accepted as a member of the community. In practice, categories did not exist. When most of the priests were away, which was much of the time, he functioned as the superior of the community. He attended chapters and had a consultative vote even before that was enacted into law.

Soon after arrival, he was told to "build us a house." He taught himself architecture and went on to build thirty-three churches, many with altars facing the people, even before the Council. He had learned about this idea during his reading in the library in Somerset. He also built the national press club in Karachi, and the central offices of the Salvation Army. Most of the men he supervised doing construction were Muslim. He commented that when he returned to his province, it was still assumed that he would do domestic work. This brother was left to "reinvent" himself. He became a campus minister at Providence College, ran the school's radio station, and served as treasurer of that large community for five years before "retiring."

This St. Joseph brother's experience of slow change at home is like that of one of the older Polish brothers. Well into the 1960s, the Polish cooperator brothers still had their own chapel where they recited their Paters and Aves or the Little Office. Most brothers did physical labor and worked very hard, dawn to dusk. A now elderly Polish brother remembers one of the "conversi" before the Council, Brother Gwala Torbiński. He did all the laundry for the huge house of studies. The brothers wore their habit all the time, even when hiking in mountains. Brother Gwala hardly ever left the laundry, but he also did all the gardening. And he was always ready to find books in the library for student brothers and deliver them to their rooms. In Poland, real changes only came in the 1970s, when the brothers were given classes in adult catechism. This brother even taught a class for three solemnly professed brothers himself.[11]

In contrast, institutional changes came earlier in Holy Name Province. In the late 1950s, that province was already sending cooperator brothers to night school to earn college degrees. One of these was a brother who entered that province in the early 1950s. In 1959, having completed his B.A. in English, the provincial told him that he was to be assigned to the high school run by the province in Los Angeles, St. John Vianney, later renamed Daniel Murphy. He objected that he did not want to be the only cooperator brother living and teaching with the priests who staffed the school. So another brother, who had also earned a degree, was sent with him. Brothers of St. Albert the Great Province, in the American Midwest, were also sent to teach at their high school, Fenwick, in the early 1960s.

Attitudes about the brothers and their education differed from province to province, even in the same country. One St. Joseph Province brother recalled the incomprehension and resistance of the local superior when his provincial sent him to get a vocational nursing degree that would prepare him to serve as infirmarian for their retirement community. That brother later went on to become a registered nurse and then to earn a doctorate in nursing.[12] At St. John Vianney High School, in contrast, the cooperator brothers were already admitted to house meetings and voting, at least on school matters, by the mid-1960s.

These developments, one Holy Name Province brother said, caused tensions. Older "conversi" brothers were skeptical about having brothers teach. Some even considered the cooperator brothers at the high school "uppity." These tensions between young and older brothers would continue into the 1970s. By the later 1960s, the cooperator brothers had become a dominant force at what was by then Daniel Murphy High School, and two of them served as principals.[13] This flourishing brother apostolate came to an end in the later 1970s, when the archdiocese of Los Angeles took over the school from the friars.

Within five years of the arrival of the cooperator brothers at what was then St. John Vianney High School, Holy Name Province began to restructure the brothers' formation, creating a program that would be held up as a model at the 1965 General Chapter. One brother, who became a postulant in 1959, remembered the formation program before the changes of the mid-1960s. As a postulant, he lived in the clerical novitiate, but very strict categories meant nearly no contact with the priests and clerical novices. There were three older cooperator brothers who did domestic work. They instructed him in laundry, cooking, and cleaning. He also served the priests' private Masses. The postulant master gave daily classes in theology, spirituality, and the constitutions.

After six months, in 1960, he moved to the province house of studies in Oakland, St. Albert the Great Priory, for his novitiate. There was a large number of professed and novice cooperators there, and, again, categories were strong. But the focus on educational preparation continued. The brothers did shifts as receptionist, as well as doing domestic work. Young cooperator novices who seemed to have academic abilities were sent to a local Catholic college to prepare for high school teaching. One of this brother's fellow cooperators in formation would later become the first brother principal of Daniel Murphy High School.[14]

These changes were profound. In past ages, as we have seen, there were highly skilled and educated lay brothers, but this training predated entry into the Order. Slowly, brother formation was assimilating to that of the clerics. Academic studies were rapidly becoming a part of brothers' training. By the mid-1960s, the Holy Name Province clerical novitiate had been moved, and that priory converted into a house for formation of the brothers. This program in Kentfield, California, very much the creation of Father Paul Scanlon (1933–2015), would be held up as a model in the 1965 Chapter.

One brother, who was ordained a priest in the 1970s, remembered his interview for admission in 1964. He was interviewed not only by the priest director of the program but also by two cooperator brothers. These friars "show-cased" their new brothers' formation program. High school was required before admission, because all the cooperators would be studying at the local community college. The new cooperator brother was to be an "educated brother." This brother praised the quality of the classes he received in Bible, constitutions, spirituality, and the history of the Order. Life at Kentfield was still quite monastic. After rising at 5:30 a.m., the brothers attended the morning Latin Office with the priests. They then recited all four of the Little Hours in English. After breakfast, there were classes and work. In the evening, they again attended the clerics' Latin Vespers, and then they recited Vespers together in English as a group. After dinner, all friars, including the young cooperators, sang Compline in Latin chant. During their time in simple profession, all the brothers did classes at the local community college, to complete the associate degree. They then commuted to a Catholic university in San Francisco to earn the bachelor's degree of their own choice. This brother went on to complete his B.A. in anthropology.[15]

A brother who entered his postulancy in 1959 remembered the shift to this new, and much more demanding, program. He too praised the quality of the teaching and the opportunities for further education. On the other hand, there was much turnover and instability among the brothers in formation.[16] For Holy Name Province, this was a peak period of recruitment for brothers—in the late sixties the number of brothers reached twenty-four in a province of 135 professed—but many left before final vows. And soon, many would leave even after final vows. For example, of the nine brother novices (with 11 clerics) who entered Holy Name Province in 1970, all left but two. And one of those two was eventually ordained a priest.[17]

In the developing world, where the manual-labor model of the brother would continue to flourish for decades, experimentation became the rule in formation. One brother of the then newly formed Province of Vietnam remembered his novitiate in 1964.[18] His was the last class to receive the black scapular. Clerics and cooperator novices were together under a single novice master, but classes were distinct. Formation was somewhat turbulent, as typical of the times, but also exacerbated by the displacement of the friars from the north to the south after the Communist takeover. Of the five cooperator novices in his class, he alone stayed.

After the novitiate, he was sent to a community in the mountains for seven months to learn auto mechanics. Reassigned to Saigon, he spent most of the rest of his life as the provincial's driver, but he also did building maintenance and supervised workers constructing the new priory. He also developed his skill as a bookbinder. So it was possible to change the structure of cooperator formation, but keep the traditional focus on manual labor.

Even in the United States, change in the traditional understanding of the cooperators could come slowly. The St. Joseph

Province brother who eventually earned a doctorate in nursing remembers his formation in the 1960s. The postnovitiate at the house of studies in Washington was still rigidly structured and focused on domestic work. He got his first taste of nursing by being assigned to tend the elderly priests retired there. He had to ask special permission to take a first-aid class at night. During the entire time there, the brothers had only one class. In addition, they had the option of reciting the Little Office privately, or, if they could, participating with the clerics in the Latin choral office.

Immediately after the postnovitiate, as had been the case for brothers in the 1950s, the brother who would later become a nurse was sent to St. Rose Priory in Kentucky. In actuality, formation stopped. This was a large community, but most priests were sick, elderly, or had limited ministries. With the parish priests very busy, internal life in the house was mostly run bythe brothers. In theory there were categories, but as in the Pakistan mission, they did not really exist because of the realities of life. As an outside job, this brother worked as a practical nurse's aide in a local hospital during the week. It was this experience that convinced him to ask permission of the provincial to get his nursing degree. At the house where he was assigned during that training in the later 1960s, the category barriers were disappearing. The focus of the brothers' life, however, remained domestic work.

Then, in 1967, when the Office switched to English, the treasurer resisted buying copies for the cooperator brothers. It was too expensive because there were too many brothers and "they did not need them." Only an intervention by the prior got the brothers their copies.[19] Another brother of that province, who had entered in the 1950s, remembers being assigned to help manage the provincial Shrine of St. Jude, in New Jersey. On arrival, he was told that his only responsibility would be domestic work in the priory. In frustration, he asked to be reassigned. But by the 1970s he was put in charge of the province Mission Office and found himself very busy, traveling to parishes and making 150 to 180 mission appeal presentations a year.[20] He would go on to become treasurer of the house of studies and then assistant to the treasurer of the province.

THE TURMOIL OF THE SIXTIES

If there is one cooperator brother who could symbolize the new freedoms and bewildering changes experienced by the brothers during the 1960s, it would be Brother Antoninus Everson, the famous San Francisco "beat poet." Antoninus is the twentieth-century cooperator brother best known to those outside the Order and has been the subject of numerous scholarly studies, including a full-fledged biography.[21] Born William Everson in 1912 to a working-class family near Sacramento, California, he began writing poetry in high school. Inasmuch as he had any, his religious beliefs were vaguely pantheistic.

He spent World War II as a conscientious objector in a Civilian Conservation Corps camp near Waldport, Oregon. There he became involved with the government-sponsored "Fine Arts Project." With other conscientious objector writers and artists, he organized dramatic productions, readings, and other cultural events. They also founded the Untide Press, and Everson developed a love of fine-art printing. Released in 1946, he moved to Berkeley, California, and rose to prominence during the "San Francisco Literary Renaissance" of the late 1940s. He received a Guggenheim Prize for his poetry collection *The Residual Years* in 1948.

The young beatnik poet underwent a religious conversion during Christmas Midnight Mass in 1948. He took catechism at St. Augustine Church, Berkeley, and became active in the "Catholic Worker" movement. One fellow catechism student remembered his iconoclastic and spontaneous outbursts. Once, when a student objected to the Real Presence in the Eucharist as "cannibalism," Everson shouted: "Of course, it's cannibalism! The Body and Blood of Christ! And that's why it's so wonderful—it satisfies one of man's strongest desires, to eat his own kind!"

After what he considered a mystical experience of light during prayer, Everson began the quest for a religious vocation. Rejecting the Benedictines and Franciscans because they would not guarantee that he could continue the art printing for which he was already famous, Everson visited the Dominicans at the Holy Name Province house of studies in Oakland. There, the regent of studies, Father Kevin Meagher, promised Everson that he could continue to print. He became a donatus brother in 1951.[22]

Now known as "Brother Antoninus," Everson continued to write poetry and established an art-printing studio at the house of studies. In 1954, he completed an autobiography, *Prodigious Thrust,* which was controversial because of its frank discussion of his sexuality. It would not be published until after his death. His hand-set letter-press printing, which included a famous version of the Pius XII Latin Psalter, made him famous. Everson's has been called the best American letter-press work of the twentieth century.[23] One brother remembers working with Antoninus in the print shop. Although they did art printing, much of the work was commercial printing work done for outsiders. This brought in money to support the venture and the community. When outside commercial printing became less expensive in the 1960s, this part of the work was phased out.[24]

In spite of his growing fame, Brother Antoninus lived an extremely cloistered life at St. Albert's Priory. Under the direction of Fr. Victor White, a psychologist, he studied Carl Jung, whose influence on his writing in the later 1950s was pronounced. His poetry took a "sensual" turn. A man of strong passions, he depended on the rigorous monasticism of the house for stability. When relaxations began in the late 1950s, for example, the introduction of a television set in the recreation room and occasional trips out to the theater, Brother Antoninus underwent a crisis. He would later write: "That television set formed a catalyst for a whole new movement; it was not just a symbol. I was clinging to the old monastic norms . . . The world was triumphing."[25]

With permission of his provincial, Antoninus began to travel widely and give public readings of his poetry. He was reabsorbed into the Beat Poetry culture of San Francisco. Then, his travel was restricted by the archbishop of San Francisco, who feared it was causing scandal. But, under a new provincial, Fr. Joseph Agius (whose secretary was a cooperator brother), he again began to travel widely after 1960. Everson had applied to the clerical novitiate in 1954, but it was mutually agreed that he should remain a donatus brother. He now continued to discern his ultimate vocation. Then, after the formality of a year of novitiate, Brother Antoninus professed simple (temporary) vows as a cooperator brother on 3 October 1964.

This was the beginning of the period when the old monastic structures of Dominican life were increasingly questioned, and a life apart from the world seemed to many obsolete. The previously cloistered brother began to do psychological counseling for lay people. Among his advisees was a young woman with whom he fell in love. His major poetic work of the period, "Rose of Solitude," was inspired by her, but he broke off their relationship. His poetry now had overtly erotic elements. In 1968 he won the Commonwealth Silver Medal for poetry.

At this time, Antoninus toured Europe, lecturing and reading poetry. On one occasion, while speaking in Hyde Park, London, a heckler shouted at him: "Christianity makes my private parts shrivel!" Antoninus retorted: "I wish it did that to me!" On his return, he entered yet another relationship with a very young counselee. Finally, he and his new provincial, Fr. Paul Scanlon, the founder of the Kentfield brothers' program, reached the conclusion that Brother Antoninus would let his temporary vows, of which about a year remained, expire and quietly leave the Order. But suddenly, on 7 December 1969, in the midst of a public reading at the University of California, Davis, Brother Antoninus threw off his habit and announced he was getting married. The provincial learned about this the next day on the evening news. Although in part a defense of his own erratic behavior, Everson would later write about the religious changes of the 1960s as the trigger of his personal confusion and spiritual crisis. He wrote:

> One of the reasons I had been dissatisfied with the Order was Vatican II's emphasis on Orders shifting over from the contemplative to social action. This meant that monasteries were being penetrated with a different spirit.[26]

The former cooperator brother became a "master printer" at the Esalen Institute, and then taught printing at the University of California, Santa Cruz. He was also poet in residence there until his death in 1994. Everson never formally left the Church, and in his post-Dominican period he was much influenced by the ideas of Teilhard de Chardin. In 1978, his collection of poetry from the time he was in the Order, *The Veritable Years*, won the Shelly Memorial Award and the Book of the Year Award of the Modern

Language Association.[27] In 1985, William Everson visited the provincial house of studies in Oakland and apologized to the community for the embarrassment his public departure had caused. And he then did the *venia*.[28] In his later years, as he was dying of Parkinson's disease, Everson was visited regularly by Father Finbarr Hayes, a Holy Name Province Dominican who had learned printing in Antoninus's shop while a student. Father Hayes ministered to him in his last illness and visited him regularly with Communion. The former brother died with the rites of the Church.[29]

RESPONDING TO THE VATICAN COUNCIL

Before turning to the constitutional changes and developments affecting the life of the brothers brought by the Second Vatican Council, we should mention something that one might think had little to do with the cooperator brothers, the crisis in the Congo from 1960 to 1965. This is because that conflict brought about the martyrdom of a good number of friars, including the most recent cooperator martyrs. This civil war was really a proxy war between the United States and the Soviet Union. As the Congo had considerable Belgian investments, Belgian troops were also involved. One of the side effects of this conflict was wholesale massacres of missionaries by the Communist-supported forces of Patrice Lamumba. Among those who gave their lives for the faith were two cooperator brothers from Belgium: Brother Petrus Maurits Broché (1898–1964), who was killed along with thirteen Dominican priests, and Brother Vincent Marcel de Doncker (1912–1964), who died along with two Dominican priests and two Order of Mary Immaculate priests.[30] Other cooperator brothers in the Congo also witnessed to the faith, although not at the cost of their lives.

Meanwhile, as the social and cultural changes of the 1960s were affecting the life of cooperator brothers in differing ways throughout the world, the bishops of the world were meeting in Rome for the Second Vatican Council (1962–1965). The General Chapter of Bogotá (1965) would coincide with the last sessions of the Council. One of the two most important Council documents for the life of the Order and the brothers, *Lumen Gentium*, had already been promulgated in 1964. The other, *Perfectae Caritatis*, would appear only after the chapter, in October 1965. Attempts by Dominican theologians to apply the teachings of the Council would be published a couple of years later.[31] These paid little attention to the life of the brothers.

Lumen Gentium 5–6 emphasized the universal call to holiness, and pointed out that religious life was not a "third way" between the lay and priestly states. The effect was to emphasize the identity of priests and brothers in their common vocation. Even more direct was the declaration of *Perfectae Caritatis* 15, which addressed the status of brothers directly:

> Those called lay brothers, assistants, or some other name should be brought into the heart of [the institute's] life and activities . . . Communities of men that are not exclusively lay in their character can admit both clergy and laity on the same basis with equal rights and duties, excepting those that result from Ordination.

The document went on to call for a renewal of the common life of religious so that it might give a greater witness in the world. The *motu proprio* of Pope Paul VI, *Ecclesiae Sanctae*, issued the year after the chapter, prescribed common prayer of clerics and lay brothers and the gradual granting of voting rights to brothers. In 1969, the instruction of the Congregation of Religious and Secular Institutes, *Renovationis Causam*, called for the end of separate novitiates.

Even before these documents, such reforms were already being discussed and instituted in the Order.[32] As the preparations for the 1965 Bogotá Chapter began, however, those developments lay in the future. Friars were still divided as to what changes in the brothers' life were necessary or useful. An anonymous document, drawn up as a working paper for the chapter, laid out the diversity of opinions.[33] Its author held a very conservative view of the brothers' vocation, but his characterization of the diverse opinions seems accurate.

The most "conservative" position described, to which the author subscribed, saw the brothers' life as essentially hidden and an exercise in humility. They had only an indirect involvement in the apostolic work of the Order: they freed priest friars of domestic drudgery so that they could dedicate themselves full-time to prayer, study, preaching, and sacramental ministry. Thus the work of the brothers was essentially manual labor. Juridically, *conversi* (his usage) are *familiares* and *servientes*. Their functions did not require training in the sacred or profane sciences. Their forms of prayer and way of life were wholly distinct from that of clerics. For these reasons, granting voting rights to the brothers is unwise, and, if done, should only occur in the most exceptional cases.

The author then identified a middle view that focused on the dwindling number of vocations to the brotherhood since the 1930s. Those of this opinion considered the "traditional" work of cooperators inside the community as less and less comprehensible to young people. These friars saw the decline in brother vocations as "deplorable," and identified a progressive involvement for them in the external apostolate as the solution. These voices did not see major constitutional changes as immediately necessary. Rather, there should first be a long period of adaption and experimentation.

Finally, there was what the author called the "radical" view. This saw the Order as fundamentally directed to the preaching apostolate. In this view, the traditional life of the brothers was a monastic relic. The constitutions needed to be changed so that the formation, work, and role in governance of the brothers would all be identical to that of the clerics. The only distinctions remaining would be those directly connected to the sacramental function of the ordained. Some of those holding this position went further and, since they viewed the preaching apostolate of the Order as essentially clerical, thought that most brothers should be ordained, at least as deacons, so that they could preach alongside the priests. Consequently, the "lay" brotherhood would eventually disappear.

These radical changes, in the opinion of those holding them, were essential to the religious life of the Church as understood by Vatican II. The author identified the first two positions as most common among the friars, but the "radical" view was not a small minority. In the end, there was a convergence between the author's "conservative" view and that of the "radicals." Both agree that the purpose of the Order is essentially clerical: administration of the sacraments and pulpit preaching. So, brothers should either do traditional domestic work or be ordained.

The same document that contains this friar's observations also includes an anonymous response to them from the "radical" perspective. That author observed that, although many innovations had been made by chapters in the life of the brothers between 1958 and 1965, nothing had been done to address developments in modern culture and society. The changes, like the name "cooperator" and the granting of the white scapular, were paternalistic, mere "crumbs" (*migahas*). *Perfectae Caritatis* 14.14 and *Ecclesiae Sanctae* 2.27, to this author's mind, demanded real *aggiornamento* and made the status quo impossible. For this writer, public preaching is the work and responsibility of the whole community, and brothers must be directly involved in it. Worrying about "dangers" (*peligros*) coming from the clerical status of the Order is misguided. All distinctions between clerics and cooperators that are not related to priestly function should be removed. Objections to such reforms were merely "practico-juridico" stonewalling.[34] These diverse opinions show that, at least in 1965, there was no consensus on how to "update" the brothers. The final frustrated question raised (in capital letters!) by the "conservative" friar was: "WHAT DOES THE ORDER WANT?"

THE BOGOTÁ CHAPTER OF 1965

The preparatory commission for the chapter received numerous petitions from individuals and groups of friars relating to the life of the brothers.[35] A good number of these strongly favored change. First, on liturgy, a French petition asked that the old office of Paters be abolished and that cooperators say the Divine Office like clerics. This, of course, presented the problem of Latin literacy. A petition from Poland urged that all cooperators with Latin be required to go to choir, and that future cooperator students all be trained to sing the Latin Office as clerics did. The theme of greater integration of cooperators with clerics was general. Individual friars from the provinces of Brazil, France, and Toulouse, as well as a group of fourteen clerics from Poland, asked that the chapter abolish as many of the distinctions between clerics and cooperators as possible.

A petition from Lyon asked that the constitutions and Order legislation be systematically revised so that the equality of the two categories would be made more evident. The most concrete symbolic act to end this distinction would be a change in the brothers' habit. A petitioner from Poland not only opposed the different forms of the habit as divisive, he called the black scapular a "relic of feudalism," unfit for the modern age. Along with individuals like that priest from Poland, others from several provinces, including twenty clerics from Brazil, asked for the same change. But the most significant of these petitions, because it was the only one from the brothers themselves, was the request to change the habit signed by fifty-five cooperators from the Province of Naples. It seems that nearly every brother in that province signed it.

Juridically, the most important changes proposed concerned voting rights and election. Support of active voice for the brothers was wide. Petitions in favor came from the provinces of France, England, Brazil, Poland, Lyon, and St. Albert the Great in the United States. The cooperators of Naples were again active: forty-four of them signed a petition asking for active voice. Passive voice, that is, the right to be elected, received less attention. Only a petition from Poland favored allowing brothers to be elected to provincial and conventual chapters.

Against the background of the diversity of opinion, the cooperator commission established by the 1961 Chapter took a "wait and see" attitude.[36] The commission agreed that the cooperator vocation should flourish, but that the time was not ripe for changes in the older juridical structures. Nevertheless, the condition of the brothers could be improved, without inventing a "new kind of cooperator brother." Their consensus was that the historical, canonical, and theological arguments for and against suggested changes were inconclusive and that the Council documents were too easily subject to arbitrary interpretation to provide any real guidance. In addition, the differences of condition and opinion among the provinces were so great that general changes seemed impossible.

Some members did favor major changes in outdated structures, a few even favoring abolition of the clerical status of the Order. Others saw no reason to modify the brothers' life at all. Still others favored "gradualism" and wanted the decisions to be devolved to the provincial level. The commission members were themselves divided between gradualists and those who wanted major changes. As they were not unanimous, the commission urged as much change as possible, but without major structural changes.

The commission was able to agree, virtually unanimously, however, on seventeen proposals for consideration by the chapter. These were grouped under three headings. The first concerned "renewal" of the cooperator formation program, in particular a six-month postulancy, a single novitiate for clerics and cooperators, a postnovitiate period in a well-functioning priory under their own master, the appointment of provincial promoters of the cooperator vocation, and finally a period of technical training following the novitiate. It is interesting that the Holy Name Province diffinitor, Fr. Finbarr Hayes, who would present the commission report to the chapter as a whole, opposed this proposal. It probably seemed to him a pulling back from the more academic program for cooperators in his own province.

The next group of proposals dealt with integration of the brothers into the life of the Order. These included continuing the consultative vote by brothers on admission of new brothers to vows, increased involvement of brothers in catechesis, permission to use vernacular versions of the Breviary instead of the Little Office, and permission for donati to wear the cooperator habit instead of the old tertiaries' habit. A motion to allow individual provinces to abolish the cooperator habit failed. This was more because members wanted to impose the clerical habit on all brothers, than because of opposition to the change itself.

Finally, there came a group of proposals to improve the quality of the cooperator brothers' life. These included annual meetings of the brothers in each province, clerical formators instilling in clerical students greater respect for the cooperator vocation, and making St. Martin de Porres a first-class feast in houses of cooperator formation.

The Bogotá Chapter met in July of 1965. The cooperator brothers were the subject of a "great and long discussion" on 17 July.[37] Given the importance of the Holy Name Province's new cooperator formation program, it is no surprise that the discussion was directed by the diffinitor from that province, Father Finbarr Hayes. He especially emphasized the needs of the modern, well-educated vocations to the brotherhood attracted by his province's program.

The first debate of the day focused on the most contentious issue: active voice in the prioral chapter.[38] Those favoring grant of voice argued from the perspective of fraternal equality as religious, while those opposed argued from the perspective of the canonical status of the Order as clerical. The grant of voice failed by 10 to 28 in a secret ballot. Fr. Hayes and the diffinitor of France, calling attention to the fact that cooperators already had consultative vote on cooperators' admission to vows, moved that a vote be taken allowing the provinces themselves to grant determinative vote to brothers as they saw fit. The vocals defeated this motion by 13 to 25. The issue of active voice, however, would not go away.

The next debate was on changing the cooperators' habit and granting the white scapular.[39] Fr. Hayes moved that the habit be changed, and that provincials and their councils be given until the next general chapter to institute the change. This motion passed and entered into the chapter acts.[40] The remaining legislation on cooperators was uncontroversial and mostly passed unanimously. These decisions included institution of a cooperator novitiate in every province, or, if vocations were insufficient, joint novitiates between provinces. Novitiate was to be followed by three years in a priory under a cooperator brother master.[41] For those finally professed, the old office of the master of brothers was abolished so that brothers now came directly under the local superior.[42]

In the light of the liturgical renewal initiated by the Council, the capitulars determined that all brothers were to be present for all liturgical functions and to participate in them. How the cooperators were to participate in the Latin choral office was left unspecified. If absent, the brothers' daily office obligation could be discharged by saying the Little Office, "any other approved office," or by saying three Rosaries.[43] This effectively abolished the old office of Paters and Aves. Finally, the constitutions and the acts of the chapter were to be redacted so that all the friars be simply called "brother," "as was done in the early days of the Order."[44] An American cooperator brother, who later served in many offices in his own Province and in Rome, later wrote that the Bogotá chapter only made three significant changes in the life of the brothers.[45] It abolished the master of cooperators, allowed final profession after only three years of simple vows (as was the case for clerics), and changed the habit.

In the end, the most visible and lasting effect of the Bogotá Chapter on the brothers was the change in their habit. One brother of Holy Name Province remembers a poll of that province's cooperators, before the Bogotá Chapter, on changing the habit. They were almost unanimously opposed to the change.[46] But when the change came, most were happy about it—as it was understood as symbolizing greater equality in the brotherhood.[47] Brothers I have spoken with all spoke very positively of the change in retrospect. A brother of the Vietnamese Province remembers being overjoyed with the adoption of the white scapular, again as a sign of acceptance and equality in the Order.[48] Enthusiastic reactions to the change were also registered by St. Joseph Province brothers who lived through it.[49] One of those brothers, while admitting that he was a bit miffed about not being consulted on the change, remembered entering the recreation room in the new habit and having a priest greet him by saying "hello" for the first time in his life. He also remarked that during his time in Pakistan during the 1950s, cooperator brothers already regularly wore the white scapular because of the heat.

For some who delighted in the change there remained a certain nostalgia for the black scapular, especially because of its (mistaken) identification with St. Martin de Porres. One Holy Name Province brother, Raymond Bertheaux (1936–2011), after a distinguished life of service in the Chiapas and Guatemala missions, at Santa Sabina, and finally as archivist of his own province, asked to be buried in the black scapular, but hidden, he specified, under the white one he had worn since 1965.[50]

CONSULTING THE BRETHREN

Unlike the Chapter of 1965, where the preparations seem to have been haphazard at best, perhaps because of the rush to respond to the work of the Council, the preparations for the River Forest Chapter of 1968 began almost immediately after the close of that at Bogotá. An important part of this preparation was the compilation of a massive survey. This consisted of some sixty-four questions on the Order, its mission, and its life. The responses to the survey are preserved in the archives of the Order at Santa Sabina.[51] Among these questions, four—N, O, P, and Q—dealt with the brothers.[52] As the responses included those of cooperators themselves, this is one of the first times we can hear brothers reflecting on themselves and the Order.

Although sent to all the entities of the Order, for consideration by all the friars, including novices, only about one-fourth of the friars responded, and only one-fifth of those solemnly professed. Only twenty-eight of the thirty-eight provincial councils replied, but something was received from every province. The questions were in Latin, which discouraged cooperator responses and produced problems even for some clerics. As answers to questions were written out, not chosen from a list, no real quantification is possible. For each question, a summary was, however, produced, outlining the spectrum of views by respondents. Even when factoring in the hesitations and problems encountered of those assembling the data, as a sampling of opinions, the material is suggestive.

Question N asked whether the cooperator vocation, as found in the legislation of the Order, was suited to the needs "of the present time."[53] If there was any general consensus, it is the more than 100 responses emphasizing that the brothers have a share in the Order's apostolate, even without being ordained, and that they should be free to choose any ministry for which they have the aptitude. On the other hand, some 70 respondents, concentrated in the English-speaking provinces, praised the brothers for their service in manual labor. Among the English-speaking respondents, there was strong support (65 replies) for abolishing, as much as possible, the distinctions between priests and brothers, and for granting the brothers active voice in elections (24).

A number of replies from Holy Name (18) and Piedmonte (12) emphasized the importance of cooperators as a reminder of the contemplative life. Some eighteen respondents scattered throughout the Order, but with a block in Spain (5), wanted more rigorous education and higher academic admissions standards. Some 25 replies urged admission of cooperators to minor orders and the diaconate, the largest block (8) being from France. This sentiment shows the massive change in the conception of the brother implied by the change of name from "lay brother" to "cooperator brother." A brother was now simply understood as a friar who was not a priest. The change meant a "cooperator" could also be a "cleric," which he would be, if advanced to minor orders and the diaconate.

Question O asked what could be done to make the Cooperator Brothers' Office (*Officium fratrum cooperatorum*) more effective. This dealt with the brothers' prayer obligations, even though a number of clerics misunderstood the Latin, and thought it was about the brothers' assigned tasks in the house.[54] The replies to this question fell into two basic groups, those who wanted greater incorporation of the brothers into the Divine Office and Mass, and those who wanted the distinct prayer requirements preserved. Over 100 respondents asked for a vernacular Office with the co-operators participating in it. Within one year, with the translation of the Office into the vernacular, and the effective end of separate prayers, this question would become moot.

Question P asked for practical changes that would make cooperator brothers' formation more effective.[55] This question produced the most scattered and diverse responses. The move toward a more academic program in Holy Name Province was reflected in responses from 15 friars from that province and the St. Joseph Province, recommending that all brothers be sent to get a university degree. But twice as many from the English-speaking provinces generally, and from Germany, favored sending the brothers to technical, not academic, programs. The Italians (21) were especially interested in requiring secondary school before admission.

If there was one educational requirement that had wide support throughout the Order (57), especially in the French Provinces, it was improving the brothers' training in theology, Scripture, canon law, and spirituality. This reflects the wide influence of the Holy Name formation program. It is interesting that many friars (67), especially the French, thought that the entire formation program should be reconfigured to match that of other brothers' orders. When mentioned, except by Holy Name and English friars, it was assumed that cooperators should have a separate house of formation from the clerics.

The last question, Q, asked, preserving the canonical status of the Order as clerical, to what extent brothers should be incorporated into governing structures and given voice. Here a generalization is possible.[56] In one way or another, respondents favored, sooner or later, granting of active voice in chapter to the brothers, as well as a vote in the election of the prior. Both positions counted over 100 replies, with the largest single block being the French. Also receiving support from over 100 friars was a proposal granting passive voice for all offices not involving jurisdiction. Only three replies mentioned service on provincial councils specifically.

The council of Holy Name Province drafted a statement on voice. Its members concluded that it was desirable, but depended on the preparation of the brothers, which differed widely from province to province.[57] The cooperators in formation at Kentfield also drew up a statement on voice. They wrote: "The brothers themselves do not wish to acquire positions as major superior. . . . But they should have as much right as anyone else in the order to choose their superiors." In fact, they opposed passive voice for cooperators as superiors.[58] I suspect this reflected the position of younger cooperators throughout the Order as a whole. Finally, appended to the summaries of the responses was a short abstract of directives for the coming chapter in light of the replies to the questions.[59] The conclusions were brief, but significant. The recommendations were four: 1. Cooperators are true religious and true members of the Order. So they should be esteemed as part of the community's work. They are intrinsic to the life, not just externally aggregated. 2. Cooperators should have a cultural formation suitable to each country before admission to novitiate, and that novitiate should be with the clerics. 3. After novitiate, they should receive three years of formation in the novitiate house or a formal priory, with spiritual, cultural, and technical training. 4. Some friars think that expansion of the rights and duties of the brothers should proceed, but with "caution" (*cautela*).

THE 1967 CONGRESS OF PROVINCIALS

In September of 1967, in preparation for the River Forest Chapter of the following year, a congress of provincials was held in Rome.[60] It included a commission on the brothers and produced working documents for the chapter. The commission was chaired by John Hislop of England, and included Hyacinth Bosco of Dacia, José Romero of Betica, and Francis Ward of Holy Name. Experts (*periti*) from Toulouse, Portugal, Netherlands, and Peru also assisted. This commission produced a general statement and a series of proposals to be voted on by the congress as a whole.

The general statement aimed to give a vision of the cooperator vocation.[61] The members all rejected the view that cooperators should only do manual labor. They admitted that they were divided on how precisely to proceed, but all agreed that the Order should recognize the "new" cooperator brothers who did things beside manual labor. The Order needed to affirm that these men were fully part of the Order. The commission praised the brothers' vocation as an antidote for the "intellectualism" rampant in the Order, and recognized their witness to the contemplative aspect of Dominican life, so threatened in an age of activism. Practically, brothers should become part of the house chapter and have active voice. Noting the many requests from friars generally, the brothers should be more fully incorporated into the apostolate of the priests. But the commission recognized that this could not happen without some change from the brothers' "traditional" role of internal domestic work.

The discussion of cooperators by the whole congress opened with a statement by the master of the Order, Aniceto Fernández.[62] He was cautious. The brothers were to be esteemed and to get good spiritual formation. He reaffirmed the clerical status of the Order because its purpose "is preaching and thus clerical." In his view, the brothers shared in this end as "auxiliaries," because they freed the priests to preach. Their formation, therefore, should be for this end, and not "clerical." If a change to direct involvement in preaching was desirable, those brothers qualified should be ordained as deacons.

For Father Fernández, to call manual labor slavery was a pagan, not Christian, view of work. Brothers are sanctified by humility. A good brother, he declared, is a treasure for the community. And the brothers of his acquaintance were happy, more so than many priests. Finally, he praised the Holy Name formation program in Kentfield, which he had just visited. Father George Perreault of Canada replied. He noted the decline of cooperator vocations in Canada and blamed this on the lack of appeal of the old model. Father Jean-Marie Tillard, a *peritus* (non-voting expert), added that, in his opinion, the Council had redefined the mission of the Word as nonclerical. The Order's conception of its end as clerical needed to be revisited. This brought a spirited rejoinder from Father Radulfo de Almeida of Portugal, who praised the simple, illiterate brothers of his province as a model that edified poor and simple people.

The commission then presented eight proposals on which they had voted.[63] The first was a restatement of the definition of the brothers' vocation as truly Dominican. They voted 6 to 2 that the cooperator novitiate be in common with the clerics, but 7 to 1 that postnovitiate formation last three years and be in a separate house from the clerics. More contentious was their failure to reach a conclusion on abolishing the practice of ranking brothers after priests in the order of religion. This proposal failed 3 to 5. Father Kevin O'Rourke, a peritus from St. Albert Province, intervened and noted that in his country young people no longer paid any attention to ceremonial orderings.[64]

The commission was able to achieve greater consensus on the motion to expand the brothers' determinative voice on cooperator admissions and vows, in force since Bogotá, to voice on all matters before the chapter. They remained uncomfortable about how to do this and how to deal with situations where the cooperators numbered over one third of the community. They unanimously agreed that the brothers should be bound to the, now vernacular, choir office. The commission was also unanimous that brothers should have passive voice for all offices not involving orders, even, with some hesitation, that of major sacristan and priory treasurer. Finally, the commission rejected 3 to 5 a recommendation that, if qualified, cooperators be allowed to advance to the diaconate.

The congress as a whole followed all the commission's recommendations on every proposal but the last. They decided to recommend the ordination of suitable brothers as deacons to the coming chapter. Discussion and voting closed with an impassioned defense of the traditional cooperator way of life by Father Vieira of Portugal. He praised the cooperators' service to the Order by manual labor and the models of holiness and humility they presented to the world.[65] The stage was now set for the coming general chapter.

RIVER FOREST AND THE NEW CONSTITUTIONS

The chapter of River Forest, that met outside of Chicago in 1968, was a pivotal one in the history of the modern Order, and of the brothers. This is less because of its acts and legislation than for the new constitutions that were appended to the acts. [66] These constitutions codified changes enacted for the brothers going back to the 1950s. The River Forest Chapter itself made, with one exception, mostly incidental changes for the brothers. In fact, the chapter did not even have a commission on them. Perhaps this is simply a result of the sense that brothers were now so fully integrated into the Order that they no longer needed to be dealt with apart from the clerics.

Some changes in the constitutions, such as providing for a common novitiate and ending division of brothers and clerics in the order of religion, had been long discussed. Much more important was the practical abolition of categories. The justification for separate recreation rooms and chapels, where they still existed, was gone. More important still was the official recognition of the brothers' active voice in chapters, and passive voice for most offices. The chapter continued, however, the disqualification of brothers from the office of prior and provincial, because these involved jurisdiction and so were considered clerical by definition. Although brothers could now serve as capitulars, they could not yet be diffinitors, as that office also involved clerical jurisdiction. It remained unclear if they could be "diffinitors" (voting delegates) at a general chapter. That brothers were, and still are, ineligible to be superiors was criticized by some then, and has remained a topic of debate to this day.[67]

Although there was no commission report and little new legislation exclusively on the brothers, the capitulars did dedicate two long sessions to them. The first of these involved the understanding of the brothers' participation in the apostolate of the Order; the second concerned their ordination to the diaconate. The first issue arose during Session 25 (8 October).[68] The issue was how to include the brothers more explicitly into the statement on the apostolic work of the Order, or to change it so that it would speak of all friars as "brothers" without distinction. A question was raised by Father Alfonso d'Amato of Lombardy. Was it enough simply to say explicitly that cooperators participated in the work of the Order? The master's opinion was that, if this were to be the case, the language should be related to friars' "common priesthood" as baptized Christians.

Father Romero asked why ordination to the diaconate was not mentioned as a means of participation in the apostolate. An objection was raised that deacons were clerics and so not really "cooperator brothers," but clerical brothers. Clearly, the "lay" model of the brother was not dead. To this objection, one vocal noted that "Deacons cooperate with priests," and so a brother-deacon was also a "cooperator." The chapter voted 33–11–3 to mention the brothers specifically, but not to elaborate on the mode of participation. Father Romero then asked that a text be added treating cooperator brothers and the diaconate. The consensus was that this was premature. The final draft of the statement passed 44 to 2.

The issue of the diaconate, however, would not go away. It came up again in Session 41 (18 October).[69] Father d'Amato moved that, in regions where the bishops allowed permanent deacons, provinces be allowed to experiment with cooperator deacons. This passed easily, 40–5–1. Father Rolo then asked how you could "experiment" with permanent deacons, because ordination is permanent. In his view, this affected the clerical structure of the Order. If brothers should be deacons, why not priests? Does the exclusion of brother deacons from the office of superior mean that the Order is not clerical, but priestly? As this debate seemed potentially endless, Master Fernández declared that he favored experimentation, especially in the missions, where there was a shortage of priests. This, he said, would be aggiornamento in the spirit of the Council. A motion to drop the issue failed, 8–38–1, and the master's proposal of experimentation where permitted, especially in the missions, then passed 38–9–0. This decision would pass into the acts of the chapter.[70]

I will close this survey of the cooperator brothers in the 1960s with a brief summary of the legislation affecting them in the constitutions of 1969. These remain, with minor changes, still in effect today. Rather than lose any of the minor later modifications in my ongoing narrative, I will include them here in this summary. These new constitutions were consciously intended to incorporate the insights of Vatican II and the work of the 1965 and 1968 chapters.

The most important change between the 1969 constitutions and those previously in force was the disappearance of a separate section on the cooperators. The constitutions are now understood to apply to cooperators and clerics together, as a whole. This is summed up in the Fundamental Constitution, which declares: "Cooperators are just as much members of the order as clerics."[71] The index of the constitutions clearly notes that, unless it is expressly stated, all laws apply equally to both clerics and cooperators.[72]

But distinctions still remain between the two groups of friars. The first distinction is in the requirements for admission. While some higher education and, in theory, some study of Latin is required of clerical vocations, cooperator applicants needed only "that level of culture" determined by the provincial chapter. By 1984, however, completion of secondary education was required of brothers before admission.[73] In fact, in some provinces, brothers usually enter with at least some college.

The 1969 constitutions provided for the option of keeping separate novitiates for clerics and cooperators. And soon, if a friar underwent a category change, this only required a decision of the provincial and his council.[74] Already in 1969, no second novitiate was needed for the new state.[75] Effectively, this ended the numerous impediments to category change that had been in effect since the 1200s. Later, in 1977, distinct novitiates were abolished and all friars now must make the same novitiate.

The longest section of the constitutions dedicated to the brothers exclusively concerned formation.[76] After novitiate, cooperator students were to have three years of formation under their own student master, at which point they could make solemn profession. Then they were to spend two years in a priory, under the direction of the local superior. During this process, they are to be formed "for their apostolate." The training is to be directed to this work, and may include technical, as well as spiritual and theological, training. Choices are to be made in terms of the needs of the province and the abilities of the brother.

There is nothing to prevent brothers from receiving the same philosophical and theological training as clerics. Indeed, in some provinces, individual brothers were already doing this by the 1970s. In 1984, it was provided that the student master of the cooperators may be a cooperator. But declines in cooperator vocations has meant that, in some provinces, the cooperator students are under the same master as the clerics. After 1992, the regent of studies became responsible for their intellectual formation, as he was for clerics. In short, after 1970, there has been a progressive assimilation of the formation programs for clerics and cooperators, but there remain large differences between provinces.

The 1969 constitutions hold up complete integration of the cooperators into the liturgical life of the community as the goal or even the norm.[77] The constitutions emphasize that the liturgy is the work of the whole community, not just of the clerics. Cooperators who must be absent from the Office are bound to recite Lauds, Vespers, and Compline privately. An exception was made so that a brother, "when there is just cause," might substitute the Rosary for the Office. This legislation appears to have been merely transitional to provide for older and infirm brothers. By 1984, specific reference to brothers had disappeared from the section on liturgy. And, by 1998, the brothers who miss Office were to recite all the hours privately, just like clerics. This completed the process of making the liturgical life of the cooperators more like that of the clerics that had begun with the introduction of the Little Office in the 1930s. The completion of the process was possible because of the near universal abandonment of the Latin Office, a form of prayer that today many, if not most, clerics would find difficult. The old distinction between the Latin and vernacular cultures that had divided the Order from the beginning was gone.

One of the most striking changes introduced by the 1969 constitutions was its discussion of the "cooperator apostolate." The constitutions read:

> Cooperators have a part in the apostolate of the whole community, not only by the labor they provide to the community, but also in the said ministry [i.e. "Holy Preaching"] by cooperating with the priest brothers and by exercising the apostolic activity innate to them.[78]

Furthermore:

> Made participants of the apostolate of the Order by profession, brothers are to be prepared to exercise suitable apostolic activity so that they be true cooperators of the priest brothers.[79]

Although the term "cooperate" is repeated, this legislation contains a tension. On the one hand, brothers "cooperate" in the ministry of their priest brothers by their labor or by assisting them directly. On the other, they may have "suitable apostolic activity" in their own right, not as "cooperating" in the priestly ministry. This reality has led some friars, some as early as the 1970s, to ask whether "cooperation" is an adequate description of the brothers' ministerial and apostolic work. Some have even suggested that the concept and the language of "cooperation" be dropped, and that all friars, ordained or not, be simply called "brothers."

A precocious example of this dedication of brothers directly to their own pastoral ministry was the experience of one brother in the Holy Name Province, himself a product of the Kentfield formation program. In 1970, he was assigned by the provincial to one of the province's university chaplaincies with the instruction to "do campus ministry." He quickly became involved in counseling, catechesis, and even preaching during Mass. He remarked that, other than not celebrating Mass and giving absolution in Confession, his work was identical to that of the priests. And those priests accepted this and received him, with no hesitation, as part of their "pastoral team." In 1977, the brother went on to do identical work in a regular parish.

After that, he became an expert in liturgy and engaged in a full-time itinerant program of liturgical workshops called "Beyond Banners." These workshops were given for both parish priests and laity. Reflecting on the turmoil that marked Church life in the 1970s, he remarked that his move from internal domestic work to public ministry involved little or no tension or conflict with the priests or laity he worked with.[80]

Juridically, the most important change introduced by the new constitutions was the abolition of formal categories and the grant of active and (most forms of) passive voice to the cooperators.[81] Henceforth, cooperators would have the same active voice as clerics in chapters. Initially there was a distinction between clerics, who received voice after ordination and any complementary studies required for faculties, and brothers. The brothers received voice after eight years of vows (or six if they were over age 21 at entrance). By 1972, however, even this distinction was gone, replaced by whatever the "common law" was. In practice, this meant active voice at solemn vows for all friars.

The constitutions retained, and still retain, a distinction as to passive voice.[82] Like clerics, cooperators were eligible to be elected to offices and positions after nine years of profession. But the requirement of priestly orders and faculties was retained for election as prior, provincial, or a diffinitor or socius of a provincial going to a general chapter. Brothers were also ineligible to serve as diffinitors (i.e., members of the governing committee) at provincial chapters. The restrictions on election as diffinitors and socii were dropped in 1974, but the restriction requiring priesthood and faculties remains for superiors.[83] This distinction, the last one dividing priests and cooperators as to voice, continues to be an issue of debate and strong divisions of opinion.

These constitutional changes may seem dramatic on paper, but I was surprised to find, speaking around the world with brothers who lived through them, that they hardly seemed so radical in practice. One brother, who later went on to be ordained a priest, remarked that the disappearance of categories mostly meant, in practice, joint recreation with the priests, something that happened intermittently much earlier. He also observed that the rules against speaking to clerics had mostly ceased to be observed before River Forest. For all intents and purposes, categories were gone in the community of his province with the largest number of brothers, Daniel Murphy High School. So this change, in his Holy Name Province, went little noticed.[84]

Another brother of that province, the one who became a liturgist, said of the granting of active and passive voice that "it just happened." The typical brother of the time, he noted, lived in a small community with no chapter and no elected prior. And, in small priories, prioral elections happened only every three years or so. He admitted that some older brothers, including Raymond Bertheaux, whom, we have noted as being nostalgic for his black scapular, did not like the changes in voice and categories because they seemed to undermine their identity, but they, too, adjusted. This same brother also said that he never felt a sense of inferiority or isolation as a brother, even in the 1950s.[85]

Even in Vietnam, where brothers of the 1970s (and after) still did, almost exclusively, manual labor and there remained a marked educational difference between priests and cooperators, older brothers observed that the constitutional changes happened there with little fanfare. One brother noted that the coming of joint prayer with clerics after the introduction of the vernacular liturgy was a delight. On the other hand, active voice did not seem much of a change from the consultative vote brothers already had.[86] Another, older, Vietnamese brother agreed. Paradoxically, he said of the end of categories and the grant of voice, "these changes had been decided by the Order and I obeyed."[87]

In St. Joseph Province, older brothers' comments differ little from those in California and Vietnam. The constitutional changes happened, and they were welcomed. There was, one brother remarked, little controversy or tension.[88] Like the brothers of

Holy Name Province, another brother noted that, since most houses had little need for chapter decisions and did not vote on students, the granting of voice went little noticed. The limits on passive voice continued to rankle, but during the 1970s it was the tardy abandonment of the term "lay brother" and occasional condescension by priests that were more painful. In particular, the brother noted the continued use of "Dominican Priests" to describe the Order in vocation literature as symbolic of the practical "invisibility" of the brothers.[89]

The "Crisis" of the 1970s

The 1960s were an age of exciting change and, for many, enormous optimism. Theologically and canonically, the brotherhood had undergone a dramatic aggiornamento. The decline in brother vocations that began in the 1930s had caused anxiety, but for most friars, this drop seemed the result of the incompatibility of the traditional life of the brothers with modern attitudes and culture. After River Forest, it seemed to most that this problem was well on the way to being addressed. What followed in the 1970s proved that optimism false. The vocations decline to the brotherhood not only continued, it became more severe, and the number of cooperator brothers began an absolute decline.

I have tabulated the number of living professed brothers as of 2015 in Appendix C (page 292).[90] This throws the brothers' vocation crisis of the 1970s into stark relief. The brothers shared this crisis with the clerics, but it was far more severe. As can be seen, the number of brothers professed before 1950 and still alive today is only 19. These are very elderly men, mostly in their 90s. Death has taken a huge toll. The professions of the 1950s and 1960s are a better benchmark for recruitment. The professions of the 1950s, most of whom are now in their 80s, number still 71, even after many deaths. Some brothers professed in the 1960s have died, and some have left the Order, but mortality has not yet affected this group drastically, as they are mostly in theirlate 60s and 70s. They total 92, the largest age cadre by far.

In comparison, there are, for the decade of the 1970s, only 19 professed brothers in the entire Order. Deaths cannot account for this, as these men are still mostly in their 60s. Contrary to most friars' impressions, recruitment after the 1970s actually improved. From the 1980s, there are 28 brothers; from the 1990s, there are 36; and from the 2000s, there are 52. Certainly, among the older brothers of those thirty years, there have been deaths and departures, but these men are not aged. And the current decade, only half over, seems comparable in numbers to the 2000s. Like the priesthood, one cooperator commented, the brothers benefited from the "John Paul II Vocations." I will say more about these developments in the Epilogue.

What can account for the brothers' demographic crisis of the 1970s? This involved not just fewer vocations. Many brothers recruited failed to profess vows. Others left after profession. And some were ordained priests. There is no question that, at least for clerics, the 1970s vocation crisis, and in particular that of the cooperator brothers, caused enormous anxiety, acrimony, and self-criticism. In contrast, conversations with cooperator brothers who lived through the period reveal little sense that this was a period of crisis.

The first meeting of cooperator brothers as a group in Holy Name Province occurred in January 1970. The "crisis" was then already under way. A brother participant recalled the very positive attitudes of those brothers involved and their good sense of identity. The latter was much the result of the large number of brothers sharing the apostolate at Daniel Murphy High School. He did note that, by the mid-1970s, brothers had absorbed a sense that there was a crisis in the brotherhood, but this was more a response to clerical perceptions and to the debates at general chapters in the period. He said: "Our question was simply, 'What does the Order want from us?'"[91]

The comments of one brother of St. Joseph Province resemble those of brothers in Holy Name Province, as well as those of brothers in Poland and Vietnam. In his opinion, he and his fellow cooperators did not experience the 1970s as a period of crisis for their vocation.[92] Yes, vocations were down, but they seemed even more down for clerics. Brothers continued their work, whether traditional internal ministry or, ever more frequently, active participation in apostolic work. Unlike priests, who were still in controversy over what Vatican II meant for the nature of the priesthood, the brothers generally adjusted and got on with their lives. Rare brothers got ordained to the priesthood; some professed brothers, unable to adjust, simply left. But, he suggested, a fixation on "the brothers' crisis" was more typical of clerics than the brothers themselves.

The depletion of the 1970s cadre of brothers deserves a study in its own right, but this is not the place to undertake it. Conversations with those who lived through the period, however, suggest a spectrum of causes, which when taken together became a "perfect storm." First, there was simply a drop in vocations to the brotherhood. Behind this lay cultural, social, and religious changes that made religious life in general, like the priesthood, less attractive to young Catholics. Men who might have become brothers, like the women who might have became sisters, found the larger choice of options in the world more attractive. Along with decline in supply, brothers noted that some vocation directors just stopped promoting the brothers' vocation. A lack of Latin skills no longer served to track potential vocations into the brotherhood. And the common negative image of the brothers as menials and domestics still remained.

There were also increasing numbers of deaths and departures. The percentage decline in brothers' vocations since the 1930s had made the brothers' age spectrum top-heavy. A group with a larger number of elderly experiences a greater number of deaths. And there were increasing numbers of departures. Some left because they did not like the changes. A historian of the Order notes that the young brothers who entered in the late 1950s and early 1960s often found the changes in their life more difficult to deal with than their older confreres. So they left.[93] In some cases, realities fell short of expectations. In Holy Name Province, a good number of the brothers of Daniel Murphy High School left after the province withdrew from that ministry. And more decided that the best use of their training was to become priests. Finally, as in any time of turmoil, many found that the controversies, arguments, and frustrations outweighed the benefits of remaining in the Order.

The first general chapter of the decade, that at Tallaght, Ireland, in 1971, almost completely ignored the brothers. Perhaps the sense of crisis had not yet set in. Their only mention of the cooperators was to advise caution and to avoid haste in any experimentation with ordination to the diaconate.[94] This negligence was remedied at the next chapter, that at Madonna dell'Arco outside of Naples, in 1974. The chapter itself enacted little concrete legislation affecting the brothers beyond expanding their active and passive voice.[95] And they also urged friars to have a greater appreciation of the brothers as an integral part of the Order.[96] But the historic development was the inclusion of a cooperator, Brother Norbert Fihn (1939–1994) of Holy Name Province, as an invited guest and secretary. At the request of his provincial, he became the first cooperator brother ever to address a general chapter.[97]

Brother Norbert addressed the chapter during Session 14, on 10 September 1974.[98] His words were short, but significant. He first thanked the fathers for allowing him to make such a historic address. He then turned to the topic that was on most friars' minds, the cooperator vocation crisis. He pointed out that his own province was blessed with numerous cooperator vocations, and that this showed that young men, although unordained, wanted to collaborate with priests in their ministry. Declaring himself and his confreres "the successors of Oderic," he observed that the modern brothers' vocation would only flourish if it fit the needs of our time as well as that of the first brother did his. The chapter had to provide ways to allow the brothers to participate fully in the life of the Order. In particular, he asked that all limitations on active and passive voice be removed, and that the brothers' presence at general chapters be institutionalized.

The discussion and questions that followed Brother Norbert's address show the diversity of views among the capitulars. A capitular from the Philippines asked about brothers' formation in Norbert's province. He replied that it was done in the context of the clerical program, but with provisions for technical training. A priest from Spain observed that, along with the vocations decline, he perceived, in his province, confusion of identity for the cooperators who studied with the clerics. Norbert clarified that conditions were different in various provinces. A father from Ecuador, from his own experience, registered grave doubts as to whether cooperators were ready for voice of any kind. He asked: "Do you think the cooperators of your province are ready for voice?" Norbert replied: "Yes. And I think that in the future they will have full passive voice, and that this will not be a big change."

The new master of the Order, Father Vincent de Couesnongle, then intervened. He thanked Brother Norbert for his reflections and promised they would be considered in deliberations. He urged Norbert and the brothers generally: "Embrace our fraternity; changes do not merely depend on me and the chapter." Real change, he implied, involved more than legislation; it required a change of hearts. As if to confirm the significance of the cooperator presence at this chapter, almost exactly one year later, on 28 September 1974, Pope Paul VI canonized St. Juan Macías. As St. Martin de Porres was technically a donatus, St. Juan became the first brother officially raised to the altar. The final action of the chapter concerning the brothers was to establish a commission of ten friars (all clerics), under the presidency of Brother Norbert Fihn, to study and report on the cooperator brothers and their vocation in the Order.[99] The work of this commission and its papers are found today in the archives of the Order, boxed with the records of the 1977 Chapter at Quezon City, where they were presented.[100]

It was probably in preparation for this project that two other leading American cooperator brothers, Ignatius Perkins of St. Joseph Province and Edward van Merrienboer of St. Albert the Great Province, joined with Brother Norbert in chairing a meeting of nine other American brothers in Oakland, California, from 8 to 10 November 1975.[101] Most of these brothers, the document they produced noted, had master's degrees. This meeting passed four resolutions defining the participants' views on the needs of the brothers. They first identified as a priority the study of Scripture and social justice as essential to any reform of the brothers' life. The next concern was the removal of all restrictions on the brothers' active and passive voice in the Order. But they observed that what was most essential was to "create a milieu of the Holy Spirit," rather than to make demands for these changes. And the brothers recognized that these changes involved complex canonical and theological issues. Third, they declared that the diaconate, which had attracted so much attention in recent discussions of the brothers, should not be viewed as essential to the vocation. Finally, they called for more meetings among the brothers themselves. The ideas ventilated in Oakland would be implicit in the work of Brother Norbert's commission.

In preparation for their report, the commission sent a questionnaire to all entities of the Order, with a request that it be completed by 5 March 1977. Twenty-five of the forty-one entities responded. The best percentage response came from South America and Asia. Oddly, no reply was received from Brother Norbert's own province, perhaps because of the 1975 meeting and its report. Canonical and theological papers were requested from experts on the issues involved in granting the brothers full passive voice.

Before examining these replies, and especially those of cooperators, it would be useful to review what statistical conclusions the commission members drew from it.[102] They reported that cooperators are older than clerics, and that most were still involved in traditional internal domestic work (313 of 447 brothers). They could find no significant differences in the numbers of vocations attracted by provinces with more "modern" formation programs and those with programs basically unchanged from before the Council. But, in terms of governance, much had changed: of 25 provinces, 15 had included cooperators in their provincial chapters, and 4 had elected them as councilors. Some 105 brothers were serving on prioral councils, and 15 held provincial offices open to them. As to the diaconate, only 3 had been ordained, but 25 had expressed interest, mostly in mission areas. In response to the move to ordain brothers to the diaconate, the "overwhelming majority" of respondents opposed making this official policy. This is significant as, among clerics, ordination of all cooperators with suitable preparation to the diaconate had, as we have seen, considerable support.

More than in the tabulated statistics, the voices of cooperator brothers are clearest in the two cases where brothers themselves decided to draft their own letters to the commission.[103] Brother Benedetto Zorcolo and four other Angelicum cooperators sent a "Letter to the Master of the Order," dated 16 December 1975.

They decried the lack of cooperators on the commission. They had no faith in it. They declared that the form of input solicited from the brothers was too restricted. On the other hand, they labelled Brother Norbert's 1974 proposal at the chapter of full passive voice for brothers "assurdo"—because the Order is clerical by nature. Instead, they listed four possible real improvements in their life: 1. Full liturgical participation by abolishing the use of Latin at Office. (The Office was, and still is, in Latin at the Angelicum.) 2. Greater integration into the apostolate after the model of Catholic Action. 3. Some institutionalized presence of brothers at general chapters. 4. Better training for the brothers and more respect for their manual work. Too often, they wrote, cooperators are treated as the *proletariato* of the Order and reduced to religious proletarians.

Brother Gerardo Beurze, a Dutch cooperator at the Angelicum, wrote directly to Norbert Fihn on 20 January 1976. He echoed the other brothers' complaint about the absence of brothers on the commission. After outlining the strictly subordinate position of the brothers before the Council, he declared that little had changed. At the Angelicum, he wrote, the brothers "do all the work to maintain house." He thinks this may be a cultural issue in Italy. In contrast, he noted, in Germany, Belgium, and the United States, clerics also work in the kitchen, refectory, and laundry. Many younger brothers ask why they cannot be elected diffinitors to general chapters, but he sees this as no solution to the problem as a whole. Solidarity and symbolic inclusion were for him meaningless gestures. Perhaps, he wrote, all those brothers with the ability should eventually be ordained priests. "Probably within twenty years there will be no brothers left in the Order." All will be dead or priests. His letter seems a counsel of despair.

The provincial of Mexico, Francisco Hernández de Viana, also wrote, questioning the whole purpose of the commission, but from the opposite perspective.[104] For him, all the recent changes had undermined and destroyed the cooperators' identity and their vocation. The downfall began in 1965. He wrote:

> Until the chapter of Bogotá, which changed their scapular, things were more or less right. Now brothers do not want to serve, but

> rather to give orders. They are neither lay brothers nor priests but a 'tertium quid'—undefined, disoriented, ambidextrous, unable to find their place or trade.

He reported that brothers of his province had told him that they could not understand why the black scapular that they wore with such joy was taken away from them. One senses that, for Father Francisco, the situation of the brothers was just as hopeless as it was for Brother Gerardo.

Given the quantity of data and the diversity of views expressed, it is remarkable that Brother Norbert's commission could draw up any conclusions for the coming chapter. But, during a meeting from 4 to 10 October 1976, they did so.[105] Given the diversity of the provinces, they had no recommendation on post-novitiate training. All, including Brother Norbert, concluded that the clerical status of the Order meant no passive voice for brothers to become superiors. Nevertheless, they urged revision of legislation to remove as many distinctions between brothers and clerics as possible. Things said about clerics that distinguish them from cooperators—the obligation to study and the choir office, use of the title "father" in legislation—should be revised to remove the seeming exclusion of the brothers. Manual labor should not be mentioned as specifically a task of the brothers. Finally, they ask whether the term "cooperator" is itself a useful term, as it seems to subordinate the brothers' work to that of priests. One observation they made was remarkably perceptive. They correctly noted that the expansion of the brothers' role in the Order and in ministry was not new. It had been going on since the 1930s.[106]

On the issue that seems to have been on everyone's mind, the diaconate, the commission produced a separate report. They noted that some thought that diaconate ordination, by making the brothers clerics, would automatically solve the problem of passive voice as superiors. They reject this instrumentalization of ordination. Although this seems mostly forgotten by modern friars, the early 1970s was a period when ordination to the diaconate seemed the wave of the future for brothers. One brother I spoke with remembered that all the cooperators of his province were specifically asked if they wanted to be ordained.[107]

Another of the same province reported the same inquiry, but noted that no pressure was involved.[108] The one cooperator of that province who was ordained a deacon said that this happened principally so that the marriages he was already performing in the Pakistan mission "would be valid." He went through a deacon training program and certification even though he had never gotten a high school diploma.[109]

The chapter held at Quezon City in the Philippines the following year would be a watershed event for the brothers. This was less for its actual legislation than for its tone. Like the general chapters for the rest of the century, this one dedicated much time and energy to drafting long position papers reflecting on issues facing the Order. One-fifth of these reflections concerned the brothers. This would be the high-water mark for attention to the brothers at a general chapter. Brothers themselves remember above all as significant one single enactment by this chapter, its apology to the cooperator brothers.[110] It reads as follows:

> This Chapter confesses, in the name of the whole order, that all have often overlooked the great patrimony of St. Dominic. We have failed in promotion of the cooperator vocation and neglected their part in the apostolate of the whole order. . . . We declare that one of the priorities of this chapter is to remedy this negligence.[111]

They went on to write, however, that the chapter intended to make no changes in the laws concerning brothers. They considered the legislation in force sufficient for future evolution and necessary growth. But they were determined to "remove all juridical impediments to the election of cooperator brothers as diffinitors to provincial and general chapters." And so they did. In their one other practical piece of legislation, the chapterrequired a single novitiate for cooperators and clerics and that all cooperators have secondary school education.[112]

The Quezon City Chapter, as was to be expected after all the preparations, had a five-member commission on the "the special vocation of the brothers," chaired by Father Christoph Schönborn, later an archbishop and cardinal. It included a cooperator brother peritus. Its reflections, the most extensive by any chapter to date, are found principally in the fifth chapter of the Proemium of the chapter acts.[113] This essay sought to place the brothers within the life of the Order historically, theologically, and practically. Some of the results seem romantic wishful thinking. For example, this declaration: "The brothers [fratres] of the order, both clerics and cooperators, have always labored together in the preaching of the Gospel and have been vigilant in prayer."[114] Given the restriction of preaching, from Dominic to the modern age, not only to the ordained, but only to those with a formal license to preach, as well as the vast difference between the choir office and the recitation of Paters and Aves, this is more a hope for the future than real history.

Nevertheless, the chapter's work reflected a clear understanding of contemporary realities. They recognized that many brothers were still engaged in internal domestic work, but that others were already involved in theological investigation, Christian instruction, spiritual counseling, and preparation for the sacraments. They also respected the long tradition of charity and service to the poor that marked the history of the brothers. While noting that "charity is not enough," they recognized that freedom from priestly ministry meant that the brothers could dedicate themselves more intensely to work "among prisoners, immigrants, and youth," and that they could serve as "probation officers, social workers, and directors of youth clubs."[115]

The chapter also insisted that the brothers' formation be adapted to the growing diversity of their mission. However, when attempting to ground this in Dominican history, the authors drift again into romanticism. They claim: "Dominic desired the vocation of the cooperators to be characterized by works of administration and charity through which, in a special way, the Order would meet its evangelical obligation to the poor." A noble vision for modern brothers, even if little evidenced in actual history.

The Quezon chapter also dealt briefly with the question of the diaconate. They provided that a prior provincial and his council might designate suitable cooperators for ordination to the diaconate.[116] Few seem to have taken this option. In the end, diaconate ordination of cooperators would happen almost exclusively in the missions—and there, rarely. In the Philippines, when the idea of deacon ordination was broached, not a single brother wanted to be ordained.[117] On the other hand, Brother Norbert Fihn, himself, in 1977, asked for a leave of absence to discern whether he should ask for dispensation from vows. He did decide to return to the Order and went on to be ordained a deacon in 1987. When he died in 1994, he was considering asking for the priesthood. Such a decision to be ordained a priest would eventually be taken by six of the other "educated cooperators" of Holy Name Province.

"THE COOPERATOR BROTHER QUESTION"

I have entitled this section "The Cooperator Brother Question" because the two decades between 1977 and 2000 were a period during which clerics, especially at general chapters, attempted to resolve, to their own satisfaction at least, the nature of the cooperator vocation in the light of the Council and modern realities. In this period, the voices of the brothers themselves became less audible than in the period of the 1960s and 1970s. The concerns of the Order's leadership itself seemed to focus elsewhere. This is not to say that the gains were lost, but that the attention of the capitulars drifted. Those who study the period have remarked on this.[118]

On the other hand, from this point forward, a cooperator peritus was always present at the chapters. Brother Edward Van Merrienboer not only was present at Walberberg (1980), but he also spoke on all issues, not just on those concerning the brothers. Petitions were regularly received from the provinces, asking that the law be changed to allow brothers to be elected superiors. This was considered again at Rome (1983), where Brother Pedro Blanco served as peritus. At Ávila (1986), the possibility of cooperators as superiors was debated inconclusively for over an hour. As a result, the master was asked to commission a study on the topic.[119] As the decade ended, the Church herself joined in recognizing the sacrifices of the brothers. On 18 October 1987, Pope John Paul II gave the Order two new brother saints by canonizing the martyr companions of St. Dominic Ibáñez at Nagasaki, St. Francis Shoyemon and St. Matthew of the Rosary Kohioye. This event doubled the number of canonized brothers.

The discussions and debates about the cooperators and their

vocation during the 1990s were well summarized as the decade was about to begin by the master of the Order, Damian Byrne, in his *relatio* for the Chapter of Oakland (1989).[120] Father Damian noted that the previous chapter of Ávila did not repeat earlier requests for a commission on the brothers. Rather, it asked the master to investigate the possibility that they be superiors. The master reported that he had carried on conversations with the superiors of various religious orders on this, but that the atmosphere was mixed, even within congregations including both brothers and priests. He emphasized that the brothers had accomplished great work for the Church and the Order. For some, he said, continual debate about passive voice is a distraction. He noted the brothers' declining numbers and called this a great loss.

In closing, Father Damian pointed out the growing variety of ministry done by brothers. Some still did domestic service. Others taught in schools or did catechesis, and some even served as deacons. In the light of this, he asked, should admissions requirements and formation be the same for all? He thought the move to require brothers to do the same "substantive" courses as clerics inflexible. Brothers needed to give "wise counsel," but not to be theologians. A reform of their formation, making it more academic, would become another concern of chapters in this period. Damian had doubts about such a change and its effect on recruitment. It would effectively eliminate older and less academically-gifted vocations. Perhaps such older men and younger vocations should be treated differently. He said: "We might even consider receiving older men as *donati* with the possibility of eventual incorporation into the Order for a particular house within the Order."

Other masters and friars made similar reflections during the successive chapters. The Mexico City Chapter published a statement on cooperators in 1992.[121] They asserted that the chapters of Madonna dell'Arco and Quezon City had sufficiently reflected on how the brothers were "complementary and in solidarity" with priests and that they "partake of the apostolate of the Order because of their vocation." So, they said, the brothers not only provide for the needs of the house but serve "also in ministry as such." They listed fields of ministry as "catechesis, academic teaching, nursing, economy, journalism, etc." But, for them, the images of Martin de Porres and Juan Macías validated a brother's work as "carpenter, mechanic, engineer, and general helper" as well. Like Master Byrne's remarks, the growing variety of work called into question the movement to create a unitary formation program. The same chapter urged promoters of cooperator vocations to emphasize their variety of service.[122]

But, as Master Timothy Radcliffe noted in his 1995 *Relatio*, this growing variety of ministry had not, at least in his opinion, stopped the decline in vocations.[123] In fact, he suggested that it had made it worse. He noted that there were only fifty-nine simply professed brothers in the Order, and that they were found in only nineteen entities. Thirty-three entities had none in formation at all. He praised the brothers and their witness. And, he said, this decline is not just because of the drop in vocations generally. "This decrease in vocations is due only in part to the shortage of applications. Many provinces do not have a clear vision of how our cooperator brothers are called to take part in the mission of the Order."

Legislation on formation mirrored the tension between the diversity of cooperator ministries and the desire for a common program of studies, or at least one less distinct from that of clerics. Mexico City (1992) directed that cooperator formation reflect Dominican life generally and include "progressive introduction into the apostolate," as was done for clerics.[124] The Provincial Chapter of the Philippines, that same year, was notable for the space devoted to the brothers.[125] The movement to assimilate their formation to that of the clerics was clear. After novitiate and a year of spiritual formation as cooperators, they were to do two years of theology, covering the same materials as the clerics. Like clerics, they were to be assigned to parishes and active houses during summers and holidays so that they would be integrated into the "full active life" of the province. The Philippine capitulars praised their one cooperator brother dedicated to full-time preaching and the two assigned to Santa Sabina. Finally, they urged the canonization of Brother Gregorio Hontomin, who had never worked outside the community and had mostly served in building maintenance. They seemed not to sense the possible irony.

The Chapter of Caleruega (1995) noted that the new *Ratio Studiorum Generalis* provided, for the first time, a single outline for clerical and cooperator studies, although it allowed provinces to adapt for specific needs.[126] The Chapter of Bologna (1998) continued the assimilation of the two formation programs.[127] Cooperators were to do the prenovitiate, as well as the novitiate, with the clerics. They were to get at least three years of philosophy and theology, as well as courses in Church history, moral theology, and the economics of pastoral practice. Brothers were also to receive instruction on the variety of ministries "and on Sacred Orders in the Church." Provincials were to see to any necessary professional or technical training, but this was to be, if possible, in the (clerical) house of studies.

This assimilation of cooperator and clerical formation does have a spiritual logic. Since the Council, Dominican reflection has focused on reappropriating "preaching" as the task, not just of the ordained, but as a responsibility of the whole community. At least one writer, however, questioned the historical basis for the assertion that the whole community "preaches." He rejected the idea that all friars "preach," that is, that an active Ministry of the Word is the defining mark of every friar. He even asserted: "If there is to be any future for lay brothers in the order, we need to re-emphasize their lay distinctiveness." That is to say, rehabilitate internal domestic service as their primary end.[128]

But this friar was a lonely voice. More common was the position that, given that the "whole community preaches," cooperators literally preach. In the context of medical and social work, and the care of poor and marginalized, not to mention "parish ministries," brothers can speak of God. They need not mount the pulpit at Mass to do this.[129] This expansion of the definition of "preaching" was adopted by the Chapter of Krakow (2004): "We are all co-operators in preaching of the Gospel . . . and some are ordained." Indeed, according to the friars at Krakow, no brother can exclude himself from the responsibility of preaching.[130]

As this movement toward ever greater convergence between clerics and cooperators in ministry and studies, at least conceptually, was occurring, another issue festered. Since the granting of active and passive voice in the 1970s, one disability remained. Brothers could not, and still cannot, be elected superiors. Only ordained priests were considered eligible to exercise jurisdiction over priests. For many, this disparity meant, for all the language of fraternity and equality, unjust discrimination. For others, the prohibition was essential to the nature and end of the Order.

Masters of the Order and chapters, beginning with Master Damian Byrne and the Chapter of Oakland, tried to find work-arounds. Four years later, the Chapter of Mexico City asked that postulations and requests for dispensations be made to the Holy See.[131] Timothy Radcliffe, at the Chapter of Caleruega (1995), reported that he was working with leaders of the other mendicant orders to have Rome allow full passive voice, and that one postulation of a cooperator as prior had been granted.[132] The Providence Chapter (2001) again asked the master to petition through the procurator general for Rome to allow brother superiors.[133] And, in 2004, the Krakow chapter, after much intense, if inconclusive, debate, again asked the master to apply for dispensations and for a formation of a commission to study "the history and precise significance that we are a 'clerical order.'"[134]

In contrast, at just about this time, the Holy See began to exhibit resistance to further dispensations. Consequently, this disability has become, and remains at least at this time, a neuralgic issue. This book is not the place to rehearse all the arguments for and against full passive voice, but I will flag the spectrum of opinions for those seeking further reading. Some have suggested that the Order ask to be reclassified as "mixed" rather than "clerical," an idea that has generated strong objections.[135] In fact, a powerful theological and historical argument has been made that the nature of the Order is not only clerical, but, in terms of its preaching mission, essentially priestly.[136]

Meanwhile, one Dominican canonist has argued that brother superiors are theoretically possible, if acts of clerical jurisdiction attached to the office were delegated to a priest.[137] In contrast, another Dominican canonist has suggested that, since ecclesiastical courts exercise jurisdiction and have lay judges, the exclusion of brother superiors is merely positive law and could be changed.[138] In any case, in the words of a distinguished cooperator brother: "At this moment, the Cooperator Brothers are as equal under our laws as Church law will permit."[139]

The last chapter of the decade, that at Bologna (1998), included in its acts a long section on the brothers, entitled "Cooperator Brothers in the Mission of the Order."[140] It is not necessary to summarize this essay as it reflects currents typical of the 1990s; that is, the struggle to provide a coherent image of the brothers' vocation that encompasses their diversity of apostolates and does not degrade domestic work. Likewise, it struggles with the relationship between these works and the ministry of Dominican priests. In the light of the changes since the Council, Bologna asserted that it is not enough to say that the brothers "cooperate in the mission of the ordained friars." Instead the capitulars declare: "Today brothers can engage in the direct and explicit preaching mission of the Order." Finally, they conclude: "We must reflect on whether the title "co-operator should not be dropped and [that we] acknowledge that we have both ordained and non-ordained friars in the Order of Preachers." Whether the brothers have to "cooperate" in priestly ministry at all was probably the central clerical question about them at the end of the millennium.[141]

THE COOPERATORS ANSWER

I have called the previous section "The Cooperator Brother Question." This section is called "The Cooperators Answer." Notice that "cooperators" is not possessive, and that "answer" is a verb. During the years after the millennium, unlike the 1990s, when discussion of the brothers seems dominated by clerics, the brothers themselves, through their own commissions and meetings, began to voice their own concerns and requests. During this period, there were two brothers' commissions that solicited input and drafted reports. Each deserves a study in its own right. I will merely summarize each of them. But first, I want to call attention to further recognition of the heroic brothers of the past by the Church herself. On 11 March 2001, Pope John Paul II beatified the six brothers martyred as companions of Bl. Hyacinth Serrano López during the Spanish Civil war. And six years later, on 28 October 2007, Pope Benedict XVI beatified the eighteen brother companions of Bl. Bonaventure Garcías y Paredes in the same conflict.

The first brothers' commission of the new millennium produced a report in 2003. This process had been mandated by the 2001 General Chapter at Providence, Rhode Island. At this chapter, three American cooperators were present and participated, Brothers Ignatius Perkins, Herman Johnson, and Angel Mendez. Brother Ignatius presented a statement on his experiences and the challenges facing the brothers.[142] In the report, he listed five "challenges to the chapter": 1. To remove barriers to the brothers' recruitment, formation, and apostolates, many of which he considered as much "attitudinal" as legal. 2. Greater respect for the differences between provinces and recognition of new initiatives. 3. Establishment of a more collaborative approach to recruitment, formation, and ministry.
4. Appointment of an assistant to the master for the brothers. And,
5. Appointment of a commission to facilitate these needs.

At the chapter, the outgoing master Timothy Radcliffe spoke of the brothers in his report on the state of the Order.[143] He decried the often overly "clerical" perception of Dominican identity and linked this to the drop in cooperator vocations. He also noted his dislike for the label "cooperator" for the brothers. He praised the meetings of brothers that were being planned in Central America and hoped they would be expanded. Finally, he registered his concern that vocation directors do not sufficiently promote the brothers' vocation. The chapter did treat the brothers, but other than providing that the director of cooperator formation after novitiate may be a cooperator, and a request that the previously mentioned commission be created to examine Order legislation to recommend possible changes, most texts addressing the brothers were hortatory.[144]

In response to Brother Ignatius's challenges and the chapter's mandate, the new master of the Order, Carlos Azpiroz Costa, appointed a commission of seven brothers. They were Pedro González (Spain), Edgardo González Falcon (Puerto Rico), Peter

Keteh (Nigeria), Joseph Nguyen Thang (Vietnam), Quirico Pedregosa (Philippines), James Ryan, and Edward van Merrienboer (both of St. Albert the Great). This commission met first in 2002, at Rome, in consultation with experts in canon law, theology, and history.[145] They decided to send a single questionnaire to the provinces. After reviewing the opinions of the experts, and the replies to the questionnaire, the commission met from 29 September to 1 October 2003 and prepared their report.

The first part of the report surveyed the results of the questionnaire, to which about one-third of the friars had responded, including 174 cooperators.[146] It was found that only forty-one entities had a program to promote cooperator vocations. Two-thirds of the entities used the term "cooperator," while the rest simply used "brother." They found that cooperators were involved in very diverse ministries. They listed them: sacristan, catechist, porter, financial administrator, secretary, education at all levels, health care, youth ministry, retreat, and social work. Two-thirds of cooperators were formed in joint programs with clerics. Fifty-eight percent of respondents favored granting dispensations so that brothers could be superiors. Finally, nearly all reported that brothers were incorporated into provincial community life, but less so into studies. The authors of the report registered concern that most respondents (who were themselves mostly clerics) were comfortable with the status of the Order as a "clerical entity," and that they accepted the linkage of authority to clerical jurisdiction as the formal reason for excluding brothers from being superiors.

The commission's recommendations were not extensive. Three involved greater involvement of brothers in formation, increased roles of leadership, and continuing petitions to dispense cooperators postulated as superiors. The two others were recommendations to encourage studies, both by cooperators themselves and by clerics, on the nature of priesthood. Finally, they requested that a history of the brothers be written and that there be more meetings of the brothers. At least in the last two cases, some progress has been made.

The second process, studying the brothers, which was much more extensive than that commissioned by Providence, was mandated by the General Chapter of 2004 at Krakow, Poland.[147] It resulted in twelve study papers, a roundtable discussion at Santa Sabina, 25 to 26 May 2006, and the issuing of a Summary Report. The Krakow chapter did not legislate extensively on the brothers, perhaps because they sensed that this could not be done until the commission completed its report. The chapter did exhort the master to ensure that brothers were present at all general chapters, and it confirmed the provision of the previous chapters allowing for a cooperator novice master for novice brothers.[148] Otherwise, the acts were mostly hortatory.[149]

The subsequent commission, which met in May of 2006, consisted of Vito T. Gomes, José Saul Hernández, Charles Morerod, Christian Steiner, and Quirico Pedregosa. None of these participants were cooperators, but one, Brother Ignatius Perkins, was invited to attend the commission meetings. I will not attempt to summarize all twelve study papers prepared for the Commission meeting, except to note that a large percentage dealt with the status of the Order as "clerical" and what that meant in historical and current canon law.[150] This reflects the continued frustration of many that this status seems to mean exclusion of brothers as superiors. The historian who wrote the historical study for the earlier commission simply resubmitted it.[151] Among the papers there are only two by cooperator brothers. Brother Betto C. Christo of Brazil prepared one on the apostolic nature of the Order, and Brother Ignatius Perkins had one on re-envisioning the cooperator vocation and ministry. Both were fundamentally "theological."

Brother Ignatius's is perhaps the most important of the twelve papers, if only because it was the most wide-ranging and practical.[152] First, he expressed frustration with the obsessive concern over the clerical status of the Order, which he did not believe needed to be changed. He noted that chapters have, since Madonna dell'Arco (1974), tried to integrate the brothers into the life, governance, and mission of the Order. For him, the problems are more attitudinal than legal. The first priority should be changing exclusivistic clerical attitudes. As a practical way to do this, he outlined a model formation program for his own province that sought to address attitudes among both clerical and cooperator students, and to foster a more collaborative approach to the ministry of "preaching" in all its forms. He also noted that the history of the brothers requested by the previous commission had not been written.

The commission's final report systematically covered several areas of concern. First, historically, it recognized that conversi existed from the beginning of the Order and were primarily dedicated to the care of the monastery's temporalities. They also recognized that brothers have, almost from the beginning, done many other things. Finally, they recognized that the brothers never preached in the formal sense, but they were considered equally religious in spite of that.

On canonical issues, the report recognized the clerical status of the Order and noted that there is no category of "mixed" congregations. As superiors exercise authority in both internal and external forums, they must be priests. But dispensations and accommodations for brothers as priors have been given. In addition, nothing prevented brothers from preaching in church, except for the homily at Mass. Theologically, the commission reaffirmed that religious life (of both priests and brothers) is rooted in our common baptism. They also observed that the term "cooperator" may not be helpful, as it might imply a hierarchy, in which the brothers find their meaning by "helping priests." They emphasize that the presence of brothers prevents communities from becoming mere priestly associations with no religious or contemplative character.

The commission also made thirteen "recommendations" for reflection or action at the next, Bogotá, chapter. In terms of their goals, one group of recommendations attempted to foster common religious identity. The next chapter, they said, should also identify the unique aspects of the cooperator vocation. The commission saw these goals as to be fostered by improving formation. Finally, some concrete actions were proposed: These were composition of a book on the history of the brothers, promotion of brother vocations, greater involvement of brothers in governance, and naming of a socius to the master for the brothers. Although not issued by the commission itself, Brother Ignatius Perkins' unofficial summary of the commission and its

Report raised the underlying question for reflection today: given the decline in the number of brothers, what does this mean for the life of the whole Order? And what would it mean for the Order to become one solely of priests?[153]

Two commissions had now presented comprehensive studies and serious reflections on the status of the brothers. To digest this material and act on it would be difficult. The next two chapters did not address this brothers' project directly. At the 2007 General Chapter in Bogotá, where Brother Ignatius represented the cooperators, the master Carlos Azpiroz Costa did not mention the brothers in his report on the state of the Order.[154] The chapter did, however, recommend that the special state of the brothers be reflected in the *Ratio Studiorum Generalis* and those of the provinces.[155] Most significantly, it declared, in the only statement on the brothers, that "We are all cooperators, with distinct apostolates, all collaborators in the same mission." The Dominican understanding of preaching needs to be "declericalized."[156]

The 2010 General Chapter of Rome included as the cooperators' representative Brother Marcel Côté of Canada, who had served nearly his entire religious life in internal ministry asa cook. Along with reviewing the work of the various commissions since 1998, and the "extensive" reflection of previous chapter on the brothers, this chapter mandated something of great importance: Regional meetings of the brothers, to be followed by a general meeting during 2013 in Lima, Peru.[157] This would be the first time that brothers throughout the world were officially to meet among themselves and speak on their vocation today.

Epilogue
Brothers of the New Millennium

In this epilogue we shall listen to the voices of the brothers today, and see how they envision themselves and their vocation. To do so, I will draw first on their own reflections, in the reports of the regional meetings and the Lima Conference of 2013. I will then draw on conversations I had with brothers around the world, in 2016, as I prepared to write this book. As for the last fifteen years, nearly all the new brothers were professed in the English-speaking, Polish, or Vietnamese provinces, my oral history focuses on them. They are, in particular, "the brothers of the new millennium."

First, however, because it sometimes dominates discussions of the cooperator vocation, we need to take a look at statistics for the brothers and brother vocations. To many friars, it seems that the brothers face continued decline in numbers and possible extinction. The statistics are actually more complex. Since the 1980s, the number of newly professed brothers has actually increased every decade (Appendix C, p. 292). New professions have gone from 28 in the 1980s, to 36 in the 1990s, to 52 in the 2000s. And the current decade seems at least equal to the previous. This does not mean that the number of brothers will not decline. Through deaths and departures, the number of brothers has declined by nearly 75% since 1967, and, even more striking, by 60% since 1980 alone. Since 1967, brothers have declined from 13% of all professed to just 5% today. We should remember that in 1931, they were still 20% of the Order. In addition, the age cadre of brothers over 75 years old accounts for about two-thirds of those alive today. Even if vocations were to double, human mortality means a declining number of brothers for at least the next fifteen years.

On the ground, the situation is vastly different according to provinces. This can be seen in Appendix A (p. 288), which like the following summaries is complied from the data available to me in 2016. Some large and growing provinces, like India or Nigeria, have no brothers or virtually none. In contrast, Canada had 23 brothers according to my most recent statistics, of which only 3 were under 70. Spain is even more aged. Of 32 brothers, only 2 were under 70, and 16 were over 80. Colombia, in contrast, had a brothers' vocations boom in the 1990s, but more recently has professed only 1 brother. France has not professed and retained (with the exception of the Scandinavian mission) a single brother since 1965. This is like Australia, where there have been no cooperator vocations since 1960, except recently in their vicariate of the Solomon Islands. In contrast, there are provinces like St. Joseph in the United States. That province went for 40 years without a cooperator vocation, but in the last 10 years, it has professed 5.

According to the statistics that I received, current as of 31 December 2015, there were, worldwide, 21 brothers in formation, of whom all but one were in Vietnam, Poland, or English-speaking entities (St. Joseph, St. Albert, and the Solomon Islands). So, the modest increase in cooperator vocations has been increasingly concentrated in a very small number of entities. I will say a little more about this at the end of this epilogue.

VOICES FROM LIMA

What did the brothers say about themselves at the regional and Lima meetings? These meetings were initiated by the General Chapter of Rome.[1] The final report on them, which included summaries of the regional meetings, the report of the Lima Meeting, and an Executive Summary, was officially issued on 1 September 2013. Copies were sent to the superiors of all provinces and entities. In his cover letter of 6 December 2013, the master of the Order, Bruno Cadoré, asked all the friars to study these documents. The following summary is not a substitute for that study.[2]

The meeting process was directed by a committee of brothers from Toulouse, Congo, Vietnam, and Poland, under the chairmanship of Brother Ignatius Perkins of St. Joseph Province. The provincials were charged with organizing the nine regional meetings. One-hundred-eighty brothers, just about half those living, attended the regional meetings, submitted written responses, or contributed reflections in some form. Considering the advanced age of many brothers, this was a good showing. The Executive Summary identified the following as the major areas of discussion at the regional meetings: Renewal of the Order and the brothers' vocation for the New Evangelization, the identity and dignity of the brothers, and their role in community life, recruitment, formation, ministry, interprovincial cooperation, and governance.[3] To those who have read my summaries of earlier commissions, these topics should not come as a surprise.

The Summary also registers the brothers' commitments and concerns: Cooperator brothers love the Church and are committed to its service. They see themselves as essential to the New Evangelization. They take personal responsibility for their own renewal and have a commitment to study. They are concerned about their dropping numbers, and with their frequent lack of integration into the apostolates of the Order and the life of their local communities.[4] In preparation for the regional meetings, facilitators sent out seven topics for discussion: 1. "Hopes and fears." 2. Cooperator identity. 3. What sustains the vocation and what is the vision of its future. 4. Elements that attract vocations. 5. How can the vocation be renewed? 6. Topics for discussion at the international congress. 7. Items to communicate to the master. A short review of the reports from the regional meetings shows that, beyond their common concerns, the cultures of the brothers throughout the world are quite diverse. This diversity is shown by the very different ways they went about this project.

The brothers meeting in Argentina, for example, in their short report, focused on their spiritual development and how they can preach. They flagged as venues of preaching the social media, arts, education, and health care.[5] The short biographies they included indicate that older brothers serve more in internal ministries, while younger ones engage more in apostolates outside the community.

The Canadian brothers chose not to compose a comprehensive statement, but to collect individual observations. These show clearly the concerns of an aging brotherhood. While they remain concerned about "clericalism," the Canadian brothers' greatest concerns involve aging. They lament the loss of visibility (e.g., not wearing the habit in public), the drastic decline in vocations, and the loss of Catholic culture in French Canada. While they note that the few new cooperator vocations do not do manual labor or domestic work, as most of the older brothers do, they are happy with that. In spite of these concerns, the older brothers are not negative; they believe their prayers are essential to the life of their communities.[6]

Very different are the responses from the meetings in areas where organized meetings and reports do not seem to fit into the cooperator-brother culture. For example, the brothers meeting in Congo supplied the schedule of their meetings and identified local needs, which are promotion of vocations, better training, and diversification of ministries.[7] That was the entirety of the report. The shortest of all the reports came from the brothers gathered in Toulouse. They sent a list of the events and a note of appreciation for the opportunity to gather and enjoy good cheer. They may have believed this sufficient because an article was to be published on the French brothers in a coming number of *Revue du Rosaire*.[8]

The brothers meeting in Mexico registered their frustrations, but they acknowledged their own responsibilities. The older brothers remarked on their own invisibility and their sense of marginalization. Formerly, they served their communities in domestic work. Now the friars hire lay people to do their traditional tasks. So the brothers are replaced by paid help. They remark on how this "secularizes their own vocation." They wonder about the lack of a clear vision for the brothers' vocation. Present needs risk turning brothers back into servants for priests, or clericalizing their functions because of a lack of priests. A separate report on the Mexican Province's formation program also flagged the tendency to use the brothers to make up for the inadequate number of priests. They identified as problematic the subtle pressure to clericalize the brothers by ordaining them deacons.[9] But mostly the brothers are positive and hope that changes in formation will address the whole person, spiritually and professionally. They are happy that more options are becoming available for them to study theology and philosophy, but according to their own abilities.[10]

Perhaps the most negative report came from the brothers of the United States, contrary to what we might expect, given the recent upturn in vocations there. This report consisted of (anonymous) quotations from brothers grouped under the discussion questions. Brothers complained that cooperators are looked down on, discriminated against, and frequently marginalized. The brothers are hurt and offended that most "reforms" of their role in Dominican life have been merely "cosmetic." At least one brother thinks that these problems are rooted in clerical misunderstandings of priestly identity. Several participants noted that the Order and the provinces have no coherent vision of a cooperator vocation. More positively, they identified and named their charism as preaching and offered suggestions for promoting vocations.[11] In addition, three jubilarian brothers from St. Joseph Province submitted their own, very positive, summary of their experiences living their vocation over many decades of change.[12] But one of the youngest, and one of the oldest, brothers both contrasted the proliferation of clerical talk about "social justice" with the continued marginalization of the brothers.[13]

In contrast to the United States, the Vietnamese brothers registered the most positive view of their vocation and life. For each of the 38 brothers present, the report gave a summary of his ministry and recent accomplishments. The image was one of prayerful, hard-working, joyful men. They noted that the average age of Vietnamese brothers has dropped since 1990 from the 60s to the 40s. They included a report on the rapidly growing devotion to St. Martin de Porres in Vietnam, a campaign begun by a cooperator brother, Joseph Nguyen Huu Hoa. If my perceptions from visiting the country are correct, St. Martin seems to have become one of the "national" saints of Vietnam. The brothers do admit that they face difficulties; too often a brother lives and works alone in a community of clerics. Vietnamese lay people, they noted, often show partiality and greater respect for priests. Finally, there is a sense that brothers often end up "just doing whatever seems useful."[14]

The international congress of brothers met in Lima, Peru, from 31 October to 2 November 2012. It included brother representatives from twenty-four entities. The summary of the conference issued as part of their report contrasts with the diversity of the regional meetings. Those assembled did reach a considerable degree of consensus on their hopes for the future. They asked for better vocation literature and the appointment of a cooperator vocation director in each entity. They desired greater flexibility in their formation programs and better preparation of formators for the specific needs of the brothers—but two representatives expressed the opinion that their program should be identical to that of clerics.

All favored more regional meetings and greater promotion of the cult of Martin de Porres. And, again, they asked for the composition of a history of the brothers. In terms of the constitutions of the Order, they urged that any structure or rule restricting the use of brothers' talents and gifts be changed. They were discouraged that chapters keep issuing recommendations that no one seems to follow. They want, instead, legislation mandating needed changes and the enforcement of that legislation. In particular, they asked that a cooperator, with full voting rights, be assigned for each general chapter. Finally, they asked all friars to pay more attention to the brothers, and that all those in formation get better instruction on the nature of the brothers' vocation.[15]

The drafters of the Executive Summary catalogued over 50 recommendations to the master of the Order, but they flagged several as most urgent.[16] First, they recommended that a renewal plan be prepared for the entire Order, including a special renewal plan for the brothers. Second, they asked that a socius of the master be appointed for the brothers. Third, they asked that the history of the brothers be completed by the Feast of St. Martin de Porres, 2016. Fourth, they requested that all legislation and chapter acts be revised to include cooperators, as much as possible, in every level of governance. Fifth, they asked that another international meeting of the brothers be planned. They recommended that, during the Eight-hundredth Jubilee of the Order, the cooperator vocation be highlighted. And finally, they asked the master of the Order to issue a pastoral letter on the brotherhood and propose to the Congregation for Institutes of Consecrated Life publication of a document on the life of brothers in the Church. And that document was issued in 2015.

A provisional version of this report was presented to the general chapter at Trogir (2013), where Brothers Joseph Mai Van (Vietnam) and Joseph Trout (St. Albert) commented on the Lima Congress. The capitulars praised the meeting's results and thanked the brothers for what they had accomplished, even if the chapter did not yet feel ready to legislate in response to it.[17]

The Lima Process and Congress was indeed a true landmark in the history of the Order. Not only was it the first international event planned and conducted by brothers themselves, it is the first time that the brothers, as a whole, have publicly reflected on their vocation and concerns in the Church.

LISTENING TO THE BROTHERS

As I have noted, according to the statistics made available to me, the young brothers in formation were concentrated in the American Provinces, Poland, and Vietnam. Time and logistics eventually determined that my visits would be to those three regions, as they accounted for 86% of the brothers in formation and a very high percentage of those brothers newly in ministry. My focus in these interviews was on how the friars were attracted to the brotherhood, how they experienced fraternal life and ministry, and what their aspirations are for the future. As it is a common concern, I also attempted to identify what might account for the successes in brothers' recruitment in those regions. Two regions, the United States and Poland, have a number of phenomena in common so I will discuss them first. Then I turn to the unique situation of Vietnam.

The brotherhood in all four American provinces shows certain qualities in common. Excluding those exclaustrated, there are today 33 cooperator brothers in the four provinces. They are concentrated in St. Joseph Province (10) and St. Albert Province (13). All four provinces had a long dry spell during which no brothers professed and persevered. As Holy Name Province pioneered modern brothers' formation in the Kentfield Program, I will begin there. Of the older cooperators in the province, the last to profess did so in 1963. The next vocations came in the 1990s. So Holy Name Province went nearly thirty years without a vocation to the brotherhood. In the 1990s, there was a sudden uptick in vocations. At one point, four student cooperators were living in their own house of formation at a parish in Los Angeles. All left. The consensus is that this was due to poor admissions screening and problems in the senior community of that house.[18] Since 2003, Holy Name Province has solemnly professed two brothers and had one other complete the novitiate. The professed brothers both have technical training and do province service. One is the province webmaster; the other is infirmarian of the house of studies in Oakland. Both entered already well educated. The novice, who was a certified public accountant, choose not to renew his simple profession. My conversations with Holy Name cooperator brothers revealed a high to very high satisfaction with their work and a joy in the vocations. If they had reservations, these seemed to be mostly about the isolation working alone at their responsibilities. This is an issue raised also in Poland and Vietnam.

The implications of modern mass education are also clear in the other three provinces. In St. Martin de Porres Province (formed out of St. Albert and St. Joseph provinces in 1980), there is no brother who made profession between 1964 and 1981. Three brothers professed between 1981 and 2000. There was thus a gap of nearly twenty years. These recently professed brothers, as well as that brother professed in 1964, are all involved in education. Two are university professors, one of Spanish and one of theology. One is a seminary professor. All have advanced degrees. The brother professed in 1964 is a high school guidance counselor. These men are all highly professional. One, Brother Herman Johnson, has served as prior, having received a dispensation to do so, the first in the history of the Order.

St. Albert the Great Province has no brothers who professed between 1963 and 2007. It went forty-four years without a professed brother who persevered. Since 2007, they have professed five cooperator brothers. The two who have finished formation are both high school teachers, with advanced teaching degrees. All the student brothers have bachelor's degrees, and at least one of them is tracked to teach high school. I spoke with him and the other teachers during a congress of religious brothers, in March of 2017.[19] They all spoke enthusiastically about their work, and it was clear that the older brother is a mentor for the two younger teachers. The sense of collegial ministry among these teachers is strong.

St. Joseph Province went from 1968 to 2008 without a profession, a period of forty-one years. Since 2008, there have been five professions. The last four professions have been since 2014, and all four are currently students. Conversation with the oldest of the five, who does pastoral ministry in a parish of the province, revealed that he found formation alone among clerics a difficult experience.[20] The St. Joseph studentate was large (over 50 students), and he felt isolated, even somewhat marginalized, by his unique status. His own formation needs as a brother were sometimes unaddressed.

He did not call the charity or intentions of the formation community into question, but he ascribed the tensions to the lack of other cooperators with whom to share his experience. The presence of an older brother in the formation program did address this somewhat. In contrast, the four brothers now in formation registered no feelings of isolation or marginalization. They clearly delighted in their vocation and, especially, that they could share the experience together. Like the St. Albert Province brothers, all four brothers have college degrees. Three of them look forward to teaching. One hopes to find a position teaching high school, perhaps at Fenwick High School, in St. Albert Province. The other two want to complete doctorates in philosophy and serve as professors at Providence College, in Rhode Island. The fourth brother is discerning, but he feels drawn to parochial ministry in some form.

When asked, none of these student cooperators expressed concerns about not having passive voice to become a superior. All four said they were comfortable with the "clerical" status of the Order. It seems that for them the lack of voice does not have the symbolic loading that it has for many older cooperators. For older brothers this exclusion appears as part of older exclusionary clerical attitudes and the treatment of brothers as menials and inferiors. One of the student brothers observed: "We don't have all the negative experiences of some of the older brothers." On the other hand, like some of the older cooperators of this province to whom I spoke, they agreed that some younger clerics might be happy to see brothers back in roles of domestic service. This attitude is sometimes signaled by a desire to bring back the old brothers' habit. One student brother interjected: "Don't ask me about the black scapular!" The others nodded knowingly.

What do my conversations with younger American brothers reveal? In background, nearly all the young vocations are either converts or had background in lay ministry. Their vocation choice was very personal, and sometimes unsupported by family and friends. Once in the Order, community and shared life with other cooperators is very important to them. So too, they value having a shared ministry with those with whom they live. Next, nearly all the brothers are highly educated. They are, in fact, as academically gifted as the clerical vocations. Although the community at Fenwick High School is predominantly clerical, the shared teaching ministry means a shared identity and life. The result is a strong tendency toward education as the field of ministry.

Finally, with a couple of exceptions, the younger brothers register relatively little resentment or frustration with the clerical status of the Order, or with their relationship to priests and clerics. I would also venture that the long dry spell in cooperator vocations was the result of increased education among vocations and the end of Latin in the classroom and liturgy. Many men who, before 1960, would have become brothers, now became priests. At the present time in the United States, there is little to distinguish the educational preparation of clerics and cooperators before entrance. These men now choose to be brothers; they are not tracked to the brotherhood because of their educational background or abilities. I would add one other observation. In recruitment, success breeds success. The more brothers there are, the easier it is to attract others. The American provinces also demonstrate that it is possible to again recruit brothers, even after many decades without a single vocation.

The religious and cultural life of Poland is vastly different from the United States. America is privately religious, but publicly more and more secularized. Catholics were, and still are, a minority. With the breakdown of ethnic neighborhoods and enclaves, most American Catholics today have a relatively weak shared religious identity. In contrast, Poland is a Catholic country with a high level of practice. Traditional observances and common prayer typify the families from which the Polish cooperator brothers come. A common phrase used by the brothers themselves was: "I came from a traditional Polish Catholic family." That meant at least weekly, often daily, Mass attendance, common family Rosary, and, under Communism, a strong sense of Catholicism as a part of national identity.

On the other hand, the Polish cooperator vocation history shows a similarity to that of the United States. The reasons, however, are different. After the World War II, the Communist regime bitterly opposed and repressed the Church. This did not mean there were no vocations; there were many, and they remain plentiful. The Dominicans seem little affected by the increased secularism of post-Communist Poland, which has had some effect on vocations to other orders. Nevertheless, from 1950 to 1990, there were few cooperator brother vocations. One brother called this "the long dry spell."

There were, at the time of writing, twenty-three cooperators in the Polish Province. All but two of these brothers professed after 1978, when John Paul II was elected pope. The Poles themselves call these men "the John Paul II Vocations." But, as some of the brothers themselves said, before the 1980s, the priority of the province itself was to recruit and train priests. This means that the "John Paul II Generation" of cooperators encountered few older brothers. And these were very elderly and had little formal education. Those men were, by all reports, very hard working and fiercely pious. They were admired as saints, but usually not as models. Modern brothers had at least high school education, and the current novices, like Polish clerical vocations since 2000, all have college degrees.

But this golden age of cooperator vocations suddenly ended soon after the millennium, just as the first Poles not rearedunder Communism came of age. From 2007 to last year, there had been only one cooperator vocation (professed 2011). Now there are three cooperator novices, all of whom are expecting to profess simple vows within the year. In this, the Polish province had its own later (and shorter?) version of the American dry spell. One Polish priest brother linked the recent drop in cooperator vocations to the end of the domestic conversus model. He said: "Recent cooperator vocations could all become priests; many have M.A. degrees. So why don't they become priests? They do!"[21] My interviews showed this shift in socio-religious background. Before 1995, brother vocations entered immediately after high school,[22] or they had technical training.[23] After 2002, they all have university educations.[24]

There was also evident a change in what attracted men to the Order. The older vocations, pre-2000, emphasized personal contacts, especially with cooperator brothers and Dominican parishes.[25] One brother smiled, remembering his contact with an elderly, saintly brother. That brother told him: "You will be a brother because you work hard and smile a lot!"[26] More recent vocations, like several in the United States, did not often mention personal contact with brothers or priest Dominicans. They mentioned reading history, the mystics, or even novels (*The Name of the Rose*!).[27] Others mentioned youth or prayer groups.[28] In contrast, the current novices identified vocation films or personal Internet research as the root of their vocations. Some American brothers encountered resistance from family or friends about religious vocation generally, but the Polish cooperators encountered such resistance because they choose not to become priests.[29]

The Polish Province modified its cooperator formation program as the nature of their vocations changed. Before the 1990s, brothers did a postulancy, then a novitiate with the clerics, and then were assigned out individually to other communities. The similarity to the pre-Vatican-II formation programs is clear. In the 1990s, a "juniorate" for simply professed brothers was established at the Freta Priory in Warsaw. But a few brothers continued to do the older individual training elsewhere. This new program included classes in theology, liturgy, Latin, spirituality, Scripture, and canon law. Brothers who went through it spoke highly of the program. [30] This program, however, was under Communism, and two brothers remembered spending long hours each day standing in line to buy staples for the community. That was a common cooperator responsibility at that time.

After 1993, the "juniorate" was merged with that of the

clerics. At first, they were under a single student master, but clerics and cooperators got different classes. Then more and more classes were in common with the clerics. Cooperators had favorable views of the joint formation program. "We have to live in houses with priests," one noted. They were less happy with joint classes. The sense was that the academic program was intended for priests, and that cooperator needs were marginalized. And the brothers in formation had additional responsibilities—sacristy, gardening, etc.—in addition to the studies.

After 2005, the current program came into force. Cooperators and clerics had the same postulancy, novitiate, and, in theory, the same academic program. Young brothers who experienced this program expressed frustration. One asked and got permission during novitiate to talk to older cooperator brothers. He did not want to have contact almost solely with clerics. But he recalled a good common life with the other novices, with no sense of exclusion or real difference from the clerics.

He then entered studies with them. That proved more problematic. There was nothing specifically for him as a cooperator brother. After two and a half years of philosophy, he went to the new provincial and expressed his desire "to do something else." He was released to learn sacristy work "by doing." He credited this with saving his cooperator vocation.[31] Conversation with the current novices, all very well educated, reflects this kind of tension. They have hesitations about a one-size-fits-all education. Two of the three felt drawn to sacristy work or service to the poor as a porter. Sacristy work is still a very common cooperator function in Poland. An older brother who works as sacristan in Krakow explained the appeal of being a "sacristan." It involves meeting people with spiritual needs and includes the traditional "porter" work of helping the poor and troubled. "I am the public face of the community," he said.[32] This still appeals to some young vocations.

One of the novices, who had a background in construction, hoped to be involved with building new churches or houses for the poor. Another, although attracted to the sacristan model, remains interested in political science, world religions, and missions. All three novices hope that the academic program will accommodate these kinds of aspirations, but they had no doubt they could complete the classes in philosophy and theology. After their formation, all sensed that they would not be able to pursue the older sacristan and porter models. They thought more probable what is now common among younger brothers, work as an administrator or treasurer. They expect also that, as was the case for a cooperator brother who runs a study center for Eastern Christian spirituality and art, it will be up to them to get training in their personal interests, and that they will have to pursue them in addition to their formal assignments.

What lessons did I draw from the Polish brothers? First, and obviously, a vital Catholic culture with a high level of practice, in which religious vocations are honored, is a royal road to vocations, both cooperator and cleric. The Polish brothers, like the Americans, also find themselves happiest when there are other brothers around. One specifically said he did not want to live as the lone brother in a house of clerics. Next, although the current brothers are highly educated, they are not attracted to academics per se. Unlike the Americans, I sense no interest in pursuing vocations in teaching or education. Although no younger Polish brothers are drawn to domestic service, some would happily choose work with a human element (sacristy or social service), if they could.

They do have hesitations. They admit that finding a way to use their secular training and skills can be difficult. The old model of cooperators is gone; the new model remains unclear. Brothers sometimes feel themselves invisible, especially when they read province vocation literature or hear vocation talks. One said: "The real issue today is for cooperators to find a new identity in Poland."

In common with their American brothers, younger Poles seem to give little thought to the debates over passive voice or over brothers doing pulpit preaching. One brother, who served on the preaching commission at the recent Bologna General Chapter, remarked that his commission put forward a motion to have cooperators preach at Mass. He, the only brother on the committee, was not in favor of this. He laughed when recounting how the master assumed that he was the force behind this motion, when, in fact, it came solely from the clerics. This is a lesson for us all. Modern brothers are their own men, and they can be very different from what clerics and priests assume them to be.

A LONG JOURNEY ENDS

The last stop on this journey was Vietnam. The historical situation there resembles that of Poland, and the contrasts with the United States are even more pronounced. Nevertheless, young Vietnamese brothers have traits in common with those of the other two regions. The first Dominicans in Vietnam were missionaries of the Lyon Province. They worked mostly in the north, the original home of most Vietnamese Catholics. After 1954, the Catholics fled the Communists to the independent state of South Vietnam. Culturally, to this day, most Vietnamese Catholics are northern, and they often comment on this. Vietnamese Catholics are a religious minority, and a persecuted one. But, in part because of this, they have an even higher sense of identity and a higher level of practice than even the Poles.

Since reunification, Roman Catholics have risen from 5% to 19% of the total population. Modern Vietnam has now transitioned to a managed capitalist economy. Among young people generally, Communism is identified with an invasive and oppressive state bureaucracy. For those who grew up under Communism, it has no appeal as an ideology. In addition, Buddhism, the other "traditional" religion of Vietnam, is not very vital. Although some 30% of Vietnamese so identify, the level of practice is rather low, syncretistic, and sometimes limited to rituals that bring good luck. On several occasions, it was remarked to me that in twenty years Vietnam may replace the Philippines as the "Catholic country" in Asia.

In addition, Catholic families (and non-Catholic families) are large. Dominicans I spoke with almost always had five to ten or more siblings. Among cooperator vocations, daily Mass and family Rosary were not merely the norm but virtually universal. Religious vocations and priesthood are not only encouraged, but considered a family honor. One brother born in 1971, among whose five siblings is a Cistercian monk, talked about growing up in a rural Catholic community. The village and its surroundings, entirely Catholic, have produced over 500 vocations to religious life or the priesthood.[33] Even in Poland, I heard nothing comparable to this. The vast majority of cooperator brothers, until very recently, came from poor peasant backgrounds. Many, if not most, had at most a secondary education. Nearly every brother I spoke with identified family encouragement as a major part of the reason for becoming priests, brothers, and sisters. It should come as little surprise that the Vietnamese Church and nearly all the Orders have been experiencing a vocation boom since the 1970s.

The Vietnamese Province had, in 2016, forty-one professed cooperator brothers. Only six professed before 1992, and of these only three professed after the Vatican Council. So there was a long "dry spell" for cooperator vocations, as in the United States and Poland. But the cause was different. Under Communism, religious vocations were always there, although subject to quotas by the government. By the late 1980s, however, the Vietnamese government, imitating their Russian allies, began to relax restrictions on religion and personal freedoms. The result was the effective end of the quota system.

Sometimes it is said that the vocations boom for Vietnamese cooperators was the result of clerics being denied ordination because of the quotas. In fact, I did meet a priest who spent twenty years as a deacon because of the ordination quota. But this explanation of cooperator numbers is not correct. Under the quota system, the province did not take cooperator vocations at all. Priests were considered essential and it would not do to fill up quotas with unordained brothers. When the quotas ended, the province started taking men who wanted to be brothers. Since the late 1990s, the Vietnamese province has consistently professed two to three new brothers every year. Oddly, none was professed in 2016 because, for the first time since the early 1990s, there were no novices. This remains an oddity and might not mean a change in cooperator recruitment. Only time will tell its significance.

Currently, there are nine brothers in formation. Already in the 1950s, Vietnamese cooperators and clerics had a joint novitiate. They still do. In those early days, cooperators were simply sent off to an assignment after novitiate, and learned the manual or technical work needed there. One of the older brothers remembers being sent out to learn automobile maintenance. Then suddenly, with the fall of Saigon, he was sent to a farm in the mountains. He worked there for twenty-five years to keep the farm running so that the government would not seize it as "unproductive agricultural land."[34]

Soon after 2000, this brother was one of those who petitioned the provincial to create a new postnovitiate formation program for cooperators, one that would have a theological and spiritual dimension as well as technical training. The goal was to allow brothers to do more than manual labor. This change brought some mitigation of the old inferior, second-class status of "conversi." The brother sees these changes as significant in triggering the cooperator vocation boom that followed.

Also a trigger for the rise in brothers' vocations was the growing Vietnamese Catholic devotion to St. Martin de Porres, something first promoted by a cooperator brother.[35] Over fifty thousand pilgrims flock to St. Martin's annual celebration in November at the province retreat house. Most brothers mentioned the model of St. Martin as one of the things that drew them to the Order and to their cooperator vocation.

After 2000, the brothers were sent, after novitiate, to a joint three-year juniorate program, in conjunction with the Dominican sisters. Educational admissions standards were also being tightened up. One brother remembers discerning his vocation while in a G.E.D. program, which he had to complete to qualify for admission.[36] Although brothers who went through this joint program gave it mixed reviews, about half were very negative. They felt marginalized among the hundreds of sisters. One of those who did not like it could only identify two positive aspects: it was easy and short.[37] On the other hand, some of the brothers spoke very positively of the contemplative and "monastic" aspects of the program. It could be spiritually very nourishing. And they were well received. "The sisters love the brothers," one brother said.[38] In theory, after the joint program, each brother was to be sent for technical or mechanical training. It seems that this was sometimes omitted and the brothers were assigned as needed immediately.

In 2006, the province decided to send the simply professed to a program with brothers from other religious orders for their instruction in spirituality and theology. This was run by the Christian Brothers. There was much dissatisfaction with the program, as it was dominated by teaching brothers and the Dominican cooperators were marginalized. In 2011, the brothers were pulled from this joint brothers program and the province set up its own program for cooperators, the "Sedes Sapientiae Institute." It is open to brothers from other congregations and lay people, but the focus is Dominican brothers' formation.

Brother Joseph Tuyen, one of the two cooperator representatives at the General Chapter of Trogir (2013), was in the first class at Sedes Sapientiae, and he was attached to the priest founder to help organize the program. This program consists of three years of spirituality, theology, liturgy, Scripture, and canon law, all adapted to the needs of the brothers. Brother Tuyen has now worked in the Sedes program for seven years, as well as teaching catechism in parishes. This kind of basic religious instruction, especially for lay people, is what he loves.[39] In theory, after three years, the brothers are sent to technical programs according to their abilities and the needs of the province.

All the brothers I spoke with had good things to say about the academic part of the Sedes program. They especially liked that it is directed to their needs and is not as academically intensive as the clerics' philosophy-theology program. They even referred to it as "Track B," in contrast to the academically focused "Track A" of the clerics. [40] One brother, who does not enjoy schoolwork, admitted that even the Sedes classes were a chore, but that he really enjoyed the practical training in Information Technology that came after. He now does publicity and media for the province, along with serving as assistant infirmarian in the retirement community. The brother's vocation allows him to do what he really loves, helping people.[41] One brother summed up his vision in a quote from John Paul II: "The Church needs less teaching and more witness."[42] One senses that, for the majority of brothers during the last fifteen years, a joint academic program with the clerics would have posed serious problems for pursuing their vocation.

One theme, more common than a disinclination for studies, came up regularly in conversations with the brothers. A large number of brothers gave as their reason for choosing the brotherhood over priesthood that they would not have to do sacramental ministry. The reason for this was not a low view of priestly work. Rather, the brothers see Vietnamese priests' time as so taken up with the sacramental demands of the laity that they cannot do much else. Brothers often mentioned their ability to spend time with people, help them, and share experiences with them as what drew them to the brotherhood. Priests, they observed, often lack the time for this human contact. That brothers do many different kinds of work and are not locked into the priestly round was commonly mentioned as a great attraction.[43] One brother put it bluntly: "We cooperators have less to do." No brother, however, complained of being underworked; indeed, all seemed very busy.

What the cooperators do in Vietnam has been changing, and over the last ten years, changing rapidly. Those professed up to about 2003 all serve in "traditional" cooperator ministries: domestic work, plant maintenance, and—this being an agricultural country—farm work. Among them, there is a librarian and an infirmarian, but they are exceptions. After 2003, things changed. Among these brothers, there is a receptionist (porter) and one brother doing mostly domestic work, but the rest work outside of those "traditional" ministries. They do adult education and general ministry in parishes, and serve as treasurers, webmasters, music directors (including composition of hymns), and nurses. Among the last, one has just been certified in traditional medicine and acupuncture.

Among the five brothers in simple vows, all anticipate ministries that require special training: health care, religious journalism, adult education, Internet evangelization. One is already training as a master catechist in the Diocesan Catechetical Program. They universally think that the Sedes Sapientiae program is well adapted to their changing needs. They complain only that some are not allowed to complete the two years of technical training before being assigned out. When I mentioned the move in the United States and Poland toward assimilation of cooperator academic formation to that of the clerics, the usual reaction was disbelief. In Vietnam, at least for the cooperators, that change is not even on the horizon.

Vietnamese brothers do, however, register concerns. Reflecting on the changes, the oldest brother of the province wondered if the young brothers have an identity problem. For him, their identity as a brother has become unclear, and they really want to be priests. This, he says, makes them dissatisfied and unhappy. He bluntly stated that brothers' jobs can be dull and monotonous. He wondered if totally separate formation programs might not be a better idea.[44] His was a single voice. When other brothers worried about clerical and cooperator identities, they remarked on the extreme prestige of the priesthood among Vietnamese Catholics. They find themselves having to explain their vocation to lay people. Several recalled the social and family pressure, sometimes not subtle, to become a priest.[45] But they add that this is more a problem with the Vietnamese laity than among the friars themselves.

This popular devaluation of the brotherhood sometimes makes them feel invisible. One brother recounted how he makes a point of wearing his habit when he goes home to his village. (Friars almost never wear habit or collar in public in Vietnam.) This, he said, caused people to ask about who he was, and that gave him a chance to explain and promote the brotherhood. He said: "Vocation directors need to talk more about the brothers."[46] Finally, in spite of the generally large Vietnamese Dominican communities, all usually with more than one brother, a brother did comment on the difficulty he faced living along with a community of priests.[47] In this, he sounded like many American and Polish brothers.

Even more than in Poland, the controversial issues of passive voice and pulpit preaching seem nonissues among the Vietnamese brothers. This was the case in all age groups. That cooperators might become superiors seemed perplexing. One simply said to me: "How? That is against canon law!" He added that the Vietnamese people in general were not ready for such a move. How could they accept seeing a brother put above a priest![48] Another objected that the brothers themselves are not prepared, and did not want, such positions.[49] One tellingly said that, although he opposed this, if the Order legislated full passive voice for cooperators, he would accept the ruling. "We Vietnamese," he said, "are not rebellious people."[50] The brothers registered similar reactions to brothers doing pulpit preaching.

In these attitudes, the Vietnamese brothers resemble the majority of younger Polish and American brothers. Voice and preaching are not central concerns, and they do not have the symbolic power that they have for some older brothers. But in Vietnam, among the youngest, these views may be changing. One student brother did remark that the Vietnamese cult of the priest can introduce inequality into our life, especially since the social backgrounds of brothers and clerics are still so diverse. [51] Another student brother saw the growing opportunities for education and professionalism for the brothers as the reason the Dominicans are drawing more brothers than other orders. He liked that. He had completed university training as a computer analyst and programer. Higher studies came naturally to him. He would clearly be very comfortable in the same academic track as the clerics. Among the five student brothers, three have equally distinguished academic backgrounds.[52] This seems the way of the future in Vietnam, although the implications are not yet clear. When I asked this student brother why he, with his educational background, choose the brotherhood, he smiled and replied: "It's a mystery."[53] As I complete this study on the brothers and their vocation, I have to agree.

Appendices

Appendix A

LAY BROTHER STATISTICS SINCE 1876

(Vowed Friars—Vowed Lay Brothers—Percentage)

Province or Entity	1876	1910	1921	1931	1949	1967	1992	2016
Under the Master	73–22-30%	54-22-37%	94-50-50%	87-11-13%	109-16-16%	0-0-0%	0-0-0%	0-0-0%
Spain								455-29-6%
Spain	257-32-10%	382-84-22%	356-87-24%	383-122-32%	518-105-20%	961-139-14%	547-62-11%	[295-25-8%]
Aragon	154-14-9%		168-7-4%	123-21-17%	151-19-13%	253-36-14%	159-2-1%	[87-3-3%]
Betica	97-4-4%	120-21-18%	121-20-17%	160-32-20%	186-27-15%	258-35-14%	155-17-11%	[73-1-1%]
Toulouse	172-26-15%	148-18-12%	118-24-20%	160-30-19%	223-35-16%	195-20-10%	158-10-6%	130-8-6%
France	[293-17-17%]	395-16-10%]	[381-43-10%]	550-36-16%]	[699-28-9%]	[781-30-7%]	[469-12-5%]	266-6-2%
France	166-25-15%	218-19-9%	238-15-6%	337-34-10%	454-32-7%	521-24-5%	321-11-3%	
Lyon-Occitania	127-24-19%	177-19-11%	143-26-18%	213-55-26%	245-33-13%	260-28-11%	148-14-9%	
St. Dominic in Italy								126-7-6%
Lombardy	113-28-25%	65-7-11%	50-6-12%	104-24-23%	143-30-21%	189-25-13%	162-13-8%	
Piedmont	92-17-18%	110-20-18%	124-12-10%	193-40-21%	201-21-10%	189-18-10%	100-9-9%	
Roman of St. Catherine								61-2-3%
Rome	150-39-26%	89-17-19%	79-9-11%	123-23-17%	166-15-9%	162-15-9%	80-3-4%	
San Marco-Sardinia	22-2-9%	58-10-17%	55-7-13%	81-15-19%	93-21-23%	87-13-15%	55-7-13%	
St. Thomas in Italy								71-11-15%
Naples-Calabria	178-39-22%	54-12-22%	44-8-18%	76-29-38%	129-25-19%	131-22-17%	106-13-12%	
Sicily	223-61-27%	101-10-10%	55-11-20%	72-7-10%	75-9-12%	83-5-6%	43-1-2%	
Austro-Hungarian Empire	118-34-29%	146-59-40%	145-45-31%	140-50-36%	[299-74-20%]	[326-73-18%]	[194-16-8%]	[143-7-5%]
Hungary					87-13-14%	97-15[a]-15%	33-1-3%	17-1-6%
Bavaria-Austria					118-31-24%	121-24-20%	64-8-13%	42-3-7%
Bohemia		82-30-37%	79-22-28%	104-43-41%	94-30-32%	108-34[a]-32%	97-7-7%	37-3-8%
Slovakia								47-0-0%
Teutonia		195-60-31%	210-38-18%	323-108-33%	294-67-23%	332-40-12%	188-14-7%	104-7-7%
Netherlands (Lower Germ.)	114-11-10%	293-47-16%	350-53-15%	415-69-16%	489-75-15%	546-81-15%	207-24-12%	49-7-14%
Flanders	79-21-27%	155-41-26%	202-41-20%	299-56-19%	379-51-13%	267-27-10%	86-10-12%	[99-0-0%]
Belgium						100-5-5%	37-0-0%	70-0-0%
Switzerland						87-6-7%	63-3-5%	29-0-0%
England	67-15-22%	114-13-11%	120-11-9%	169-25-15%	186-32-17%	234-43-18%	111-10-9%	72-1-1%
Ireland	104-14-13%	174-35-20%	169-25-15%	181-37-20%	332-51-15%	413-49-12%	280-33-12%	150-6-4%
Poland	140-28-20%	125-42-34%	114-33-29%	159-49-31%	142-43-30%	210-37-18%	320-29-9%	398-23-6%
Croatia (Dalmatia)	43-4-9%	59-7-12%	63-8-13%	67-10-15%	73-9-12%	117-13-11%	81-6-7%	64-3-5%
Portugal						80-20-25%	64-9-14%	48-2-4%
Brazil						97-8-8%	52-7-13%	52-4-8%

Province or Entity	1876	1910	1921	1931	1949	1967	1992	2016
Mexico	49-8[b]-16%	30-8-27%				96-14-15%	139-18-13%	100-9-9%
Peru	17-2-12%	65-3-5%	51-6-12%	58-13-22%	79-13-16%	74-16-22%	63-6-10%	56-6-11%
Colombia	38-5-13%	73-10-14%	81-16-20%	106-25-24%	103-24-23%	143-31-22%	116-8-7%	160-10-6%
Ecuador (Quito)	47-6-13%	83-19-23%	90-24-27%	116-51-44%	122-35-29%	128-37-29%	71-13-18%	38-3-8%
Chile	85-24-29%	72-15-21%	49-5-10%	53-8-15%	40-4-10%	39-6-15%	21-3-14%	14-1-7%
Argentina	51-6-12%	94-8-9%	77-11-14%	59-9-15%	69-4-6%	71-9-13%	91-7-8%	60-5-8%
Rosary	284-31-11%	532-61-11%	504-59-12%	537-58-11%	523-77-14%	800-89-11%	329-31-9%	218-17-8%
Philippines							159-13-8%	138-8-6%
Central America	18-0[c]-0%						60-7-8%	57-1-2%
Puerto Rico								17-1-0%
Bolivia								50-0-0%
St. Joseph (all)	80-23-29%	187-15-8%	291-20-7%	486-40-8%	[837-47-6%]	[1262-76-6%]	[708-53-8%]	[455-23-5%]
Eastern US					580-33-6%	703-58-8%	331-17-5%	234-10-4%
Central US					257-14-5%	559-18-3%	235-26-11%	131-13-10%
Southern US							142-10-7%	90-5-6%
Western US	27-5-19%	45-5-11%	63-4-6%	75-13-17%	93-13-14%	175-24-14%	168-11-7%	126-6-5%
Malta	46-4-9%	67-11-16%	72-16-22%	95-21-22%	105-14-13%	130-17-13%	80-5-6%	47-5-11%
Canada		100-22-22%	135-21-16%	246-56-23%	365-77-21%	477-104-22%	269-62-23%	122-23-20%
Australia						91-14-15%	90-9-10%	67-10-15%
Congo (Central Africa)						13-0-0%	47-3-6%	48-3-6%
Nigeria							90-5-6%	121-4-3%
South Africa							44-3-7%	22-0-0%
West Africa								68-0-0%
Vietnam							121-11-9%	297-41-14%
Pakistan							33-2-6%	32-1-3%
India							51-0-0%	103-0-0%
China							16-2-13%	25-0-0%
TOTAL VOWED FRIARS	3289	4272	4510	5800	7123	9640	6520	5715
TOTAL VOWED LAY B.	567 (18%)	863 (20%)	739 (18%)	1182 (20%)	1101 (15%)	1219 (13%)	599 (9%)	310 (5%)

[a] 1967 figures for Hungary and Bohemia are actually of 1949, but the novices are assumed to have all professed.
[b] Includes the Provinces of Oaxaca, and Puebla; both extinct by 1910.
[c] Includes the Provinces of Guatemala and Chiapas, both extinct by 1921.

Appendix B
Brother Saints and Blesseds

SAINTS

Martin de Porres, d. 3 Nov. 1639, Lima, Peru.
Canonized 6 May 1962. Celebrated 3 November.

Juan Macías, d. 16 Sep. 1645, Lima, Peru.
Canonized 28 Sep. 1975. Celebrated 18 September.

The martyr companions of St. Dominic Ibáñez, Nagasaki, Japan:
Francis Shoyemon, d. 14 Aug. 1633
Matthew of the Rosary Kohioye, d. 19 Oct. 1633
Canonized 18 Oct. 1987. Celebrated 28 September.

BLESSEDS

The companion martyrs of Bl. Sadoc, traditionally known as:
Andrew of Sandomierz, d. c. 1260
Peter of Sandomierz, d. c. 1260
Cyril of Sandomierz, d. c. 1260
Jeremiah of Sandomierz, d. c. 1260
Thomas of Sandomierz, d. c. 1260
Mass and Office approved, 18 Oct. 1807.
Celebrated 2 June.

Simon Ballachi, d. 3 Nov. 1319, Rimini, Italy.
Mass and Office approved, 25 Sep. 1818.
Celebrated 5 November.

James Griesinger of Ulm, d. 11 Oct. 1491, Bologna, Italy.
Mass and Office approved, 3 Aug. 1825.
Celebrated 11 October.

The companion martyrs of Bl. Alphonsus Navarrete, Nagasaki, Japan:
Dominic of the Rosary Magoshichi, d. 10 Sep. 1622
Peter of Saint Mary, d. 29 Jul. 1627
Mancio of the Cross, d. 29 Jul. 1627
Anthony of Saint Dominic, d. 8 Sep. 1628
Thomas of Saint Hyacinth, d. 8 Sep. 1628
Beatified 7 May 1867. Celebrated 6 November.

The companion martyrs of Bl. Hyacinth Serrano López, Spain:
Gumersindo Soto Barros, d. 29 Jul. 1936, Calanda
Matthew (Santiago) de Prado Fernández d. 30 Jul. 1936, Miguelturra
Arsenius de la Viuda Solla, d. 14 Aug. 1936, Almagro
Ovidius Bravo Porras, d. 14 Aug. 1936, Almagro
Dionisius Pérez García, d. 14 Aug. 1936, Almagro
Rafael Pardo Molina, M., d. 26 Sep. 1936, Valencia
Beatified Mar. 11, 2001. Celebrated 22 September.

The companion martyrs of Bl. Bonaventure García y Paredes, Spain:
Hyacinth García Riesco, d. 20 Jul. 1936, Madrid
Hyginus Roldán Iriberri, d. 25 Jul. 1936, Madrid
John Crespo Calleja, d. 25 Jul. 1936, Madrid
Edward González Santo Domingo, d. 5 Aug. 1936, Madrid
Abilius Sáiz López, d. 18 Aug. 1936, Navelgas
Nicasius Romo Rubio, d. 30 Aug. 1936, Madrid
Theophilus Montes Calvo, d. 14 Sep. 1936, Madrid
Christopher Iturriaga-Echevarrí Irazola, d. 31 Aug. 1936, Sama de Langreo
Peter (Santiago) Vega Ponce, d. 31 Aug. 1936, Sama de Langreo
Eugene Andrés Amo, d. Sep. 1936, Satillo
Cyprian Alguacil Torredenaida, d. 15 Oct. 1936, Madrid
Victorian Ibáñez Alonso, d. 22 Oct. 1936, Santander
John Herrero Arroyo, d. 28 Nov. 1936, Torrejón, Madrid
Bernardine Irurzun Otermín, d. 23 Dec. 1936, Santander
Eleuterius Marne Mansilla, d. 23 Dec. 1936, Santander
Peter Luis, d. 23 Dec. 1936, Santander
Joseph-Mary García Tabar, d. 23 Dec. 1936, Santander
Joseph-Mary Laguía Puerto, d. Sep. 1937, La Felguera
Beatified Oct. 28, 2007. Celebrated November 6.

Appendix C
Brothers by Decade of Profession since 1940

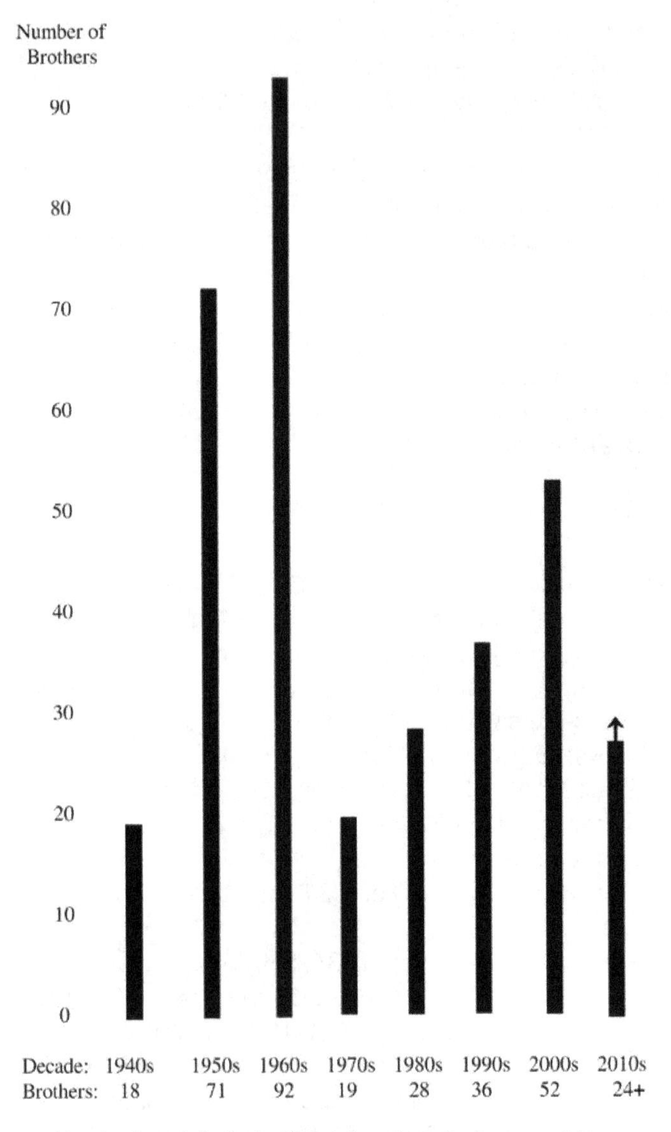

Note that the statistics for the 2010s only represent the six years to date.

Appendix D
Oral History Interviews

An [Bro. Gioan Baotixita] (interview), Dao Thien. St. Martin de Porres Priory, Bien Hoa, Vietnam. 23 February 2017.

Buda (conversation), Jacek. Dominican House of Studies, Washington DC, 8 October 2016.

Cao [Bro. Dominic] (interview), Pham Thanh. St. Albert the Great Priory, Ho Chi Minh City, Vietnam. 20 February 2017.

Central Province Brothers (Conversation). Joseph Trout, Stephen Peterson, John Steilberg. Notre Dame University, Notre Dame, IN. 25 March 2017.

Dang [Bro. Joseph] (interview), Nguyen Ba. Provincial Curia, Ho Chi Minh City, Vietnam. 24 February 2017.

Dinh [Bro. Peter] (interview), Nguyen Van. St. Albert the Great Priory, Ho Chi Minh City, Vietnam. 21 February 2017.

Dolen (interview), Thomas Aquinas. St. Catherine of Siena Priory, NY. 12 December 2016.

Downey (interview), Michael. St. Vincent Ferrer Priory, NY. 12 December 2016. Duong [Bro. Peter] (interview), Vo Ta. Provincial Curia, Ho Chi Minh City, Vietnam. 24 February 2017.

Eastern Students (interview). Thomas Martin Miller, James Wallace, Martin David, Daniel Traceski. Dominican House of Studies, Washington, DC. 27 October 2016.

Eli (interview), Jude. St. Albert the Great Priory, Oakland, CA. 28 December 2016.

Han [Bro. Joseph] (interview), Dinh Van. St. Albert the Great Priory, Ho Chi Minh City, Vietnam. 20 February 2017.

Hayes (interviews), Finbarr. St. Albert the Great Priory, Oakland, CA. Several occasions, 2015.

Hoang [Bro. Augustin] (interview), Tran The. St. Martin de Porres Priory, Bien Hoa, Vietnam. 23 February 2017.

Kennedy (Conversation), Paul M. Dominican House of Studies, Washington, DC. Fall 2016.

Khanh [Bro. Peter] (interview), Nguyen Phi. St. Albert the Great Priory, Ho Chi Minh City, Vietnam. 21 February 2017.

Kołtyś (interview), Marek. Klasztor Ojców Dominikanów, Krakow, Poland. 15 February 2017.

Krus (interview), Jarolslaw. Klasztor Sv. Józefa, Służew, Warsaw, Poland. 8 February 2017.

Long [Bro. Francis] (interview), Mai Thanh. St. Martin de Porres Priory, Bien Hoa, Vietnam. 23 February 2017.

Manh [Bro. Peter] (interview), Pham Van. Provincial Curia, Ho Chi Minh City, Vietnam. 24 February 2017.

McCarthy (interview), Damian. St. Vincent Ferrer Priory, NY. 13 December 2016.

Mochoń (interview), Tomasz. Klasztor Sv. Józefa, Służew, Warsaw, Poland. 9 February 2017.

Morris (oral communication), Glenn. Province of India, Angelicum, Rome, Italy. 13 January 2017.

Mszyca (interview), Jan. Klasztor Sv. Józefa, Służew, Warsaw, Poland. 8 February 2017.

O'Leary (interview), Mark. St. Albert the Great Priory, Oakland, CA. 27 December 2016.

Pastuła (interview), Andrzej. Klasztor Ojców Dominikanów, Krakow, Poland. 14 February 2017.

Patalano (interview), Anthony. Holy Rosary Priory, Portland, OR. 19 July 2017.

Perkins (interviews), Ignatius. St. Catherine of Siena Priory and St. Catherine of Siena Priory, NY. 12–13 December 2016.

Polish Novices (interview). Adam Jastrzebski, Bartlomiei Gorski, Marcin Marzalek. Klasztor Sv. Józefa, Służew, Warsaw, Poland. 10 February 2017.

Skowrónski (interview), Manusz. Klasztor Sv. Józefa, Służew, Warsaw, Poland. 6 February 2017.

Strycek (interview), Robert. Sw. Jacka, Freta, Warsaw. Poland. 9 February 2017.

Tam [Bro. Francis Xavier] (interview), Nguyen Thanh. St. Albert the Great Priory, Ho Chi Minh City, Vietnam. 20 February 2017.

Tam [Bro. Peter] (interview), Nguyen Thanh. St. Albert the Great Priory, Ho Chi Minh City, Vietnam. 20 February 2017.

Thai [Bro. Dominic] (interview), Do Van. Provincial Curia, Ho Chi Minh City, Vietnam. 24 February 2017.

Thomas (interview), Daniel. St. Dominic Church, Benicia, CA. 27 December 2016.

Tien [Bro. Peter] (interview), Ha Anh, Albert the Great Priory, Ho Chi Minh City, Vietnam. 21 February 2017.

Tuan [Bro. Francis Xavier] (interview), Tran Duc. St. Martin de Porres Priory, Bien Hoa, Vietnam. 23 February 2017.

Tuong [Bro. Dominic] (interview), Nguyen Minh. Provincial Curia, Ho Chi Minh City, Vietnam. 24 February 2017.

Tuyen [Bro. Joseph] (interview), Mai Van. St. Albert the Great Priory, Ho Chi Minh City, Vietnam. 20 February 2017.

Vietnamese Students (interview), Joseph Nguyen Van Nghi, Joseph Nguyen Quoc Huy, Joseph Le Hoang Nguyen, Peter Hoang Chien Thang. St. Albert the Great Priory, Ho Chi Minh City, Vietnam. 21 February 2017.

Wichrowicz (interview), Cyprian. Klasztor Ojców Dominikanów, Krakow, Poland. 15 February 2017.

Wtyło (interview), Piotr. Klasztor Sv. Józefa, Służew, Warsaw, Poland. 7 February 2017.

Notes

Prologue The First Conversi

1. Mulhern, v–vi; cf. Tugwell (2002).
2. E.g., Magboo, 503–14; Hinnebusch, 1: 288–90.
3. Tugwell (2002), 1–2; Mulhern, 3-16.
4. See Louis J. Lekai, *The Cistercians* (Kent, OH, 1977), 21–32.
5. Osheim, 371, 380.
6. Osheim, 382–83: Gilles-Gérard Meersseman, *Ordo Fraternitatis* (Rome, 1977), 1: 294–99.
7. Thompson (2012), 19–34.
8. Thompson (2005), 69–103.
9. Tugwell (2002), 3; MOPH 25, n. 29.
10. *CNDP* 2: 1, 2, 6, 8, 48, 53, 189; Vicaire, 109, 124; cf. Mulhern, 89–93.
11. Osheim, 374.
12. Vicaire, 124, f.n. 110: Jean Guiraud, *The Medieval Inquisition* (London, 1980) 1: 348.

Chapter 1 Early Dominican Brothers, 1216–1300

1. Gy, 3; Vladimir J. Koudelka, "Notes sur le cartulaire de s. Dominique," *AFP* 28 (1958): 92–100.
2. Tugwell (2002b), 2.
3. Thompson (2012), 34–54.
4. Tugwell (2002b), 1, f.n. 1.
5. Tugwell, *AFP* 71 (2001): 138.
6. Gy, 4–6; *Constitutiones Concilii Quarti Lateranesis*, ed. A. García y García (Vatican City, 1981) 58–59.
7. Gy 3; X 5.8.14 (Friedberg 2: 789); *Hostiensis, Summa Aurea* (Lyon, 1556), 354vb.
8. Michele M. Mulchahey, *First the Bow is Bent in Study* (Toronto, 1998) 130–67.
9. Tugwell (2002b) 2.
10. Raymond Creytens, "Les convers des moniales dominicaines au moyen âge," AFP 19 (1949), 5–48, esp. 7–16; CNDP 2: 9 n. 106, CNDP 1: 256;

    Tugwell (2002) 4; Vicaire 124; Mulhern 89–93.
11. Tugwell (2002) 3; MOPH 25 f.n. 73.
12. Jordan, *Libellus* 51, 50 (Lehner trans. 48), MOPH 22, 149–57, BGF 45, Fiamma 344; Vicaire 215 (correct form of his name).
13. AD 2.1: 152; Mortier 1: 28; Mulhern 36; cf. Tugwell (2002) 4.
14. Jordan, *Libellus* 49, 48 (Lehner trans. 47).
15. Jordan, *Libellus* 59; Ferrandus 40, 238; Vicaire 251; Mulhern 37.

16. Jordan, *Libellus* 55, 51 (Lehner trans. 50); Caesarius of Heisterbach, *Homiliae Festivae*, ed. J. A. Coppenstein Cologne, 1615).

17. Fiamma 321, 344, 348; Pio 102; AD 4.2: 697; Vicaire 247–50; Mulhern 36–37.

18. NDO 68.

19. AD 4.2: 667 (Pio); O'Daniel (1921) 64.

20. Vicaire 278.

21. VF 2.8, 72–73 (Conway trans. 47); Vicaire 268.

22. Fiamma 20; Mulhern 37.

23. BOP 1: 16 n. 33 (7 Oct. 1225).

24. Cecilia, *Miracles*, 14, 182–83; Vicaire 348–50; cf. Tugwell (2002) 3.

25. Tugwell (2002) 19. VF 231–35; MOPH 1: 231–35; 2: 22–24; BGQ 24; BOP 4: 565; Venchi 128–29. Cf. O'Daniel (1921) 79.

26. Venchi 133–34; Klemens Chodykiewicz, *De rebus Gestis in Provincia Russae Ordinis Praedicatorum* (Berdyczów, 1780); cf. AD 6.1: 47, f.n. 1.

27. ACD, Bologna, n. 26, 144–45 (Lehner trans. 116); Gy 2–7; Mulhern 24–25; cf. Vicaire 311.

28. Tugwell (1996) 63–64. Cf. Galvano Fiamma, MOPH 2: 27.

29. Rule of Grandmont: PL 204: 1135–62; Tugwell (2002) 2–3: Thomas of Cantimpré, *Bonum Universale de Apibus* (Douay, 1627) 111; Mulhern 26–27.

30. Golding 46–51; M. D. Knowles, "The Revolt of the Lay Brothers of Sempringham," *English Historical Review* 50 (1935): 465–87; R. Foreville, "La Crise de l'ordre de Sempringham au XIIe siècle," *Anglo-Norman Studies* 6 (1963): 39–57.

31. Cf. Hinnebusch (1965) 1: 289.

32. Osheim 379.

33. BGF 97, 161–229.

34. BGF 265–71.

35. *Pace* Tugwell (2002) 10.

36. BGF; cf. later ACPR 347 (Gubbio, 1334): 3 of 13. 37. NSMN 1: 3–21.

38. NDO: 23 of 144 (16%); NSC 402–80: 18 of 118 (15%).

39. Tugwell (2002) 6–7, and esp. 20, f.n. 70; Gómez (2006) 1–3.

40. Mulhern 21–23. 41. COP (1241) 26.

42. COP (1228) 37 (De Conversis, 7), (Lehner trans., 251).

43. COP (1228) 37 (De Conversis, 6), (Lehner trans. 251).

44. COP (1228) 37 (De Conversis, 8), (Lehner trans. 251, 45. PL 188: 1118.

46. COP (1241) 67–68.

47. ACG (1249–1251) 1: 46, 51, 56.

48. E.g., ACPH (Palencia 1249), passim., esp. 413.

49. ACPR (Rome 1244); ACPL (Bologna 1275) 153.

50. ACG 1: 116 (Bologna 1262); ACG 1: 119 (London 1263).

51. Humbert of Romans, "De Modo Prompte Cudenti Sermones: Sermo ad Conversos de Ordine Praedicatorum,"*Maxima Biblioteca Veterum Patrum* 25: 470; translation: Mulhern 33.

52. Mulhern 32: ACP (Douais) 1: 19.

53. Osheim 377; cf. Hinnebusch (1965) 1: 287.

54. COP (1228) n. 37, 368–69; ACG (Paris 1236) 1: 6; cf. Mulhern 39.

55. E.g., ACPD (Odense 1252) 553, (Lund 1254) 556.

56. ACG (Trier 1249) 1: 44; ACG (Strasbourg 1260) 1: 102; ACG (Pest 1272) 1: 169; ACG (Vienna 1282) 1: 217; ACG (Montpelier 1283) 1: 222; cf. Hinnebusch (1965) 1: 288–89.

57. Cf. Mulhern 39.

58. ACG (London 1250) 1: 49–50; ACPL (Padua 1289) 163.

59. ACPR (Rieti 1305) 153; Hinnebusch (1965) 1: 289.

60. ACPR (Pisa 1298) 128.

61. Cf. Hinnebusch (1965) 1: 288–89; Mulhern 40–41.

62. Humbert 2: 209; cf. Mulhern 39.

63. ACG (1233) 1: 3; cf. Mulhern 39, Gómez (2006) 3; Hinnebusch (1965) 1: 289 (Provence 1254).

64. ACG 53 (London 1250), f.n. 1; cf. Mulhern 53.

65. Mulhern 57.

66. Humbert 2: 235; Hinnebusch (1965) 1: 290; Mulhern 58. 67. COP (1228) n. 37, 368–69.

68. Humbert 2: 327.

69. ACG (Trier 1266) 1: 133; Hinnebusch (1965) 1: 341.

70. ACPR (Viterbo 1261) 25.

71. ACPH (Palencia 1256) 417.

72. ACG (Metz 1251) 1: 57; ACG (Buda 1255) 1, 76; ACG (Paris 1256) 1: 81; ACG (Paris 1257) 1: 84.

73. ACG (Florence 1257) 1: 87; ACG (Valencia 1259), 1: 95; ACG (Strasbourg 1260) 1: 102.

74. Gómez (2006).

75. ACG (Trier 1289) 1: 253.

76. ACG (Montpellier 1294) 1: 274. 77. ACG 2: 18 (Paris 1306).

78. Tugwell (2002) 7, f.n. 23; Hinnebusch (1965) 1: 341; cf. Mulhern 54–55.

79. AD 9.1: 253–54 (López).

80. Tugwell (2002) 12.

81. VF (Conway trans. 170–71) 4.16.3, 198.

82. Humbert 2: 235.

83. BGF 105.

84. Humbert 2: 234; Tugwell (2002) 11–12; Gómez (2006) 4; cf. Mulhern 59.

85. ACPH (Léon 1275) 419.

86. Tugwell (2002) 10.

87. Humbert 2: 233–36.

88. Tugwell (2002) 11–16; Mulhern 30–33.

89. Thompson (2005) 343–54.

90. Humbert 2: 234; Hinnebusch (1965) 1: 289.

91. ACPR (Anagni 1256) 19.

92. Humbert 2: 234–35; Mulhern 62; Gómez (2006) 4.

93. Jordan, *Epistolae* 21, 25.

94. COP (1228) n. 37, 368–69; Tugwell (2002) 7–8.

95. Hinnebusch (1965) 1: 290; Mulhern 42–43. 96. Gómez (2006) 3.

97. ACG (London 1250) 1: 51; ACG (Metz 1251) 1: 56; ACPR (Todi 1266).

33; ACG (Valencia 1291) 1: 262.

98. NDO 68.

99. NDO 79.

100. Tugwell (2002) 16.

101. ACG 1: 219 (Vienne, 1282); Mulhern 47. 102. ACG 1: 219 (1289); Mulhern 47.

103. ACPR 124 (Viterbo, 1296).

104. Galbraith 214.

105. Cf. ACPR (Viterbo 1258) 23.

106. Humbert 2: 78–79.

107. Mulhern 64–65.

108. CDO (Buda 1254) 85.

109. E.g., ACPR (Anagni 1270) 37; ACPL passim.

110. COP (1228) n. 37, 368–69; Thompson (2005) 251–53.

111. COP (1228) n. 37, 368.

112. Mulhern 61.

113. COP (1228) n. 37 (De Conversis, 5) 369 (Lehner trans. 251).

114. Mulhern 63.

115. AD 3.1: 151 (BGF); O'Daniel (1921) 65.

116. AD 5.2: 699 (BGF).

117. Pio 138; AD 10.2: 654; O'Daniel (1921) 64.

118. Without Aves: ACG (Pest 1272), 1:165 (for a cardinal); ACPH (Léon 1275) 420; ACG (Bologna 1252) 1: 62; ACG (Ferrara 1290) 1: 259); including Aves: ACG (Piacenza 1292) 1: 265; ACG (Besançon 1303) 1: 323; ACG (Vienne 1282) 1: 220; ACG (Ferrara 1290) 1: 259; ACG (Rome 1292), 1: 267; without Aves: ACG (Montpellier 1292) 1: 275.

119. ACPD (Lund 1252) 558; ACPD (Vesteras 1291) 565.

120. 120. VF 5.7.5, 289.

121. Razzi 281; AD 4.2: 596; O'Daniel (1921) 65.

122. VF 1.6.6, 43 (Conway trans. 26).
123. VF 1.6.19, 53 (Conway trans. 33).
124. VF 2.42, 97 (Conway trans. 67–68).
125. VF 5.1.3, 244 (Conway trans. 211).
126. Vigna 13; AD 11.2, 767.
127. VF 4.25.9, 228 (Conway trans. 196).
128. VF, 5.2.6, 259–62 (Conway trans. 227).
129. Cf. AD 12.2: 581; O'Daniel (1921) 64.
130. O'Daniel (1921) 64.
131. AD 2.1: 119–20; O'Daniel (1921) 64
132. VF 5.9.14, 303 (Conway trans. 260).
133. NSC 432. LII.
134. Tugwell (2002b) 2; Mulhern 24.
135. Bennett 149.
136. Humbert 2: 209; Mulhern 38.
137. Tugwell (2002) 14, f.n. 46 (Thomas of Cantimpré, Bonum Universale 2.5.1).
138. Tugwell (2002) 14.
139. Tugwell (2002) 11–16.
140. AS 25 (Jun. V): 360, f.n. 45; Hinnebusch (1965) 1: 289.
141. ACPR (Rome 1263) 27; ACG (Florence 1281) 1: 214.
142. Humbert 1: 560–61; Bennett 152.
143. Humbert 2: 288–94; Mulhern 75–77; Hinnebusch (1965) 1: 289–90; Tugwell (2002) 20–21.
144. Tugwell (2002) 16.
145. Humbert 2: 288–94; Mulhern 75–77.
146. Humbert 2: 317–19; Mulhern 79–80.
147. ACG (Paris 1286), 1: 234; Gómez (2006) 4–5.
148. AD 10.2: 655 (Razzi); O'Daniel (1921) 65.
149. Alberti 162–63; Pio 111–12; Choquet 134–36; AD 12.1: 19–20.
150. Humbert 2: 320–22; Mulhern 80–81.
151. NSC 574, CCLVI.
152. Humbert 2: 333–36; Mulhern 78–79.
153. NSD 14.
154. NSC 571, CCXLIX.
155. Alberti 159–61; Razzi 279–81; AS 66 (Nov. II): 211–12; "Il b. Simone Ballachi di s. Angelo nel sesto centenario della sua morte (1319–3 novembre 1919)." *Il Rosario-Memorie domenicane* 36 (1919): 537–44; AD 11.1: 59–62; Venchi 221; Tugwell (2002) 19.
156. ACPL 146.
157. Humbert 2: 323–29; Mulhern 81–83.
158. NDO 71.
159. NDO 101–02.

160. Humbert 2: 327–30; Mulhern 83–84.
161. NSC 415, XI; NSMN 1: 15 (149).
162. Humbert 2: 330–31; Mulhern 84.
163. NSC 410, VI; AD 5.2: 459; O'Daniel (1921) 64.
164. NDO 84.
165. Mulhern 32: ACP (Douais), 1: 77, 110.
166. Humbert 2:301–04; Mulhern 77–78.
167. E.g., ACG (Valencia 1647) 7: 224.
168. ACPR (Viterbo 1296) 123.
169. NSMN 1: 5 (30), 2: 220; Tugwell (2002) 15.
170. AD 1: 512 (Razzi).
171. VF 5.3.6, 259 (Conway trans. 226).
172. Humbert 2: 347–53.
173. NSC 411, VIII. 174. Gómez (2006) 5.
175. NSMN 1: 4 (13), 2: 216.
176. Humbert 2: 272–74; Mulhern 74–75; ACPL (Cremona 1284) 159.
177. AD 4.2: 631 (Pio).
178. NDO 74,
179. AD 1: 477; O'Daniel (1921) 64.
180. E.g., ACPR (Florence 1254) 17.
181. Razzi 282; AD 6.1: 77; O'Daniel (1921) 65.
182. AD 9.2: 815; O'Daniel (1921) 66.
183. NSC 482, CXXII.
184. AD 1: 850 (Razzi); Daniel 64.
185. 185. NSMN 1: 73 (350).
186. AD 2.1: 295–96 (Pio, Razzi).
187. AD 5.2: 587.
188. AD 12.2: 733 (BGF); O'Daniel (1921) 64.
189. AD 9.2: 518.
190. AD 11.2: 638.
191. Prudlo 1–8 (youth and murder), 9–12 (conversion), 12–21 (cult): Razzi 77; AD 11.1: 423–46.
192. Tugwell (2002) 18–19.

CHAPTER 2 BEYOND THE MONASTERY, 1300–1500

1. Hinnebusch 1: 161.
2. ACG 1: 29 (Bologna 1264); ACPR (Orvieto 1275) 45; ACPL 158 (Milan 1283).
3. ACPL 171 (Ferrara 1312).
4. Tugwell (2002) 14, f.n. 51; VF 1.5.3, 28–29 (Conway trans. 18–19); Vicaire 333.
5. AD 9.2: 1003.

6. AD 4.1: 337 (BGF); O'Daniel (1921) 64.
7. Humbert 2: 285–88; Mulhern 68–70.
8. Tugwell (2002) 11–16.
9. Tolomeo of Lucca, *Annales,* MGH.SS, n.s., 8: 178, 216; Tugwell (2002) 8; cf. Mulhern 70.
10. NSMN 1: 110–11 (467), 2: 577.
11. NSMN 1: 174 (678), 2: 290–91.
12. NSC 554, C.
13. NSMN 1: 192 (716).
14. NSC 563, CCXXXV.
15. NSC 500, CLIII.
16. NSC 484, CXXIX.
17. NSD 39.
18. NSMN 1: 148 (588), 2: 77.
19. NSMN 1: 128 (501).
20. E.g. ACPA 25: 337 (Lérida 1357).
21. Humbert 2: 274–79; Tugwell (2002) 15; Mulhern 70–72.
22. ACG 1: 46 (Trier 1249); cf. Gómez (2006) 3–4; 1250, ACG 1: 52 (London 1250); ACG 1: 57 (Metz 1251); ACG 1: 66 (Buda 1254).
23. Humbert 2: 310–16; Mulhern 72–73.
24. André de Resende, *A santa vida e religiosa conversão de Frei Pedro* (Rio de Janeiro, 1947); English trans. John R. C. Martyn, *Biographies of Prince Edward and Friar Pedro* (Lewiston, 1997); Pio (1607), 69–70; AD 1:404–14.
25. Razzi 282; AD 4.1: 292.
26. NDO 114.
27. NSMN 1: 9 (114), 2: 228.
28. NSMN 1: 47 (267), 2: 340.
29. NSMN 1: 150 (592), 2: 126.
30. E.g. BGF; ACPA.
31. See NDO.
32. NSC 475–582.
33. NSMN 1: 3–21 (1200s), 1: 21–141 (1300s), 1: 142–203 (1400s).
34. NSMN 142–205.
35. Mulhern 67–68.
36. Tugwell (2002) 22–23 "Appendix I."
37. BGL 6: 406; cf. Mulhern 38. 38. NSMN 1: 43 (251), 2: 331. 39. NSMN 1: 58 (306), 2: 276.
40. NSMN 1: 108 (100–01); Tugwell (2002) 17–18.
41. ACG 3: 124, 309; Hinnebusch 1: 270.
42. Tugwell (2002) 17; cf. Mulhern 85. 43. NDO 78–79.
44. NSC 520, CLXXVII, CLXXVIII.

45. NDO 104. 46. AD 1: 714.

47. NSMN 1: 117 (482).

48. Marchese 1: 29–210; Mulhern 86–87.

49. NSMN 1: 14 (145), 2: 241 (Sisto); NSMN 12 (133), 2: 236–38 (Ristoro); Tugwell (2002) 16. See also Marchese 1: 37–63; AD 3.1: 313–22; O'Daniel (1921) 48–49; Mulhern 86.

50. NSMN 1: 28 (197), 2: 261; Marchese 1: 66.

51. NSMN 1: 31 (210); Marchese 1: 66.

52. NSMN 1: 35 (219), 2: 273–75; O'Daniel (1921) 65.

53. NSMN 1: 52 (284), 2: 348ff.; Marchese 1: 135–62: cf. NSMN 1: 63 (316), 2: 373.

54. MOPH 20: 86.

55. NSMN 1: 67 (328); Marchese 1: 163–65.

56. NSMN 1: 94 (423), 2: 524; Marchese 1: 135–62.

57. NDO 84.

58. NDO 94.

59. Marchese 1: 73.

60. NSC 467, CVIII; Marchese 1: 442–43; AD 8.2: 681–85; Mulhern 87–89.

61. NSC 504, CLX; Marchese 1: 113.

62. Valle (1651) 175; AD 9.2: 1004–04.

63. Marchese 1: 203–04.

64. *Fra' Bartolomeo e la scuola di San Marco*, ed. S. Padovani (Venice, 1996); "Fra' Bartolomeo," *Wikipedia: L'enciclopedia libera*, Wikimedia Foundation, 2 Apr. 2017 (31 May 2017); AD 10.2: 843–52.

65. NSD 36: 1425.

66. "Fra Damiano da Bergamo," *Wikipedia: L'enciclopedia libera*, Wikimedia Foundation, 2 May 2017 (31 May 2017); Marchese 2: 214–38; Vittorio Polli, *Le tarsie di San Bartolomeo in Bergamo del Frate Damiano Zambelli* (Clusone, 1995).

67. Ambrogino of Soncino, *Vita del beato fra' Giacomo d'Alemagna* (Bologna, 1613), Latin trans. Isidoro of Milan, AS 53 (Oct. V): 793–803; Razzi 294–91; Hieronymus Wilms, *Der selige Jakob Griesinger aus Ulm* (Dülmen, 1922); English trans. *Lay Brother, Artist and Saint* (London, 1957); Alfonso D'Amato, *Un maestro nell'arte delle vetrate istoriate* (Bologna, 1991); *Butler's Lives* 4: 89–90.

68. Venturino Alce, "Il beato Giacomo da Ulma, maestro di vetrate a Bologna tra il 1453 e il 1476," *Memorie domenicane*, 78 (1961): 128–51.

69. Alberti 262v; Pio 188; AD 2.1: 153–54; "Ambrosino da Tormoli," *Wikipedia: L'enciclopedia libera*, Wikimedia Foundation, 20 Nov. 2015 (31 May 2017).

70. Jordan, *Libellus* 88, 67 (Lehner trans. 72). 71. AD 3.1: 138.

72. NSMN 15: 147.
73. NSMN 15: 148.
74. Venchi 133.
75. Jordan, *Libellus*, n. 55; HOPD 501; Vicaire 364.
76. AS 25 (Jun. V), n. 70, 360; AD 11.1: 259–60; Hinnebusch 1: 289.
77. NSMN 1: 84–85 (401), 2: 435–38; Loenertz 173–74; Hinnebusch 1: 290.
78. BOP 2: 286.
79. ACG 2: 317 (Bologna 1347).
80. See Bennett, esp. 155.
81. ACG 2: 51 (Naples 1309).
82. ACG 2: 51 (Naples 1309).
83. ACPR 140 (Todi 1301).
84. ACPA 20: 277 (Pamplona 1304).
85. ACG 2: 358 (Narbonne 1354); ACG 2: 365 (Pamplona 1355); ACG 2: 386 (Prague 1359).
86. ACPCL 211–49; legislation: ACPCL 211–306. 87. NSC 530–546; NSMN 65–84.
88. NSC 539, CCII.
89. NSD 5–6.
90. NSMN 97ff.
91. NSMN 185 (705).
92. ACG 3: 137 (Bologna 1410).
93. NSMN 97 (433).
94. NSMN 138 (526).
95. ACPA 32: 366 (Huesca 1378); ACG 3: 380 (Rome 1484); ACG 3: 391 (Venice 1487).
96. ACG 2: 364 (Pomplona 1355); ACG 3: 243 (Savigliano 1439).
97. ACG 3: 152 (Strasbourg 1417).
98. ACG 3: 23–24 (Avignon 1387).
99. ACG 3: 38 (Rouen 1388).
100. ACPA 35: 356–57 (Balaguer 1399).
101. ACG 3: 16 (Avignon 1386).
102. ACG 3: 115–28 (Nuremberg 1405); ACG 3: 81–84 (Poitiers 1407).
103. ACG 3: 158.
104. Vargas 130, 135.
105. ACPA 24: 285 (Lérida 1354).
106. ACPA 24: 267–68 (Játiva 1353); Vargas 138.
107. Vargas 180.
108. ACG 2: 302 (Le Puy 1344).
109. ACPA 25: 348 (Lérida 1357); Vargas 135.
110. ACPA 25: 359 (Lérida 1357).
111. E.g., ACPR; ACPLI (1307).
112. E.g., ACPR 184 (Lucca 1312); ACPHo 160 (Bremen 1488).

113. Gómez (2006) 4: examples 1282 (Vienne), 1283 (Montpellier).
114. ACPR 153 (Rieti 1305); ACPR 165 (Fuligno 1307), etc.
115. CDO 114; Jasinski 101; Hinnebusch 1: 289; Gómez (2009) 5.
116. ACPCL 262 (Como 1490).
117. ACPHo 98 (Leeuwarden 1479).
118. ACG 2: 411 (Bruges 1369); Hinnebusch 1: 290; ACG ROME, 3: 93 (Venice 1394); ACG 4: 18 (Rome 1501).
119. ACG 1: 322 (Besançon 1303); ACPH 151 (Nizeux 1487).
120. ACPH 294 (Rotterdam 1510); MOPH 17: n. 96, 48; MOPH 17: 41 (n. 52); MOPH 17: 131 (n. 176).
121. ACPHo 416 (Visitation report, Lille, Belgium, 22 Jun. 1489).
122. ACPCL 257 (Brescia 1486).
123. ACG 2: 147 (Barcelona, 1323).
124. ACG 2: 360 (Narbonne 1354). 125. ACG 2: 406 (Genoa 1366).
126. ACG 2: 415 (Valencia 1370),
127. ACPH 33–34 (Douay 1470); ACPH 52 (Zutphen 1471).
128. ACPH 24 (Rotterdam 1468); ACPH 52 (Zutphen 1471. 129. ACG 3: 36 (Rouen 1388).
130. ACPA 34: 299 (Pomplona 1392).
131. CDO 214–15 (Narbonne 1392).
132. ACPA 23: 309 (Balaguer 1351),
133. ACPCL 264 (Como 1490).
134. ACPCL 286 (Bologna 1510).
135. ACPCL 285 (Bologna 1510).
136. ACG 3: 132 (Nuremberg 1405).
137. ACG 1: 133 (Trier 1266); Mulhern 61.
138. ACG 2: 7 (Toulouse 1304); ACG 2: 27 (Strasbourg 1307); ACG 2: 44 (Zaragoza 1310); ACG 2: 68 (Metz 1313); ACG 2: 74 (London 1314), etc.
139. ACPA 21: 138 (Valencia 1314); ACPA 22: 142 (Valencia 1327); ACPA 22: 152 (Huesca 1328), etc.
140. ACG-1407 200 (Bologna); ACG-1413 312 (Genoa); ACG 3: 180 (Metz 1421); ACG 3: 202 (Bologna 1426); ACPH 493 (Cordoba 1464), etc.
141. ACG-1473 499 (Basel 1473).
142. E.g., ACG 3: 372 (Rome 1481) for Sixtus IV; ACG 3: 421 (Ferrara 1494) for Alexander VI.
143. ACG 3: 436 (Ferrara 1498). 144. Valle 238; AD 6.1: 293.

CHAPTER 3 REFORMERS, MISSIONS, AND MARTYRS, 1500–1650

1. Hinnebusch (1975) 127–30.
2. NRP v.

3. ACG 4: 186, 193 (Valladolid 1523).
4. ACG 5: 4, 9–79 (Bologna 1564).
5. E.g., ACG 4: 70 (Pavia 1507); AGC 4: 234 (Rome 1530); ACG 6: 69 (Valladolid 1605).
6. Clement VIII, BOP 8: 112, no. 45 (19 May 1603); ACG 6: 360 (Toulouse 1628).
7. ACG 6: 264 (Bologna 1615).
8. ACG 6: 367 (Toulouse 1628).
9. ACG 7: 31 (Rome 1629).
10. CDO 114 (Bologna 1706); CDO 114: Benedict XIII, BOP 6: 683 (Dec. 20, 1728); CDO 114 (Rome 1777).
11. ACG 5: 194 (Rome 1530); ACG 5: 166 (Barcelona 1574).
12. ACG 5: 331 (Venice 1592).
13. *Dominican Penitent Women* esp. 5–7; TOP Rule (1415): 41–48.
14. Thompson (2005) 69–103.
15. TOP Rule (1415) 5–7.
16. ACG 6: 121 (Rome 1608).
17. TOP Rule (1415) 3–4.
18. TOP Rule (1415) 13, cf. 14.
19. TOP Rule (1415) 20, 39
20. TOP Rule (1415) 25.
21. TOP Rule (1415) 32.
22. ACG 7: 398 (Rome 1656).
23. ACG 5: 368 (Valencia 1596); ACG 5: 394 (Naples 1600).
24. CDO 114; CDO 477.9–10 (Rome 1670, Rome 1756).
25. Gómez (2006) 5.
26. ACG 7: 109–10 (Rome 1644).
27. CDO 116 (Rome 1650, Rome 1656, Rome 1756).
28. ACG 7: 353 (Rome 1650); AD 6.2: 524.
29. ACG 6: 60 (Valladolid 1605); ACG 6: 94–95 (Rome 1608).
30. ACG 6: 61 (Valladolid 1605); CDO 117 (Rome 1777).
31. CDO 117 (Rome 1670); Hinnebusch (1975) 127.
32. AD 5.2: 523 (Sousa).
33. AD 10.2: 775.
34. ACG 7: 224 (Valencia 1647). 35. ACG 7: 356, 360 (Rome 1650).
36. ACG 7: 354 (Rome 1650); AD 10.2: 824.
37. AD 12.1: 160.
38. ACG 5: 277, 282 (Rome 1589).
39. ACG 6: 133–34 (Paris 1611).
40. ACG 6: 243 (Bologna 1615).
41. CDO 117 (Rome 1694).
42. ACG 5: 368 (Valencia 1596).
43. "Historical Notes" 3.

44. CDO 85 (Salamanca 1551).
45. 45. ACG 6: 243 (Bologna 1615).
46. 46. ACG 4: 176 (Rome 1518).
47. 47. Gómez (2006) 6.
48. ACG 5: 64 (Bologna 1564); CDO 118 (Bologna 1564, Barcelona 1574, Rome, 1580, Naples 1600, Rome 1608, Paris 1611, Bologna 1615). BOP 8: 144, no. 4 (1630).
49. CDO 118 (Bologna 1564, Barcelona 1574, Rome 1580, Rome 1589).
50. CDO 117–18 Alexander VIII (21 Sep. 1663); Clement VIII (10 Mar. 1693).
51. ACG 7: 18 (Rome 1629).
52. ACG 4: 177 (Rome 1518); ACG 4: 193 (Valladolid 1523); AGC 4: 215 (Rome 1525); ACG 4: 289 (Rome 1539); ACG 4: 301 (Rome 1542).
53. ACG 4: 322 (Salamanca 1551); Gómez (2006) 5.
54. ACG 5: 48 (Avignon 1561); ACG 5: 78 (Bologna 1564); ACG 5: 115 (Rome 1569); ACG 5: 148 (Rome 1571); ACG 5: 187–89 (Barcelona 1574); ACG 226 (Rome 1580).
55. ACG 5: 146 (Rome 1571).
56. ACG 5: 175–76 (Rome 1574).
57. ACG 5: 261 (Rome 1583); ACG 5: 307 (Rome 1589); ACG 5: 346 (Venice 1592); ACG 5: 378 (Naples 1596); ACG 5.5: 405 (Naples 1600).
58. ACG 6: 42 (Rome 1601); ACG 6: 51 (Valladolid 1605); ACG 6: 82–83 (Valladolid 1605); ACG 6: ACG 126 (Rome 1608); ACG 6: 180 (Paris 1611); ACG 6: 229–30 (Rome 1612); ACG 6: 294–95 (Bologna 1615); ACG 6: 319 (Lisbon 1618); ACG 6: 350–51 (Milan 1622); ACG 6: 377 (Toulouse 1628); ACG 7: 74 (Rome 1629); ACG 7: 214 (Rome 1644); ACG 7: 274–75 (Valencia 1647); ACG 7: 374 (Rome 1650); ACG 7: 485 (Rome 1656).
59. AD 6.2: 618–19.
60. AD 1: 186.
61. AD 7.2: 762–68.
62. AD 7.2: 68 (Archives du Rhône, Fonds des Jacobins, Inventaire 4, fo. 262).
63. AD 12.1: 205–06 (Sousa).
64. ACG 5: 120 (Rome 1571).
65. AD 2.2: 453–54.
66. ACG 7: 282, 300 (Rome 1650).
67. AD 1: 99.
68. AD 7.1: 26.
69. AD 10.2: 663–66.
70. AD 5.2: 686.
71. CDO 190 (Rome 1670).
72. ACG 6: 102 (Rome 1608).
73. ACG 7: 203 (Rome 1644).
74. ACG 7: 482 (Rome 1656).

75. AD 4.1: 310–11; inscription: AD 4.1: 311.
76. AD 9.1: 90.
77. AD 9.2: 566.
78. Nicolas Le Roux, *Un Régicide au nom de Dieu* (Paris, 2006). 79. AD 2.2: 731.
80. AD 10.1: 100–01.
81. AD 1: 831.
82. Joseph Hyacinth Albanès, *Couvent royal de Saint-Maximin* (Nîmes, 2002); AD 4.1: 427.
83. AD 9.1: 66.
84. NRP 6; "Frà Angiolo Marchissi speziale e aromatario in Santa Maria Novella nel xvi secolo," Aneddoti e curiosità, Officina Profumo Farmaceutica di Santa Maria Novella, 2013 (7 Jun. 2017).
85. NRP 53.
86. NRP 8.
87. NRP 43.
88. AD 11.1: 194; AD 9.2: 520.
89. ACG 7: 30 (Rome 1629).
90. Razzi 283; AD 4.1: 356.
91. Valle 256–57; AD 8.2: 573.
92. ACG 7: 353 (Rome 1650).
93. AD 1: 513–14.
94. ACG 7: 205 (Rome 1644).
95. AD 7.1: 250.
96. AD 10.2: 488–92; text: AD 10.2: 491–92.
97. ACG 5: 116–17 (Rome 1569); ACG 5: 149 (Rome 1571); ACG 5: 262–63 (Rome 1582).
98. ACG 5:308 (Rome 1589); O'Daniel (1921) 77.
99. Thomas Burke, *Hibernia Dominicana* (Cologne [i.e. Kilkenny], 1762); John O'Heyne and Ambrose Coleman, *The Irish Dominicans of the Seventeenth Century* (Dundalk, 1902); M. H. MacInerny, *A History of the Irish Dominicans* (Dublin, 1916); Daphne Pochin Mould, *The Irish Dominicans* (Dublin, 1957); Thomas S. Flynn, *The Irish Dominicans*, 1536–1641 (Dublin, 1993).
100. ACG 7: 468–79 (Rome 1656).
101. ACG 7: 206 (Rome 1644); Burke 563; Moulde 228.
102. Burke 562; Moulde 228.
103. ACG 7: 471 (Rome 1656), cf. ACG 7: 364 (Rome 1650); Burke 570; O'Heyne 191; Moulde 229; O'Daniel (1921) 79, f.n. 5.
104. ACG 7: 365 (Rome 1650); ACG 7: 475 (Rome 1656); Burke 565; Moulde 288; cf. AD 4.2: 650, AD 6.2: 393.
105. Burke 575; AD 12.1: 133–34.
106. Burke 556; O'Heyne 265; Moulde 228.
107. ACG 7: 471 (Rome 1656); Burke 573; O'Heyne 265; Moulde 229; cf. AD 9.2: 568.

108. ACG 7: 475 (Rome 1656); AD 3.1: 324
109. See Piotr Stolarski, *Friars on the Frontier* (New York, 2016).
110. ACG 6: 283 (Bologna 1615); AD 3.1: 327–37, esp. 333–35.
111. AD 11.1: 406.
112. ACG 7: 368–70 (Rome 1650); AD 3.1: 327–37; Klemens Chodykiewicz, *De Rebus Gestis in Provincia Russae Ordinis Praedicatorum Commentarius*, 2 vols. (Berdyczow, 1780).
113. Cf. O'Daniel (1921) 79, f.n. 4.
114. AD 11.2: 562.
115. Three friars: Nizhyn; Lubartów (Poland); 2 friars: Potok (Poland); 1 friar: Kolomyia, Sokolov (Poland), Rohatyn, Morakw, Zboriv.
116. AD 8.2: 888; Fontana 652–54, 673.
117. ACG 5: 149–53 (Rome 1571).
118. ACG 5: 227–30 (Rome 1580).
119. AD 2.2: 583–84.
120. AD 4.2: 897 (Sousa).
121. AD 4.1: 94 (Sousa).
122. Venchi 247–49; Francisco Carrero, *Triunfo del S. Rosario y Orden de S. Domingo en los reinos del Japón (1617–1624)* (1626; rpt. Madrid, 1993); Carlo Longo, *Giordano Ansalone e i martiri giapponesi del 1633* (Reggio Calabria, 1980); J. Delgado García, *Fr. Juan de la Badía, O.P.*, misionero del Japón y Domingo Castellet, O.P., misionero mártir del Japón (Madrid, 1986); Ceferino Puebla Pedrosa et al., *Witnesses of the Faith in the Orient*, trans. Maria Maez, 2. ed., ed. George G. Christian (Hong Kong, 2006); Fidel Villarroel, *Lorenzo de Manila* (Manila, 1988).
123. Venchi 247–46.
124. Venchi 249.
125. ACG 7: 208 (Rome 1644).
126. C. R. Boxer and J. S. Cummins, *The Dominican Mission in Japan* (1602—1622) and Lope de Vega (Rome, 1963); C. R. Boxer, *The Christian Century in Japan, 1549–1640* (Berkeley, 1967), esp. 342–61; Neil Fujita, *Japan's Encounter with Christianity* (New York, 1991); Jurgis Ellisonas, "Christianity and the Daimyo," *Early Modern Japan*, The Cambridge History of Japan 4, ed. John Whitney Hall (Cambridge, 2008), 301–71.
127. AD 9.1: 337–78; Puebla 30.
128. AD 7.2: 803–06; Puebla 46, 48.
129. AD 9.1: 257–63, esp. 261–63; Puebla 52, 54.
130. AD 8.2: 711–25.
131. AD 10.2: 587–92 (Aduarte).

CHAPTER 4 IBERIA AND NEW WORLDS, 1550–1700

1. Ruiz 4–5.
2. ACG 8: 251 (Rome 1686).
3. AD 4.2: 566–67 (AGC 1644).
4. AD 6.1: 59.
5. AD 4.1: 248 (López).
6. AD 4.1: 452.
7. AD 2.1: 22.
8. AD 4.2: 699 (López).
9. AD 5.1: 173–74.
10. Tomás Fuster, *Resumen historico de los prodigios acaecidos en el Monasterio y Monte Santo de Luchente y de los varones santos de este devotissimo santuario* (1691; rpt. Valencia, 1997), 2.4; AD 12.1: 80.
11. AD 2.1: 255–56.
12. ACG 7: 361 (Rome 1650).
13. AD 1: 258.
14. AD 8.1: 502.
15. ACG 7: 200 (Rome 1644).
16. AD 1: 331.
17. AD 3.1: 285–86 (López).
18. AD 4.1: 93–94 (López).
19. ACG 7: 427 (Rome 1644); AD 8.1: 417–27l.
20. ACG 7: 201 (Rome 1644).
21. AD 1: 77.
22. AD 5.2: 701; AD 5.1: 222.
23. ACG 7: 364 (Rome 1650); AD 9.1: 132.
24. AD 1: 113–17 (López).
25. ACG 7: 364 (Rome 1650); AD 6.2: 393.
26. ACG 7: 361 (Rome 1650).
27. AD 5.2: 482 (López).
28. AD 9.2: 815 (López).
29. AD 9.1: 816.
30. AD 1: 852.
31. Jerónimo Moreno, *La vida y muerte de y cosas milagrosas que el Señor ha hecho por el venerable Fray Pablo de Santa María* (Seville, 1609); Ramón Freire Gálvez, "Fray Pablo de Santa Maria, dominico ecijano, venerado por su ejercicio de la caridad en Sevilla, durante el siglo XVI," Página de un Ecijano, March 2014 (13 Jun. 2017); AD 12.2: 752.
32. ACG 7: 359–60 (Rome 1650); ACG 7: 420 (Rome 1659).
33. Ruiz 5, esp. f.n. 22 & 23.
34. O'Daniel (1921) 77.
35. AD 4.1: 377–78 (López).

36. ACG 4: 327–28, 347 (Salamanca 1551).

37. Ruiz 6–12.

38. Francisco Hernández de Viana, "Report on Granting Passive Voice to the Cooperator Brothers" 2 (AGOP III.7.1977.2, packet 7).

39. ACG 7: 338 (Rome 1650).

40. Ruiz 16.

41. ACG 8: 100 (Rome 1670).

42. AD 8.1: 345.

43. AD 10.2: 623 (Dávila).

44. AD 6.2: 605–06 (Dávila).

45. Pio 32–35; AD 4.1: 254 (Dávila).

46. See Michael Gannon, *The Cross in the Sand* (Gainesville, 1965). 47. AD 12.1: 80–82 (Dávila); O'Daniel (1930) 1116–19, 130–35. 48. O'Daniel (1930) 185–88; Franco 156–60.

49. AD 11.1: 404; O'Daniel (1930) 102–09 (Dávila).

50. O'Daniel (1930) 86–98 (Dávila 1.1.60; Franco 558).

51. O'Daniel (1930) 186.

52. Poole 91.

53. ACG 8: 202 (Rome 1677); O'Daniel (1921) 71.

54. ACG 5: 564 (Valencia 1596).

55. Aduarte 1: 203–05; AD 12.1: 231–33.

56. ACG 6: 173–74 (Paris 1611).

57. ACG 6: 280 (Bologna 1615).

58. ACG 6: 374 (Toulouse 1628).

59. Aduarte (1640) 1: 395–97; AD 6.2: 423.

60. ACG 6: 379 (1628); Aduarte (1640) 2: 255–56; AD 6.1: 204–05.

61. ACG 7: 482 (Rome 1656); AD 9.1: 419–20; AD 5.1: 429–30.

62. AD 9.1: 163–65.

63. AD 11.2: 791–92.

64. ACG 9: 289 (Rome 1756).

65. Poole 55–63; James Lockhart, *Spanish Peru*, 1532–1560 (Madison, 1968); Luis Martin, *The Kingdom of the Sun* (New York, 1974).

66. Ruiz 20–21.

67. ACG 5: 135 (Rome 1571).

68. Cussen 31-63

69. Cooperator Brothers Study (2013) 108–10 (Appendix—M).

70. Cussen 38–39.

71. AD 9.1: 254–55 (Meléndez).

72. ACG 1642, 1656 (MOPH 12: 96–97, 479–80); *Proceso de beatificación de Fray Martín de Porres 1: Proceso diocesano, años 1660, 1664, 1671*, J. Prieto, ed. (Valencia, 1960); AS 68 (Nov. III): 108–25; Bernardo de Medina, *Vida prodigiosa del venerable siervo de Dios Fr. Martin de Porras, natural de Lima, de la tercera Orden de N.P. Santo Domingo* (Madrid, 1675).

73. See also: Giuliana Cavallini, *Vita di S. Martino de Porres, O.P.* (Rome, 1962), English trans. *St. Martin de Porres* (London, 1963); Salvador Velasco, *San Martín de Porres* (Madrid, 1992); Reginaldo Frascisco, *Il primo santo dei negri d'America* (Bologna, 1994); Alex García-Rivera, *St. Martin De Porres* (Maryknoll, 1994); Joan Monahan, *Martin de Porres* (New York, 2002); Brian J. Pierce, *Martin de Porres* (Hyde Park, 2008). Bibliography: Venchi 222–23; *Butler's Lives* 4: 269–70.

74. Cussen 11–12.

75. ACG 6: 65 (Valladolid 1605).

76. 76. ACG 6: 171 (Paris 1611).

77. ACG 6: 268, 271 (Bologna 1615).

78. ACG 6: 311 (Lisbon 1618).

79. ACG 6: 343 (Milan 1622); ACG 6: 373 (Toulouse 1628).

80. ACG 7: 55 (Rome 1629).

81. Cf. AS 68 (Nov. III): 115.

82. Cussen 27.

83. Cussen 39–40.

84. Cavallini 46; Pierce 77.

85. 85. AS 68 (Nov. III): 111, 115.

86. See Pierce, chapter 3; Cavallini 45–46; Cussen 30; Monahan 31–32.

87. Cussen 54–84.

88. Cussen 132–42.

89. Cussen 61–63.

90. Cussen 85–100.

91. ACG 7: 96–97 (Genoa 1642); ACG 7: 479–80 (Rome 1656).

92. ACG 9: 317–18 (Rome 1777).

93. "Ad Perennem Sancti Martini de Porres Canonizationis Memoria." ASOP 70 (1962): 551–84.

94. ACG 7: 83 (Genoa 1642).

95. ACG 8: 97 (Rome 1670).

96. Cussen 153–78; Aurelio Miró Quesada Sosa, *Martín de Porres en el arte y en el folklore* (Lima? 1939).

97. AD 4.1: 146 (Meléndez).

98. AD 8.1: 99–103 (Meléndez); cf. AD 1: 775.

99. AD 2.1: 163–66 (Meléndez).

100. Velasco 148.

101. AD 3.1: 101–02 (Meléndez).

102. AD 9.2: 567 (Meléndez).

103. Tarsicio Piccari, *Orme di un esule* (Rome, 1975); Salvador Velasco, *San Juan Macías* (Guadalajara, 1975); Reginaldo Frascisco, *San Giovanni Macías* (Rome, 1976); Mary Fabyan Windeatt, *Warrior in White* (New York, 1944); John C. Rubba, *St. John Macias*, 1585–1645 (New York, 1975). Also: AD 10.1: 71–90; Venchi 191–92; *Butler's Lives* 3: 593–94.

104. Piccari 45–50; MOPH 12: 381 (AGC Rome, 1656; Acta of Lima Provincial Chapter, Lima, 1649); *Limana canonizationis Beati Joannis Macias, religiosi professi O.P. (1585–1645)* (Rome, 1973).
105. ACG 7: 381, 404 (Rome 1656).
106. ACG 9: 317–18 (Rome 1777).
107. ACG 7: 97.
108. ACG 7: 210 (Rome 1644).

CHAPTER 5 REVOLUTION AND RESTORATION, 1700–1960

1. John McManners, *Church and Society in Eighteenth-Century France*, 2 vols. (Oxford, 1998); Nigel Aston, *Religion and Revolution in France, 1780–1804* (Basingstoke, 2000); *Enlightenment, Re-Awakening and Revolution*, Cambridge History of Christianity 7, ed. Stewart Brown and Timothy Tackett, (Cambridge, 2006); David Hempton, *The Church in the Long Eighteenth Century* (London, 2011).
2. ACG 9: 96 (Bologna 1725); ACG 9: 165 (Bologna 1748); ACG 9:267 (Rome 1756).
3. ACG 9: 253 (Rome 1756).
4. AD 11.1: 88.
5. AD2 1: 834–35 (Brunone Faraudy, *Vita Patris Antonii a Sanctissimo Sacramento Ordinis FF. Praedicatorum* (Avignon, 1756), ch. 29).
6. ACG 9: 297 (Rome 1756).
7. ACG 9: 285 (Rome 1756).
8. ACG 9: 285 (Rome 1756).
9. ACG 9: 187 (Bologna 1748).
10. Jean-Philippe Rey. "Frère François Romain," *Memoire dominicaine* 2 (1993): 119–34; AD2 1: 162–69; Francesco Milizia, *The Lives of Celebrated Architects, Ancient and Modern* (London, 1826) 304; Leonardo Fernández Troyano, *Bridge Engineering* (London, 2003) 130–35; Charles Smith Whitney, *Bridges of the World* (Mineola, 2003) 144–46.
11. ACG 9: 331 (Rome 1777).
12. ACG 9: 298–392 (Rome 1777).
13. ACG 9: 324, 362 (Rome 1777).
14. ACG 9: 374–92 (Zaragoza 1832); 9: 377, 393 (Rome 1838).
15. ACG 9: 407 (Rome 1838); ACG 9: 14 (Rome 1841).
16. Noble 25.
17. AD2 1: 222–25.
18. AD2 1: 364–78.
19. Paragot esp. 1–9.
20. COP (1867) nn. 1149–50, 297–300.
21. COP (1867) nn. 2468–69, 679–80.
22. COP (1867), D. 2 c. 15 "De Conversis," 678–79.

23. CDO 395 (7 Feb. 1862).
24. COP (1867) no. 2475–77, 680–81.
25. Vilarrasa 68–71.
26. COP (1867) 681–82.
27. COP (1867) no. 2434, 682, cf. ibid. 678, f.n. 2; Vilarrasa 63–64.
28. COP (1867) 679 f.n. 1, 685; Vilarrasa 95.
29. CDO 115.
30. COP (1867) nn. 2489–90, 684.
31. COP (1867) 678, f.n. 1, cf. COP (1867) n. 2483, 682.
32. COP (1867) 683–86.
33. O'Daniel (1921) 112–17.
34. O'Daniel (1921) 126–38.
35. Vilarrasa iii.
36. Vilarrasa 89–90.
37. Vilarrasa 23–25.
38. Vilarrasa 92–94.
39. Vilarrasa 94.
40. Vilarrasa 22.
41. Vilarrasa 36–37.
42. Vilarrasa 38–41.
43. O'Daniel (1921) 144–51.
44. Lacroix 289–302.
45. Lacroix 336–42.
46. Lacroix 343–48.
47. Paragot 16–19.
48. Paragot 18.
49. Paragot 13–15.
50. Paragot 16.
51. Lacroix 349–64.
52. See CGOP (1876), index 165–240; CGOP (1910) esp. 386–87; CGOP (1921) 442–43; CGOP (1931) 605–06; CGOP (1949) 947–54; CGOP (1967) 686–705; CGOP (1992) 642–69.
53. Magboo 503.
54. E.g. COP (1886) 678–86; *Index* 114 (Ávila 1895); *Index* n. 88 (Viterbo 1909), 82.
55. *Index* n. 76 (Rome 1910), 143.
56. ACG 1913 (Venlo) n. 39, 94.
57. McCarthy (interview).
58. ACG 1913 (Venlo) 99.
59. ACG 1913 (Venlo) n. 107, 181.
60. Bro. Peter Yost (b. 1929) of Holy Name Province.
61. COP (1924) 47–51 "De Conversis." 62. COP (1924) n. 156, 47.

63. ACG 1938 (Rome) n. 43, 71.
64. COP (1924) nn. 169–72, 50–51.
65. COP (1924) nn. 157–62, 47–48.
66. COP (1924) nn. 163–65, 48–49.
67. E.g., ACG 1935 (Rome).
68. COP (1932) 2.1.5.4 "De Fratribus Conversis."
69. ACG 1938 (Rome) n. 45–46, 77; ACG 1938 (Rome) n. 60, 83.
70. O'Daniel (1921) 37–38.
71. O'Daniel (1921) 40.
72. Noble 5–7 (I cite the English version). 73. O'Daniel (1921) 39.
74. Noble 29.
75. O'Daniel (1921) 159–60.
76. Noble 9–11.
77. Noble 14–15.
78. O'Daniel (1921) 43–44.
79. Noble 12–13.
80. Noble 17–20.
81. Noble 23–24.
82. Lacroix 327–35.
83. Lacroix 320–25.
84. Paragot 17.
85. Wichrowicz (Interview).
86. Lacroix 303–13.
87. Magboo 525–29.
88. See Luis Gettino, *Martires Dominicos de la Curzada Española* (Salamanca, 1950).
89. Benedict M. Ashley, *The Dominicans* (Eugene OR, 2009) 229.
90. "Mártires del Siglo XX: Biografías," Oficina de Comunicación Dominicos, 21 Jun. 2007 (21 Jun. 2017).
91. Gettino 387.
92. Gettino 38–43.
93. Gettino 205–07.
94. Jonathan Luxmoore, "Beatification Starts for Dominican Martyrs," The Tablet Publishing Company, 18 Nov. 2006 (20 Jan. 2017).
95. ACG 1946 (Rome) n. 46, 52.
96. ACG 1949 (Washington) nn. 96–99, 67–68.
97. AGOP III.2.1949 "Transcriptum Actorum Commissionum," Commission 5: "De Vocationibus Ordinis" 13–14.
98. AGOP III.2.1949: "Textus Officialis Sessionum Commissionum," "De Vocationibus Ordinis" 5–6.
99. "Insufficiens adaptio conversationis ipsorum ad hodiernam mentem adspirantium."

100. AGOP III.2.1949: "Processus Verbalis," Session 9 (23 Sep. 1949) 90–96.

101. ACG 1949 (Washington) n. 987, 67.

102. Downey (Interview).

103. McCarthy (interview).

104. Downey (Interview).

105. Dolen (interview).

106. O'Leary (interview).

107. COP (1954) nn. 192–96, 74–76.

108. COP (1954) n. 192, 74.

109. COP (1954) n. 194, 74–75.

110. COP (1954) n. 185, 172.

111. ACG 1955 (Rome) n. 180, 99.

112. Lacroix 54–55.

113. Lacroix 169.

114. Lacroix 127–34.

115. Lacroix 167–233.

116. Lacroix 182.

117. Thomas (interview).

118. Downey (Interview).

119. McCarthy (interview).

120. McCarthy (interview).

121. O'Leary (interview).

122. Thai [Bro. Dominic] (Interview).

123. AGOP III.2.1958.2: "Processus Verbalis Sessionum," Second Session (25 Sep. 1958) 10–12.

124. AGOP III.2.1958.2: "Processus Verbalis Sessionum" 9.

125. AGOP III.2.1958.2: "Processus Verbalis Sessionum" 37; ACG 1958 (Caleruega) n. 211, 93.

126. ACG 1958 (Caleruega) n. 118, 65.

127. AGOP III.2.1958.2: "Processus Verbalis Sessionum," 10–11.

128. ACG 1958 (Caleruega) n. 235, 100.

129. AGOP III.2.1958.1: "De Constitutionibus et de Regulari Observantia," "De Questionibus in Proximo Capitulo de Fratribus Conversis."

130. AGOP III.2.1958.2: "Processus Verbalis Sessionum" 10; ACG 1958 (Caleruega) n. 113, 63.

131. Dolen (interview).

CHAPTER 6 THE BROTHERHOOD IN THE AGE OF VATICAN II

1. Documents: *Vatican Council II*, rev. ed., 2 vols., ed. Austin P. Flannery (Northport, 1999). John W. O'Malley, *What Happened at Vatican II* (Cambridge, 2010); Giuseppe Alberigo and Joseph A Komonchak, eds, *The*

History of Vatican II, 5 vols., trans. (Maryknoll, 1998–2006); Giuseppe Alberigo, *A Brief History of Vatican II* (Maryknoll, 2006); Roberto de Mattei, *The Second Vatican Council*, trans. Michael M. Miller (Fitzwilliam, 2012); Matthew Lamb and Matthew Levering, *The Reception of Vatican II* (Oxford, 2017).

2. ACG 1961 (Bologna) nn. 58–59, 57.

3. ACG 1961 (Bologna) n. 81, 69.

4. ACG 1961 (Bologna) n. 60, 58.

5. See AGOP III.2.1961.1–2.

6. AGOP III.2.1961.1, "Petitions."

7. AGOP III.2.1961.2 (Processus Verbalis) 31.

8. "In nostris regionibus causa cooperatorum perdita est."

9. See AGOP III.2 (1962) 1–3.

10. Dolen (interview).

11. Wichrowicz (Interview).

12. Perkins (interview).

13. O'Leary (interview).

14. Thomas (interview).

15. Eli (interview).

16. Thomas (interview).

17. Patalano (interview).

18. Tam [Bro. Francis Xavier] (Interview).

19. Perkins (interview).

20. Downey (Interview).

21. *The Collected Poems of William Everson*, 4 vols. (Santa Barbara CA, 1997); *Prodigious Thrust* (Santa Rosa CA, 1996). Lee Bartlett, *William Everson* (New York, 1988).

22. Barlett 112–27.

23. Barlett 130–40.

24. Thomas (interview).

25. Bartlett 163.

26. Bartlett 219.

27. Barlett 220–34.

28. Patalano (interview).

29. Hayes (interview).

30. "Democratic Republic of the Congo," The Hagiography Circle, 12 May 2017 (27 Jun. 2017).

31. Paul Hinnebusch, *Renewal in the Spirit of St. Dominic* (Washington, 1968); Valentine Walgrave, *Dominican Self-Appraisal in the Light of the Council* (Chicago, 1968).

32. See Van Merrienboer 1; Magboo 514–16.

33. Documentos (1965–67) 1–8 "Animadversiones circa Quaestiones de Fratribus Cooperatores (a. 1965)."

34. Documentos (1965-67) 2-5.
35. AGOP III.2.1965.1, 75-84.
36. AGOP III.2.1965.2, "Relatio R. P. Praesidis Commissionis de Fratribus Coopertoribus"; Documentos (1965-67) 5-8.
37. AGOP III.2.1965.3, "Processus Verbalis" 13-18 (17 Jul. 1965).
38. AGOP III.2.1965.3, "Processus Verbalis" 14-17.
39. AGOP III.2.1965.3, "Processus Verbalis" 17. 40. ACG 1965 (Bogotá) n. 198, 99.
41. ACG 1965 (Bogotá) nn. 128-29, 75-76.
42. ACG 1965 (Bogotá) nn. 254-55, 116.
43. ACG 1965 (Bogotá) n. 276, 123; ibid. n. 130, 76.
44. ACG 1965 (Bogotá) n. 275, 121.
45. Van Merrienboer 1.
46. O'Leary (interview).
47. Thomas (interview).
48. Tam [Bro. Francis Xavier] (Interview).
49. Dolen (interview); Perkins (interview); McCarthy (interview).
50. Eman Bonnici, "Br. Raymond Charles Bertheaux," Find A Grave, 1 Dec. 2011 (28 Jun. 2017).
51. ACOP III.3.1966.1-65.
52. ACOP III.3.1966.15-18; Documentos (1965-67) 8-23.
53. III.3.1966.15 "Summarium N"; III.4.1968.1.9.
54. E.g., III.3.1966.16 (O), 32. d.5, e.1, e.7, e.9, e.15, e.16, f.2, f.8.
55. ACOP III.3.1966.17 "Summarium P"; Documentos (1965-67) 11-22.
56. ACOP III.3.1966.17; Documentos (1965-67) 16-23.
57. ACOP III.3.1966.18.32.a.
58. ACOP III.3.1966.18.32.b1.
59. AGOP. III. 1968/3 Cartella 3; Documentos (1965-67) 23-25.
60. AGOP III.4.1968.3.
61. AGOP III.4.1968.3 Cartella 2.
62. AGOP III.4.1968.3 Cartella 4.
63. AGOP III.4.1968.3 Cartella 2.
64. AGOP III.4.1968.3 Cartella 4.
65. AGOP III.4.1968.3 Cartella 4.
66. ACG 1968 (River Forest) nn. 46, 38.
67. Van Merrienboer 1-3.
68. AGOP III.4.1968.18, 204-06.
69. AGOP III.4.1968.18, 323-34.
70. ACG 1968 (River Forest) n. 83, 56.
71. COP (1969) n. 1, sect. VI, IX, 18, 21.
72. COP (1969) 238.
73. COP (1969) n. 169, 71.
74. Naples (1972), n. 82.

75. COP (1969) n. 179, 74.
76. COP (1969) nn. 217–20, 85–86.
77. COP (1969) n. 63.2, 43.
78. COP (1969) n. 100.2, 54.
79. COP (1969) n. 219.2, 86.
80. Thomas (interview).
81. COP (1969) nn. 440–43, 147–48.
82. COP (1969) n. 443, 148.
83. Madonna dell'Arco (1974) n. 218.
84. Eli (interview).
85. Thomas (interview).
86. Thai [Bro. Dominic] (Interview).
87. Tam [Bro. Francis Xavier] (Interview).
88. Downey (Interview).
89. Perkins (interview).
90. Statistics are from the most recent province directories available.
91. Eli (interview).
92. McCarthy (interview).
93. Tugwell (2002b) 1.
94. ACG 1971 (Tallaght) n. 147, 89; cf. Van Merrienboer 3.
95. 95. ACG 1974 (Madonna dell'Arco) n. 118. 218; n. 218, 144.
96. ACG 1974 (Madonna dell'Arco) n. 222, 134.
97. Van Merrienboer 3–4.
98. AGOP III.6.1974.11, packet 2, 113–16.
99. ACG 1974 (Madonna dell'Arco) n. 207, 130.
100. AGOP III.7.1977.2.
101. AGOP III.7.1977.2 folder 2.
102. AGOP III.7.1977.2, folder 1.
103. AGOP III.7.1977.2, folder 2.
104. AGOP III.7.1977.2, packet 7, 3.
105. AGOP III.7.1977.2, Folder 1.
106. AGOP III.7.1977.2, Folder 1, 32.
107. McCarthy (interview).
108. Downey (Interview).
109. Dolen (interview).
110. Ignatius Perkins, email communication, 7 Feb. 2017; Magboo 520.
111. ACG 1977 (Quezon City) n. 62.3, 43.
112. ACG 1977 (Quezon City) n. 235, 120.
113. ACG 1977 (Quezon City) nn. 62–63, 42–46; Van Merrienboer 4.
114. ACG 1977 (Quezon City) n. 62.2, 42.
115. ACG 1977 (Quezon City) n. 62.5, 43–46.
116. ACG 1977 (Quezon City) n. 63, 46.
117. Magboo 521.

118. Commission Report (2003) 1–2; Documentos (1965–67) 25.

119. ACG 1986 (Ávila) n. 168, 94. Length of debate: oral communication to author, Basil Cole of St. Joseph Province.

120. ACG 1989 (Oakland) Section IV, 119–20.

121. ACG 1992 (Mexico City) n. 36.1.4, 30.

122. ACG 1992 (Mexico City) n. 43, 38.

123. ACG 1995 (Caleruega) 120–21.

124. ACG 1992 (Mexico City) n. 31, 25.

125. Magboo 522–25.

126. ACG 1995 (Caleruega) n. 100.2, 69.

127. ACG 1998 (Bologna) nn. 140–45, 66–67.

128. Tugwell (2002b) 2–3.

129. Perkins (2006b) 7–8.

130. ACG 2004 (Krakow) n. 250–54, 72–73.

131. ACG 1992 (Mexico City) n. 44, 38.

132. ACG 1995 (Caleruega) 121.

133. ACG 2001 (Providence) n. 290, 94.

134. ACG 2004 (Krakow) nn. 256–58, 73.

135. Esposito esp. 3.

136. Gy, esp. 9: "Letter to Azpiroz-Costa and Javier González."

137. Ombres 2–5.

138. González 2–8.

139. Van Merrienboer 6.

140. ACG 1998 (Bologna) nn. 135–37, 64–65.

141. Cf. Gy 1–7.

142. Perkins (2001) 1–6.

143. ACG 2001 (Providence) 173–226.

144. ACG 2001 (Providence) n. 217, 154; ACG 2001 (Providence) n. 289, 93.

145. Expert reports: Tugwell (2002); Tugwell (2002b); Esposito; Gy.

146. Commission Report (2003) 4–7.

147. 2004 (Krakow) 257–58.

148. ACG 2004 (Krakow) n. 295, 83; ACG 2004 (Krakow) n. 358, 95.

149. ACG 2004 (Krakow) 72–74.

150. Ombres; Gómez (2006); González; Perkins (2006).

151. Tugwell (2002).

152. Perkins (2006b). 153. Perkins (2006) 5–6.

154. ACG 2007 (Bogotá) 133–202.

155. ACG 2007 (Bogotá) n. 212, 91.

156. ACG 2007 (Bogotá) n. 165, 72.

157. ACG 2010 (Rome) n. 152, 176.

EPILOGUE BROTHERS OF THE NEW MILLENNIUM

1. AGC 2011 (Rome) n. 218, 82.
2. Friars who have not read the report should request it from their regional superior.
3. Cooperator Brothers Study (2013) 3–4.
4. Cooperator Brothers Study (2013) 9–10.
5. Cooperator Brothers Study (2013) 3-5 (Appendix—A), 28–43 (Appendix—P).
6. Cooperator Brothers Study (2013) 7–18 (Appendix—B).
7. Cooperator Brothers Study (2013) 20–23 (Appendix—C).
8. Cooperator Brothers Study (2013) 45 (Appendix—G).
9. Cooperator Brothers Study (2013) 96–101 (Appendix—L).
10. Cooperator Brothers Study (2013) 35–43 (Appendix—D).
11. Cooperator Brothers Study (2013) 47–64 (Appendix—H).
12. Cooperator Brothers Study (2013) 112–15 (Appendix—N).
13. Cooperator Brothers Study (2013) 160 (in Appendix—S); Cooperator Brothers Study (2013) 151–52 (in Appendix—R).
14. Cooperator Brothers Study (2013) 66–74 (Appendix—I).
15. Cooperator Brothers Study (2013) 25–33 (Appendix—D); Yefrey A. Ramirez, "A Chronicle of the Meeting of Cooperator Brothers," Order of Preachers, 3 Nov. 2012 (3 Jul. 2017).
16. Cooperator Brothers Study (2013) 4–8.
17. ACG 2013 (Trogir) n. 80–82, 32.
18. Eli (interview).
19. Central Province Brothers (Conversation).
20. Kennedy (Conversation),
21. Buda (interview).
22. Wtyło (Interview); Pastuła (Interview); Skowrónski (Interview).
23. Mszyca (Interview)—plumbing; Strycek (Interview)—construction; Kołtyś (Interview)—metalworking.
24. Krus (Interview)—hotel; Mochoń (Interview)—law; Polish Novices (interview).
25. Wtyło (Interview); Strycek (Interview).
26. Pastuła (Interview).
27. Kołtyś (Interview); Skowrónski (Interview).
28. Krus (Interview); Mochoń (Interview).
29. Pastuła (Interview); Strycek (Interview); Kołtyś (Interview).
30. Pastuła (Interview); Wtyło (Interview); Mszyca (Interview).
31. Mochoń (Interview).
32. Strycek (Interview).
33. Dang [Bro. Joseph] (Interview).
34. Tam [Bro. Francis Xavier] (Interview).

35. E.g., An [Bro. Gioan Baotixita] (Interview); Long [Bro. Francis] (Interview).
36. Manh [Bro. Peter] (Interview).
37. Quang [Bro. Peter] (Interview).
38. Long [Bro. Gioan Baotixita] (Interview).
39. Tuyen [Bro. Joseph] (Interview).
40. Hoang [Bro. Augustin] (Interview).
41. Long [Bro. Francis] (Interview).
42. Tuan [Bro. Francis Xavier] (Interview).
43. E.g., Tien [Bro. Joseph] (Interview).
44. Thai [Bro. Dominic] (Interview).
45. Long [Bro. Gioan Baotixita] (Interview); Quang [Bro. Peter] (Interview); Cao [Bro. Dominic] (Interview).
46. An [Bro. Gioan Baotixita] (Interview).
47. Hoang [Bro. Augustin] (Interview).
48. Dang [Bro. Joseph] (Interview).
49. Manh [Bro. Peter] (Interview).
50. Tam [Bro. Peter] (Interview).
51. Duong [Bro. Peter] (Interview).
52. Vietnamese Students (Interview).
53. Khanh [Bro. Peter] (Interview).

Bibliography

Unpublished Documents

AGOP Archivum Generale Ordinis Praedicatorum
General Curia, Santa Sabina, Rome, Italy
General Chapter of Washington (1949)
AGOP III.2.1949: All materials
General Chapter of Caleruega (1958)
AGOP III.2.1958.1: Petitions and Commissions
AGOP III.2.1958.2: Processus Verbalis
General Chapter of Toulouse (1961)
AGOP III.2.1961.1: Petitions
AGOP III.2.1961.2: Processus Verbalis
General Chapter of Bogotá (1965)
AGOP III.2.1965.1: Petitions
AGOP III.2.1965.2: Commissions
AGOP III.2.1965.3: Late Petitions, Processus Verbalis
Chapter of River Forest and Preparatory Materials (1965–68)
ACOP III.3.1966.1–65: Questionnaire on Order and Replies
ACOP III.3.1966.15–18: Questions N, O, P, Q (On Cooperators)
ACOP III.4.1968.1.9: Digested Questions on Cooperators
AGOP III.4.1968.1–3: Congress of Provincials in Rome (1967)
AGOP III.4.1968.4–18: Chapter of River Forest (1968)
AGOP III.4.1968.18: Processus Verbalis
Chapter of Madonna dell'Arco (1974)
AGOP III.6.1974.1–12: Chapter of Madonna dell'Arco (1974)
AGOP III.6.1974.6: Petitions
AGOP III.6,1974.11: Processus Verbalis
Chapter of Quezon City (1977)
AGOP III.7.1977.1–11: Chapter of Quezon City (1977)
AGOP III.7.1977.2: Commission of Cooperator Brothers

Byrd, Paul. "Dominican Cooperator Brothers: Saints—Blesseds—Martyrs." Unpublished document. In Cooperator Brothers Study (2013), Appendix—J, 73–78.

Commission Report (2003). "Report of the Commission on the Cooperator Brothers." Ed. Pedro Luis González. Commissioned by 2001 General Chapter (Providence), n. 289. Unpublished document, 1 October 2003.

Cooperator Brothers Study (2013). Dominican Cooperator Brothers Study—2013: "Dedicating Ourselves to God, Following Christ to Lead an Evangelical Life in the Order (LCO 189, I). Ed. Ignatius Perkins et al. Privately printed, 2013.

Documentos (1965–77). "Documentos sobre los hermanos cooperadores [1965–77]." Ed. Lázaro Sartre from the Archives of the Order, 12/12/2005. Unpublished

documents, in Report (2006), Appendix A—3.
Esposito, Bruno. Letter to Pedro González and Commission on Cooperator Brothers. Unpublished document, 20 March 2002.
Final Report (2013). Final Report with Recommendations and Appendices: Presented to the Master of the Order and the General Curia (1 September 2013). Privately printed, 2013.
Gómez, Vito T. "Hermanos cooperadores de la Orden de Predicadores repaso de fuentes primitivas." Unpublished document. In Report (2006), Appendix A—2.
González, Javier. "The Dominican Cooperator Brothers: Their Role and Mission in the Clerical Order of Preachers." Unpublished document, in Report (2008), Appendix B—3.
Gy, Pierre-Marie. "Paper about the Dominican Cooperator Brothers." Unpublished document, 24 April 2002, with Letter to Carlos Aspiroz-Costa and Javier Gonzalez, 12 April 2002.
Ombres, Roberto. "Frati domenicani in un ordine clericale: Riflessioni canonistiche." Unpublished document, in Report (2006), Appendix B—1.
Paragot, V. "Les Fréres convers de la province d'Occitania et Lyon (1856-1953)." Typescript (1 Jan. 1954). Paris (Le Saulchoir): Archives Province Dominicaine Lyon, B 1501.
Perkins (2001), Ignatius. "Called to Preach: Brothers of the Order of Preachers: Reflections Presented to the Elective Chapter, Friars of the Order of Preachers, 4 August 2001, Priory of St. Thomas Aquinas, Province, Rhode Island." Unpublished document, 2001.
Perkins (2006), Ignatius. "Krakow Commission: Clerical Nature in the Order of Preachers and the Role of the Cooperator Brothers: Summary Report." Unpublished document, 2006.
Perkins (2006b), Ignatius. "The Dominican Cooperator Brother: Re-visioning the Vocation and Ministry of the Cooperator Brother for the Third Millennium." Unpublished document, in Report (2006), Appendix C—5.
Report (2007). "Report of the Commission on ACG, Krakow, Numbers 257-258." Unpublished report, with an appendix of 12 documents, submitted to the General Chapter of Krakow, 2007.
Ruiz, John Martin. "Evangelization in the New World: The Role of the Dominican Convent." Unpublished article. Received from the author, 7/20/16.
"Historical Notes" "Some Historical Notes on the Dominican Cooperator Brothers." Unpublished essay. Prepared for the Commission on Cooperator Brothers (2002).
Tugwell (2002), Simon. "Dominican Conversi in the Thirteenth Century." Istituto Storico Domenicano, March 2002. In Report (2006), Appendix A—1.
Tugwell (2002b), Simon. "A Personal Response to the Commission's Questions." In Report (2006).
Van Merrienboer, Edward. "The Legislative Development of the Dominican Cooperator Brothers." Unpublished document, ca. 1990.

PUBLISHED SOURCES AND REFERENCE WORKS

ACD *Acta Canonizationis Sancti Dominici* [Bologna Process]. Ed. Angelus Walz. MHSPND 2. MOPH 26.2. Rome: Institutum Historicum, 1935: 123–67. English Translation: *Saint Dominic: Biographical Documents*. Ed. Francis C. Lehner. Washington, DC: Thomist, 1964: 95–135.

ACG *Acta Capitulorum Generalium Ordinis Praedicatorum*. MOPH 3–4, 8–14. Ed. Benedictus Maria Reichert. 9 vols. Rome: In Domo Generalitiae, 1898–1904. Vol. 1: 1220–1303; vol. 2: 1304–1378; vol. 3: 1380–1498; vol. 4: 1501–1553; vol. 5: 1558–1600; vol. 6: 1601–1628; vol. 7: 1629–1656; vol. 8: 1670–1721; vol. 9: 1725–1844.

ACG 1407. "Fragmenta Actorum Cap. Gen. Bononiae an. 1407. celebrati." Ed. G. Meersseman. AFP 22 (1952): 196–200.

ACG 1413. "Acta Cap. Gen. Celebrati Genuae an. 1413." Ed. S. L. Forte. AFP 26 (1956): 291–313.

ACG 1473. "Supplementum ad Acta Cap. Gen. O.P." Ed. G. M. Löhr. AOP 18 (1927–28): 494–505.

ACG 1913 (Venlo). *Acta Capituli Generalis Diffinitorum Ordinis Praedicatorum Venlonae . . . 1913*. Sub H.-M. Cormier. Rome: Typis Polyglottis, 1913.

ACG 1938 (Rome). *Acta Capituli Generalis Diffinitorum Sacri Ordinis Praedicatorum Romae, 1938*. Sub M.-S. Gillet. Rome: Ex Domo Generalitiae, 1938.

ACG 1946 (Rome). Acta Capituli Generalis Electivi Sacri Ordinis Ff. Praedicatorum Romae, 1946. Sub E. Suarez. Rome: Ad S. Sabina, 1947.

ACG 1949 (Washington). *Acta Capituli Generalis Diffinitorum Sacri Ordinis Ff. Praedicatorum Washingtonii, 1949*. Sub E. Suarez. Rome: Ad S. Sabina, 1949.

ACG 1955 (Rome). *Acta Capituli Generalis Electivi Sacri Ordinis Ff. Praedicatorum Romae, 1955*. Sub M. Browne. Rome: Ad S. Sabina, 1955.

ACG 1958 (Caleruega). *Acta Capituli Generalis Diffinitorum Sacri Ordinis Ff. Praedicatorum Caleruegae, 1958*. Sub M. Browne. Rome: Ad S. Sabina, 1958.

ACG 1961 (Bologna). *Acta Capituli Generalis Diffinitorum Sacri Ordinis Ff. Praedicatorum Bononiae, 1961*. Sub M. Browne. Rome: Ad S. Sabina, 1961.

ACG 1962 (Toulouse). *Acta Capituli Generalis Electivi Sacri Ordinis Ff. Praedicatorum Tolosae, 1962*. Sub A. Fernandez. Rome: Ad S. Sabina, 1962.

ACG 1965 (Bogotá). *Acta Capituli Generalis Diffinitorum Sacri Ordinis Ff. Praedicatorum Bogotae, 1965*. Sub A. Fernandez. Rome: Ad S. Sabina, 1965.

ACG 1968 (River Forest). *Acta Capituli Generalis Provincialium Ordinis Ff. Praedicatorum, River Forest, 1968*. Sub A. Fernandez. Rome: Ad S. Sabina, 1968.

ACG 1971 (Tallaght). *Acta Capituli Generalis Diffinitorum Fratrum Ordinis Praedicatorum Tallaghtae, 1971*. Sub A. Fernandez. Rome: Ad S. Sabina, 1971.

ACG 1974 (Madonna dell'Arco). *Acta Capituli Generalis Electivi Ordinis Fratrum Praedicatorum, Madonna dell'Arco, 1974*. Sub V. de Couesnongle. Rome: Ad S. Sabina, 1974.

ACG 1977 (Quezon City). *Acta Capituli Generalis Diffinitorum Ordinis Praedicatorum Quezonopoli, 1977*. Sub V. de Couesnongle. Rome: Ad S. Sabina, 1978.

ACG 1980 (Walberberg). *Acta Capituli Generalis Provincialium Ordinis Praedicatorum,*

Walberberg, 1980. Sub V. de Couesnongle. Rome: Ad S. Sabina, 1980.

ACG 1983 (Rome). *Acta Capituli Generalis Electivi Ordinis Praedicatorum Romae, 1983*. Sub D. Byrne. Rome: Ad S. Sabina, 1983.

ACG 1986 (Ávila). *Acta Capituli Generalis Diffinitorum Ordinis Praedicatorum Abulensis, 1986*. Sub D. Byrne. Rome: Ad S. Sabina, 1986.

ACG 1989 (Oakland). *Acta Capituli Generalis Provincialium Ordinis Praedicatorum: Oakland, 1989*. Sub D. Byrne. Rome: Ad S. Sabina, 1989.

ACG 1992 (Mexico City). *Acta Capituli Generalis Electivi Ordinis Fratrum Praedicatorum Mexici, 1992*. Sub T. Radcliffe. Rome: Ad S. Sabina, 1992.

ACG 1995 (Caleruega). *Acta Capituli Generalis Diffinitorum Ordinis Fratrum Praedicatorum Calerogae, 1995*. Sub T. Radcliffe. Rome: Ad S. Sabina, 1995.

ACG 1998 (Bologna). *Acta Capituli Generalis Priorum Provincialium Ordinis Praedicatorum Bononiae, 1998*. Sub D. Byrne. Rome: Ad S. Sabina, 1998.

ACG 2001 (Providence). *Acta Capituli Generalis Electivi Ordinis Praedicatorum Providentiae, 2001*. Sub C. Azpiroz Costa. Rome: Ad S. Sabina, 2001.

ACG 2004 (Krakow). *Acta Capituli Generalis Diffinitorum Ordinis Praedicatorum Cracoviae, 2004*. Sub C. Azpiroz Costa. Rome: Ad S. Sabina, 2004.

ACG 2007 (Bogotá). *Acta Capituli Generalis Priorum Provincialium Ordinis Praedicatorum Bogotae, 2007*. Sub C. Azpiroz Costa. Rome: Ad S. Sabina, 2007.

ACG 2010 (Rome). *Acta Capituli Generalis Electivi Ordinis Prædicatorum Romae, 2010*. Sub B. Cadoré. Rome: Ad S. Sabina, 2010.

ACG 2013 (Trogir). *Acta Capituli Generalis Diffinitorum Ordinis Praedicatorum Traugurii, 2013*. Sub B. Cadoré. Rome: Ad S. Sabina, 2013.

ACG 2016 (Bologna). *Acta Capituli Generalis Priorum Provincialium Ordinis Praedicatorum Bononiae, 2016*. Sub B. Cadoré. Rome: Ad S. Sabina, 2016.

ACP (Douais) *Acta Capitulorum Provincialium Ordinis Fratrum Praedicatorum: Primière Province de Provence, Province Romaine, Province d'Espagne (1239–1302)*. Ed. Célestin Douais. Toulouse: Privat, 1894.

ACPA Acta Capitulorum Provincialium Aragoniae. "Actas de los Capítulos Provinciales dela Provincia Dominicana de Aragón, Correspondientesalos Años 1302, 1399." Ed. V. T. Gómez García [aa. 1302–1366] and A. Robles Sierra [aa. 1368–1394]. *Escritos del Vedat* 20 (1990): 237–85 [aa. 1302–1307]; 21 (1991): 105–54 [aa. 1310–1321]; 22 (1992): 131–78 [aa. 1327–1331]; 23 (1993): 257–333 [aa. 1345–1351]; 24 (1994): 229–98 [aa. 1351–1355]; 25 (1995): 327–74 [aa. 1357–1358]; 26 (1996): 91–140 [aa. 1363–1366]; 27 (1997): 251–87 [aa. 1368–1370]; 31 (2001): 199–242 [aa. 1371–1373]; 32 (2002): 341–86 [aa. 1376–1370]; 33 (2003): 389–430 [aa. 1381–1388]; 34 (2004): 275–332 [aa. 1389–1394]; 35 (2005): 305–60 [aa. 1395–1399].

ACPCL Acta Capitulorum Provincialium Congregationis Lombardiae. "Les actes capitulaires de la congrégation dominicaine de Lombardie (1282-1531)," Ed. R. Creytens and A. D'Amato. AFP 31 (1961): 249–306.

ACPD Acta Capitulorum Provinciae Daciae. "Brottstychen av en Dominickaner-Ordens eller Predikare-Brödernas Statut-eller Capitel-Bok infran XIII: Arhundradet, och gällande för 'Provincia Dacia' eller de Nordiska Riken." Ed. G. Stephens. *Kirkenhistoriske Samlinger* 1 (1849–52): 545–642; 2 (1853–56): 128–29.

ACPH Acta Capitulorum Provincialium Hispaniae. "Monumenta Provinciae Hispaniae: Acta Capitulorum." Ed. H. D. Christianopolis. AOP 3 (1897–98): 411–36; 4 (1899–1900): 479–93.

ACPHo Acta Capitulorum Provinciae Hollandiae. Ed. A. De Meyer. La Congrégation de Hollande; ou, La Réforme dominicaine en territoire bourguignon, (1465-1515): Documents inédits. Liege: Solidi, 1947.

ACPL Acta Capitulorum Provincialium Lombardiae. "Acta Capitulorum Provinciae Lombardiae (1254–93) et Lombardiae inferioris (1309–1312)." Ed. T. Käppeli. AFP 9 (1941): 138–72.

ACPLI (1307) "Atti del capitolo provinciale della Lombardia Inferiore celebrato a Vicenza nel 1307," ed. A. D'Amato. AFP 13 (1943): 139–48.

ACPLI (1465) Acta Capituli Provincialium Lombariae Inferioris, 1465. "Atti del capitolo della Provincia di S. Domenico [Lombardi inferioris] celebrato a Novara nel 1465." AFP 29 (1959): 153–67.

ACPR Acta Capitulorum Provincialium Provinciae Romanae. *Acta Capitulorum Provincialium Provinciae Romanae.* Ed. T Kaeppeli and A. Dondaine. MOPH 20. Rome: Institutum Historicum, 1941.

AD *L'Année dominicaine; ou, Vies des saints, des bienheureux, des martyrs et des autres personnes illustres ou recommendables par leur piété, de l'un et de l'autre sexe de l'Ordre des frères-prêcheurs: distribuées suivants les jours de l'année.* 24 vols. Lyon: Jevain, 1883–1909.

AD[2] *L'Année dominicaine; ou, Vies des saints et illustres personnages de l'un et de l'autre sexe de l'Ordre des frères-prêcheurs: distribuées suivants les jours de l'année de 1700 jusqu'à nos jours.* Vol 1: Janvier. Only one volume published. Grenoble: Vallier Edouard, 1912.

AFP *Archivum Fratrum Praedicatorum.*

AOP *Analecta Sacri Ordinis Fratrum Praedicatorum.*

Aduarte, Diego. *Historia de la provincia del Santo Rosario de la Orden des Predicadores en Filipinas, Japon, y China.* 2 vols. Ed. Manuel Ferero. Manila, 1640; new ed. Madrid: Departamento de Misionologia, 1962–63.

Alberti, Leandro. *De Viris Illustribus Ordinis Praedicatorum.* Bologna: Platonis, 1517.

AS Acta Sanctorum quotquot Toto Orbe Coluntur vel a Catholicis Scriptoribus Celebrantur. 69 vols. Paris: Palmé, 1863– .

BGF Bernard Gui. *De Fundatione et Prioribus Conventuum Provinciarum Tolosanae et Provinciae Ordinis Praedicatorum.* Ed. P. A. Amargier. MOFPH 24. Rome: Institutum Historicum, 1961.

BGL Bernard Gui. *Libellus de Magistris Ordinis Praedicatorum necnon Priorum Provincialium Provinciae et Tolosanae.* Edmond Marténe and Ursin Durand, eds. Veterum Scriptorum Et Monumentorum Historicorum, Dogmaticorum, Moralium, Amplissima Collectio. Paris: Montalant, 1724: 397–436.

BGQ Bernard Gui and Stephen of Salagnac. *De Quatuor in quibus Deus Praedicatorum Ordinem Insignivit.* MOFPH 22. Rome: Institutum Historicum, 1949.

BOP *Bullarium Ordinis Fratrum Praedicatorum.* Ed. Thomas Ripoll and Antonin Brémond. Rome: Mainardus, 1730.

Burke, Thomas. *Hibernia Dominicana: sive, Historia Provinciae Hiberniae Ordinis Praedicatorum*. Cologne [i.e. Kilkenny], n.p., 1762.

Butler's Lives of the Saints. 4 vols. 2. ed. Ed. Herbert Thurston and Donald Attwater. London: Burns & Oates, 1956.

CCQL *Constitutiones Concilii Quarti Lateranesis*. Ed. A. García y García. Vatican City: Biblioteca Apostolica Vaticana, 1981.

CDO *Constitutiones, Declarationes, et Ordinationes Capitulorum Generalium Sacri Ordinis Fratrum Predicatorum ab anno 1220 ad, 1862*. Ed. Vincenzo Fontana et al. Rome: Morini, 1862.

Cecilia, Sister. *Miracles of St. Dominic*. In *St. Dominic: Biographical Documents*. Ed. Fr. Lehner. Washington: Thomist Press, 1964, 163–84.

CGOP (1876) *Catalogus Omnium Conventum et Domorum Provinciarum et Congregationum Sacri Ordinis Praedicatorum Fratrumque in Eisdem Commerantium una cum Eorum Dignitatibus et Officiis anno 1876*. J. Sanvito jussu ed. Rome: Morini, 1876.

CGOP (1910) *Catalogus Omnium Conventum et Domorum Provinciarum et Congregationum Sacri Ordinis Praedicatorum necnon Fratrum in Eisdem Commrantium anno 1910*. H. Cormier jussu ed. Rome: Garroni, 1910.

CGOP (1921) *Catalogus Omnium Conventum et Domorum Provinciarum et Congregationum Sacri Ordinis Praedicatorum necnon Fratrum in Eisdem Commrantium anno 1921*. L. Theissling jussu ed. Rome: Garroni, 1921.

CGOP (1931) *Catalogus Omnium Conventum et Domorum Provinciarum et Congregationum Sacri Ordinis Praedicatorum necnon Fratrum in Eisdem Commrantium anno 1931*. M. Gillet jussu ed. Rome: Manuzio, 1931.

CGOP (1949) *Catalogus Generalis Ordinis Praedicatorum (Mense Aprili 1949)*. E. Suarez jussu ed. Rome: Typis Castaldi, 1949.

CGOP (1967) *Catalogus Generalis Ordinis Praedicatorum*. A. Fernandez jussu ed. Rome: Typis Polyglottis, 1967.

CGOP (1992) *Catalogus Generalis Ordinis Praedicatorum: Conspectus Generalis Ordinis Fratrum Praedicatorum necnon Index Monasteriorum Congregationum et Fraternitatum*. D. Byrne iussu exaratus et T. Radcliffe auctoritate editus. Rome: Curia Generalitia, 1992.

Chodykiewicz, Klemens. *De rebus Gestis in Provincia Russae Ordinis Praedicatorum*. Berdyczów: Typis Fortalitii Beatissimae Virginis Mariae, 1780.

Choquet, François Hyacinthe. *Sancti Belgi Ordinis Praedicatorum*. Douay: n.p., 1618.

CNDP Cartularium Nostrae Dominae, Prouille. *Cartulaire de Notre-Dame de Prouille*. Ed. J. Guiraud. 2 vols. Paris: Picard, 1907.

Constantine of Orvieto. *Vita Beati Dominici*. Ed. H.-C. Sheeben. MHSPND 2. MOPH 26.2. Rome: Institutum Historicum, 1935: 286–352.

COP (1228) "Constitutiones Primitivae Dominicanae." *De oudste Constituties van de Dominicanen*. Ed. A. H. Thomas. Louvain, 1965, 309–69. English translation: "The Primitive Constitutions of the Order of Preachers." Trans. F. Lehner. *Saint Dominic: Biographical Documents*. Washington: Thomist, 1964: 209–51.

COP (1241) *Constitutiones Ordinis Fratrum Praedicatorum secundum Redactionem Sancti Raimundi de Penafort*. Ed. Raymond Creytens. "Les Constitutions des fréres

Prêcheurs dans la rédaction de s. Raymond de Peñafort," *Archivum Fratrum Praedicatorum*, 18 (1948): 30–68.

COP (1867) *Constitutiones Fratrum Ordinis Praedicatorum*. Ed. nova. Poitou: Oudin, 1867.

COP (1886) *Constitutiones Fratrum S. Ordinis Praedicatorum*. Ed. nova. Paris: Poussielgue, 1886.

COP (1924) *Constitutiones Fratrum Sacri Ordinis Praedicatorum*. Sub fr. Ludovico Theissling. Rome: Garroni, 1925.

COP (1932) *Constitutiones Fratrum S. Ordinis Praedicatorum*. Martini Stanislai Gillet iussu editae. Rome: Apud Domum Generalitiam, 1932.

COP (1954) *Constitutiones Fratrum S. Ordinis Praedicatorum*. Rome: Apud Domum Generalitiam, 1954.

Dávila Padilla, Agustín. *Historia de la fundación y discurso de la provincia de Santiago de México de la Orden de Predicadores*. 1659; rpt. Mexico City: Academia Literaria, 1955.

Dorcy, Mary Jean. *St. Dominic's Family: The Lives of Over 300 Famous Dominicans*. Dubuque: Priory Press, 1964.

Ferrandus, Peter, *Legenda Sancti Dominici*. Ed. M.-H. Laurent. MOFPH, 16: MHSPND, 2. Rome: Institutum Historicum, 1935: 209–60.

Fiamma, Galvano. "La Cronaca Maggiore dell'Ordine Domenicano di Galvano Fiamma." Ed. Gundisalvo Odetto. AFP 10 (1940): 297–373.

Fontana, Vincenzo Maria. *Monumenta Dominicana Breviter in Synopsim Collecta*. Rome: Tinassius, 1675.

Franco, Alonso. *Segunda parte de al historia de la Provincia de Santiago de México, Orden de Predicadores en la Nueva España*. Mexico City: Museo Nacional, 1900.

Friedberg *Corpus Juris Canonici*. 2 vols. 2. ed. Ed. Emil Friedberg. Leipzig: Tauchnitz, 1879–1881.

HOPD *Historia Ordinis Praedicatorum in Dania, 1216–1246*. Ed. J. Langebek and P. F. Shum. Scriptores Rerum Danicarum Medii Aevi 5. Copenhagen, 1783.

Humbert of Romans. *Opera de Vita Regulari*. Ed. Joachim Joseph Berthier. 2 vols. Turin: Marietti, 1956.

Index of Matter Contained in Dominican General Chapters, 1885–1916. Hinckly, Eng: Walker, 1918.

Jasinski, Camillus. *Summarium Ordinationum Capitulorum Generalium Ordinis Praedicatorum*. Krakow, 1638/Brescia 1654.

Jordan of Saxony. *Epistolae*. Ed. A. Walz. MOFPH 23. Rome: Ad S. Sabinae, 1951.

————. *Libellus de Principibus Ord. Praedicatorum*. Ed. M.-H. Laurent. MOFPH, 16: MHSPND, 2. Rome: Institutum Historicum, 1935: 25–88.

Lacroix, Benoît. *Compagnon de Dieu*. Montreal: Éditions du Lévier, 1961.

López, Juan. *La Historia general de sancto Domingo y de su Orden de Predicadores*. 5 vols. Madrid: Sanchez, 1584–1621.

MGH.SS Monumenta Germaniae Historica: Scriptores.

MHSPND Monumenta Historica Sancti Patris Nostri Dominici.

MOPH Monumenta Ordinis Praedicatorum Historica.

Marchese, Vincent. *Memorie dei più insigni pittori, scultori e architetti Domenicani.* 2 vols. Florence: Parenti, 1845. English Translation: Lives of the Most Eminent Painters, Sculptors and Architects of the Order of S. Dominic. Trans. C. P. Meehan. Dublin, Duffy, 1852.

Meléndez, Juan. *Tesoros verdaderos de las Yndias en la historia de la gran provincia de San Iuan Bautista del Perú de el Orden de Predicadores.* 1671–72; rpt. Lima: Universidad Nacional Mayor de San Marcos, 2010.

NDO Necrology, Dominicans, Orvieto. Joannes Matthaei. *Chronique du couvent des prècheurs d'Orvieto.* Ed. A. Viel and P. Girardin. Rome/Viterbo: Agnesotti, 1907.

NRP Necrology. Dominicans. Roman Province. Ed. Isnardo P. Grossi. *Necrologio della Provincia Romana O.P. dal 1656 al 1694.* Florence: n.p., 1978.

NSC Necrology, Santa Caterina, Pisa *Cronaca del Convento di s. Caterina dell'Ordine dei Predicatori in Pisa.* Ed. F. Bonaini. Florence: Franceschini, 1845, 399–593.

NSD Necrology, San Domenico, Siena. *I necrologi di san Domenico in Camporegio (Epoca Cateriniana).* Ed. M.-H. Laurent. Fontes Vitae S. Catharinae Senensis Historici, 20. Siena: Univ. di Siena, 1937: 1–45: Necrologio dei religiosi.

NSMN Necrology, Santa Maria Novella, Florence. *Necrologio di S. Maria Novella,* Ed. Stephen Orlandi. 2 vols. Florence, 1955.

Noble, Henri-Dominique. *Le Frére-Convers dominicain.* Kain, Belgium: Saulchoir / Paris: Lethielleux, 1920. English translation: *The Lay-Brother: A Short Account of the Life and Status of a Dominican Lay-Brother.* Trans. A. Swinstead. Ditchling: St. Dominic's Press, 1931.

O'Daniel (1921), Victor F. *The Dominican Lay Brother.* New York: Holy Name, 1921.

O'Daniel (1930), Victor F. *Dominicans in Early Florida.* New York: Catholic Historical Society, 1930.

Ojea, Hernando. *Libro terecero de la Historia religiosa de la Provincia de México de la Orden de sto. Domingo.* Mexico City: Museo Nacional, 1897.

PDL Province Directory. Lombard Province. 2012. *Catalogo della Provincia San Domenico in Italia: Anno Domini 2012.* Milan: Santa Maria delle Grazie, 2012.

PDT Province Directory. Teutonia Province. 2013. *Katalog der Dominikaner-Provinz Teutonia [2013].* Cologne: Provinzialat, 2013.

Pio, Michele. *Delle vite de gli huomni illustri di s. Domenico.* Bologna: Bellagamba, 1607.

PL *Patrologia Latina: Patrologiae Cursus Completus.* 221 vols. Ed. Jacques-Paul Migne. Paris: Migne, 1841–1865.

Razzi, Serafino. *Vite de i santi, cosi huomini, come donne, del sacro Ordine de Frati Predicatori.* Florence: Sermartelli, 1577.

Saint Dominic: Biographical Documents. Ed. Francis C. Lehner. Washington, DC: Thomist, 1964.

Sousa, Manuel de Faria. *Historia del reyno de Portugal.* 5 vols. Lisbon: Joan-Francisco e Diego Borel, 1779.

Thomas of Cantimpré. *Bonum Universale de Apibus.* Douay: Bellerus, 1627.

TOP Rule (1415). "Regula di Munio da Zamora per i penitenti di san Domenico (1285)." Ed. G. G. Meersseman. *Ordo Fraternitatis: Confraterite e pietà deo laici nel medioevo.* Rome: Herder, 1977, 1:401–08.

Valle, Teodoro, and Secondino Roncagliolo. *Breve compendio de gli più illustri padri nella santità della vita, dignità, uffici, e lettere ch'ha prodotto la provincia dell'Ordine de Predicatori*. Naples: Roncagliolo, 1651.

Venchi, Innocenzo. *Catalogus Hagiographicus Ordinis Praedicatorum*. Rome: Postulatio Generalis, 2001.

VF *Vitae Fratrum Ordinis Praedicatorum*. Ed. Benedictus Maria Reichert. MOFPH 1. Louvain: Charpentier et Schoonjans, 1896. English translation: *Lives of the Brethren of the Order of Preachers, 1206–1259*. Trans. Placid Conway. London: Blackfriars, 1955.

Vigna, Raimondo Amedeo. *I domenicani illustri del convento di Santa Maria de Castello in Genova*. Genoa: Lanata, 1886.

Vilarrasa, Francis-Sadoc. *Religious Institutions of the Lay Brothers of the Order of Preachers*. San Francisco: Wallace & Hassett, 1879.

SCHOLARSHIP
(SEE ALSO NOTES ON BROTHERS AND EVENTS)

Beltrán de Heredia, Vicente. *Historia de la Reforma de la Provincia de España*. Rome: S. Sabina, 1939.

Bennett, R. F. *The Early Dominicans: Studies in Thirteenth-Century Dominican History*. Cambridge: University Press, 1937.

Cavallini, Giuliana. *St. Martin de Porres: Apostle of Charity*. Trans. Caroline Holland. St. Louis: B. Herder, 1963.

Creytens, R. "Les convers des moniales dominicaines au moyen age." AFP 19 (1949): 5–48.

Cussen, Celia. *Black Saint of the Americas: The Life and Afterlife of Martín de Porres*. Cambridge: Cambridge Univ. Press, 2014.

Dominican Penitent Women. Ed. Maiju Lehmijoki-Gardner et al. Classics of Western Spirituality. Mahwah NJ: Paulist Press, 2005.

Duffy, Eamon. *The Stripping of the Altars: Traditional Religion in England, 1400 to 1580*. 2. ed. New Haven: Yale Univ. Press, 2005.

Eire, Carlos. *Reformations: The Early Modern World, 1450–1650*. New Haven: Yale Univ. Press, 2016.

Galbraith, Gretchen R. *The Constitution of the Dominican Order, 1216–1360*. New York: Longmans Green, 1925.

Golding, Brian. *Gilbert of Sempringham and the Gilbertine Order, c. 1130–c. 1300*. Oxford: Clarendon Press, 1995.

Hinnebusch (1965), William A. *The History of the Dominican Order*. 2 vols. Staten Island: Alba House, 1965.

Hinnebusch (1975), William A. *The Dominicans: A Short History*. Staten Island: Alba House, 1975.

Jedin, Hubert. *Geschichte des Konzils von Trient*. 4 vols. Freiburg im Breisgau, 1957–1975; rpt. Darmstadt: Wissenschaftliche Buchgesellschaft, 2017. Incomplete English translation: *A History of the Council of Trent*. 2 vols. Ernest Graf, trans. London: T. Nelson, 1957–1961.

Loenertz, Raymond-Joseph. *La Société des Frères Pérégrinants: Étude sur l'Orient dominicain.* Institutum Historicum FF. Praedicatorum: Dissertationes historicae, 7 Rome: S. Sabina, 1937.

Magboo, Cecilio, and Rolando V. de la Rosa. "Lay Brotherhood in the Dominican Order." *Philippiniana Sacra* 45 (2010): 503–29.

Mulchahey, M. Michele. *First the Bow is Bent in Study: Dominican Education before 1350.* Toronto: PIMS, 1999.

Mulhern, Philip F. *The Early Dominican Laybrother.* Washington D.C.: n.p., 1944.

O'Daniel, Victor F. *The Dominican Laybrother.* New York: Holy Name, 1921.

Osheim, Duane J. "Conversion, *Conversi,* and the Christian Life in Late Medieval Tuscany." *Speculum* 58 (1983): 368–90.

Puebla Pedrosa, Ceferino, et al. *Witnesses of the Faith in the Orient: Dominican Martyrs of Japan, China, and Vietnam.* Trans. Maria Maez. 2. ed. Ed. George G. Christian. Hong Kong: Provincial Secretariat of Missions, Dominican Province of Our Lady of the Rosary, 2006.

Prudlo, Donald S. "The Assassin-Saint: The Life and Cult of Carino of Balsamo." *The Catholic Historical Review,* 94 (2008): 1–21.

Thompson (2005), Augustine. *Cities of God: The Religion of the Italian Communes, 1125–1325.* University Park PA: Penn State Univ. Press, 2005.

Thompson (2012), Augustine. *Francis of Assisi: A New Biography.* Ithaca, NY: Cornell Univ. Press, 2012.

Tugwell (1992), Simon. "Notes on the Life of St Dominic." AFP 66 (1996): 5–200.

Vargas, Michael A. *Taming a Brood of Vipers: Conflict and Change in Fourteenth-Century Dominican Convents.* Leiden: Brill, 2011.

Vicaire, H.-M. *Saint Dominic and His Times.* Trans. Kathleen Pond. New York: McGraw-Hill, 1964.

Index

Note: friars who died before 1700 are alphabetized under first names.

CPSIA information can be obtained
at www.ICGtesting.com
Printed in the USA
LVHW012026111022
730463LV00009B/666